D0968631

The Life
And Teachings
Of Jesus

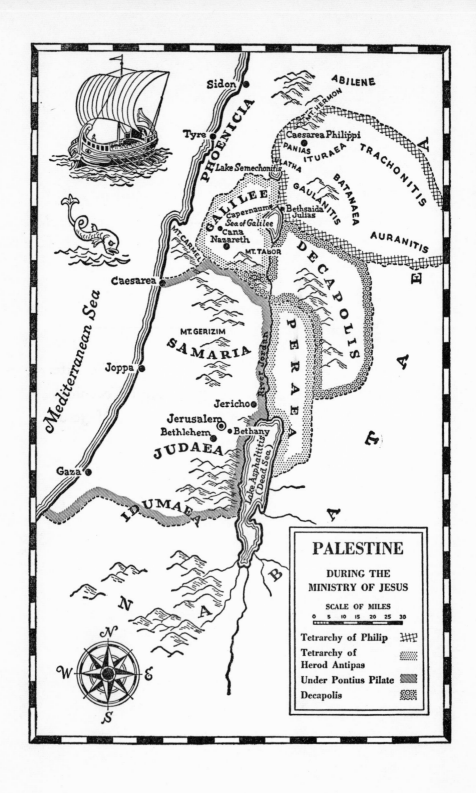

Sidon

ABILENE

Tyre

PHOENICIA

MT. HERMON

Caesarea Philippi

PANIAS

ITURAEA

TRACHONITIS

LATHA

Lake Semechonitis

BATANAEA

GAULANITIS

GALILEE

Capernaum

Bethsaida
Julias

AURANITIS

Sea of Galilee

Cana
Nazareth

MT. CARMEL

MT. TABOR

DECAPOLIS

Caesarea

MT. GERIZIM

SAMARIA

PERAEA

River Jordan

Mediterranean Sea

Joppa

Jericho

Jerusalem

Bethlehem

Bethany

JUDAEA

Lake Asphaltitis
(Dead Sea)

Gaza

IDUMAEA

N

A

B

A

T

A

E

A

N   W   E   S

PALESTINE

DURING THE
MINISTRY OF JESUS

SCALE OF MILES

0   5   10   15   20   25   30

Tetrarchy of Philip

Tetrarchy of
Herod Antipas

Under Pontius Pilate

Decapolis

The Life
And Teachings
Of Jesus

Revised Edition

CHARLES M. LAYMON

ABINGDON PRESS

NASHVILLE • NEW YORK

THE LIFE AND TEACHINGS OF JESUS
REVISED EDITION

Copyright © 1962 Abingdon Press
Copyright 1955 by Pierce and Washabaugh

ISBN 0-687-21768-7

Library of Congress Catalog Card Number: 62-7439

SET UP, PRINTED, AND BOUND BY THE
PARTHENON PRESS, AT NASHVILLE,
TENNESSEE, UNITED STATES OF AMERICA

This Book
is dedicated to

MY STUDENTS
in many lands

Preface

WHEN ONE ATTEMPTS TO WRITE A BOOK ON THE LIFE AND TEACHINGS OF JESUS AT THIS POINT IN THE TWENTIETH CENTURY, HE faces a unique situation in biblical attitudes and conclusions. Earlier studies in this field were quite optimistic in their view that the gospel records contained "a story" that could be put together with sufficient historical validity that the title *Life of Jesus* was decidedly in order. Schweitzer's *Quest of the Historical Jesus* and Cadbury's *The Peril of Modernizing Jesus* modified this confidence in some and discouraged it in others. The work of Rudolf Bultmann, with its emphasis upon myth, further questioned the biblical foundations for drawing a picture of the historical Jesus, stressing instead the Lord who confronts us existentially in the living present. Recently, however, the work of Günther Bornkamm, a follower of Bultmann, has begun to move away from the extreme historical skepticism of his teacher and to suggest certain lines within which a historical portrait can be reconstructed. His study *Jesus of Nazareth,* while setting forth specific limits, marks a positive change in the climate of biblical research in this area.

The present volume takes the position that the Jesus of history may be found within the Gospels. Theological interests and the development of a kerygma, or preaching message, have inevitably been active in the formulation of the gospel accounts, but that these have been of such a character as to obliterate or effectively efface the image of the historical Jesus is an unrealistic judgment. Although their first concern was for the significance of Jesus for faith and experience, it should not be assumed that the early Christians, on the whole, were completely disinterested in the kind of person Jesus was in the days of his flesh.

In spite of this, a book on the life and teachings of Jesus cannot be written as one would tell the story of a contemporary person. Many of the facts are missing, facts concerning his boyhood, youth, and mature career. And those that are given in the Gospels are related so losely to each other, because of the way the literary units are edited, that a final chronology is out of the question. The portrait still remains, however, of a genuinely historical person who fulfilled a ministry of teaching and preaching, of service, and of healing. We have, therefore, approached Jesus' work according to these major areas rather than in terms of sequence or periods of activity.

In this same sense Jesus' teachings are also found within the traditions of the church as reported in the Gospels, and these may be considered as we have done in this book under such selected headings as God, the Kingdom, earthly goods, prayer, love, and immortality. Jesus himself did not present them in this systematic fashion, but this need not deter us from thus organizing them for study purposes.

I have not hesitated on occasion to attempt a reconstruction of certain situations in the experience of Jesus on the basis of the data at hand, our knowledge of the times in which he lived, and the character of his mind and spirit as these are made known to us in the Gospels. This is offered as historical probability. The writing of all history involves numerous such analyses, groupings, and orientations of data. To fail to do this would relegate to historical studies the task of listing data only.

In this revision one will find particular emphasis upon the Dead Sea Scrolls, commensurate with the increasing realization of their significance; renewed stress upon the Christian Community as the matrix of the Gospel tradition; and a more detailed consideration of the character of the individual Gospels themselves.

The title of the original has been retained. Even though the character of our sources makes a biography as such impossible, a large majority of college courses continue to be offered under the subject, *The Life and Teachings of Jesus.* The familiar wording has, therefore, been followed with the expectation that the special connotation of the phrase as developed herein will be kept in mind.

The reading lists have been updated to include significant titles that have come from the press since the original compilation was made. They have been numerous, and have added considerably to the enrichment of study in this field. Some of the older works that are still in our libraries have been of necessity deleted. It is hoped that they will not be completely neglected for they contain many valuable insights.

In some instances calling for interpretation, after presenting different points of view, I have not urged a particular conclusion. This is not because I do not hold one, but in order to invite individual judgment. In other cases which are basic to a development of the theme, conclusions have been drawn, but only after a consideration of differing views. What is intended in a book of this character, in any case, is not to prove a point but rather to understand it.

The questions at the close of each chapter are a part of the work in its total conception. Answers to many of them will not be found expressly stated in the book. They are intended to encourage independent thinking. Frequently they refer the student to the implications of the Gospel for contemporary living.

This study is prepared for persons who have done introductory work in Bible or religion. For those who have not had such an opportunity the background chapters have been provided. These may also be read for review purposes.

I am indebted to many persons who have done research in this field. This has been recognized, as far as this is possible, in the footnotes. I owe a particular debt to William J. Lowstuter, now deceased, who first awakened in me a zeal for the quest of the gospel portrait of Jesus.

CHARLES M. LAYMON

Contents

11

Contents

PART I

THE BACKGROUND

1

The World
In Which Jesus Lived

THE SETTING FOR THE LIFE AND TEACHINGS OF JESUS WAS FIRST-century Palestine. The contour of the land and the thinking of its people contributed to his ministry. He did not proclaim the good news of the kingdom of God in a geographical and historical vacuum. All about him was a world of activity, demanding in its tensions and varied in its expressions.

Palestine was a part of the Greco-Roman world, in which the culture of the Greeks had combined with that of the Romans. This fusion of ideas and ideals made its impact upon the region mostly through the presence of appointed Roman officials, foreign armies which were quartered on its soil, and merchants who traveled the trade routes which crossed its terrain. The large numbers of Jews who lived abroad, and who returned periodically to Jerusalem to attend the religious festivals of their people, brought also the outside world with them. These persons are referred to usually as Hellenists. Although they still held to the religion of their fathers, the fact that they lived beyond the borders of Palestine meant that they would be subject to liberalizing contacts with Gentiles. Some, no doubt, were more open to these relationships than others.

The immediate environment of Jesus, however, was more Jewish than Greco-Roman. Palestine was located at a great distance from the city of Rome itself, and world centers such as Ephesus, Alexandria, and Corinth were not close at hand. In addition to this, most of the Jews among whom Jesus lived resisted Gentile influences with studied determination. Home life and worship were predominantly Jewish. Much in Jesus' surroundings was anti-Roman in this respect.

I

The land of Palestine contributed to the making of the mind of Jesus. Its seas provided opportunities for recreation (Luke 8:22), and its mountains invited meditation and prayer (Luke 9:28). The agricultural and pastoral life which it afforded was a constant

reminder of the presence of God in the affairs of men, and supplied
many metaphors and similes for his teaching. Temperatures were
moderate with just enough variation to be stimulating. An outdoor
life such as Jesus was called upon to live was not too difficult in
such a physical environment.

Palestine's more than 10,000 square miles extend about 270
miles, north and south, along the eastern shore of the Mediterranean Sea. Its width varies between slightly over 100 and about
175 miles. The Jordan River bisects much of it with a larger area
(6,000 square miles) on the west than on the east (4,000 square
miles). On either side of the river, whose headwaters are north of
the Sea of Galilee and which continues to flow from it to the Dead
Sea, lies the Jordan Valley. The climate here is hot, encouraging
tropical growth. The valley is flanked on both sides by mountains.
Far to the north are the Lebanon Mountains. Of particular interest
in this area is Mount Hermon, which has a height of 9,300 feet and is
the probable site of Jesus' transfiguration experience.[1] In the extreme south lie the Deserts of Paran and Arabia.

There are frequent references to the Sea of Galilee in the gospel
accounts of the ministry of Jesus. Resting 686 feet below sea level,
it is about 6 to 8 miles wide and 14 miles long. A prosperous fishing
industry developed around its border since from its waters many
varieties of fish were drawn. Josephus records that some of these
were particularly choice.[2] Several of Jesus' disciples were Galilean
fishermen (Luke 5:1-11). The Dead Sea into which the Jordan
flows is approximately 1,300 feet below sea level. It has no outlet and
its waters contain tar, salt, phosphorus, and bitumen.

There are plains of great fertility in Palestine. One of these, in
the southern part of Galilee, is the Plain of Esdraelon, which is
about 9 miles wide. Just north of this area lies Nazareth where
Jesus was reared, and we may assume that he played here as a boy.
Then there is the Maritime Plain, or Coastal Plain. It begins where
the coast widens at Mount Carmel and extends southward for
about 150 miles along the sea. The ancient Philistine tribes occupied most of this narrow strip, which averages from 10 to 12½

---

[1] Cf. later reference, pp. 244-46.
[2] Josephus *Wars* III. 10. 8.

miles in width, the wider sections being in the southern area. East of the Dead Sea are the Plains of Moab.

The eastern plateau of Palestine begins with the Anti-Lebanon mountain range in the north and extends southward to the Arabian Desert. About midway lies Mount Gilead, which rises to a height of 3,597 feet. North of it is the Plain of Bashan. This general area contains some very fertile land.

The effect of such a varied landscape as Palestine upon the people who lived there is a matter of conjecture. Modern study applies the term "human geography" to attempts to relate geography to the development of peoples. At best it cannot be an exact science. As Chester C. McCowan says in his study "The Geographical Conditioning of Religious Experience in Palestine," "Mathematics and things of the spirit are incommensurable. Mechanistic and, consequently, deterministic interpretations of history are excluded because history is human experience." [3] And yet, the fact that there is a relation between geography and personality would seem to be established.

It may be suggested quite generally that the geographical variety of Palestine was stimulating to the minds of those who lived there. It produced a ruggedness of character and the capacity to adapt to different patterns of living. Throughout the centuries changing circumstances required the people to move sometimes from place to place. This nomadic existence, in turn, affected the development of the law of the nation, especially during the early days of the Hebrews. A further influence of the land upon the outlook of the people was due to the poverty it produced in times of drought or pestilence. Hopelessness under these conditions led to trust in God and contributed to the faith that he would intervene in the affairs of men to save them. This impact of geography upon personality produced, in part, the spiritual environment within which Jesus lived.

II

There were political as well as geographical divisions in the Palestine of the first century. The major ones were Galilee, Samaria,

[3] This essay is found in Harold S. Willoughby (ed.), *The Study of the Bible Today and Tomorrow*, pp. 233-34. The above discussion is indebted to this essay.

Judea, and Perea. Besides these there was the region of the ten cities, sometimes called Decapolis, which overlapped both Perea and Galilee, and a general territory north of Perea and east of the Sea of Galilee which was inhabited by undisciplined Gentile groups. In this latter area were such districts as Gualanitis, Ituraea, Auranitis, Trachonitis, and Batanaea.

Galilee was predominantly Jewish in population in the time of Jesus, although it contained more Gentiles than Judea. Its people were passionately patriotic and many were the descendants of the followers of John Hyrcanus, who had sought to establish an independent Jewish kingdom in the region a little over a hundred years earlier. They were more liberal than their brothers in Judea due to their contact with Gentiles and, in part, because of their distance from Jerusalem, which was the seat of Judaism. The Synoptic Gospels place most of Jesus' ministry in Galilee. Here Nazareth was located, as well as Capernaum, Cana, Bethsaida, and Chorazin—all of which are mentioned in the gospel accounts.

Immediately to the south of Galilee was Samaria. The people here were descendants of the colonists who had been imported to this region by the Assyrians after the fall of the northern kingdom of Israel (*circa* 722 B.C.), and of the Hebrew natives who remained. They were of mixed blood, therefore, and were despised by the orthodox Jews. In spite of this, many of the Samaritans took pride in their Hebrew ancestry and promoted the supremacy of Mount Gerizim over Jerusalem as the holy site (John 4:20). At one time they built a temple on the mountain. It was no longer standing in Jesus' day for it had been destroyed by John Hyrcanus in 128 B.C. Sometimes in passing through Samaria, Jews met with difficulties because of the enmity which existed between the two peoples. Jesus himself was refused lodging in this region on one occasion when he and the disciples were recognized as being Jews (Luke 9:51-56).

Judea was the political division of Palestine in which Jewish traditions and customs were most zealously kept. At its heart lay the city of Jerusalem, the scene of great events in the nation's past and the site of the historic Temple, first built by Solomon. For all Jews, whether of Palestine or of the Diaspora, it remained the Holy City; and in the thinking of Jesus it held a significant place. The priests and rabbis of the Jews centered their activities in Jerusalem, and their influence went out to all Judea and beyond.

The mountain upon which Jerusalem stood had certain military advantages. Rising to about 2,400 feet above sea level, it would be difficult to attack. The city itself was surrounded by valleys which led to mountain ridges on three sides. All approaches were rugged except from the north. In A.D. 70 only an extended siege led to the city's downfall. It was a walled city and several gates made entrance possible. Within these walls were two mountain ridges or hills, and the Temple was built on the eastern one. Ravines cut across both of these ridges so that the landscape was irregular.

III

The political outlook of the Jewish people was so much a part of their religious viewpoint that what happened in government was of more than usual concern to them. Prior to the time of Jesus, Palestine had experienced tremendous crises in this area. It has been estimated that during the thirty years (67-37 B.C.) preceding the rise of Herod the Great considerably more than 100,000 Jews had been killed.[4] These men had lost their lives in resistance movements.[5] The country had been conquered by Rome under Pompey in 63 B.C., marking the end of the Maccabean kingdom with its turbulent expression of Jewish independence. Subjugation under Rome and the rulers she supported in Palestine was not accepted easily, and the Jewish nationalistic uprisings which followed were costly. It was not only a terrific loss in numbers but in strength and spirit as well, for those who died were the young men for whom the Jewish cause was a religious concern.

Although he was an efficient ruler in many respects, Herod, the Edomite Jew, was never popular with the Jews. His supreme loyalty was to Rome from whom he received his authority to rule in Palestine, first from Antony and later from Augustus. In some respects he held the Jewish people in contempt, while in others he sought to win their favor. The building of the Temple at Jerusalem, an undertaking of great expense, was intended to gain their

---

[4] Joseph Klausner, *Jesus of Nazareth*, p. 144.

[5] Before this time there had been the Maccabean Wars for independence from Syrian rule. These will be referred to later, cf. pp. 32-33.

approval. His love of Greco-Roman culture, however, stood in the way of their acceptance of him.[6] He was a Greek at heart.

The building activities of Herod extended beyond the city of Jerusalem. He constructed aqueducts, gymnasiums, amphitheaters, and even cities. The latter include Phaselis, Agrippium, and Antipatris. The erection of the harbor-city Caesarea Stratonis was particularly outstanding. He spent twelve years upon this project and the result was magnificent. It became the capital city. Herod's building interests led him to beautify communities outside of Palestine itself. Josephus wrote of this activity, "And are not the Athenians, and Lacedemonians, and Nicopolitans, and that Pergamus which is in Mysia, full of decorations that Herod presented them withal!"[7] His reputation in this regard was widespread in the Roman world.

It required great sums of money to construct such public works. Huge taxes were levied upon the Jews to finance these interests of Herod. Properties of the wealthy were confiscated, and bribes and the collection of fines resorted to when the occasion necessitated them.[8]

In order to keep a strong hand upon the government, Herod did not hesitate to put to death those whom he regarded as a threat to his rule of the nation. Among those whom he killed were Aristobulus III, his brother-in-law; Joseph, who had married his (Herod's) sister Salome; Hyrcanus II, who had once saved him from death; his wife Mariamne; and his mother, Alexandra. Even his own sons Alexander and Aristobulus were strangled at his order (*circa* 7 B.C.), and five days before his death he commanded that his son Antipater should be killed.

Josephus summarized the rule of Herod in these words:

He was not a king but the most barbarous of tryrants who had ever sat on a throne. He had slain men innumerable, but the lot of those which survived made them envy those that were slain. He not only tortured his subjects individually, but oppressed entire cities. Foreign cities he adorned

---

[6] Herod placed a golden eagle in honor of Rome over the east gate of the Temple. The Jews could not forgive this indignity.

[7] Josephus *Wars* I, 21. 8.

[8] Yet he was swift to help his people in time of famine, and in 20 B.C. reduced the taxes 23 per cent and in 14 B.C. lowered them 25 per cent.

but his own he destroyed; foreign peoples he enriched with the blood of
the Jews. So, in place of the former wealth and good laws, there came
utter proverty and bad laws. In short, the Jews suffered more in a few
years from Herod than their fathers had suffered since they left Babylon
and returned in the reign of Xerxes.[9]

These dark words should not close our eyes to the abilities and
achievements of Herod. Some religious prejudice may have gone
into the writing of them. They were strenuous days in which to
rule, and the Jews with their intense nationalistic background were
a rebellious people, difficult to govern.

At his death Herod's kingdom was governed by his three sons
Archelaus, Antipas, and Philip. Archelaus did not receive from Augustus the title 'king" which his father had willed to him. He
was called "ethnarch" (leader of the people) instead, and was
given the responsibility of ruling in Judea, Samaria, and Idumea.
Antipas was placed in control of Galilee and Perea, while Philip
was appointed to reign in Batanaea, Trachonitis, Gaulanitis,
Panias, Ituraea, and the Hauran. The latter two sons were known
by the title "tetrarch" (chief of four).

After ten years of a tumultuous rule during which he had incensed the Jews by a bad marriage [10] and further impoverished
them with a large building program, Archelaus was called to Rome
by the emperor, where he was deposed and sent into Gaul as an
exile.[11] Representatives of both the Jews and Samaritans had complained to Rome concerning his conduct in office. The territory
ruled by Archelaus was joined to Syria, and a Roman governor
was placed over the whole. At the same time a special officer
called a "procurator" was given charge of Archelaus' realm. The
best known of these was to be Pontius Pilate (A.D. 26-36), under
whose order Jesus was crucified.

Although the Jews of Judea were rid of the Herods, they were
far from free politically. The procurator resided at Caesarea and
a Roman army was quartered at Jerusalem. Taxes were collected
still by a special group known as publicans, whose reputation for

[9] Josephus *Antiquities* XVIII. 11. 2; *Wars* II. 6. 2.
[10] He married Glaphyra, daughter of Archelaus, king of Cappadocia, in disregard of the levirate law.
[11] Josephus *Antiquities* XVII. 13. 1-2; *Wars* II. 7. 3.

dishonesty was exceeded only by the hatred with which the Jews regarded them. We meet this group rather frequently in the Gospels, and Jesus chose one of them as a disciple (Luke 5:27-32).

Under the procurators the office of the high priest was appointive, even as it had been under Herod and before him under the Syrians. This meant that the chief officer in Judaism was subject to a foreign overlord, and that his independence as a Jewish leader was conditioned by political privilege. He presided over the Jerusalem Sanhedrin, a Jewish court composed of seventy members (seventy-one including the high priest) chosen from the elders, scribes, and high-priestly families. This court constituted a kind of limited Jewish government. Its jurisdiction was confined to concerns among the Jews only. In smaller communities there were local sanhedrins, or courts, set up to care for minor legal disputes among the Jewish citizens.[12] Roman courts passed upon Gentile cases, as well as upon those where both Jews and Gentiles were involved.

Herod Antipas, who ruled in Galilee and Perea, was a Jew, and this gave his Jewish subjects some satisfactions not felt in Judea. In many ways, however, he disregarded their particular sensitivities. He built the city of Tiberias in honor of the emperor [13] and seemed to favor Greek principles of government. It was he who beheaded John the Baptist, and Jesus referred to him once as a fox (Luke 13:32). When Pilate sent Jesus before him at the time of the trial, the ruler sought only to see a miracle and refused to pass judgment (Luke 23:7-12). In many ways Antipas resembled his father, Herod the Great.

Philip, who was tetrarch in the region east and northeast of the Sea of Galilee, has been called the best of the Herods. It was into his territory that Jesus went to escape the dangerous attention of Antipas, and to avoid momentarily the storm of enmity from the religious leaders which was developing around him (Mark 8:22-30). His name is associated with the building of Caesarea Philippi. He built Bethsaida also, sometimes called Julias. It was intended to honor Augustus' daughter. Since most of his subjects were

---

[12] Following the deposition of Archelaus, Judea was divided into eleven toparchies. In each of these there was a local court of twenty-three members which handled the less significant cases.

[13] The city was constructed on the site of a cemetery, which made it ceremonially unclean to orthodox Jews.

non-Jews, Philip's predilection for things Roman and Grecian did not give offense.[14] Josephus dealt more kindly with Philip than he did with his father. He said that Philip "had shown himself a person of moderation and quietness in the conduct of his life and government," and stressed his sense of justice in ordering the guilty that were convicted to be punished, and in absolving those that had been accused unjustly.[15]

The political situation which has been outlined briefly in this section provided a background for the ministry of Jesus. The dissatisfactions which it created in the minds and hearts of many of the Jews caused them to long for the advent of a deliverer, the Messiah, whom the fathers in Israel had believed was to come. This will be considered in greater detail in succeeding chapters. In the opinion of Joseph Klausner the effect of these conditions was "to beget either utterly fanatical seekers after freedom who turned into actual rebels, or utterly despairing visionaries, extreme moralists and mystics, who waited for nothing less than the mercy of Heaven. . . ." [16] It is clear that Jesus came preaching at a time when the national issue, which for the Jew was a religious issue essentially, was uppermost in the minds of many. And this made a difference in the way in which they listened to what he had to say.

IV

The social and economic conditions of first-century Palestine affected also the reception the people gave to Jesus. They heard him speak in the midst of their particular environment. Whether they were poor or rich, slave or free, Jew or Gentile, their own needs and interests influenced their response.

Slavery was an accepted practice in the Greco-Roman world. Prisoners of war were forced often into servitude. Josephus reports that when Titus destroyed Jerusalem, he took 97,000 Jewish captives.[17] Without large numbers of such laborers the extensive building program of the Empire would not have been possible.

[14] Philip placed images of both Augustus and Tiberius upon copper coins in order to honor the emperors.

[15] Josephus *Antiquities* XVIII. 4. 6.

[16] *Op. cit.*, p. 169.

[17] Josephus *Wars* VI. 9. 3.

The Jews owned slaves also. From very early times special legislation concerning this group was a part of Hebrew legal codes.[18] Although there was a distinctly humanitarian interest behind most of these laws, the slave was still under the immediate control of his master during the period of enslavement. Some slaves were persons of culture and possessed unusual abilities. They became teachers of nobility and even managers of estates on occasion. Others were of limited mentality and served as menial servants. All longed for personal freedom to direct their own lives.

The status of women was low in the Greco-Roman world. Not many were given the opportunities of an education. Girl babies were often exposed to die since boys were preferred. These were retrieved sometimes and reared to become temple women. It has been estimated that there were one thousand sacred prostitutes at Corinth alone in connection with the worship of Aphrodite. Marriage and divorce were not matters of state supervision. The individual married at will and was divorced in the same manner. The man of the household was at liberty to divorce his wife, but the wife did not have the same freedom to divorce her husband. Among the Jews the conditions of marriage required a betrothal, which was regarded more seriously than engagements in the modern world. This was arranged usually through a person other than the bride and groom. It was customary, however, for the girl to give her consent and to bring to her husband a dowry.

There were other social lines of difference besides those which existed between a slave and free men, and those between the sexes. The publicans were regarded by the Jews as persons of a base order. These were the tax collectors in the service of Rome and, therefore, particularly despised. They were grouped with the sinners who neglected the teachings of the rabbis and cared little for the heritage of their people. One of the objections which the Jews voiced most loudly against Jesus was that he fraternized with publicans and sinners (Luke 15:1-2).

Taxation itself was an ever-present burden. Duty was levied on exports and imports. Josephus mentions such taxes as those required on salt, water, food, roads, and houses.[19] It has been noted

[18] Cf. Exod. 21:1 ff.
[19] Josephus *Antiquities* XIX. 6. 3.

already that Herod taxed the people heavily in order to maintain his government and to carry out the extensive building projects, both at home and abroad, which delighted him. The taxes which were collected at "frontiers" as the people traveled from place to place added greatly to the cost of living, but enriched the coffers of the Empire. Such a taxation program was not only a great financial hardship upon the people of Jesus' day, but also awakened in them deep resentments against a foreign power, which they regarded as an idolatrous nation.

The economic pursuits of Palestine were varied in the time of Jesus. Although the country was predominantly rural, many made their living through fishing, craft-working, selling, and other trades.[20] Wages were often as low as nineteen cents a day. Grain, vegetables, fruit, and oil were produced in considerable amounts, while cattle and sheep were raised on the green and sometimes stony slopes.

The land in Palestine was held by several groups. Among the Jews there were mostly small tractholders, few being prosperous enough to own sizable estates, although some were able to do so. Many persons served as land tenants and others rented the fields they tilled or upon which they pastured their flocks.

Reference has been made already to the taxes placed upon exports and imports. Some of the Jews made their living as foreign traders. Frequently it was a lucrative occupation. Jewish ships sailed most of the seas on voyages that took them on occasion to distant ports. Items for import included special dainties which only the rich could afford.[21] Export commodities were those in which the country specialized, the products of the fields and of the sea.

The people lived both in the country and in towns, villages, and cities. Several of the latter had rather large populations. Jeru-

[20] Klausner, op. cit., p. 177, lists more than forty kinds of craftsmen as belonging to this period. Included are such workers as carpenters, barbers, bloodletters, coopers, makers of glass and glassware, jewelers, hairdressers, and well-diggers.

[21] Cf. Alfred Edersheim, The Life and Times of Jesus, I, 116. The list given here includes "exquisitely shaped, curiously designed and jewelled cups, rings . . . glass, silks, fine linen, woollen stuffs, purple, and costly hangings; essences, ointments, and perfumes, as precious as gold."

salem has been estimated to have held over 100,000 persons in Jesus' time. Some have suggested more than twice this number.[22] Houses were built along the sides of narrow streets. With their flat roofs of varying heights, although most of the dwellings were but one story high, and their stone walls, they were informal and picturesque.

The sounds which filled the busy streets were such as belonged to human activity. Although Greek was the language spoken throughout the Empire, the Jews of Palestine, on the whole, spoke Aramaic; and this, we believe, is the language Jesus used. In matters of state Latin was the official tongue.

V

Palestine was a part of the Greco-Roman world, and, as such, the religion of its people was not untouched by the religious beliefs and practices which prevailed throughout the Empire. In its broad outlook Rome encouraged a syncretism of different faiths. A citizen might, and frequently did, become a devotee of several religions at the same time. Such crossing of the lines was facilitated by the policy of tolerance on the part of the government toward the religions within its far-flung borders.

There was a place for each: hero cults, emperor worship, the religion of philosophy such as in Stoicism and Epicureanism, the mystery religions, including the Dionysian cult, Orphism, the Eleusinian mysteries, the worship of Isis and Osiris, of Attis and Cybele, and of Mithra. In addition to these there was the popular worship of the gods of Olympus and the Capitoline. Such a variety suggests the extent of religious longing which characterized the times, as the people were looking for a basis for living beyond that which the material order provided.

Since the ministry of Jesus as presented in the Gospels was largely within Galilee and Judea where Judaism was strong, and since his own religious experience and that of most of those to whom he spoke matured within this same tradition, a detailed study of the religions of the Greco-Roman world would take one

[22] *Ibid.*

too far afield at this point.[23] It is important to recognize, however, that religion was a matter of vital concern in the world in which Jesus lived.[24]

The immediate impact of Judaism, both upon Jesus and upon those who heard his message was so marked that a particular study of the religions of the Jew is necessary if the life and teachings of Jesus are to be understood and appreciated. Attention will be given to this consideration in the chapter which follows.

Palestinian life within these geographical, political, social, economic, and religious expressions might appear to be a simple and uncomplicated existence when compared to contemporary living; but the tensions that are found in all human associations were present in the first century also. There was thievery, deceit, unscrupulous practice, and chicanery. The uncertainties of an economy under a foreign rule and with heavy taxation on the one hand, and large numbers of small wage earners, hirelings, and slaves on the other, made for feelings of deep insecurity. Belief in a God who cared for the daily lot of his children was needed desperately, such a one as Jesus was to present in his teaching concerning the kingdom of God.

QUESTIONS FOR DISCUSSION

1. The teachings of Jesus contain many references to nature which reflect the countryside of Palestine. Had he lived in another part of the earth, may we assume that such references would have been in harmony with its particular natural scene? Why?

2. Had Jesus lived outside of Palestine, in Egypt or Rome, would his *ideas* have differed from those found in the Gospels? To what extent does environment color the thinking of even an original and altogether unique mind?

3. What elements in the political situation within Palestine at this time would have made the people eager for the Messiah to come?

4. Galilee was recognized as a cradle of political uprisings. Would this

[23] It is known that northern Palestine was somewhat under the influence of the religions of the Greco-Roman world. The worship of Dionysius was practiced prominently at Scythopolis, just eighteen miles from Nazareth, and it is quite likely also that Herod Antipas promoted emperor worship.

[24] The Christian Church was to find it necessary later to present its faith to the larger Greco-Roman world in terms which the people, as adherents of the religions of the day, could understand.

have made a difference in the reception which the people of this region gave to the message of Jesus? Explain.

5. Some historians have emphasized the idea that economic interests are the leading motives which move men to act. Assuming that this is true, for the sake of argument, is there reason to believe that the acceptance of Jesus' teachings by the people may have been conditioned by the economic background of the times?

6. In line with the previous question, why was it that the poor were more open to Jesus' message than the wealthy among the Jewish hierarchy?

7. What parallels can be found in contemporary life to the lines of social distinction which existed in Jesus' day, as between the Jew and the Gentile, the outcast and the righteous, the male and the female, and the slave and the free?

8. What values are there in religious syncretism such as Rome favored at this time, in which an individual in his personal religion might combine the ideas and practices of different faiths? Does this procedure weaken one's convictions since his creed is exceedingly broad, or does it strengthen one's beliefs since several religions are united into one all-encompassing whole?

9. Would you conclude that the fact that there were a number of competing religions in the Greco-Roman world hindered or helped Jesus as he presented his teachings? Explain.

10. Some of the questions in this list might lead one to decide that environment is the sole factor in understanding Jesus and the response of the people to his teachings. What factors other than environment may be suggested in this connection?

SUGGESTIONS FOR READING

I. The geographical background

Baly, Denis. *The Geography of the Bible.* New York: Harper Brothers, 1957. Selected readings.

McCown, Chester C. "The Geographical Conditioning of Religious Experience in Palestine," *The Study of the Bible Today and Tomorrow,* ed. Harold R. Willoughby. Chicago: University of Chicago Press, 1947. Pp. 231-46.

Smith, George Adam. *The Historical Geography of the Holy Land.* New York: Harper & Brothers, 1932. Selected readings.

Wright, G. E., and Filson, F. V. *The Westminster Historical Atlas to the Bible.* Philadelphia: The Westminster Press, 1945. Selected readings.

II. The political background

Enslin, Morton S. "Palestine," *The Interpreter's Bible.* Nashville: Abingdon Press, 1951. VII, 100-113.

————— *Christian Beginnings.* New York: Harper & Brothers, 1938, Pp. 3-77.

—————. *The Prophet from Nazareth.* New York: McGraw-Hill Book Company, Inc., 1961. Pp. 17-35.

Kee, Howard C. and Young, Franklin W. *Understanding The New Testament.* Englewood Cliffs, N. J.: Prentice-Hall, Inc., 1957. Pp. 22-32.

Klausner, Joseph. *Jesus of Nazareth.* New York: The Macmillan Company 1929. Pp. 135-73.

Pfeiffer, R. H. *History of New Testament Times.* New York: Harper & Brothers, 1948. Pp. 5-45.

Simkhovitch, V. G. *Toward the Understanding of Jesus.* New York: The Macmillan Company, 1947. Selected readings.

Snaith, Norman H. *The Jews from Cyrus to Herod.* Nashville: Abingdon Press, 1956. Pp. 7-50.

III. The social and economic background

Dill, Samuel. *Roman Society from Nero to Marcus Aurelius.* New York: The Macmillan Company, 1905. Selected readings.

Grant, F. C. *The Economic Background of the Gospels.* New York: Oxford University Press, 1926. Selected readings.

Klausner, Joseph. *Jesus of Nazareth.* New York: The Macmillan Company 1929. Pp. 174-92.

Mathews, Shailer. *New Testament Times in Palestine.* New York: The Macmillan Company, 1934. Selected readings.

IV. The religious background

Charles, R. H. *Religious Development Between the Old and the New Testaments.* New York: Henry Holt & Company, 1914. Selected readings.

Glover, T. R. *The World of the New Testament.* New York: The Macmillan Company, 1936. Selected readings.

McCasland, S. Vernon. "The Greco-Roman World," *The Interpreter's Bible.* Nashville: Abingdon Press, 1951. VII, 75-99.

Metzger, Bruce M. *An Introduction to the Apocrypha.* New York: Oxford University Press, 1957. Selected readings.

2

The Religion of the Jew

JESUS CARRIED OUT HIS MINISTRY IN A SOCIETY WHICH WAS MOSTLY
Jewish. He addressed himself to people with many centuries of
religious history behind them. Certain ideas, ideals, practices, and
customs had been established long since. Their world view provided
the background for their acceptance or rejection of his message.
It is important, therefore, in understanding the life of Jesus that
we should know something of the religion of the Jew in that day.

In the first place there was a basic pessimism in the outlook of
the Jew. His political status had risen and fallen, mostly the latter,
with more or less regularity during the preceding seven centuries.
At first these misfortunes seemed to imply that Jehovah was inadequate. This was because a free, independent, national life and
the sovereignty of the Jehovah were regarded as going hand in
hand. The roots of this idea extended far back into the days when
many gods were recognized. Under this philosophy the superiority
of a given god depended upon the political status of his people.

The great prophets of the nation saw deeper than this popular
world view, however, and interpreted the political misfortunes
of the people as a punishment by Jehovah for their sins. It was
thus that the tragedy of their enslavement by the Babylanions
(586 B.C.) was explained. (Isa. 40:1-2.) It was within this framework also that the Book of Judges was written. When Israel was
loyal, she prospered among the nations; when she forgot her god,
she was turned over to her enemies (Judg. 2:11-15). As the Jew
of Jesus' day reviewed his history, he saw a succession of tragic
defeats and centuries of servitude under foreign powers. The
Assyrians, Babylonians, Persians, Greeks, Egyptians, Syrians, and
now the Romans had been their overlords. It was difficult not to
be pessimistic. Surely the nation had not been that sinful! The
familiar formula was being questioned.

I

There was another rule, however, by which the Jews of Jesus'
day had come to interpret contemporary events. It was a world-
view which their fathers had discovered when they were under

the domination of the Persians. There they came into contact with the religion of Zoroaster and its teaching that behind the universe there was a basic dualism in which good and evil, and light and darkness, were opposed in spiritual warfare against each other. This dualism, it was thought, was expressed on earth in the evil experiences of men, as well as in the good. Much of the suffering and many of the misfortunes of life were regarded as due to the demoniacal forces in the universe. They believed that God would one day overthrow this dark rule, but in the meantime, the world was under the control of demons and the Prince of Evil. These ideas influenced the Jews profoundly.[1]

Accordingly, the individual Jew explained certain sicknesses and some of the personal disasters which came to him in terms of the evil work of demons or of actual demon possession. One cannot read far in the Gospels before coming across references to this fact. The first impression Jesus made upon the common people of the day was in regard to his power to cast out demons. We have such stories as the casting out of the demons in the man at the synagogue (Luke 4:31-37), of the sending of the demons into the herd of swine at Gadara (Mark 5:1-20), and of the evil spirit who ventured to return with reinforcements to the body from which he had been evicted, so that he might not again be dislodged so easily (Luke 11:24-26). Most, if not all, of the conditions which we would account for today in terms of mental sickness or neuroses, the people of that day referred to as demon possession.

On a national scale this belief in the kingdom of evil spirits modified considerably the messianic hope of the Jews. An early view represented the Messiah as a king who would be raised up from among the people to rule with justice and mercy (Isa. 9:6-7; 11:1-9). A reign such as David's was to be restored on the earth, and the political enemies of the nation were to be put down. Later,

---

[1] In the Letter to the Ephesians, a Christian writing of the second half of the first century, we read: "Put on the whole armor of God, that you may be able to stand against the wiles of the devil. For we are not contending against flesh and blood, but against the principalities, against the powers, against the world rulers of this present darkness, against the spiritual hosts of wickedness in the heavenly places (6:11-12). This is a clear reference to the belief of the day among both Jews and Christians in the organized kingdom of unseen demoniacal forces which was responsible for many of the misfortunes and tragedies of earth.

belief in the sway of unseen spiritual forces of evil, which had present control over the universe, enlarged this conception of the Messiah's task. It was thought that he would engage in a cosmic battle between good and evil, and that he would overcome all hostile agencies, not only on earth but also in the universe itself. He was conceived now to be a heavenly being. World judgment, the destruction of the sinful, and the resurrection of the righteous dead were to be a part of the final issue.[2]

A program of this character is called apocalyptic. The word comes from a root term meaning "to unveil," and as used means an unveiling of a hidden future. This future is conceived usually in terms of a great cosmic upheaval in which the forces of the universe are employed as agents for expressing the judgment of God. Such judgment does not come upon men and nations, however, until times have grown steadily worse and have reached an hour so dark that human help on earth will avail nothing. Only a divine intervention from above can save the good.

Apocalyptic thinking thrives on adversity. It grows out of darkness and blooms under despair. For this reason the Jews began especially to think in these terms during the persecutions of Antiochus Epiphanes toward the middle of the second century B.C. (175-164). This Syrian ruler sought to force Greek culture upon the Jews, an interpretation of life and ethics which was repugnant to them and ran counter to their legal restrictions.[3] The extreme indignity was when Antiochus sacrificed swine's flesh upon an altar raised to Olympian Zeus on the very site of the altar of burnt offerings in the Temple at Jerusalem.[4] The Book of Daniel refers to this act as the "abomination that makes desolate" (11:31). An uprising followed which is known in Hebrew history as the Maccabean Revolt. It was begun by the rebellion of Mattathias, an aged priest, and carried on with vigor by his son Judas Maccabaeus. These days of bitter revolt gave new impetus to the apocalyptic outlook.

---

[2] Between these two views of the Messiah there were intermediary ones in which the Hebrew people, or the spiritual core among them, suffering vicariously (Isa. 53) and later glorified (Dan. 7:13-14), were regarded as messianic. Cf. later references to this development, pp. 107-11.

[3] I Macc. 1:44-53.

[4] II Macc. 6:2.

Apocalyptic thinking expressed itself very soon in apocalyptic writing. The Book of Daniel belongs to this time of persecution. First Enoch likewise is composed of materials coming from this general period.[5] Writings of this character continue to appear in days of stress and strain.[6]

All of this was a part of the religious outlook of the Jews in Jesus' day. It did not influence the Pharisees and the Sadducees overmuch, for their approach was of a different order. But because of these apocalyptic writings, the man on the street who galled under Roman oppression was strengthened to hope for better things to come through divine intervention. Jehovah would act when the time was right. It was encouraging to remember this— encouraging in an age of disillusionment.

II

The tensions in the historical background of the Jewish people resulted in the development of different religious viewpoints among them. These various viewpoints, in turn, led to the formation of certain groups, some of which continued to exist in New Testament times. We can see this clearly in the case of the Pharisees and the Sadducees.

The origin of the Pharisees goes back probably to the pre-Maccabean Hasidim, a group which supported the cause of religious and political freedom, led by Judas Maccabaeus (167 B.C.), which cause was referred to in the previous section. As was noted there, Antiochus Epiphanes, the Syrian ruler, had sought to Hellenize the Jews, and Judas led a violent revolt against him. When victory had been won through military efforts, the Hasidim, who had been fighting on Judas' behalf, returned from combatant service to their religious (pious) interests and stressed again the keeping of the law. Only thus could a strong national life be maintained, they believed. It is thought by some that these Hasi-

---

[5] Cf. R. H. Charles, *The Apocrypha and Pseudepigrapha of the Old Testament*, II, 170-72 for dates on the various sections of I Enoch, e.g. chaps. 1-36 (before 170 B.C.), 37-71 (94-64 B.C.), 72-82 (*ca.* 110 B.C.), 83-90 (166-161 B.C.), 91-104 (104-95 B.C.).

[6] Within Christian literature there is the Apocalypse of John which should be dated at the time of the persecution under Domitian (*ca.* A.D. 96). It grew out of the same psychology of despair which gives rise to brilliant flames of hope for deliverance from above, but extreme pessimism regarding this earth.

dim became, in turn, the forerunners of the party in Jesus' day referred to as the Pharisees.[7] They were influential exceedingly in their stress upon the law and the Sabbath. As separatists or purists they sought to keep their heritage sacred, free from the taint of contemporary cultural contacts.

The program of the Pharisees in Jesus' day was to observe the commandments with such thoroughness that the Messiah would come. Jesus took issue with them because of their legalistic stress upon the letter of the law and their neglect of human values, which were forgotten in the process. They accepted not only the five books of the Law but also the tradition of the rabbis which had developed during the centuries through interpretation, somewhat as English law has evolved. Belief in divine providence, life after death, and the existence of angels were found in their official tenets also. Because of their opposition to the free spirit of Jesus, they do not appear in their best light in the Gospels. This fact should not blind us to the sincerity of many of them, nor to their contribution to Judaism.

Not all of the Jews reacted negatively to the Hellenistic culture which was being forced upon the people by Antiochus Epiphanes. There were some pre-Maccabean Hellenists among them who favored it, not that they intended in the least to be disloyal to their own religion. Rather, it was their conviction that a broadening interest in the world of that day was wholesome and desirable. Their leaders were the priests of the line of Zadok. It was from this group probably that the Sadducees came. Many centuries before, David had appointed one Zadok as priests (II Sam. 8:17; 20:25). We find that Solomon continued him in office, elevating him perhaps to the position of high priest (I Kings 4:4). A priestly line of succession became an important matter in the nation, and at this time of the rebellion against Hellenism, the old ruling party claimed to belong to the line of Zadok. From this personal name it has been suggested that the term "Sadducees" developed, although this point is not established finally.[8]

---

[7] Klausner, *op. cit.*, p. 202, subscribes to this view. Cf. Herford, *The Pharisees*, pp. 30-35. Enslin, *Christian Beginnings*, p. 112, concludes that their origin is unknown.

[8] Another suggestion is that the term "Sadducee" came from *Zaddikim*, a

As a group the Sadducees stressed certain tenets of belief. They did not accept the rabbinic traditions based upon an interpretation of the Law which the Pharisees regarded as binding upon the Jew. This made them legally severe. The survival of the soul after death[9] and belief in the existence of angels were rejected by them likewise. They did not think of God as closely related to the affairs of men, and denied divine providence for the individual. The Temple rather than the synagogues provided their chief sphere of operation. They did not win the same respect from the people as a whole which was accorded the Pharisees.

Sometimes the high priests were Sadducees, but not always.[10] Holders of this office became very powerful in the life of the nation. The temple system of taxation brought them wealth, and their fraternizing with governmental officialdom gave them prestige among certain people. Until the days of Antiochus Epiphanes, the office of high priest was hereditary. At that time, however, the Syrian court appointed whom it pleased. Later Herod continued this practice and used this appointing power for political advantage. This was displeasing to many Jews. The fact that the high priests could be removed from their position by the civil authorities predisposed them sometimes to be too friendly with the rulers.

III

The Jewish citizen who was alert to the issues of the day in his religion was faced not only with the differences in point of view between the Pharisees and Sadducees, but also with the individualistic outlook of other groups within the nation. One of these groups was the Essenes. They were extreme ascetics who withdrew from the usual contacts of daily living and set up colonies where they shared a communal life.[11] Many of these cells were in the

---

Hebrew word meaning "the righteous." This group felt that they were particularly righteous because they accepted the law only, and refused to admit the validity of oral tradition.

[9] See Luke 20:27-40, where they argued with Jesus against belief in the bodily resurrection of the dead.

[10] Several high priests were appointed from the Boethusians, who seem to have been a Sadducaic family. The name was taken from Boethus, who had been appointed high priest by Herod in 26 B.C.

[11] Although they are referred to sometimes as pacifists, Josephus *Wars* II. 8. 10, 4, implies that they participated in the Jewish wars with the Romans.

region near the Dead Sea. John the Baptist has been said to have been a member of this group because of his ascetic interests, but other aspects of his ministry would not indicate such affiliation. Like the Pharisees, their origin goes back to the Hasidim of the Maccabean days. They became even more rigid, however, than the Pharisees themselves. They were eclectic in the sense that some of their tenets came from Greek thought, while others suggest oriental mysticism. Many of their practices resembled the Christian monastic movements which were to develop later in the church.

Specifically, this was a celibate movement,[12] for the most part composed of those who shared their properties, practiced silence at their common meals, and indulged in frequent baths. They wore white robes, observed the Sabbath on the seventh day, and recognized the Temple to the extent of sending some offerings to it. Many of their doctrines were known only to the initiated. They were supposed to be acquainted with the secret names of angels with which other sects were unfamiliar. The immortality of the soul apart from the body was one of their beliefs likewise. It has been suggested that in the time of Philo and Josephus there were in all Palestine about four thousand Essenes, so that their influence on the thinking of the time was not inconsequential.

Our knowledge of the Essenes has been enlarged due to the recent (1947) discovery of the Dead Sea Scrolls. A community of this group had been established near the Wady Qumran, just a few miles south of the northwest corner of the Dead Sea, where they lived until the Romans destroyed it at the time of the war against the Jews (A.D. 66-70). The first scrolls were found in a cave near this site, and other caves in the area have since yielded additional manuscripts. Through the use of pick and shovel some of the building foundations have been excavated.

The importance of these scrolls lies in the fact that they give us insights into an aspect of Judaism, other than that of the Pharisees and Sadducees, concerning which we had only limited information. The date of the Qumran writings is *circa* 170 B.C.-A.D. 68. The scrolls include the "Book of Isaiah" (one complete and

---

[12] Their fellowship included men only. Some of them forbade marriage altogether, while others permitted it only for the procreation of children.

one incomplete), the "Commentary on Habakkuk," the "Lamech or Genesis Document," the "Manual of Discipline" (regulations for life in the order), the "War between the Sons of Light and the Sons of Darkness" (an allegorical writing that is a kind of apocalypse), and a "Book of Hymns" (a collection of psalms). Since the original find, additional search has brought to light multiple fragments of biblical writings.

The influence of the Essenes upon early Christianity is a study of great interest. Extreme claims, in this regard, followed the discovery at the beginning. These have since been modified, but it is becoming increasingly evident that in assessing the origins of the Christian movement, the Essenes must be considered as a part of the picture.[13]

In striking contrast to the Essenes there was a group of revolutionists known as the Zealots. These were the patriots who regarded Roman rule as the outstanding evil of the day. Their methods involved the use of force and violence. Josephus suggests that their origin goes back to a resistance or revolt against the census of Quirinus in A.D. 6 or 7 which was taken as a basis for levying taxes.[14] Under one Judas of Galilee (or Gamala) and Zadok the Pharisee, a movement was started which grew rapidly, especially in Galilee. One of Jesus' disciples was Simon "who was called the Zealot" (Luke 6:15). It is interesting that Jesus should have chosen an intense nationalist as one of the Twelve; it is indicative of his deep appreciation for his own people and their future. The Zealot cause remained alive for several decades, expressing itself in the middle of the century in a band of assassins known as the Sicarii or "dagger carriers."[15] This political agitation led ultimately to the uprisings of A.D. 66-70 and to the destruction of Jerusalem in A.D. 70.

Three other groups remain to be mentioned, the Zadokites, the Herodians, and the scribes. The Zadokites represented a reform movement among the priests, begun more than a hundred years

[13] Cf. Sherman Johnson, *Jesus in His Homeland,* chs. IV and V.

[14] Josephus *Antiquities* XVIII. 1. Some, however, find their origin in the Maccabean period and see in this group an extreme expression of the Hasidim. Cf. Klausner, *op. cit.,* p. 202. "They were the Hasidim for whom politics became an actual religion."

[15] Cf. the reference to an outburst led by a self-claimed messiah in Acts 21:38.

before Jesus and directed toward the worship at the Temple. Being unsuccessful they left Jerusalem and set up quarters at Damascus. Later, they returned to Jerusalem to challenge both the Pharisees and Sadducees who opposed them bitterly.[16] The Herodians were a group who favored the continuation of the Herod party in power after Archelaus was deposed in A.D. 6 and a governor appointed by Augustus. It is interesting to note that this party sided with the Pharisees against Jesus (Mark 3:6; 12:13). It would appear that they feared he was inciting a nationalistic uprising which might interfere with their interests and play into the hands of those who opposed them. While they were political in character largely, it should not be forgotten that among the Jews the political and the religious were all but synonymous.

The scribes did not constitute a special party although they are referred to as a group. In the time of Jesus most of them were Pharisees.[17] They should be thought of as scholars rather than as copyists. Mainly, they were regarded as authorities in the law. They taught frequently at the synagogues where the law was interpreted. The origin of the scribes goes back probably to the days of Ezra, when interest in the law was so marked that a group of persons known as the "Sopherim" came into being, whose responsibility it was to copy, but most of all, to interpret the law. Their successors were called "Hakamim."

IV

Religious points of view manifest themselves usually, sooner or later, in such concrete forms as buildings, institutions, and ritual. It was thus among the Jews. The Temple, the synagogues, and the great religious feasts brought into outward expression the religious longings and ideals of the nation. In the time of Jesus the Temple which served the people had been built by Herod. Begun in 20 B.C. it was not completed until A.D. 64, although it was in use most of the intervening period. Constructed of white marble and ornately decorated, it was a structure of impressive beauty as it

---

[16] Cf. Book of Zadok in R. H. Charles, *Apocrypha and Pseudepigrapha of the Old Testament.*

[17] Cf. Mark 2:16 and Acts 23:9, where "scribes of the Pharisees" is used.

rose from the summit of Mount Moriah.[18] From a distance the pilgrim en route to Jerusalem saw it as an imposing and beautiful edifice. Its size has been estimated as 750 feet wide and 1,000 feet long. Porches, colonnades, and a series of courts for the women, men, and priests, gave dignity to this house of Jehovah. Here too was the holy of holies, which the high priest entered once a year to stand before the Lord.

As a place of sacrifice, services were held daily in the Temple. The blowing of the silver trumpets and the chanting of the choirs to the accompaniment of music lent solemnity to the offerings which were presented here. Not all the Jews could attend regularly, many of them being able to come only at the great festival seasons since they lived abroad. It has been estimated that there were between five and six thousand priests attached to the Temple. Their lineage to Aaron was checked carefully, and they were divided into twenty-four courses. In their work they were assisted by the Levites, subordinate officials, who were supposed to be descendants of Levi. This was the atmosphere within which the Jews worshiped. Through the payment of the temple tax and the multiple offerings, great wealth was poured into the sacred precincts.

There were three great feasts yearly: Passover, near the first of our April; Pentecost, fifty days after Passover, toward the end of our May; and Tabernacles, near the first of our October. The Feast of Passover (Lev. 23:5) celebrated the deliverance of the Hebrews from Egypt. Pentecost (Lev. 23:9-21) was a harvest festival, but it came to be a time for recognizing the giving of the Law also. Tabernacles (Lev. 23:33-34) commemorated the providential care of Jehovah during the wilderness wanderings. Two other occasions which should be mentioned also are the Feast of Purim, near our March 1, and the Feast of Dedication, in our December. In comparison with the three already noted, these were minor celebrations and late in origin. Purim recognized the victory of the Jews over Haman as related in the Book of Esther, and the Feast of Dedication was held in honor of the rededication of the Temple after it had been defiled by the Syrians (*circa* 165 B.C.). Feast-time was an occasion of drama, pagentry, and deep religious

[18] It has been urged by some that the mount upon which the Temple stood was called Zion.

feeling. The nationalistic hopes of the people rose high at these gatherings as they remembered their past and contemplated Jehovah's action on their behalf in the future.

Just as the priests presided over the functions of the Temple, the Pharisees concerned themselves with the synagogues. There was but one Temple, but synagogues were very numerous. Their origin is thought to have been during the days of the captivity in Babylon when the Jews needed a meeting place where they might consider their common interests in Jehovah-religion. Although some worship was conducted here, its chief function was that of being a school where the Law could be interpreted. For this reason the scribes or lawyers, as the official teachers, achieved great importance in the synagogue.

Wherever there was a sufficient number (ten male members) to establish one,[19] a synagogue could be set up. Regular meetings were held on the Sabbath and during the week on Monday and Thursday. The synagogue provided a place where Jesus could address the Jewish people in formal meeting, and later it gave an opportunity for the first Christian preachers to present their cause. Although its first simple services lacked the colorful accompaniments of the Temple, its teachings made for ethical stability in the life of the nation.

The religion of the Jew with its various expressions through the messianic hope, the apocalyptic expectations, the several groups— Pharisees, Sadducees, Essenes, Zealots, Zadokites, Herodians, and scribes—and the institutions of the Temple and synagogue presents a complicated picture. It possessed the strength of contradictory and varied points of view. Within it were the seeds of survival, particularly in its ethical and moral earnestness. But it contained the seeds of dissolution likewise. Apocalyptic pessimism and an arid legalism threatened to stultify it.

When we read the Gospels, we tend to regard the religion of the Jew as an opposing force to the ministry of Jesus. That there was opposition is clear, but also there was in active Judaism a living religion that gave background to the message of Jesus.

---

[19] It was expected that these should be men of leisure (batlanim) who had time to devote to administration and worship. The Jews regarded ten persons as necessary to compose a congregation. Cf. the Talmudic tractate Sanhedrin 1.6.

QUESTIONS FOR DISCUSSION

1. Which of the following reactions to dark and discouraging situations impresses you as most desirable?

    a) A quiet waiting upon God to act in ways that will brighten the dark picture?

    b) The building of a program of action by which to change the situation?

    c) A concentration upon life in the next world where the ills of the present do not exist?

    d) A turning to special rules for living which takes one's attention away from the darkness?

    e) A withdrawing from normal human associations?

2. Which of the above alternatives did the Pharisees take? the Essenes? the Apocalyptists? the Zealots?

3. Be prepared to defend the thesis that there is a historical explanation for the rise and development of each of the dominant religious groups among the Jews. To what extent does this explain their opposition to Jesus?

4. If you had been a Jewish intellectual in Jesus' day, would you have regarded the varied religious viewpoints among the Jews as challenging or confusing? Explain. How would it have seemed to you had you been an unschooled person of the streets?

5. To what extent, if any, does the situation of Protestantism today with its multiple denominations parallel the situation in the religion of the Jew in Jesus' day?

6. Would the religion of the Jew in Jesus' day have been stronger had it been more personal and less institutionalized, since there would have been less stress upon religious exercises and more emphasis upon individual faith and devotion?

7. The religious institutions of the Jew helped to preserve his national consciousness at a time when the nation was subject to a foreign government. Was there or was there not great value in them for this reason?

8. Which do you regard as making the greater contribution to the religion of the Jew in Jesus' day, the Temple where worship was central or the synagogues where instruction predominated?

9. As between the Pharisee with his emphasis upon conformity to the Law, and the Sadducee with his regard for ritual and ceremony, which was more valuable to the nation? Give reasons for your decision.

10. Does the religion of the Jew impress you as being a vital and living expression or an empty and sterile one?

SUGGESTIONS FOR READING

I. Hebrew Apocalypticism

Enslin, Morton S. *Christian Beginnings*. New York: Harper & Brothers, 1938. Pp. 141 ff.

Frost, S. B. *Old Testament Apocalyptic*. London: Epworth Press, 1952. Selected readings.

Grant, F. C. *Ancient Judaism and the New Testament*. New York: The Macmillan Company, 1959. Pp. 84-94.

II. The several religious groups within Judaism

Beck, Dwight M. *Through the Gospels to Jesus*. New York: Harper & Brothers, 1954. Pp. 20-26.

Burrows, Miller. *The Dead Sea Scrolls*. New York: The Viking Press, 1955. Selected readings.

Dana, H. E. *The New Testament World*. Nashville: Baptist Sunday School Board, 1937. Pp. 116-17.

Enslin, Morton S. *Christian Beginnings*. New York: Harper & Brothers, 1938. Pp. 111-28.

Gaster, Theodor H. (ed.). *The Dead Sea Scriptures*. New York: Doubleday & Company, 1956. Selected readings.

Johnson, Sherman E. *Jesus in His Homeland*. New York: Charles Scribner's Sons, 1957. Selected readings.

Klausner, Joseph. *Jesus of Nazareth*. New York: The Macmillan Company 1929. Pp. 201-27.

III. The place of the synagogue, Temple, and the Sanhedrin in Judaism

Dalman, G. *Sacred Sites and Ways*. New York: The Macmillan Company, 1935. Ch. 16.

Enslin, Morton S. *Christian Beginnings*. New York: Harper & Brothers, 1938. Pp. 129-37.

Grant F. C. *Ancient Judaism and the New Testament*. New York: The Macmillan Company, 1959. Pp. 38-56.

Kee, Howard C. and Young, Franklin W. *Understanding the New Testament*. Englewood Cliffs, N. J.: Prentice-Hall Inc., 1957. Pp. 32-45.

Johnson, Sherman E. *Jesus in His Homeland*. New York: Charles Scribner's Sons, 1957. Selected readings.

IV. The Jewish feasts

Dana, H. E. *The New Testament World*. Nashville: Baptist Sunday School Board, 1937. Pp. 113 ff.

Guignebert, C. A. H. *The Jewish World in the Time of Jesus*. New York: E. P. Dutton & Company, 1939. Selected readings.

3

The Christian
Community and the
Gospel Tradition

THE STORY OF JESUS IS THE MOST FAMILIAR STORY IN THE WORLD although it is not always the best understood. To know it fully one must become acquainted with a great many facts. For instance, it must be known that behind the account of Jesus' life are the documents which tell the story, and behind these records is the Christian community and its varied interests.

Our knowledge of the early Christian community depends largely upon the writings it produced. There is little in contemporary Greco-Roman history to enlighten us concerning the church and its beginnings, as well as little concerning the personality and works of Jesus.[1] Christianity was an obscure movement in a far-off corner of the Empire, and its founder was crucified as a common criminal. There was nothing here to attract the attention of the literati of the day. In the face of these facts, we are fortunate that in due time after the death of Jesus, his followers themselves turned to writing.

I

The motives which prompted the preparation of the story of Jesus were multiple. The simplest assumption is that when the witnesses to the events in his life began to die, one by one, it was feared that the information about him would be lost. This concern, however, is not likely to have influenced overmuch a people who expected the end of the world in their own lifetime, as the first Christians did. There was to be no posterity, no extended history. A more realistic insight is that the early church gathered together the tradition concerning Jesus in order to meet the needs of a growing fellowship.[2] It has been proposed that this under-

[1] Cf. Josephus *Antiquities* XX. 9. 1; XVIII. 3. 3 (writing completed A.D. 93); Tacitus *Annals* XV. 44 (writing A.D. 110-20); Suetonius *Lives of the Caesars* ch. 25 (writing A.D. 98-138). Pliny (writing to Trajan A.D. 112) said that Christians sang a hymn to Christ as God.

[2] The word "tradition" does not mean "traditional." As used in a study of the Gospels, it refers to the developing story of Jesus, both oral and written.

43

taking was to provide a brief for missionary preaching,[3] and also
that debates within the Palestinian communities concerning Christian faith and practice made necessary a formulation of the story.[4]
An additional suggestion is that the tradition concerning Jesus
took shape for the strengthening and instruction of the members
of the fellowship itself.[5] All of these considerations have the merit
of insisting that the origin of the gospel tradition was functional
in character—that is, that it was rooted in the actual needs of a
living society.

In the beginning many of the converts to the faith had not seen
or heard Jesus. The majority of those who responded to Peter's
preaching at Pentecost, fifty days after the Crucifixion, were Jews
who had come to Jerusalem for the feast (Acts 2). Some lived
great distances from the Holy City and would have had little
opportunity to hear Jesus during his ministry. They were moved
by Peter's sermon and responded with deep earnestness. What
this new experience meant for them, as far as their living was concerned, they could have had few ideas on the day when they
became a part of the Christian fellowship.

With the passing of time certain questions would come naturally
to the minds of these Christian converts from Judaism. Some
of them would be such inquiries as: What should be their relation
to the Jewish religious system of the day, now that they had become followers of Jesus? What of the traditional expectations
concerning the coming of the Kingdom? Were they valid still?
What was to be the status of earthly possessions in the new fellowship? To what extent were outcasts and non-Jews to be included in the movement? Was the Law of Moses to be superseded
by the teachings of Jesus? These and other questions would press
themselves for answers.[6]

A special subject of inquiry which called for a particular reply
had to do with the death of Jesus. The Law said that anyone dying
as Jesus had done was accursed (Deut. 21:22-23). In spite of this

---

[3] Martin Dibelius, *Gospel Criticism and Christology*, ch. ii.

[4] Bultmann, "The Study of the Synoptic Gospels," in F. C. Grant, ed. and
trans., *Form Criticism.*

[5] Albertz, *The Synoptic Disputations*, p. 101.

[6] Cf. Acts 1:6; 2:44-45; 4:32–5:11; 10 for indications of these issues in the early
church.

the followers of Jesus were announcing that the crucified One was the Son of God, and saying that it was the purpose of God that he should die in this fashion for the sins of the world, and that the Scriptures had foretold it (Acts 2:23-47; 3:18). For the Jews there was a contradiction here basically, and those among them who become Christians found that they were in need of satisfying answers for themselves and those whom they sought to persuade.

It was in answering such questions as these that the Christian tradition concerning Jesus probably first took form. What better way to make reply than to turn to the words and deeds of their leader himself? In one sense these reminiscences might be called curriculum material for the growing Christian fellowship. It was basic instruction quite as much as inspiration that was needed.

II

In the collecting and formulation of the tradition concerning Jesus theological consideration also played a part. The early Christian community was a fellowship in Christ. Its experience of the Resurrection and Pentecost (Acts 2:1 ff.) had established him as exalted Lord in their midst, and it was within this conviction and from this premise that the church undertook to gather together the stories about Jesus and his ministry.

Sometimes it has been assumed that the early Christians gradually developed the high view of Jesus that the New Testament holds, moving from a humanistic to a divine conception of his person. The usual process that leads to the canonization of a saint does not apply here, however. Jesus' followers in the church experienced their Lord in the highest terms at the very outset. Although their thinking about him was enriched and deepened through subsequent years, it should be noted that their new life in the church began with a view of Jesus as exalted and glorified Lord. This was because of their experience at his hands through the Resurrection and at Pentecost when he indwelt their lives through the Holy Spirit.

When biblical writers refer to the early church as an eschatological community it is because of the character of the experience that brought it into existence and the convictions that it held

concerning itself and its future. It believed that in Christ it had
known a divine visitation that had established it and that it was
living in the last days when God's purpose in history would be
fulfilled. In the account in Acts (2:17-21) this is the interpretation
that Peter placed upon Pentecost as he quoted from the prophet
Joel.

One of the most important facts about the Christian community
is that with its exalted view of Jesus Christ, and its high understanding of itself, it did not lose an interest in the earthly life of
its Lord. In fact, it was the reality of his historical existence that
highlighted the glory of his person as revealed in the Resurrection
and at Pentecost. Here was the wonder of it. That the transcendant
Christ should have humbled himself to the level of a servant while
on earth was a fact that continued to astound the church,[7] and this
provided a theological motive for gathering together the tradition
about Jesus. These stories illustrated the divine humiliation of the
Lord Jesus Christ when he appeared on earth as a servant.

III

We have been taking note of the fact that certain practical and
theological motives led to the collecting and formulation of the
tradition concerning Jesus during the period before the appearance
of the canonical gospels. They were seen to be related directly to
the experience, needs, and theological understandings of the Christian community. There was nothing artificial or doctrinaire about
the process. A deep moral and spiritual concern moved the church
in a serious quest to present and interpret Jesus and his place in
the life and faith of his followers.

Because of the personal nature of the church's interest in Christ,
the question as to whether it was writing objective history in its
account of Jesus is a logical one to raise. In the scientific understanding of this expression, it should be said that this was not its
chief interest. It would be more correct to call it faith history or
even theologized history, for the facts and their meaning for faith
are usually closely intertwined. This is the only way it could have

---

[7] This divine humiliation was the theme of one of Paul's most significant passages. In what might be called an expression of the kerygma or preaching message of the church, the apostle dramatically stated this theme (Phil. 2:5-11).

been done in presenting Jesus within a movement such as the Christian community. And it was in this sense that the gospel writers understood history.

When we refer to the gospel records as faith histories we do not mean that no knowledge can be found in them of the Jesus of history. The conclusion of Robert H. Lightfoot who closes his volume on the gospels with these words "For all the inestimable value of the gospels, they yield us little more than a whisper of his (Jesus') voice, we trace in them but the outskirts of his ways" [8]— this conclusion is excessively negative.[9] A more reasoned judgment is that the Jesus of history is actually to be discovered within the kerygma or preaching message of the church. It was his historical life that gave meaning to the message of faith that was preached.[10]

In assessing the validity of the gospel portrait of Jesus a recognition of the above approach by the church is basic. Their insistence that fact and meaning belong together so that the portrait and the message become one is sound. So closely are they united that it is sometimes impossible to separate them. But a real person, Jesus of Nazareth, may be found vividly alive within the reports that the Gospels lay before us.

Before leaving this question reference should be made to the place of "prophets" in the early church. In referrring to the several gifts of the spirit the apostle Paul lists the ability to prophesy (I Cor. 12:10, 28-29). This leads us to inquire as to the function of these "prophets"; what did they do? May we assume that they were like the Seer of Patmos to whom came the visions of the Revelation to John? Persons such as these were sensitive to the Spirit through whom they heard the living Christ speak. And the words of the exalted Lord, raised and ascended into heaven, may well have been regarded as a valid teaching of Jesus, even more significant than those that he had spoken in the flesh. If this assumption is correct, there is the possibility that both words were sometimes combined, or the former taken as the latter in the reporting of the tradition.

[8] *History and Interpretation in the Gospels*, p. 225.
[9] For other expressions of historical skepticism cf. the writings of Rudolf Bultmann, particularly *Kerygma and Myth*.
[10] Günther Bornkamm has said this lucidly in his *Jesus of Nazareth*, "Our task, then, is to seek history in the Kerygma of the Gospels, and in this history to seek the Kerygma." P. 21.

Once again, fact and meaning would be joined together in a reported teaching of Jesus. Great care should be taken in interpreting
any specific teaching in this light, but its possibilities are important,
particularly in relation to passages where great significance is as-
signed to the person of Jesus.

<h2 style="text-align:center">IV</h2>

At first most of the reminiscences concerning Jesus and his teachings were expressed orally. This might be called the fluid period
during which men were searching their memories for sayings and
parables of Jesus which they might use in the administration of the
church, in preaching, and in the teaching of new converts. If a word
of their leader could be found as a guide, the authority of the
teaching would be enhanced. We can see this process at work in the
Pauline letters. In giving advice concerning marriage, Paul said in
one place: "To the married I give charge, *not I but the Lord,* that
the wife should not separate from her husband . . ." (I Cor. 7:10).
The very next paragraph begins: "To the rest I say, *not the Lord,*
that if any brother has a wife who is an unbeliever, and she con-
sents to live with him, he should not divorce her." [11] Clearly Paul
is falling back on a remembered word of Jesus in the first instance
and giving his own best judgment in the second. A third illustration,
again from Paul, indicates this tendency as it existed toward the
mid-fifties A.D.: "Now concerning the unmarried, *I have no command of the Lord, but I give my opinion* as one who by the Lord's
mercy is trustworthy" (I Cor. 7:25).[12] At this time no one of our
Gospels had yet been written, and the practice of Paul indicates
a procedure which had grown up during the years since the death
of Jesus.

An important factor in this gathering of the tradition concerning
Jesus was the tendency, through repetition and a developing sense
of orthodoxy, to fix the *form* of the sayings or story reported so that
variations would be unacceptable. This insistence on conformity
was not completely rigid, for Matthew and Luke both felt free to
change some phrases and to omit others in copying from Mark.

[11] Italics mine.
[12] Italics mine.

But even with these changes, often the original phrasing can be recognized.

The study of this tendency to arrive at more or less fixed forms in reporting the tradition concerning Jesus is known as Form Criticism (*formgeschichte*). It was applied first to the Old Testament in connection with a study of the Psalms and the life-situations out of which they came.[13] The study proceeds on the assumption that biblical tradition in its literary expression follows the same laws of transmission and formulation that are to be found in other areas of literature.[14]

The point of greatest difference among scholars in the field of form criticism has to do with the place which the Christian community played in the formulation of the tradition. Some see the community in the role of an inventor freely composing the stories or sayings in order to meet current needs for authoritative statement. Others see the community as fixing the form of the tradition as it was passed on to them from the original witnesses who heard and saw Jesus himself, in the interests of authority and orthodoxy. This latter view would fit better the account of the collection and use of the tradition as presented already at some length in this chapter.

As has been noted, the earliest tradition concerning Jesus was transmitted by word of mouth. The large place which was made for memory work in the educational procedures of Jewish society at this time facilitated this process. Sometime before our canonical Gospels, however, the tradition began to take written form.[15] Although the date of the first written material of any substance or size which lies behind our Gospels has been thought by some to be around A.D. 50,[16] literary activity began probably before this. It

[13] H. Gunkel, *What Remains of the Old Testament*, pp. 70 ff. Other specialists in this field are Albertz, Bultmann, Dibelius, Grant, Redlich, and Taylor.

[14] E. F. Scott, *The Validity of the Gospel Record*, p. 119, has listed the main forms found in the Gospels as: " (1) miracle stories; (2) 'paradigms' or 'pronouncement stories'; (3) aphorisms; (4) tales; 5) legends; (6) controversies; (7) apocalyptic utterances." Each scholar writing in this field today, however, has his own list of classifications.

[15] "When our Gospels emerge, some forty to fifty years after the events they narrate, they give clear evidence of resting upon already written records." Alfred M. Perry, "The Growth of the Gospels," *The Interpreter's Bible*, VII, 61.)

[16] This refers to the material common to Matthew and Luke largely and referred to as "Q." Cf. the discussion of this document in the following chapter, pp. 59-60. Streeter, *The Four Gospels*, p. 150, dates Q at A.D. 50. Moffatt places Q not

is possible that small collections of sayings dealing with specific subjects, as well as selected stories centering in certain issues of interest,
were written out earlier for practical usage as men of well-trained
memories recalled them. In all probability the passion narratives
circulated separately before becoming a part of the Gospels. The
same is true of the set of stories found in Mark 2:1–3:6, which deal
with conflicts between Jesus and the religious leaders. There are
other blocks of material found in Mark which are of this same
character (4:1-32) [17] We might call these brief collections "tracts"
if we do not press the modern term too far.

What we have then, during the period between A.D. 30 and A.D.
65-70 (date of Mark), is a development of the tradition concerning
Jesus which was thoroughly functional in character. It was remembered, collected, and its character established in the interest of
actual needs in the church. These needs were educational, homiletical, theological, and polemical. At first the tradition was oral.
Later, however, it was put into writing in connection with specific
interests—the death of Jesus, conflict between Jesus and the religious leaders, the nature of the kingdom of God. These small
blocks of tradition were similar to our "tracts" and were used in
much the same way. As the church grew and extended its interests
far beyond the borders of Palestine, it was felt that a more inclusive
statement was needed and this is how the first full-sized Gospel came
to be written.

QUESTIONS FOR DISCUSSION

1. To what extent would you judge that the Christian church through
its interests and needs influenced the character of the tradition (narratives
—teachings) concerning Jesus which was preserved? To what extent did
the tradition concerning Jesus contribute to the making of the church?
Which of these two influences would you think was the greater?

2. Which motive seems to you to be the most influential in the collecting of the tradition: theological considerations, to meet the needs of

---

later than the seventh decade of the first century and possibly within the sixth,
saying, "It reflects the faith, mission and sufferings of the primitive Jewish
Christian Church of Palestine long before the crisis of A.D. 70 began to loom at
the horizon." Cf. Moffatt, *Introduction to the Literature of the New Testament*,
p. 203.

[17] See Harvie Branscomb, *The Gospel of Mark*, pp. xxii ff. for a fuller discussion of these materials.

missionary preaching, to supply arguments for defending the faith, or to provide materials for Christian education?

3. In accounting for the putting of the tradition into writing, which of the following would have been, in your judgment, most prominent: the human desire to keep records, the realization that Jesus was not returning as soon as they had expected, the deaths of many of the original witnesses, the desire to illustrate the divine humility of Jesus, or the need for a practical medium for circulating the message?

4. In preserving the tradition which is most important: the exact words of Jesus in a given situation, an accurate representation of the gist of what he said, or the record of his attitude and spirit? Which of these represented the main concern of the Christian community?

5. The pragmatic test of usefulness was responsible for the preservation of tradition that was vital because it kept the selection close to the actual needs of people. Might not these conditions of choice have limited the scope of the selection, however, because *first century* needs determined the results? Is it possible that twentieth-century men would have chosen differently?

6. How do you account for the fact that the twentieth century finds the tradition selected by the first century to be as challenging as it is? Is is because human nature and its needs do not change materially through the centuries, or is it because Jesus was so great that his teachings are timeless?

7. The statement was made in the chapter that the fixing of the form of the tradition tended to make for orthodoxy because it ruled out radical variations. Was this a good thing in that it kept the tradition from being amplified by irresponsible writers, or was it a bad thing since it might result in limiting individual preference?

SUGGESTIONS FOR READING

I. The nature of the early Christian community

Enslin, Morton S. *Christian Beginnings.* New York: Harper & Brothers, 1938. Pp. 169-85.

Laymon, Charles M. *Christ in the New Testament.* Nashville: Abingdon Press, 1958. Pp. 22-37.

Scott, E. F. *The Validity of the Gospel Record.* New York: Charles Scribner's Sons, 1938. Pp. 85-109.

II. The character of the tradition concerning Jesus

Branscomb, B. Harvie. *The Gospel of Mark.* New York: Harper & Brothers, 1937. Pp. xviii-xxii.

Grant, Frederick C. *The Earliest Gospel.* Nashville: Abingdon Press, 1943. Pp. 58-75.

III. The historical reliability of the tradition concerning Jesus

Gealy, Fred D. "The Ipsissima Verba or the Ipsissimus Spiritum," *New Testament Studies,* ed. Edwin Prince Booth. New York and Nashville: Abingdon-Cokesbury Press, 1942. Pp. 115-38.

Major, H. D. A., Manson, T. W., and Wright, C. J. *The Mission and Message of Jesus.* New York: E. P. Dutton & Company, 1938. Pp. xvii-xxxi.

Scott, E. F. *The Validity of the Gospel Record.* New York: Charles Scribner's Sons, 1938. Pp. 1-24.

Robinson, James M. *A New Quest of the Historical Jesus.* Napierville, Ill.: Alec E. Allenson, Inc., 1959. Selected reading.

IV. The fixing of the tradition into definite literary "forms" according to a universal law of transmission.

Dibelius, Martin. *Gospel Criticism and Christology.* London: Ivor Nicholson & Watson, Ltd., 1935. Pp. 27-43.

Filson, Floyd V. *The Origins of the Gospels.* New York: The Abingdon Press, 1938. Pp. 85-114.

Redlich, E. B. *Form Criticism.* New York: Charles Scribner's Sons, 1939. Pp. 9-80.

Taylor, Vincent. *Formation of the Gospel Tradition.* New York: The Macmillan Company, 1933. Pp. 1-43.

V. The characteristics of a gospel

Bornkamm, Günther. *Jesus of Nazareth.* Translated by Irene & Fraser McLuskey and James M. Robinson. 3rd ed. New York: Harper & Brothers, 1960. Pp. 13-26.

Cadbury, Henry J. "The New Testament and Early Christian Literature," *The Interpreter's Bible.* Nashville: Abingdon Press, 1951. VII, 32-42.

Goguel, Maurice. *The Life of Jesus.* New York: The Macmillan Company 1944. Pp. 134 ff.

Scott, E. F. *The Purpose of the Gospels.* New York: Charles Scribner's Sons, 1949. Pp. 50-73.

4

The Four Gospels

A GOSPEL IS A COMPELLING LITERARY FORM. IT IS NOT A FORMAL treatise, a history, or a homily. Neither is it a biography as we know such writings today. The usual background material and the developmental approach to life which we are accustomed to associate with biographical studies are missing completely in the Gospels. For instance, Luke moves from the birth stories to a single incident in the life of Jesus as a twelve-year-old boy. Then he passes over the next eighteen years in his life, in some ways the most important for Jesus himself, and introduces him to his readers as a mature man "about thirty years of age." The account of the ministry in all of the Gospels is segmented and sketchy. Incidents follow one another in a kind of disjointed sequence. Background references to time and place are general, and we find ourselves in the last week at Jerusalem before we know it. This is unlike biography as it is written today.

In spite of the differences between biography and the Gospels, we see in the latter a directness and moving character not found in lengthier writings. In a series of staccato sketches they present Jesus both as teacher and helper in such a way that he emerges from the writings a real person of energy and spirit. The general treatment of the background gives to the teachings of Jesus a universality which brings to the reader a feeling that they are contemporary with himself. The impact of the Gospels is heightened by the terseness of their form. Each incident is a dramatic situation, and every teaching a word spoken out of life.

Before considering the origin of the gospels which have been accepted by the church for inclusion in the New Testament and are known as the canonical Gospels, we should take brief note of the fact that there are others which were written and rejected as unworthy. We call these the uncanonical Gospels by which, in this case, we mean writings of uncertain value, if not altogether heretical. In them legend overbalances fact largely.

Most of the uncanonical writings belonging to the New Testament period were written in the second century. Of these there are several which are found in the New Testament Apocrypha and are titled "gospels." Some of them are The Gospel According to the Egyptians which stresses asceticism, The Gospel According to the Hebrews whose authors were Nazarenes and Ebionites, and The Gospel of Peter which the Syrian Christians used. Another of these writings is The Gospel of Thomas. It is interesting especially because of the fanciful stories it relates concerning the infancy and childhood of Jesus. This should be distinguished from the Gnostic *Gospel of Thomas,* included in the Secret Sayings of Jesus, discovered about 1945 near the modern village of Nag Hammadi in Egypt. Based upon our Gospels, the writing is Gnostic in outlook and shows how this group approached the teachings of Jesus.[1]

The material in these writings is of little value in supplying data for a life of Jesus. When compared with the canonical Gospels, the latter stand out impressively in their reasonableness and ethical balance. It is indicative of the sound thinking of the Christian church that they repudiated these questionable writings in which a premium is placed upon magic and superstition.

I

The period before the writing of the canonical Gospels was one of growth and development for the church. It was a time of great activity—educational, homiletical, polemical, and missionary. These interests led to the collecting, editing, and recording of the tradition concerning Jesus of Nazareth. The literary product which resulted ultimately is found in the New Testament Gospels—Matthew, Mark, Luke, and John. We are able to assess their true character better since we are becoming more familiar with the life-process which brought them into being. There is a further literary study, however, that is necessary if we are to use them with understanding as sources for a life of Jesus. It is concerned with the structure of each individual Gospel, its rootage in the immediate background out of which it came, and its relationship to the other Gospels as well.

The Gospel of Mark has been dated variously between 65 and shortly after A.D. 70. In Mark 13:14 a reference is made to a desolat-

---

[1] Cf. the commentary on *The Secret Sayings of Jesus,* Robert M. Grant in collaboration with David Noel Freedman, with an English translation by William R. Schoedel. New York: Doubleday & Company, 1960.

ing sacrilege standing "where it ought not be." This is taken usually
to refer to a desecration of the Temple by the Romans and to suggest that the Temple was still standing. Accordingly, the book
would then be regarded as having been written before the destruction of Jerusalem in A.D. 70. It was said by Irenaeus (*circa*
A.D. 180) [2] to have been written after the deaths of Peter and Paul,
both of whom lost their lives probably in the mid-sixties during
the Neronian persecutions. First Peter 5:13 suggests that Mark was
in Rome, and this Gospel in the tradition is thought of as Roman.
Its author is considered to be John Mark, a well-known figure in
the Scriptures (Acts 12:12; 15:37; Col. 4:10; II Tim. 4:11; Philem.
24).

Papias of Hierapolis (*circa* A.D. 140) explains the origin of the
Gospel by saying that Mark became the interpreter of Peter, and
that he wrote all that he could remember from his preaching concerning the Lord's sayings or doings.[3] This would seem to be an
oversimplification of the process by which the Gospel of Mark came
into being, in view of its fragmentary character and the indications
that sections of it circulated independently before they were collected together to form a gospel proper. But it does associate
the Gospel with John Mark and imply a connection with firsthand
sources. The Gospel was written for Gentile readers. It both trans-
lates Aramaic words and explains Jewish customs (Mark 7:3-4, 11;
14:12; 15:42) and names (Mark 3:17). This is sometimes done in-
correctly. The difficult days following the persecutions under Nero
called for a lengthier statement concerning Jesus than had yet been
made, and Mark stepped into the picture and produced his Gospel.
That it found an important place for itself in the life of the church
is evidenced by the fact that both Matthew and Luke copy large
portions of it in preparing their own Gospels two decades or so
later. It was a success definitely.

Each Gospel has its own individuality growing out of the personality of the author, the situation to which it is addressed, and the
specific ideas which the writer wishes to emphasize. In the case of
Mark which should probably be read as over against a background

[2] *Against Heresies.* III. 1.1.
[3] Eusebius *Church History* III. 39. 15.

of Hellenistic Judaism,[4] Jesus is presented as the Son of God. He shows himself by loving deeds to be victor over demons, who alone recognize his divine status. In this regard he is seen as a supernatural being in conflict with supernatural powers. The stress is placed upon action rather than upon teaching. In its fast-moving narrative it provides a suggestive but incomplete order of events for the ministry of Jesus. Both Matthew and Luke follow Mark's chronology. Some scholars regard this scheme of happenings as a theological construction intended to set forth the thesis of the messianic secret.[5] Others find it historically logical and psychologically satisfying, but would not press for the exact location of the incidents as found in any indicated sequence.

II

The Gospel of Matthew is significant also as background material in preparing a life of Jesus. Standing in its position as the first book in the New Testament, it commands unusual attention, altogether apart from its own merits which are great. Traditionally it was regarded as having been written by Matthew the apostle. The statement of Papias, bishop of Hierapolis, to the effect that Matthew in the Hebrew language composed the sayings (the logia) and each one interpreted them as he was able,[6] was taken to refer to the Gospel. Actually these words may point to an earlier work composed of the sayings of Jesus, sometimes referred to as the "Logia."

Scholars agree largely today that the Gospel was not written by Matthew the apostle. Some of the reasons for this conclusion follow: Papias says that the sayings of Matthew were written in the Hebrew language (Aramaic); our Gospel, however, was written in Greek and was based largely upon Greek sources. Again, the Gospel of Matthew is didactic in character and shows an interest in rabbinical thought to an extent not to be expected from a practical publican. Furthermore, the Gospel itself does not claim Matthew as its author.

---

[4] Hellenistic Judaism represents the views of Jews who lived in the Greek world. It was more liberal than rabbinical Judaism. F. C. Grant, however, regards the theology in Mark as that of the Greek-speaking Gentile church. Cf. *The Interpreter's Bible*, VIII, 640.

[5] Cf. the discussion of the messianic-secret idea in a later chapter, p. 242.

[6] Eusebius *op. cit.* 16.

There is reflected also in the writing a development in church life more mature than that of the primitive period when Matthew would have worked. Finally, it might be asked whether the apostle Matthew, had he written the Gospel, would have depended as largely upon Mark who was not one of the Twelve? Taken together these reasons against regarding Matthew the apostle as the author of the Gospel are impressive.

Matthew depends so considerably upon Mark, even though he seriously sought in his revision to replace it, that it must have been written later. Sufficient time must have elasped for Mark to gain a reputation that would warrant the great use made of it. On the other hand, it was not written later than Ignatius (A.D. 110-115) and the Didache (*circa* A.D. 150) since both show acquaintance with it. Its reference to persecutions (Matt. 5:11; 10:18; 25:36, 39) and its concern with the end of the world (Matt. 24–25) bring it into rather close touch with the Revelation to John (*circa* A.D. 96). All in all, a date between A.D. 80-90 would seem probable.

This Gospel was intended for both Jews and Gentiles. It roots in Hellenistic Judaism and stresses what might be called the "ethics of obedience," not, however, in a legalistic sense to the exclusion of such inner qualities as knowledge and faith. Jesus is presented as a teacher, Son of God, and Son of man; he is also a new Moses, revealing a new Torah and establishing a new covenant that makes Christianity a successor to Judaism.[7] In all of this his authority comes from God (11:27; 28:18 ff.).

An interesting feature of the Gospel of Matthew is the alternation of blocks of teaching material with narrative,[8] as well as its fivefold divisions, suggesting a parallel to the five books of Moses. Each division closes with the words: "And when Jesus finished these sayings" (Matt. 7:28; 11:1; 13:53; 19:1; 26:1). Certain special emphases of this Gospel were for Jewish readers particularly, such as the idea that events in the life of Jesus fulfilled the Scriptures, and that his teachings and presence represented a new dispensation in contrast

---

[7] Cf. Edward P. Blair, *Jesus in the Gospel of Matthew,* for a development of the background of Matthew in terms of Hellenistic Judaism of the type found in Stephen whose sermon before the council is recorded in Acts 7.

[8] Matt. 5–7 (Teachings); 8–9 (Narrative); 10 (T); 11–12 (N); 13 (T); 14–17 (N); 18 (T); 19–22 (N); 23–25 (T); 26–28 (N).

to the old.[9] Syrian Antioch is suggested usually as the place where the Gospel was written. It was an important community where large numbers of both Jews and Gentiles were to be found.

III

The Gospel of Luke is another writing of importance as a source for the life of Jesus. The attention which it gives to prayer, the significance of women, loyalty to the state, sinfulness of a love for riches, and the place of all men—saints and sinners, Jews and outcasts—in the kingdom of God, make it an outstanding writing. This broad humanitarianism in Luke has sometimes obscured its Hebraic accents that suggest a relation to Hellenistic Judaism. Jesus is not represented as turning from either synagogue or Temple. He is seen to be a man, anointed by God, who performs miracles through God's power working within him. In Christianity is to be found the true Israel.

The author of this Gospel has been regarded rather consistently as Luke, the traveling companion and doctor-friend of the apostle Paul. Since there is no dogmatic purpose served by this particular identification, the tradition would not seem to have been invented. Such references to Luke as are made in Colossians (4:14), Philemon (24) and II Timothy (4:11) may have contributed to the tradition likewise. Scholars today regard the Gospel of Luke as part of a larger work which includes the book of Acts.[10] In the latter half of Acts there are several passages in which the author speaks in the first person.[11] If Luke is the author of these passages, and he is usually so regarded, then he is the author of the rest of Acts and of the Gospel as well. Similarities of language and style would indicate common authorship for both writings.

Taken together Luke-Acts tells the story of the movement which began with the birth of a baby in Bethlehem, and continued to spread and develop through the ministries of Jesus, the Apostles, and the missionary preachers, until it reached the center of the Empire, the city of Rome itself. Others had written the first part of

[9] This theme is found in the Sermon on the Mount, Matt. 5-7.
[10] See the introductory passage Acts 1:1-2; also Cadbury, *The Making of Luke-Acts.*
[11] We call these the we-passages: Acts 16:10-18; 20:5-16; 21:1-18; 27:1–28:16.

this story dealing with the career and ministry of Jesus, but Luke did not feel satisfied with their accounts (Luke 1:1-4). He wanted to start from the beginning himself. His writing was intended to be a great apologetic for the faith in the face of persecution, disillusionment, and skepticism. It is addressed to the Gentile world primarily. Antioch, Ephesus, and Rome have been suggested as the city of its origin, with either one of the last two more favored. The date of composition may be said to be A.D. 85-90, not long before the writing of Acts which may be dated at about the year 90 or shortly thereafter.

While both Matthew and Luke contain stories and sayings which are special to themselves, Luke has one section of his Gospel given over particularly to this material.[12] It is called sometimes the "greater interpolation" and is found in 9:51–18:14.[13] The Perean minstry of Jesus is its chief concern. Of particular interest also is Luke's neglect of a specific section of Mark—Mark 6:45–8:26. This material is referred to as the "great omission." Various theories concerning these two sections and their relation to the Gospel of Luke are treated in the commentaries and in the important New Testament Introductions. They are mentioned here to suggest the individuality of this writing.

IV

A close study of Matthew and Luke will show that frequent use was made of Mark by the authors of these two Gospels. Various estimates have been made as to the extent of this usage. Matthew reproduces about eleven-twelfths of Mark. Luke, on the other hand, uses rather more than half of Mark. Both writers are selective in this choice and individualistic in their adaptations of it to their own purposes. They are not mere copyists in this regard.[14] Because of this practice there is a large amount of material in these writings which is common to all three, common because two of them took the material from the third. It is called the "triple tradition."

In addition to the stories and sayings which are common to

[12] His special material is not limited to this section, however.
[13] Another section is known as "the lesser interpolation." Cf. Luke 6:20–8:3.
[14] These differences have led some scholars to suggest either a use of different copies of our canonical Mark, or the use of a possible earlier edition of Mark referred to as Ur-Marcus.

all three of these writings, there is another body of material found in two of them which we called the "double tradition." Primarily this material is common to Matthew and Luke and is of the nature of sayings or teachings largely. It shows evidence of being copied from a third writing, obviously not Mark. Scholars believe that this was a written document which they designate by the initial "Q." [15] Streeter considered it to have been written originally in Aramaic about the year A.D. 50 and at Syrian Antioch. We do not have a copy of this writing today, except as it appears in Matthew and Luke. The extent of this work is regarded variously by scholars. Moffatt lists a number of different reconstructions in his *Introduction to the Literature of the New Testament.*[16]

Besides the triple and the double traditions, there is other material which goes to make up the "single tradition." It refers to the stories and sayings which only one of the Gospels possesses. In Matthew we designate this by the letter "M" and in Luke by the letter "L." [17] Roughly speaking, a little less than half of Matthew is of this character while a little more than half of Luke is comprised of it. About seven per cent of Mark is peculiar to itself. The single-tradition material contains highly interesting tradition, and we would be ever so much poorer without it in arriving at our portrait of Jesus. For instance, in Matthew such parables as the tares (13:24-30; 36-43), the pearl of great price (13:45-46), and the wise and foolish maidens (25:1-13) belong to this Gospel alone; and in Luke the parables of the good Samaritan (10:25-37), the prodigal son (15:11-32) and the rich man and Lazarus (16:19-31) are its special possession.

In these brief paragraphs on the triple, double, and single tradition we have been considering the data which introduces us to what is known as the "Synoptic Problem." Matthew, Mark, and Luke are called the Synoptic Gospels because they look at the portrait of Jesus with unusual similarity, and employ frequently the same

[15] "Q" is the first letter of the German word *Quelle,* meaning source. Some identify it with the Logia in the Papias quotation previously mentioned in our discussion of the authorship of Matthew, cf. pp. 56-58. This view has been rejected by Alfred M. Perry, *op. cit.,* p. 64, who thinks Q to have been written in Greek.

[16] Pp. 197 ff. Matthew and Luke may have used different copies of Q, in the first instance to be signified as Qmt and in the second as Qlk.

[17] This material may have come from both oral and written sources.

words in describing his work, person, and message. In the midst of this marked similarity, however, there are striking dissimilarities. These similarities and dissimilarities, taken together, constitute the Synoptic Problem. How are we to account for them?

This is not the place for a lengthy discussion of this question. It is sufficient to indicate here that it exists and to suggest quite generally the line along which its solution has moved. The similarities among all three Gospels grow out of the fact that Matthew and Luke draw heavily upon Mark for their material. The particular similarities between Matthew and Luke exist because each used a writing we designated as Q in composing their Gospels.[18] The dissimilarities among the three Synoptic Gospels are due to the special material, oral or written, which each possessed, as well as to their individualistic use of common material. In the main this is known as the "two-source theory" because it suggests *two main written sources* for Matthew and Luke—Mark and Q.[19]

A fuller refinement of this theory has been suggested by B. H. Streeter as the "four-source theory." [20] It adds to the above the suggestion that M (Matthew's special material) and L (Luke's special material) came also from *written documents* (M from Jerusalem (A.D. 65 and L from Caesarea A.D. 60).[21] Besides this there was an Antiochian source for Matthew (tradition including the birth stories, probably oral) and another written source (the birth stories in Luke 1 and 2) used by Luke. Streeter suggests also an earlier edition of Luke known as Proto-Luke, composed of Q and L to which Mark and the source of Luke 1 and 2 were added later, expanding it into our larger Gospel of Luke in the New Testament.[22]

V

The Gospel of John presents an interpretation of Jesus which is unique in character. It is concerned primarily with the Jesus of

[18] Mark's use of Q is debatable.

[19] It does not exclude other sources, written or oral, but insists on two main written ones.

[20] *Op. cit.,* ch. ix.

[21] Insistence upon M and L as *written* documents, each complete in itself, is pressing the available data quite far. Some of this special material may have been oral.

[22] Cf. F. C. Grant, *The Growth of the Gospels,* p. 66, for another multiple source theory of the origin of the Gospels.

religious experience. As a book of religious insight it has great
value.[23]

We may date this writing at the close of the first century (A.D.
100-110). Seventy years of Christian experience lay behind it. The
author was interested in presenting Jesus to his day as a solution
to its disillusionment and cynicism. There was discouragement in
the church because the promises of the Revelation to John seemed
not to have been fulfilled. The Roman Empire had not been judged
and destroyed; Jesus had not returned as pictured. There were
other interests behind the writing of this Gospel also. The question
as to the relation between Jesus and John the Baptist was a matter
of concern, since there were those who were urging the supremacy
of the baptizer (John 1:19-23; 3:25-30), as was also the issue of the
reality of Jesus' life in the flesh (John 1:14). Jewish groups were
continuing to put forth objections to Jesus as the Messiah (John
7-8). The Gospel deals with all of these problems.[24]

As one compares the Fourth Gospel with the Synoptic Gospels
one is impressed with the differences between them. The vocabulary at many points is not the same; the form of statement differs
likewise. Again, the setting varies considerably,[25] and the chronology of events is different sometimes.[26] There are only a few incidents presented in John, compared to the many in the Synoptics.
At the same time it contains several lengthy sermonic discourses
not found in the others (6:25-59; 14–17).

John's Gospel is an extended dramatic meditation on the glory
of Jesus, the Son of God.[27] Written in the Hellenistic world it possesses a fine feeling for drama. In its relentless movement toward
the crucifixion of Jesus, it is reminiscent of the best in Greek
tragedy. Whereas this gospel has usually been considered Hellenistic and to be interpreted within the thought-forms of the Greek

[23] See C. H. Dodd, *The Interpretation of the Fourth Gospel,* pp. 444 ff.

[24] See E. Colwell, *John Defends the Gospel,* for a valuable discussion of the
In John's Gospel it is at the beginning of Jesus' ministry; in the Synoptics it is at
the Fourth Gospel," *The Interpreter's Bible,* VIII, 449 ff.

[25] In John's Gospel, Judea is the setting for most of the incidents; in the
Synoptics it is Galilee.

[26] An outstanding illustration is the position of the cleansing of the Temple.
In John's Gospel it is at the beginning of Jesus' ministry; in the Synoptics it is at
the close.

[27] "These are written that you may believe that Jesus is the Christ, the Son of
God, and that believing you may have life in his name." John 20:31.

world, the Jewish elements it contains should not be passed over lightly. The Judaism of the Dead Sea Scrolls substantiates this view, for it is also reflected in certain areas of this book.[28] The Fourth Gospel is against traditional Gnosticism, but there is within it a Hellenization of some of the main themes of Gnosticism.

As the author of this Gospel meditated long on the stories and sayings of the Synoptic tradition, mystic that he was, he did not always distinguish between what Jesus *said* in the flesh and what he was *now saying* to him in religious experience. It is not possible always, therefore, to tell whether it is a word of Jesus out of the past which John records, or whether it is the inspiration of the exalted present.

There is a philosophical background to the Fourth Gospel that contributes further to its uniqueness. The Logos philosophy of Philo appears in its Prologue (1:1-18),[29] although John himself was not a philosopher. The eternal struggle between light and darkness is here also. New birth is an ever-present theme in its chapters, reminding us of the interest in the Greek mystery religions which his readers possessed (3:1-15).[30]

The author of the Fourth Gospel is unknown. John the Elder has been suggested most often by liberal scholars as a candidate, partly on the basis of a quotation from Papias which mentions him as residing in Ephesus.[31] Traditionally John the disciple of Jesus has been regarded as the writer. Primarily because of the differences between this Gospel and the Synoptics, it is difficult to hold this

[28] Cf. Frank Moore Cross, Jr., *The Ancient Library of Qumran and Modern Biblical Studies,* pp. 153-62.

[29] Cf. vss. 1-3, in particular. Heraclitus (*ca.* 500-450 B.C.) , as well as the Stoics (*ca.* 300 B.C.) , employed the term "Logos" also. As used by Philo (*ca.* 20 B.C.-A.D. 50) in his attempt to Hellenize Judaism, it refers to the "reason" through which God created the world. John represents the Logos as becoming flesh in the historical Jesus, e.g., "The Word became flesh" (1:14). It is this life in the flesh which interested John most, however, not speculations concerning its origin.

[30] Cf. John 6:53-56 where the language concerning the Eucharist is reminiscent of the sacred meals of the mysteries. Cf. a reference to the mystery religions in chap. 1, p. 26.

[31] Most scholars consider Ephesus as the place where this book was written although Alexandria in Egypt has been suggested, largely because of the philosophical tradition which is associated with this city. Antioch has been suggested also as the place of writing, because of the similarities of thought and expression between the letters of Ignatius, bishop of Antioch, and the Fourth Gospel. Cf. Eusebius *op. cit.* III. 39, for the Papias quotation.

view. An actual disciple of Jesus would have stayed more consistently [32] by the main stream of the tradition found in Matthew, Mark, and Luke.

QUESTIONS FOR DISCUSSION

1. Which of the following seems to you to argue most for the importance of the Gospel of Mark in the literary composition of the Gospels?

   a) The fact that both Matthew and Luke follow its order of events, returning to it whenever they digress to present their own material?

   b) The great use made of it by Matthew and Luke in copying from it almost verbatim?

   c) The traditional association of the Gospel with Peter through John Mark who was said to have been the interpreter of the apostle?

2. What do you think of the argument that Matthew and Luke did not copy from each other because they would not have omitted as much of each other's material, as is the case, had they done so?

3. Since Matthew's and Luke's use of Q is verbally so similar in many places, does it suggest that this source was written or oral material? Explain.

4. Does the fact that Matthew's and Luke's Q material varies in form on occasion imply that they had different versions of Q, or do you think that their own individuality in the use of the same material would take care of the situation adequately?

5. Characterize each of the Four Gospels so as to highlight the individuality of each.

6. What is the Synoptic Problem?

7. What do we mean by the two-source theory?

8. What is meant by the four-source theory?

9. Explain the term "canonical Gospels."

10. Read the first two chapters of Mark and John, noting the differences in style of writing, the number of incidents included, and the emphasis placed upon ideas and narrative in each. Do these differences illuminate Clement of Alexandria's statement that John composed a "spiritual gospel"?

SUGGESTIONS FOR READING

I. The date, authorship, place of composition, and individual characteristics of each of the Gospels

[32] For a detailed study of the authorship of the Fourth Gospel consult the *Introductions to the Literature of the New Testament* and other selected books in this field.

A. Matthew

Barnett, Albert E. *The New Testament: Its Making and Meaning.* Rev. ed. Nashville: Abingdon Press, 1958. *Ad. loc.*

Blair, Edward P. *Jesus in the Gospel of Matthew.* Nashville: Abingdon Press; 1960. Selected readings.

Johnson, Sherman E. "Matthew: Introduction," *The Interpreter's Bible.* Nashville: Abingdon Press, 1951. VII, 231 ff.

Knox, Wilfred L. *The Sources of the Synoptic Gospels.* London: Cambridge University Press, 1957. Vol II, selected readings. Use also in connection with Luke.

McNeile, A. H. *Introduction to the Study of the New Testament.* New York: Oxford University Press, 1927. Pp. 3-72.

B. Mark

Barnett, Albert E. *The New Testament: Its Making and Meaning.* Rev. ed. Nashville: Abingdon Press, 1958. *Ad. loc.*

Goodspeed, E. J. *An Introduction to the New Testament.* Chicago: University of Chicago Press, 1937. Pp. 125-57.

Grant, F. C. "Mark: Introduction," *The Interpreter's Bible.* Nashville: Abingdon Press, 1951. VII, 629 ff.

McNeile, A. H. *Introduction to the Study of the New Testament.* New York: Oxford University Press, 1927. Pp. 3-72.

Robinson, James M. *The Problem of History in Mark.* Napierville, Ill.: Alec R. Allenson, Inc., 1957. Selected readings.

C. Luke

Barnett, Albert E. *The New Testament: Its Making and Meaning.* Rev. ed. Nashville: Abingdon Press, 1958. *Ad. loc.*

Gilmour, S. MacLean. "Luke: Introduction," *The Interpreter's Bible.* Nashville: Abingdon Press, 1952. VIII, 3 ff.

Laymon, Charles M. *Luke's Portrait of Christ.* Nashville: Abingdon Press, 1959. Pp. 1-12.

McNeile, A. H. *Introduction to the Study of the New Testament.* New York: Oxford University Press, 1927. Pp. 3-72.

D. John

Barnett, Albert E. *The New Testament: Its Making and Meaning.* Rev. ed. Nashville: Abingdon Press, 1958. *Ad. loc.*

Dodd, Charles H. *The Interpretation of the Fourth Gospel.* London: Cambridge University Press, 1953. Selected readings.

Howard, Wilbert F. "John: Introduction," *The Interpreter's Bible.* Nashville: Abingdon Press, 1952. VIII, 437 ff.

McNeile, A. H. *Introduction to the Study of the New Testament.* New York: Oxford University Press, 1927. Pp. 255-78.

II. The Synoptic problem

Burch, Ernest Ward. "The Structure of the Synoptic Gospels," *Abingdon Bible Commentary*. Nashville: Abingdon Press, 1929. Pp. 867-73.

Filson, Floyd V. *The Origins of the Gospels*. New York: The Abingdon Press, 1938. Pp. 115-41.

Perry, Alfred M. "The Growth of the Gospels," *The Interpreter's Bible*. Nashville: Abingdon Press, 1951. VII, 60-74.

Sanday, William (ed.). *Studies in the Synoptic Problem*. New York: Oxford University Press, 1911. Selected readings.

III. The four-source theory of the composition of the Synoptic Gospels

Streeter, B. H. *The Four Gospels*. New York: The Macmillan Company, 1952. Pp. 227-28.

IV. The nature and extent of Q

Moffatt, James, *Introduction to the Literature of the New Testament*. New York: Charles Scribner's Sons, 1911. Pp. 194-206.

Streeter, B. H. *The Four Gospels*. New York: The Macmillan Company, 1952. Pp. 182-86.

V. Ur-Marcus and Proto-Luke

Menzies, Allen. *The Earliest Gospel*. New York: The Macmillan Company, 1901. P. 34, n. 2.

Moffatt, James, *Introduction to the Literature of the New Testament*. New York: Charles Scribner's Sons, 1911. Pp. 191-94.

Streeter, B. H. *The Four Gospels*. New York: The Macmillan Company, 1952. Ch. viii.

Taylor, Vincent. *Behind the Third Gospel*. New York: Oxford University Press, 1926. Selected readings.

VI. The uncanonical gospels

Goguel, Maurice. *The Life of Jesus*. New York: The Macmillan Company, 1944. Pp. 157-61.

James, M. R. *The Apocryphal New Testament*. New York: Oxford University Press, 1950. Selected readings.

VII. Later writings

Grant, Robert M. and Freedman, David Noel. *The Secret of Sayings of Jesus*. New York: Doubleday & Company, 1960. Selected readings.

Grobel, Kendrick. *The Gospel of Truth*. Nashville: Abingdon Press, 1960. Selected readings. (A Valentinian meditation on the Gospel written *circa* A.D. 150.)

PART II

THE LIFE AND TEACHINGS

5

Bethlehem and Nazareth

THE ACCOUNTS OF JESUS' BIRTH HAVE STIRRED THE IMAGINATION and enriched greatly the devotional experience of Christians. Almost from the first the unusual character of his life was reflected in the stories of his coming into the world. This was true in spite of the fact that Jesus made no reference to this occasion, and only two of the twenty-seven documents of the New Testament contain narratives of his advent.

Matthew (1:18–2:23) and Luke (1:26–2:20) have preserved for us accounts of rare beauty in which the songs of angels, a virgin birth, the visitation of magi and shepherds, and the guiding light of a brilliant star commingle to tell of the joy and hope which Jesus' coming brought to man. It signaled the dawning of a new age in history. This manger-cradled babe, the angel said to Mary, "will be great, and will be called the Son of the Most High; and the Lord God will give to him the throne of his father David, and he will reign over the house of Jacob for ever; and of his kingdom there will be no end" (Luke 1:32-33).

A sense of expectancy pervades the birth stories from first to last, giving to them a religious spirit which marks them as prophetic literature. It is difficult to tell where history ends and poetry and legend begin in writing of this kind. Some would regard these accounts as historical throughout; others would think of them as wholly poetry and legend in which the significance of Jesus for life has been given a symbolical representation, following the Hebrew practice of expressing dogma in narrative form.

Reference is made sometimes to the similarity of the stories of Jesus' advent to the legends of the Greco-Roman world concerning the births of their leaders. For instance, there is the legend of Perseus born of Danaë, a virgin who was impregnated by a shower of gold. Then there is the story of Attis, whose mother, Nana, became pregnant as the result of eating a pomegranate. A comparison of these accounts with those of the New Testament will show that quite a different ethical ideal and spirit is found in the Christian records of the birth of Jesus. The Christian stories are highly moral and ethical and in harmony with the character of the life they celebrate, altogether apart from the historical question. The historicity of the stories, however, is not to be decided on the basis of the moral tone or ethical level of the New Testament accounts.

The Greco-Roman world found the idea of a virgin birth congenial. At the time when first the birth stories were being circulated, God's relation to the earth, both among the Jews and the Greeks, was considered to be remote. During the period before the birth of Jesus, the Jews had come to think of God in transcendental terms. So exalted above the earth was he that angels served as messengers to bridge the gap between heaven and the sphere of man. The Greeks, also, because of their view of the evil character of the material world, had elevated pure deity to a realm beyond the earth, and accordingly, had to make room in their thinking for intermediary beings, aeons, or subordinate divinities of different orders so that the two might be related. In view of this outlook we can understand how the stories of the virgin birth of Jesus would have made an impression upon the Greco-Roman world. In them they found God the remote One making contact with the earth through the birth of Jesus.

Today, philosophy of the divine immanence has made us sensitive to the idea of the divine presence throughout the universe.[1] In this light we think of God as related personally to his world at all times. In addition to this, we hold to the concept of natural law in the universe, by which we mean that all life, everywhere, proceeds in causal sequence through uniform and orderly processes. These can be observed, charted, tested, and validated through the application of the scientific method.

A virgin birth, as such, lies beyond the scope of these processes as we know them today. Strictly speaking, on these terms one may accept such an occurrence only by positing the existence of unknown modes of procedure, not yet observed and validated. Some choose to do this. Others reject such an event outright, and still others reserve judgment in the expectation of further knowledge. Through the centuries the church in its historic creeds has affirmed its belief in the virgin birth.

Persons will accept or reject the virgin birth of Jesus in accord-

[1] The term "divine immanence" refers to the indwelling of God, complete (pantheism) or partial, in the world.

ance with (1) their philosophical world view, (2) their scientific outlook, (3) their conception of Jesus, (4) their knowledge of the New Testament, and (5) their theory of the inspiration of Scripture. One has no other course in assessing matters of this character. In the final analysis it is well to remember that regardless of the means by which Jesus entered the world, the luminous impact of his mind and spirit upon history remains to this hour. No decision as to the mode of his birth can either add or detract from the brightness of that impression.

I

The date of Jesus' birth has been computed variously. Luke the historian introduced customarily significant happenings with a reference to contemporary events. In presenting the Jordan Valley religious awakening under John the Baptist he says (3:1-2):

> In the fifteenth year of the reign of Tiberius Caesar, Pontius Pilate being governor of Judea, and Herod being tetrarch of Galilee, and his brother Philip tetrarch of the region of Ituraea and Trachonitis, and Lysanias tetrarch of Abilene, in the high-priesthood of Annas and Caiaphas, the word of God came to John the son of Zechariah in the wilderness.

Tiberius Caesar was made emperor on August 19 in A.D. 14. The fifteenth year of his reign would be a date between August 19, A.D. 28, and August 18, A.D. 29.[2] Luke notes also that Jesus was "about thirty years of age" when he began his ministry (3:23). Putting these two statements together would place Jesus' birth broadly between 6 and 2 B.C. (allowing four years for the word "about").

Matthew records that Jesus was born "in the days of Herod the king" (2:1). This is a reference to Herod the Great, who died in 4 B.C. Accordingly Jesus would have been born before or during the year 4 B.C.

These figures are reached without too great difficulty. The situation is complicated, however, by the reference in the biblical account to the census which was taken when Quirinus was governor

---

[2] Tiberius was associated with Augustus for the last two or three years of his reign. His rule may be figured from A.D. 11 or 12 on this basis. The fifteenth year would then be A.D. 26 or 27.

of Syria, at which time Mary and Joseph are represented as going
to Bethlehem to register (Luke 2:1-5). Josephus records that this
census of Quirinus occurred in A.D. 6 or 7.[3] This date is too late to
fit the earlier figure computed on the basis of Jesus' age at the time
he was baptized by John the Baptist. Attempts to place Quirinus
in Syria at an earlier period in connection with a census have been
inconclusive.[4]

The available evidence leads most scholars today to locate the
birth of Jesus in the years 6-4 B.C. The date of December 25 was
fixed at Rome after long uncertainty in the first quarter of the
fourth century.

The place of Jesus' birth has been regarded traditionally as
Bethlehem in Judea because of the biblical account and of Luke's
reference to the enrollment under Quirinus. By this same rule, however, Bethlehem has been questioned as the birthplace of Jesus.
The usual Roman method of registration in such matters was to
require individuals to register in their home community, and Luke
makes it clear that Mary and Joseph lived in Nazareth (2:4). Why
then should they have gone to Bethlehem? Josephus knew only
the later census under Quirinus, and an earlier universal enrollment at the time of Augustus is not mentioned in secular Roman
history. The question is complicated further by the tendency in
the early church to relate the Old Testament to events in the life
of Jesus in a prophecy-fulfillment sequence. Since Micah had said
that out of Bethlehem the ruler of Israel would come (5:2),[5] it
could be concluded that locating the birth at Bethlehem was an
outgrowth of this passage rather than historical fact.[6] For some,
these considerations are not sufficiently conclusive to cancel the
biblical tradition altogether.[7] Others regard this part of the story
as legendary or an open question at best.

Both Matthew and Luke present genealogies of Jesus, Matthew
beginning with Abraham and coming down through David, and
Luke beginning with Jesus and extending back through David to

---

[3] Josephus *Antiquities* XVIII. 2. 1. Quirinus was legate in Syria between A.D.
6-9.
[4] See H. K. Luce, *St. Luke*, pp. 14-15.
[5] Cf. John 7:42.
[6] See Ramsay, *Was Christ Born at Bethlehem?* for a discussion of this subject.
[7] E. J. Goodspeed, *A Life of Jesus*, p. 29.

Adam the son of God (Matt. 1:1-17; Luke 3:23-38). The lines of descent are different in the two accounts.[8] As far back as Julius Africanus (third century A.D.) these differences were discussed with various solutions being offered. The levirate law, by which a dead brother's childless widow might be married to the living brother, to raise up children in the name of the deceased, and the difference between legal and actual parentage have both been suggested as solutions.[9] Most probably we have two separate traditions coming from different sections of the Christian Church. An acceptance of this conclusion delivers one from the necessity of harmonizing them. In any case, such record keeping as scientific genealogical research requires today was unknown in those distant days. In traditional lists such as these complete accuracy could not be expected.

Although both accounts present David as pivotal in the sequence, indicating the conviction of the early church that Jesus as Messiah was the son of David,[10] Luke, by carrying the genealogy back to Adam the son of God, is suggesting the universal significance of Jesus. His concern extended beyond the Hebrew people to include all mankind.

II

Life in Nazareth where Jesus was reared was varied and interesting. This small community was nestled in the hills, historic hills, which were crowned with tradition. Near by was the Plain of Esdraelon, famed as a scene of great battles in the nation's past. The names of Barak, Gideon, and Saul came easily to the lips as one gazed over the landscape, for here they fought for the glory of Israel and Israel's God. It has been said that from the hills above Nazareth "you see thirty miles in three directions. It is a map of Old Testament history." [11] This was the country of Elijah also, the idol of adventurous Jewish boys.

To grow up in the midst of such surroundings, and to play on

---

[8] Luke has forty-two names after David's; Matthew has twenty-seven. Vs. 23 reads "Heli" instead of "Jacob." The immediate ancestors of Zerubbabel are different in Luke, where also Nathan, instead of Solomon, is the son of David through whom the line of descent runs.

[9] Cf. Eusebius *op. cit.* 1. 7.

[10] See Goguel, *The Life of Jesus,* pp. 255-58, for a fuller discussion of the Davidic origin of Jesus.

[11] G. A. Smith, *Historical Geography of the Holy Land,* pp. 432 ff.

the tops of these hills, was an experience sure to influence a sensitive boy such as Jesus must have been. His adult references to Old Testament characters are imaginative and colorful, and it is reasonable to suppose that they became vivid to him in his youth. It may not be going too far afield to suggest that the boy Jesus and his Nazareth friends re-enacted the historical events which had occurred on the very soil where they were standing.

It was not only an appreciation for the past, which the view from the hills awakened in the minds of the boys who played in this locale. There was much to be seen in the present, also, which would be exciting and stimulating. Near by were the arterial roads which tied together the East and the West, and which united the lands beyond the Mediterranean with Egypt. Caravans in procession moved slowly along them, colorful in character and dramatic in form. These presented to Jesus a constant pageantry, suggesting strange peoples, distant places, and unknown experiences. There was a world beyond Nazareth, a Gentile world of splendor and power. Merchants, soldiers, priests, slaves, and itinerant vagrants tramped the stony roads. The very rich and the desolate poor were there. Spices, gold, precious stones, fragrant woods, and rare textiles were transported along these traffic lanes. All of this brought "the kingdoms of the world and the glory of them" close to Nazareth. Behind Jesus' statement that in the last days "many will come from east and west and sit at table with Abraham, Isaac, and Jacob in the kingdom of heaven" (Matt. 8:11) may be such scenes as Jesus witnessed of the coming and going of many peoples along the highway near by. The temptation which he was to know later in the wilderness, suggesting that he use worldly means to win the nations, could have come easily from the impression this passing show had made upon him.

Life within the village was interesting also. Its streets were narrow, bringing the villagers near to one another; while the small homes, often having but a single room, added further to the close proximity in which the people lived. These houses were built usually of stone and mud. They may have had an unglazed window, or they may had have none at all (Luke 15:8-10) .[12]

---

[12] The woman had to light a candle in order to see sufficiently to look for the lost coin.

Hard-packed earth provided the floor. Occasionally straw was scattered about for purposes of warmth and covering. The family livestock occupied a part of the house. If it were a one-room dwelling, there would be a raised platform on which the family slept. This kept them off the cold floor and apart from the animals. They were crowded, and sometimes the atmosphere was malodorous; but, withal, it was friendly and homelike. An oven in which the cooking was done provided some heat, while a grindstone turned whatever grain was available into meal for the baking. The cooking utensils were crude earthenware, but sturdy and serviceable.

The houses were topped with flat roofs which were put frequently to other uses than coverage. It was an ideal place for visiting with one's friends at the end of the day, for above were the stars which hung so low they seemed to be within one's reach. The wind, which would blow unexpectedly and just as suddenly die out (John 3:8), made it delightfully cool after the hot days. This roof was reached by an outside staircase. It has been suggested that the meeting of Jesus with Nicodemus may have occurred on a rooftop such as this (John 3:1-15). These were the selfsame housetops where the secret counsels of the home were revealed in open conversation (Luke 12:3). The paralytic who was brought to Jesus by his four friends was carried up a flight of outside stairs to such a rooftop. Then he was lowered into the room through an opening made by removing the tiles which served as the covering (Luke 5:17-26).

It was within such a home as this that Jesus grew up with his parents, brothers, and sisters. That it was a happy home is evident from the joyful references to home life in the statements of Jesus. Neighbors came in to help with the grinding of the grain (Luke 17:35); fragrant dough rose slowly as it rested on the back of the oven (Luke 13:21); torn garments were mended (Mark 2:21); and bowls were washed both inside and out (Luke 11:39). Hens sat on their eggs, and little chicks peeped their stifled cries from beneath the feathered wings of the biddies which mothered them (Matt. 23:37).

Best of all were the times at the end of the day when the folklore of Israel was recalled in stories of dramatic intensity. Jesus heard them again and again as a boy, and told them over and over as a man. It was here that his native gifts as a storyteller first found an outlet. One can speculate that some of his parables, with which he was later to hold the attention of the Galilean multitudes, awakened first the interest of the family circle in his Nazareth home. It was on Sabbath eve that these tales were most usually told as a preparation for the holy day. The food had been prepared for the morrow, and its fragrance filled the room as it was being kept warm for eating on the Sabbath (Exod. 35:3).

Reference has been made to the brothers and sisters of Jesus. We are told that the names of the boys were James, Joses, Judas, and Simon (Mark 6:3). The names of the girls are not given. That these are children of Mary would seem to be clear from the fact that Jesus is referred to in Luke as her firstborn son" (Luke 2:7). In spite of these statements, the question has been raised by the Roman Catholic Church as to their actual relationship to Jesus. This religious communion has not accepted the belief that Mary gave birth to additional children. That there were blood brothers and sisters of Jesus, children of Mary, has seemed to them to be sacrilegious. The perpetual virginity of Mary could not be held if this were true.

To meet this situation, certain suggestions have been made from time to time. One was that these children were cousins of Jesus.[13] A second proposal is that the children were sons and daughters of Joseph by a former wife.[14] This would make them stepsons of Mary, and they would be referred to as relatives of Jesus. Such suggestions as these are not convincing to those who have no dogmatic reasons for objecting to Jesus' having brothers and sisters of his own.

A preferred stating of the case would be to say that these are children of Joseph and Mary, and were born after Jesus. This is the view Protestants hold, by and large. It brings normalcy into the family experience of Jesus and helps to explain his kinship with the entire human race. The beauty of his mind and spirit, the supernal wonder of his life, and the altogether uniqueness of his

[13] This is the view of the Latin Church and was suggested by Jerome.
[14] The Greek Church holds this view. See the Protevangelium, or Gospel of James (8:13) for the earliest witness to this idea.

revelation of God are not dimmed in the least by the fact that he had blood brothers and sisters.

We do not know whether any of Jesus' brothers were married during the Nazareth years, but it is not unlikely that this was the case. If so, the preparation for the wedding which the times required was made. When his brothers' brides became a part of the household, it necessitated probably the building of an addition to the home, and Jesus the carpenter would have entered into this project with zest.

Sometimes there may have been family differences. That these were painful to Jesus is reflected in his reference to divisions (Luke 12:52-53):

In one house there will be five divided, three against two and two against three; they will be divided, father against son and son against father, mother against daughter and daughter against her mother, mother-in-law against her daughter-in-law and daughter-in-law against her mother-in-law.

These words referred to the days before the judgment at the end of the age, but they have a note of realism about them that indicates they may have come from experience.

All in all, however, we can be certain that Jesus' home life was a happy one. When it is remembered that the family pattern was chosen by Jesus to illustrate best the relationship between God and his children, this fact becomes clear. His favorite word for God was Father, and this would not have been true had Jesus been unhappy in his own home.

It was a fully normal Jewish household where traditional family life was at its best. A young boy could do a lot of growing up in such surroundings. There was give and take under the benign authority of the head of the house. Jehovah was honored and his Law was kept. A deep piety gave significance to simple family procedures and provided confidence in the goodness of living.

QUESTIONS FOR DISCUSSION

1. As you read the birth stories in the Gospels (Matthew 1–2; Luke 1–2), what do you conclude their main emphasis to be, judging from the content of the songs?

    a) The manner of conception and birth?

    b) The portent in the heavens?

    c) The new age which the coming of the babe will inaugurate?

    d) The love of God for his people?

2. What does the fact that the birth stories were written after Jesus had completed his ministry suggest concerning the impression his life had made upon his followers?

3. What is the religious value of the birth stories for today? As a symbol of the fact that God is at work in the universe for the enrichment of man's spiritual life, do they carry a vital religious message?

4. Is there an adequate answer which can be given to the remark one hears occasionally that, considering the limitations of Nazareth where Jesus was reared, they do not understand the broad outlook he had upon life?

5. What do you think Jesus' playmates contributed to his life as a boy in Nazareth?

6. What do you think Jesus learned in his own home which enriched his ministry?

7. Had Jesus been reared in a less colorful environment than that which surrounded Nazareth, do you think it would have made a difference in his preaching?

8. During Jesus' active ministry it is clear that his kinsfolk did not understand him. How far back in his life would you judge this misunderstanding to extend? Would it have begun in boyhood, youth, or young adult life?

SUGGESTIONS FOR READING

I. The virgin birth

    Beck, Dwight M. *Through the Gospels to Jesus.* New York: Harper and Brothers, 1954. Pp. 344-347.

    Gilbert, G. H. *The Student's Life of Jesus.* 3rd ed. New York: The Macmillan Company, 1900. Pp. 1-11.

    Orr, Thomas. *The Virgin Birth.* Selected readings.

    Taylor, Vincent. *The Life and Ministry of Jesus.* Nashville: Abingdon Press. 1955. Pp. 51-54. *The Virgin Birth.* Selected readings.

    Worcester, Elwood. *Studies in the Birth of the Lord.* New York: Charles Scribner's Sons, 1932. Selected readings.

II. The genealogy of Jesus

    Johnson, Sherman E., and Buttrick, George A. *The Interpreter's Bible.* VII, 250-51.

    Luce, H. K. *St. Luke.* "Cambridge Bible Series." Pp. 32-33.

Montefiore, C. G. *The Synoptic Gospels.* New York: The Macmillan Company, 1927. II. 450-51.

Stauffer, Ethelbert. *Jesus and His Story.* Translated by Richard and Clara Winston. New York, Alfred A. Knopf, Inc. 1960. Pp. 13-42. This section also considers the virgin birth, the site, census, et cetera.

III. The date of Jesus' birth

Goguel, Maurice. *The Life of Jesus.* New York: The Macmillan Company, 1944. Pp. 230-31.

Manson, William. *The Gospel of Luke.* New York: Harper & Brothers, 1930. Pp. 16-17.

IV. The place of Jesus' birth

Luce, H. K. *St. Luke.* "Cambridge Bible Series." Pp. 14-15.

Ramsay, William. *Was Christ Born at Bethlehem?* Selected readings.

V. The geography of Palestine

Baly, Denis. *The Geography of the Bible.* New York: Harper & Brothers, 1957. Selected readings.

Smith, George Adam. *The Historical Geography of the Holy Land.* New York: Harper & Brothers, 1932. II.

Westminster Historical Atlas to the Bible, ed. G. Ernest Wright and Floyd V. Filson. Philadelphia: The Westminster Press, 1956. Selected readings.

VI. The family of Jesus

Case, S. J. *Jesus.* Chicago: University of Chicago Press. 1927. Pp. 160-212.

Glover, T. R. *The Jesus of History.* New York: Harper & Brothers, 1950. Ch. ii.

Warschauer, Joseph. *The Historical Life of Christ.* New York: The Macmillan Company, 1926. Pp. 27-31.

6

The Maturing Years

A N ATTEMPT TO RECONSTRUCT THE MATURING YEARS IN THE experience of Jesus must, of necessity, take us beyond the data at hand since we have no records of these days, except for his visit to Jerusalem at the age of twelve (Luke 2:41-51). At best, historical probability is all that we may hope to achieve. Yet we are not without guideposts along the way. We know something about the country, times, and customs of the homeland in which Jesus matured. We also know something of our Lord's mind as an adult as this "comes through" the gospel accounts of his ministry. Not to make use of this knowledge is to be guilty of a too extreme historical skepticism. To make too much of it is to be guilty of historical irresponsibility. It is our intention in this chapter not to err in either direction.

Hebrew boys were taught early the religion of their people. This began in the home with the telling of Old Testament stories. The father was given the responsibility of teaching his sons the Shema found in Deut. 6:4-5: "Hear, O Israel: The Lord our God is one Lord; and you shall love the Lord your God with all your heart, and with all your soul, and with all your might." That this should be done was commanded in the Law where it was written: "You shall teach them diligently to your children, and shall talk of them when you sit in your house, and when you walk by the way, and when you lie down, and when you rise" (Deut. 6:7).

Formal teaching was given at the synagogue. Judged by present-day methods, the instruction was quite likely too rigid. Seated on the ground with their legs folded under them, the class repeated after the teacher phrases and verses from the Scriptures. How far Jesus went in school is a matter of conjecture. The local teaching program did not carry one very far beyond what we would regard as the elementary level. It was Hebrew education, strictly and solely. The breadth of Jesus' outlook as we meet him in adult life is all the more remarkable when we consider the educational system under which he was taught. His reading of the Scriptures shows a grasp of the historical situation such as the teaching techniques of the day would not have been likely to foster. In this regard Jesus was not limited by his background but rose above it.

I

Not only did Jesus attend the synagogue school; he went regularly to its religious services as well. Just how the Nazareth synagogue looked, it is impossible fully to say. That there was one in this community is evident clearly. One Jewish scholar has written, "There was then practically no Jewish town without its synagogue." [1] We have in the Gospels an account of Jesus' visit to the Nazareth synagogue, a visit which did not turn out in his favor since some of the angered gathering, resenting his words, sought to throw him headlong from the brow of the hill (Matt. 13:54-58; Mark 6:1-6; Luke 4:16-24). Upon entering, the father of the family would wash his hands so that he might participate as one ceremonially clean. Those under the legal age of twelve sat in the gallery with the women. Peering through the rails, they could see what was happening below. In the center of the floor was a rack for the scrolls called the "ark." Sometimes it was referred to as the "press." The ruler of the synagogue was in charge of these sacred documents.[2] It was he who selected the one to be read according to the day and gave it to the reader. Another of his duties was the counting of the congregation, for at least ten men must be present. He was responsible, also, for the keeping of good discipline.

The service itself followed a rather fixed form. This included the saying of the Shema, prayer, the reading of the Law in Hebrew,[3] which in Palestine was then translated into Aramaic, and the delivery of a treatise or interpretation of the passage. Some of these statements were boresome with their pedantic legalistic definitions. How much inspiration they contained is open to question. It is possible that Jesus' impatience with the empty dialectic of the lawyers in Israel began as he listened to their hairsplitting discourses in the Nazareth synagogue.

There was much, however, in the service to interest a growing boy, in spite of its shortcomings. The voice of the reader was sonorous and dignified.The pageantry associated with the handling

---

[1] Joseph Klausner, op. cit., pp. 234-35.
[2] This was probably the attendant mentioned in Luke 4:20.
[3] Reading from the Prophets followed sometimes the reading of the Law.

of the scroll was impressive also, as it was lifted from the silver cylinder which held it, a kiss was placed upon the silk which encased it, and it was unwound with a great show of reverence. Even the bells which were attached to the knobs of the rollers were said to ring gently as the parchment was turned. When the reading was ended, the document was prepared for its place in the ark with similar solemnity. All of this gave an air of importance to the service which a sensitive boy would not fail to notice.

How shall we assess the contribution of the synagogue to Jesus? There are persons who are greater than any institution which touches their lives, but this does not mean that they are not influenced by such contacts. Undoubtedly, the habits of worship and the attitudes toward life which continued association with the synagogue fostered, made their impression upon Jesus. Foremost is the fact that it was here he became acquainted with his Scriptures. In all probability he did not own any scrolls of the Old Testament, nor even fragments of a scroll covering any part of it. Yet he knew his way about in the story it told, was familiar with its greatest passages, and turned to it for guidance in the hours of great decision. The synagogue, had it done nothing more than this for Jesus, has justified its existence in history.

A second contribution of the synagogue to Jesus was the fact that here he found answers to the questions that plagued his developing mind. Not all of the answers were satisfactory, and some of them he had later to reject; but they helped him along the way at a time when they were needed. It was no small factor in his development that there was in his own home community an institution which stood for a definite way of life and provided guideposts for thought and action.

The social contacts at the synagogue were not without their contribution also. Here the Jewish people gathered.[4] It was their meeting, their school, and their center of worship. As a people apart, the Jews did not participate in Gentile village activities. Their place in society was circumscribed, so they were compelled to make the most of what they had. In the synagogues they met with their own kind of people under conditions of their own making. All of

---

[4] Sometimes Gentile visitors attended the services also.

this would bring to the boy Jesus a feeling of national pride that deepened his appreciation for the finest traditions of his people.

The fact that as an adult Jesus continued to attend the synagogue services speaks well of what they meant to him during his boyhood. Even though he may have found many of the sermons dull, he was in his place regularly. Here he had realized the presence of the heavenly Father. This was in itself a witness to its worth.

II

At the age of twelve Jesus went to the Feast of the Passover with his parents (Luke 2:41-51).[5] Three yearly visits to Jerusalem were required by the Law, but it is doubtful if more than one was made usually by most Jews (Exod. 23:14-17). The practical requirements of earning a living and managing a household made it difficult to keep the commandment in this case.

At the festival seasons caravans of Jewish pilgrims traveled toward the Holy City throughout the length and breadth of Palestine. There was much excitement for a young boy of twelve in this experience. New places and new faces, open campfires at night, sleeping under the stars, singing the songs of Zion, and playing games among the rocks that lined the roads—all these made the journey festive and adventurous.

There was more to this visit for the boy Jesus, however, than a holiday. It was a religious celebration which he was attending. The scene of David's reign was Jerusalem. Here Solomon had built the Temple, and here the religious system which gave unity to the consciousness of the nation had its seat. The story which depicts Jesus in the Temple on this visit, asking questions of the teachers, is one of unusual significance, if it is interpreted thoughtfully. It was very natural for Jesus to be in the Temple. He had been taught that it was the house of his heavenly Father and he felt at home where his Father was concerned. It is quite conceivable also that Jesus had questions to ask the learned doctors. His growing mind was an inquiring one. It was not out of line with his years that in the intense concentration of early adolescence he should forget his parents and the homeward journey. And the

[5] Luke alone gives us the account of this visit. It is the only experience of the boyhood of Jesus recorded in the Gospels.

reply which he gave to his distracted mother, who imagined him
to have been lost, was typical, likewise, of a boy with his background
and training: "How is it that you sought me? Did you not know
that I must be in my Father's house? (Luke 2:49.) Clearly it is a
boy speaking in the language of a boy, intending to say just what
he said and nothing more.

In the interest of dogma Jesus is regarded by some as speaking
theologically when he replied to his mother. Especially is this the
case if the King James Version of the statement is insisted upon:
"How is it that ye sought me? wist ye not that I must be about
my Father's business?" (Luke 2:49) . This, it is held, is an assertion
by the boy of his call to a divine mission. More than this, it is
insisted that when he spoke these words, he knew he was to be
crucified on a cross for the sins of the world. Such thoughts do not
belong to childhood, and to place them there is questionable historical interpretation. What we have in Jesus' statement is an expression of delight at being in his Father's house by a boy who
had been brought up to regard God as his heavenly Father. His
questions to the learned doctors, likewise, were those of an amazing,
alert, and precocious boy, and not those of a miniature adult.

III

Jesus returned to Nazareth with Mary and Joseph after the
feast, and was "obedient to them" (Luke 2:51) , like any other boy.
The years between this time and the occasion of his baptism have
been called the "hidden years," because there are no direct sources
of information concerning them. This is an exceedingly important
period in the growth and development of persons. It is during
these years that young people mature, choose their mates, select
their professions, and build the philosophy in terms of which they
shall live their adult lives. And it is these very years in the life of
Jesus which are wreathed in silence.

Piety sought early to fill in some of the missing details. These
attempts are found in the apocryphal gospels.[6] In them we read
stories of the youthful Jesus represented as modeling clay birds
which came to life;[7] speaking sharp words to a young boy who had

---

[6] Cf. previous reference pp. 53-54.
[7] See Thomas' Gospel of the Infancy of Jesus Christ, 1:4-10.

angered him, whereupon the lad died;[8] and miraculously causing
dye to leave material which he had introduced prankishly into a
dying vat.[9] Such imaginary accounts are unhistorical completely,
but they are part of an attempt to read back into the boyhood of
Jesus the wonder-deeds which were found in the record of his mature
ministry. These stories represent a sincere desire to glorify Jesus.
That the stories fail to do this for today is not out of line with the
thinking of the church which regarded them as spurious and kept
the books in which they were found from becoming a part of the
canon.

Luke makes a statement which deserves to be noted at the close
of his story concerning Jesus' visit to the Temple at the age of
twelve. He says: "And Jesus increased in wisdom and in stature,
and in favor with God and man." (2:52.) This suggests that Jesus
developed in successive stages as is normal for all growing youth.
Furthermore, it says that this development was along four lines.
It was mental, physical, religious, and social. An ever-enlarging
circle of knowledge and realization was his from year to year. Adolescence passed into young manhood, and then into adult life. What
this development meant in regard to his conception of God, his
convictions regarding the destiny of the Hebrew people and the
coming of the Messiah, we can only surmise from the kind of person
he later became.

There is some possibility that Jesus had some contact with
John the Baptist during these years, so that when they met later at
the Jordan River, they were not strangers to each other's thinking.
Their developing interest in religion would be a natural subject
of conversation on such occasions. One can imagine that as young
men in their late teens they often had heated and sometimes raptur-
ous discussions of the great issues of the day.

Joseph Klausner argues against any close relationship between
Jesus and John. Because of the fact that John's movement continued
after the preaching of Jesus began, and that it was found to be active
some twenty years later in Ephesus, Klausner concludes: "It is
obvious, therefore, that John had no personal acquaintance with

[8] *Ibid.*, 2:7-9.
[9] See the First Gospel of the Infancy of Jesus Christ, 15:8-15.

Jesus and did not recognize his messiahship." [10] This would not seem to be a necessary conclusion. Acquaintance does not mean similarity of viewpoint. Differences between Jesus and John do not rule out the possibility of their growing up as friends who shared their developing outlook through the years.

This period during which Jesus matured was a time of great political upheaval, and events of stirring character were happening not far from where Jesus lived. That these made their impression upon him seems altogether reasonable. The destruction of the nearby city of Sepphoris by the Romans because of its revolutionary activity under Judas, was a terrifying example of ruthlessness. Jesus was only a small boy at the time, but the occasion was discussed for many years afterwards. It was the capital of Galilee until the seat of government was moved to Tiberias. The holocaust offended greatly the pride of the Jews who lived there, and the issue of Hebrew nationalism was kept alive through this experience. Later, the city was rebuilt and because of its nearness to Nazareth, being less than an hour's walk from the village, it has been suggested that the carpenter Jesus may have worked there.[11] Whether or not this is true is a matter of conjecture, but the effect of these events upon the mind of Jesus would seem to be inescapable. The fact that in his ministry he spiritualized the political issue may be due to his conviction, based upon such examples as the destruction of Sepphoris in his boyhood days, that the nation must seek a higher ideal than political independence if it were to save itself and fulfill its service to men.

That Jesus may have had some intimations of his own mission during these years is highly probable. This too would have been a growing realization, subject to his own critical judgment step by step, until the time of his baptism, when the preaching of John the Baptist in the South Jordan Valley called him from the carpenter's bench at Nazareth and catapulted him into public life. It is not unusual for young people of superior talents to feel the stirrings of future greatness during adolescence and in their early twenties. To notice that their talents are greater than those of their fellows is not a sign of egotism. Rather it is the mark of alertness and discrimination in self-analysis. Jesus could not help realizing that the concerns of Israel and

[10] *Op. cit.*, p. 249.
[11] Cf. S. J. Case, *Jesus*, pp. 204 ff.

his heavenly Father were more acutely real to him than to others. He did not become aware suddenly of his calling at the time of his baptism. That he might have sensed it during the years of his maturing is a reasonable conclusion.

QUESTIONS FOR DISCUSSION

1. Environment has a profound influence upon the development of personality in growing children and youth. Would this have been true for Jesus, or was his young life untouched by the events which surrounded him?

2. How do you think the synagogue service of Jesus' day compares with the worship services which children attend in our time? Which would be more inclined to make a lasting impression upon young life?

3. In adult life Jesus made practically no pronouncements of a political character. Does this indicate that he took little interest in current events as a growing boy? What does it suggest?

4. What is meant when it is stated that Jesus' experience in the Temple at the age of twelve was a normal one for an unusually alert lad?

5. Does the conception of a developing mind in the boy Jesus detract from the high view of the church concerning him? Or does it account realistically for his firmness of conviction as an adult person?

6. To what extent shall we regard Jesus as a child of his own age in his conception of the authorship of scripture, the origin of life, and the nature of the physical world? Would he have had a special knowledge in regard to these matters such as belong to a scientific age nearly two thousand years later?

7. If you conclude that Jesus shared the views of his day in regard to the above, how do you account for his outdistancing his own generation, and those which followed, in moral and spiritual insight?

8. Would a gradually developing realization of his mission in life be as religious and spiritual as a sudden awakening to this fact, on the one hand, or a full knowledge of it since boyhood, on the other?

SUGGESTIONS FOR READING

I. The educational experience at the synagogue and Temple
   Bailey, A. E. *Daily Life in Bible Times*. New York: Charles Scribner's Sons, 1943. Pp. 250-72.
   Barton, G. A. *Jesus of Nazareth*. New York: The Macmillan Company, 1931. Pp. 84-85.
   Bosworth, E. I. *The Life and Teaching of Jesus*. New York: The

Macmillan Company, 1935. Pp. 26-27.

Schürer, Emil. *The History of the Jewish People in the Time of Jesus Christ*. New York: Charles Scribner's Sons. Div. II, II, 1-83.

Stauffer, Ethelbert. *Jesus and His Story*. Translated by Richard and Clara Winston. New York: Alfred A. Knopf, Inc., 1960. Pp. 43-62.

II. The character of Jerusalem

Baly, Denis. *The Geography of the Bible*. New York: Harper & Brothers, 1957. Ch. XIV.

Dalman, G. *Sacred Sites and Ways*. New York: The Macmillan Company, 1935. Ch. xv.

Kraeling, Emil G. *Bible Atlas*. Chicago: Rand McNally & Company, 1956. Pp. 364-67.

Macalister, R. A. S. "The Topography of Jerusalem." *Cambridge Ancient History*. III, 333-53.

Smith, George Adam. *Jerusalem*. II, 495-555.

III. Jesus and the crisis at Sepphoris

Case, S. J. *Jesus*. Chicago: University of Chicago Press, 1927. Pp. 202-7.

IV. The apocryphal stories of the boyhood of Jesus

M. R. James. "Infancy Gospels." *The Apocryphal New Testament*. New York: Oxford University Press, 1950.

7

The Religious Awakening
In the South Jordan Valley

J ESUS ENTERED PUBLIC LIFE AT A TIME OF GREAT RELIGIOUS FERVOR. The preaching of John in the wilderness had awakened the nation to a realization of the riches of its heritage, and to an acute sense of its destiny in the immediate future. Expectation was high, and moral earnestness made living meaningful for the Jews, who responded to the stirring messages.

Who was this preacher? They called him John the Baptizer, because he urged his followers to be baptized as they repented and made their hearts ready for the coming of the Messiah, who would judge the nation. John's origin is relatively obscure. All we know about him is that he was the son of Zechariah, a priest, and of Elizabeth, referred to the Gospel of Luke as the kinswoman of Mary the mother of Jesus.

The Gospel of Luke dates John's ministry in the fifteenth year of the reign of Tiberius Caesar, which would be somewhere around the year A.D. 29.[1] In poetry of rare beauty his mission is made clear. The song of Zechariah concerning him says (Luke 1:76-79):

And you, child, will be called the prophet of the Most High;
for you will go before the Lord to prepare his ways,
to give knowledge of salvation to his people
in the forgiveness of their sins,
through the tender mercy of our God,
When the day shall dawn upon us from on high
to give light to those who sit in darkness and in the shadow of death,
to guide our feet into the way of peace.

As in the cases of Samson (Judg. 13) and Samuel (I Sam. 1-2:10), the Scriptures discover a divine purpose in the birth of John. He was born to introduce the Messiah to public life by awakening the nation to its responsibilities before God, and by making "ready for the Lord a people prepared" (Luke 1:17).

[1] There is a possibility that the date was earlier. Cf. footnote p. 71.

I

John preached in the wilderness region of the South Jordan Valley. The ruggedness of the terrain matched the severity of his message. Though he lived somewhat like the Essenes, probably he was not one of them, although speculation on this point continues in the face of the revelation of the practices of the Dead Sea community of the scrolls. It has even been suggested that John was expelled from the Qumran order, prior to the baptism of Jesus.[2] His dress was different, however, and his baptism was unlike their daily washings. He did not worship angels as they did. In some ways he resembled the Nazarites, but it is not likely that he belonged to their group. John was himself, unique, original, and impressive.

His clothes were the skins of animals and his food such fare as the desert would offer. When he preached, the people were captivated by the commanding character of his voice and the burning earnestness of his countenance. Fasting and solitary living had contributed to the awesomeness of his personality, while prayer and meditation had sharpened the edge of his message.

John the Baptist resembled Elijah in many ways. Some thought that he was this ancient prophet returned, as Malachi had said he would before the advent of the day of Jehovah (Mal. 4:5). Like Elijah, John challenged the religious leaders of his day, even confronting a king with a demand for repentance. This made him feared by his contemporaries. Although he was the son of a priest, he acted more like the prophets. The cadence of chanted ritual would have faded before his rugged and staccato calls for righteousness.

What was it that led John to begin his preaching mission when he did? The distresses of the time were such that the coming of the Judgment seemed inevitable. It appeared to offer the only solution to conditions under the Romans which were growing more intolerable daily. Conventional religion had reached a point also where a direct moral challenge could no longer be postponed. Long vigils in prayer and meditation, during which time these things had been faced before God, brought into the soul of this

[2] Cf., however, the article by Cullmann "The Significance of the Qumran Text," *Journal of Biblical Literature*, 74 (1955), pp. 218 ff.

rugged man a sense of great urgency. His became a prophetic responsibility to speak out, announcing boldly the doom of the wicked and the deliverance of the righteous in the nation. As Luke put it, "The word of God came to John the son of Zechariah in the wilderness" (3:2), so he began to preach.

The audience which John drew was both varied and large. People of many interests came to this outdoor meeting to hear the message. They went to him from Jerusalem, Judea, and all the region around about the Jordan. Some were curious only, being the kind of people who are drawn always to great gatherings. Others were resentful of the reports which had reached them concerning what was being said. These were mostly the professional religious leaders who could not regard favorably this outsider and the inroads he was making into their field. Then, there were the people from all walks of life who had been left behind or pushed unnoticed to one side as the official religious interests of the temple system of the day were administered. Their hungering and thirsting for great truths by which to live had not been satisfied, and John's ringing announcement of the coming visitation from the Lord promised a new life. And so they came: Pharisees, Sadducees, soldiers, tax collectors, carpenters, fishermen, the rich and the poor.

II

What was it that these people heard as the prophet John came forth to preach, following his nightly vigils in prayer, and faced the crowds by the side of the Jordan? The message was practical and almost blunt in its directness. Josephus said that John "incited the Jews to practice virtue, to be just towards one another, and pious towards God." [3] When the soldiers asked what it was that they must do, he told them to extort from no man by violence. This was common practice on the part of soldiers quartered on foreign soil and in charge of a subject people. Likewise they were warned against making false accusations when arresting a man or testifying against him before a superior officer. One thing more, the soldiers were advised to be content with their wages, the im-

[3] *Antiquities* XVIII. 5. 2.

plication being probably that they were not to add to their income through bribes and threats (Luke 3:14).

When the Pharisees and Sadducees came to his baptism, John was ruthless almost in his insistence that they bring forth fruits worthy of repentance. He was not suggesting that they would be forgiven in proportion to the quality of their deeds, but rather was demanding that their character be in harmony with their religious profession. Some of them had been counting upon their nationality as Jews to secure their standing before God, saying, "We have Abraham as our father" (Matt. 3:9). Nationality would not give them position on the day of Jehovah's visitation. They were to be judged as individual persons in the presence of God and not as members of a particular group. God could and would raise up new sons unto Abraham out of the rocks if he needed them, John said.[4]

When the people heard John preach, they were moved by the language which he used. He did not speak in the studied phrases of the priests. He chose, rather, words from the everyday experiences of the people, employing their own phrases which had the flavor of forest and field upon them. For instance, when he wanted to announce the nearness of the judgment, he said, "Even now the ax is laid to the root of the trees; every tree therefore that does not bear good fruit is cut down and thrown into the fire" (Luke 3:9). And when he wished to bring home to his hearers the exciting news that the coming of the Kingdom and of the Messiah were at hand, he cried out, "His winnowing fork is in his hand, to clear his threshing floor, and to gather the wheat into his granary, but the chaff he will burn with unquenchable fire" (Luke 3:17).

John's ideas concerning the Judgment, the advent of the Messiah, and the coming of the Kingdom were apocalyptic. This means that he believed these great events would enter the present world-order directly from the hand of God. They would not grow up within society but would burst upon it from above. Human instrumentality was ruled out. Man had no part in the process. All he could do was get himself ready, to wait expectantly, and to receive it gratefully when it came.

[4] Mark does not record these antinationalistic words of John. He may not have known them since they are found only in Q.

III

The dramatic words of John stirred the people greatly. They rejoiced when they thought of the deliverance from Roman rule which the Messiah's coming would bring. At last they would be free! Their expectation, however, was deeper than the political aspect. God himself was going to act within history. To be ready for this divine intervention was the greatest challenge they could imagine. No cost was too exacting; no sacrifice was too demanding.

What John required them to do, as a preparation to receive the Messiah and the new day, was not new actually. It had been urged upon the nation by the prophets again and again. Even the priests of their own day regarded it as essential. They were to repent of their sins, sincerely repent. Only this time repentance looked toward the immediate advent of the Judgment, the Messiah, and the Kingdom. What others had foreseen in the future, or regarded in formal and priestly terms, was now to be an immediate actual event.

As an expression of this repentance, John called the people to the banks of the Jordan River where he baptized them in its muddy waters. This was not an unfamiliar ceremony among the Jews.[5] Proselytes from other religions were required to be baptized. They were by this rite born anew and their prebaptismal sins were effaced. By it also they were admitted to the Hebrew community so that they belonged now where they had been outsiders before. Some among the Jews thought of baptism as sacramental cleansing;[6] others regarded it as ethical renewal.[7] Three witnesses, usually of the Sanhedrin, were present at the rite.[8] The immersion was complete, so that all parts of the body were covered. Benedictions and exhortations accompanied the ceremony.[9]

When John called upon the Jews to submit to baptism, he was giving to the rite a new emphasis. It became a dedication to the

[5] Cf. Lev. 14:9, Num. 19:7-8, where ablutions were prescribed to overcome certain impurities. It was practiced also in Mithraism.

[6] See Oesterley and Box, *Religion and Worship of the Synagogue*, p. 264.

[7] Edersheim, *The Life and Times of Jesus*, II, 746.

[8] Yebam. 47b.

[9] For possible parallels between the baptism of John and the ritual of the Essenes cf. Duncan Howlett, *The Essenes and Christianity*, pp. 139 ff.

approaching Kingdom, involving repentance from sin and com-
mitment to the coming Messiah. It was related to an anticipated
movement in history. This took it out of the realm of traditional
ritual and made it uniquely a kingdom-of-God expression.

Some of the Jews resented the fact that John asked them to be
baptized. Too long they had associated the act with the admission
of Gentiles to the Hebrew community. Was it not insulting to
ask one already an acceptable Jew to submit to it? While this
seemed unorthodox to them, to John it was a reasonable demand.
Great events were to take place in the immediate future, and
baptism was the way to prepare oneself to participate in these
significant days.

The Jordan River is not large in the area where John was
preaching, so that great numbers of people could not enter it at
one time. Probably they came singly or in small groups when they
were moved to respond. As in all such meetings, there were out-
bursts of emotion and expressions of praise and joy on the lips
of those who participated. Jesus himself was to have a profound
religious experience when he was baptized by John, and those who
preceded and followed him into the water were touched deeply
likewise.

John's baptism was in the form of immersion quite likely. This
was the method which was practiced most by the Jews in their
ablutions. Later the Christian Church adopted sprinkling in places
where there was an insufficient supply of water. Within the New
Testament there does not seem to be any argument concerning
the proper form of water baptism. All of this was to come later
when the church grew to be increasingly sacramentarian.

IV

The place of John the Baptist in history is an interesting one.
The New Testament presents his movement in such close proximity
to Jesus and the development of the Christian community, that by
comparison, it loses something of its originality and force. Besides
this, there was an interest on the part of the author of the Fourth
Gospel to keep the person of John in the background as he stressed

the pre-eminence of Jesus.[10] Through the years the church has continued to follow the New Testament in the neglect of John. This is understood readily even if it is to be regretted. Jesus, on the other hand, said of John that he was as great as the greatest man ever born of woman (Luke 7:28). He said this at a time when John was expressing some doubt as to whether or not he was the Messiah he had once thought him to be. This makes his compliment concerning John all the more significant.

Jesus was not alone in his recognition of the greatness of John. The people who were drawn to Jordan's banks to hear him were so impressed by his conviction, and moved by the power of God which rested upon him, that some wondered if he could be the Christ. Such recognition is not to be thought unlikely. A voice as challenging as the baptizer's had not been heard in Israel since the great age of prophetic preaching, presented in the Old Testament, had come to an end. An unordained preacher, speaking in his own right, had awakened in them a nostalgia for the old days and a hope for the future. Was this man the Christ? He did not dress like the kingly Messiah, nor did he live like the royal messianic ruler; yet when he spoke, there were deep stirrings in their hearts. His simple rejoinder that he was not the Christ did not dampen their enthusiasm for him. Some continued to follow him even when Jesus appeared on the scene. And after he was beheaded, there were others who concluded that Jesus was John the Baptist risen from the dead (Matt. 16:14). So great was the impression which this wilderness preacher had made, that even the genius of Jesus did not seem beyond him.

The religious awakening at the Jordan Valley which John inspired was of such proportions that it drew the attention of Herod, an attention that resulted in the preacher's death. According to Josephus, this ruler feared that a political revolt would develop from the new movement. That this would happen was unlikely, for John's call was not to rise up against the government, but to repent and wait for God to act. Herod could not understand such an outlook. His own political wiliness made him suspicious of

[10] See John 3:25-30. It has been suggested that a John the Baptist movement in Asia at the time this book was written is responsible for this overemphasis upon the retiring character of John. The writer of the Fourth Gospel is thought to have wished to discourage this movement.

others, and he suspected that John had hidden motives. It would be easy to use such a following for political gain, he thought.

The gospel writers, however, do not explain Herod's enmity toward John in political terms.[11] They point out, rather, that Herod disliked him because the prophet had disapproved of his marriage (Matt. 14:1-12; Mark 6:14-29; Luke 9:7-9). The ruler had deserted his own wife in order to marry Herodias, the wife of Herod of Rome, his half brother.[12] This was immorality to John, and like the prophets of the past in Israel, who did not hesitate to take kings to task for their personal sins, this new preacher of the desert pointed an accusing finger at Herod. The ruler struck back by having John arrested and later beheaded.

The killing of John by Herod was mentioned in contemporary history by the historian Josephus. He explained the defeat of Herod at the hands of Aretas IV, king of Ababia, by saying, "Many Jews saw in the destruction of Herod's army a just punishment from God for the killing of John who was called 'The Baptist'; Herod had slain this just man who had called upon the Jews to follow the way of righteousness." [13]

It was important that John the Baptist had awakened the nation to its destiny, and attracted many to accept baptism unto repentance for the remission of sins. It was significant, also, that John's influence had reached even to the chambers of the palace. It was of even greater moment, however, that the voice of John preaching in the wilderness was heard in the village of Nazareth by a young carpenter who was so moved with its eloquence and message that he made the journey southward and stood one day among his brethren on the banks of the Jordan River. Because this young man came, John's movement is remembered today; and its preacher has achieved great recognition wherever the story of Jesus is told.

QUESTIONS FOR DISCUSSION

1. Considering that he was reared in the home of a priest, how are we to account for the unpriestly character of John the Baptist? Could

---

[11] The Gospels were written at a time when the good will of the Roman state was a needed asset because the political status of the Christians was unsettled.

[12] The Gospels mistakenly refer to her as the wife of Philip the tetrarch.

[13] Josephus *Antiquities* XVIII. 5.2. In the light of this passage the historical existence of John the Baptist is established, apart from the New Testament.

it be that he reacted against the formalism of ritual and ceremony because by nature he was the outdoor type of person?

2. Beneath John's rugged exterior can you detect any of the personality traits of a priest?

3. Prepare a personality study of John the Baptist.

4. Prepare a digest of the message John preached.

5. Can you see any relationship between the austerity of his sermons and the kind of life he lived?

6. What was it that drew the people to hear John:

   a) A deep-seated unrest and spiritual longing in their lives?

   b) The love of excitement and a natural curiosity?

   c) An interest in the messianic Kingdom?

   d) Jealousy on the part of the religious leaders among the Jews?

7. Did the people present themselves to John for baptism in order to confess their sins, unite with the Kingdom movement John proclaimed, or because they were impressed with the magnetism of the preacher?

8. The Kingdom which John preached was apocalyptic, that is, it was wholly the gift of God through divine intervention. Does this mean that John believed men were to do nothing at all along the lines of social service?

9. Have there been religious movements involving a profound spiritual awakening similar to John's revival meeting since that day? Were the Protesant Reformation, the John Wesley Awakening in England, and the Moody revivals in America of similar character and intent? Can you name other comparable religious expressions today?

SUGGESTIONS FOR READING

I. Jewish references to John and the rite of baptism as practiced by the Jews

Abrahams, Israel. *Studies in Pharisaism and the Gospels.* I, ch. iii, iv.

Herford, R. T. *Judaism in the New Testament Period.* New York: The Macmillan Company, 1917-24. Selected readings.

Sandmel, Samuel. *A Jewish Understanding of the New Testament.* Cincinnati: Hebrew Union College Press, 1956. Selected readings.

The Jewish Encyclopedia. I, 68 ff.

II. The site of the John the Baptist revival

Kraeling, Emil G. *Bible Atlas.* Chicago: Rand McNally & Company, 1956. Pp. 367-71.

Smith, George Adam. *The Historical Geography of the Holy Land.* New York: Harper & Brothers, 1932. Pp. 482-96.

III. The character and rule of Herod

Enslin, Morton S. *Christian Beginnings.* New York: Harper & Brothers, 1938. Pp. 63 ff.

Josephus, F. *Antiquities* XVIII. 5. 4.

Mould, E. W. K. *Essentials of Bible History.* New York: The Ronald Press, 1951. Pp. 473 ff.

IV. The character and work of John the Baptist

Kraeling, Carl H. *John the Baptist.* Charles Scribner's Sons, 1951. Selected readings.

Parsons, Ernest William. "The Significance of John the Baptist for the Beginnings of Christianity," *Environmental Factors in Christian History,* eds. McNeill, Spinka, and Willoughby. Chicago: University of Chicago, 1939.

Rollins, W. E. and M. B. *Jesus and His Ministry.* Greenwich, Conn.: The Seabury Press, 1954. Ch. II.

8

The Baptism

CARPENTRY IN NAZARETH WAS A RUGGED PROFESSION. ONE DID NOT order his timber ready-cut and in convenient lengths. There were trees to fell, logs to haul, and boards to hew. The output of a carpenter's shop was varied. Ox yokes, hand plows, carts, and plank doors were made here. In addition there was the hand-hewn furniture such as was used in the village homes and throughout the surrounding countryside. This would have included beds, low tables, benches, and stools. Some of the basic utensils which were necessary in the cooking were fashioned also after the manner of the times. Many of these items were made-to-order, custom-built, while others represented standard stock. It was interesting work with the human touch adding to the joy of labor. These products were more personalized than modern ones. The feeling of the craftsman for his work was reflected in the form and character of the objects made.

There was time for talk at a carpenter's bench. What conversation there must have been in the Nazareth shop with Jesus as the chief conversationalist! He would have listened with interest as those who dropped in to pass the time related the latest news. Some of the parables with which he was to move his hearers in the days to come may have had their origin here as events in the changing human scene were reported.

It may be assumed that there came a day when travelers passing through Nazareth brought astounding news of the religious awakenings in the South Jordan Valley, and of the new preacher who had begun to preach in the wilderness. As was indicated in the previous chapter, John was no ordinary speaker, and his words were arousing many throughout the country. Jerusalem had sent a representation to look into this latest development in the religious life of the people, and soldiers had been dispatched to keep order lest an uprising should occur. Roman decorum must be preserved, come what may. This new preacher used none of the formal rhetoric of the scribes and Pharisees. Speaking in the language of the common people, he did not care whether the religious officials approved of what he said or not. In this respect he resembled an ancient

prophet—Elijah, perhaps. He announced the coming of both the
Messiah and the Judgment in the immediate future, and commanded men to prepare for the Kingdom by repentance and baptism as a sign of committal to the great cause. All of this would
have been in the report which came to Nazareth from the South
Jordan Valley.

What did the news from the southland mean? This was the
question which must have confronted Jesus. It is reasonable to
assume that he had been living with great expectations in his soul,
and that the dreams of his youth for a better day in Israel were
still alive. For some years now he had been engaged in his work
in Nazareth. Assuming that Joseph had died, Jesus was faced with
a family responsibility, and he would not have taken this duty
lightly. As was stated previously, intimations of a great mission in
life may have come to him already, but in all probability Jesus
had not reached a final conclusion as to what the Father would have
him do.[1] In the face of the reports of John's preaching, however,
it is quite likely that he experienced deep stirrings of heart, and
that questions filled his mind as to whether his own lifework and
the Jordan Valley awakening were related. He would go to see
John at once!

I

When Jesus reached the Jordan where John was baptizing, it is
not probable that he presented himself immediately for baptism.
All the journey through we may assume that he had been thinking
vigorously of what he had heard concerning the religious awakening. As travelers from the south passed him on the way, we can
imagine that he interrogated them eagerly. Were there any new
developments? What had John been saying when they had last
heard him? Did they think it was a temporary outburst of fanatic
enthusiasm, or was there a core of reality in the happenings that
had permanent value? Throughout his entire ministry Jesus was
interested in what everyday people had to say. Their reactions to
human situations impressed him. He believed that God spoke

[1] Cf. pp. 86-87.

through them, and therefore he paid attention to their judgments. In this particular situation he would have wanted to know what the people had concluded about John, just as later he was interested in their conclusions concerning himself (Luke 9:18).

When he arrived on the scene, we may surmise that Jesus continued to observe the men and women of his nation as they listened to this prophetic voice in the wilderness. He would have looked into their faces as they came from the waters of baptism. What was to be read in their expressions? We can assume, likewise, that Jesus was interested in the reactions of the religious leaders of the nation. While he himself was not authoritarian in regard to religion, it would be significant to learn what these officials had to say. They were men of great responsibility, and some were quite learned. Since they knew the Scriptures as they did, their reactions were worthy of consideration. The conclusion of both the people and the religious officials concerning the preaching of John would be important to Jesus as he made up his own mind in regard to what was happening.

That Jesus was affected greatly by what he saw and heard is evident from the fact that he presented himself for baptism. This was a genuine religious revival. God was present in it. The spiritual authority of John was seen clearly in his preaching. The moral earnestness of the people and their hungering and thirsting for righteousness were real undeniably. This was the time of God's visitation. It was the hour of destiny for the nation. Was it God's will for him to identify his life with these decisive events? Jesus concluded that it was, approached John, and requested baptism.

Matthew indicates that there was some conversation between Jesus and John before the latter would baptize him (3:14-15). The wilderness prophet did not feel worthy to do so. He recognized Jesus as his superior, saying, "I need to be baptized by you, and do you come to me?" At Jesus' insistence, however, he performed the rite. It is possible that John's reticence was read into the tradition, or at least stressed purposefully by the early church in order to safeguard the pre-eminence of Jesus. Followers of John were urging the priority of their leader throughout the first century, and the record of this interview would discourage them.

II

Baptism was an exalted experience for Jesus. In language of re-strained simplicity, Mark (1:10-11) described it in these words: "And when he came up out of the water, immediately he saw the heavens opened and the Spirit descending upon him like a dove; and a voice came from heaven, 'Thou art my beloved Son; with thee I am well pleased.' " This account states that the Father had designated Jesus as the "beloved Son," and that the Spirit came upon him in full measure.

The gospel writers regarded the baptism of Jesus as the occasion when he received his call to be the Messiah.[2] It may be assumed that they were interpreting it as Jesus himself had taught his fol-lowers to understand it. At some appropriate time when it would have been exceedingly helpful, he probably shared with his dis-ciples the inner meaning of this high hour. The very personal character of a religious experience such as this, which brought to him a definite consciousness of specific mission, made such a shar-ing necessary if it were to be understood. The baptism was Jesus' own experience primarily. John and the multitudes participated in it only secondarily. It does not seem that the people realized fully what was happening to Jesus, if they grasped it at all, since they did not instigate a popular following at this time. And the fact that many of John's disciples did not leave him to go with Jesus, and that John himself continued his own work, suggests that even he had only a partial understanding of what had happened.

The voice of the Father which Jesus heard spoke to him within his own soul. These "inner voices" are the dominating influences in human life. They are the real voices that reach the heart and determine the direction in which the life shall move. As such, they are far more significant than those which are audible to the out-ward ear. The words, "Thou art my beloved Son; with thee I am well pleased" (Mark 1:11), are based upon two Old Testament

---

[2] The chapter which follows will consider in detail the traditional conceptions of the office of Messiah and Jesus' attempt to understand his relationship to them. It is sufficient to indicate here quite generally that the Messiah was thought of as the One whose coming would inaugurate a new age for the Hebrew people in which the righteousness of God would be revealed and in which the glorification of the nation under the messianic rule would become a reality.

passages.[3] Although in the past the phrase "my beloved Son" was not a messianic designation,[4] the expression "Son of God" had come to carry this high significance in the early Christian community; and Mark regards it as conveying to Jesus the call to be the Messiah.

Not only did Jesus receive his commission to be the Messiah at the time of his baptism; he experienced also the coming of the Spirit of God into his life to empower him for the fulfillment of his vocation. This was not a radically new conception of the function of the Spirit in Israel. Prophets and servants of God in the past had received an anointing of the Spirit for their work (Isa. 61:1-2). This experience does not suggest that God was not in Jesus' life continually. It does indicate, however, that his personal relation to God was very real, and that from time to time he knew crisis moments in which new insights were born and new decisions were made. There were others which were to come in the days ahead, but this one in particular was outstanding, occurring as it did at the beginning of his ministry.

Mark and Matthew use the symbol of the day in describing the coming of the Spirit into the life of Jesus.[5] This calls to mind Noah's sending out the dove from the ark to fly over the surface of the flood (Gen. 8:8-12), and suggests also the statement in the story of creation which says, "And the Spirit of God was moving over the face of the waters" (Gen. 1:2). The dove as a symbol of the Holy Spirit expresses poetically the inner experience of the indwelling Spirit which came to Jesus at this time. We should not attempt to interpret these suggestive words as referring to the concrete form of a bird.

The day that Jesus was baptized began as any other day at the South Jordan Valley. When it closed, it may have seemed to many to have been no different than the rest. John the Baptist, however, had been impressed with the greatness of Jesus, and the carpenter from Nazareth had begun to walk the road that took him ultimately

---

[3] Ps. 2:7, "He said to me, 'You are my son, today I have begotten you.'" Isa. 42:1, "My chosen, in whom my soul delights; I have put my spirit upon him, he will bring forth justice to the nations."

[4] Cf. William Manson, *Jesus, the Messiah,* pp. 149-50.

[5] Luke objectifies this spiritual experience for purposes of literary effect, adding the words "in bodily form."

to the Cross. There were no thoughts of death, however, in the mind of Jesus this eventide. Instead there was an elevation of soul such as he had not known before, and bright dreams of the coming of the kingdom of God, which as the Messiah he had been called upon to inaugurate, filled his mind.

III

The church has held to the dogma of the sinlessness of Jesus down through the years, but it has seemed to some that Jesus must have had sin in his life since he presented himself for baptism. This idea was stated clearly by Middleton Murry when he wrote:

He [Jesus] had come as more than a sinner, but as a sinner he had indeed come. Whatever this man was, he was the incarnation of honesty. He would have sought no baptism for the remission of sins had he not been conscious of sin. He came out also to see and to hear a prophet; he would have seen him and heard him, but he would not have sought his baptism for no cause, and become one with the outward ritualists whom he so passionately condemned.[6]

A related view is found in an early apocryphal writing, the Gospel According to the Hebrews, which represents Jesus as explaining that it was possible for him to repent only for sins committed in ignorance.

Although this is not the place for a lengthy discussion of the subject, a brief word concerning the dogma of the sinlessness of Jesus is in order. This idea may be understood passively as referring to the complete absence of sin in his life. On the other hand, it may be interpreted actively as indicating the actual and continuous identification of his will with the Father's.[7]

The religious consciousness of Jesus as seen throughout the gospel accounts shows an awareness of unbroken union with God. This is an unusual situation when compared with the fact that the religious expressions of the greatest persons of faith and practice throughout the centuries abound in protestations of moral failure and unworthiness. The more saintly among them are the

---

[6] *Jesus, Man of Genius*, pp. 22-23.
[7] In this discussion sin is taken to mean the conscious and deliberate rejection of the will of God.

more outspoken in this regard. This comparison between Jesus and the saints of the church may be said to constitute, in part, the moral or religious argument for the sinlessness of Jesus.

There are those for whom the sinlessness of Jesus is a major consideration. Jesus to them is not *Jesus* unless he is without sin. Others are drawn to him more closely if they can believe that on occasion he knew what it meant to miss the mark. For still others this is an academic question largely, one for theologians to consider, and possessing little or no practical implications. In the final analysis the dogma of the sinlessness of Jesus lies beyond the area of demonstrable fact. One will accept or reject it depending upon his total view of Jesus and his philosophy in general. The impression Jesus makes upon one's moral sensitiveness will contribute much to the conclusion he reaches.

Whatever view one holds concerning the sinlessness of Jesus, it seems justifiable to conclude, in the light of what followed his baptism, that Jesus asked John to baptize him in order that he might identify himself with the religious movement the prophet was proclaiming. He believed in it and wanted to become a part of it. In this sense baptism for him was a dedication ritual by which he committed his life to the Father for the coming of the Kingdom.

QUESTIONS FOR DISCUSSION

1. Why did Jesus make the journey to the Jordan Valley to hear John:
   a) Because of a general interest in the reports which had come to Nazarth concerning the character of the revival?
   b) Because in prayer he became convinced that it was his Father's will for him to go?
   c) Because he concluded that the religious awakening provided a dynamic background for beginning his ministry as the Messiah?

2. What logic do you find in the suggestion which is made sometimes that since John did not disband his following at once, he did not grasp really the greatness of Jesus at the baptism?

3. How does the idea appeal to you that since John was later to question the messiahship of Jesus, he could not have been impressed with his greatness at the time of his baptism? Must we allow for the possibility that John developed honest questions concerning Jesus when he was languishing in Herod's prison and Jesus did not turn a hand to free him?

4. What is meant by the statement that Jesus' religious experience at

the Jordan was his own primarily, that the voice and the vision were for himself? If you decide that this is true, what would you say to the person who said that Jesus was baptized for the sole purpose of setting a noble example for his followers?

5. What happened in the soul of Jesus at his baptism? Was anything added to his consciousness and outlook which had not been there before this event occurred?

SUGGESTIONS FOR READING

I. The relationship between Jesus and John

Goguel, Maurice. *The Life of Jesus.* New York: The Macmillan Company, 1944. Ch. x.

II. The sinlessness of Jesus

Bundy, Walter. *The Religion of Jesus.* Indianapolis: The Bobbs-Merrill Company, 1928. Pp. 160 ff.

Major, Manson, and Wright. *The Mission and Message of Jesus.* New York: E. P. Dutton & Company, 1938. Pp. 22-23.

Rollins, W. E. and M. B. *Jesus and His Ministry.* Greenwich, Conn.: The Seabury Press, 1954. Pp. 36-40.

III. The title "Son of God"

Cadoux, C. J. *The Historic Mission of Jesus.* New York: Harper & Brothers, 1943. Pp. 27-33.

Dalman, Gustav. *The Words of Jesus.* Pp. 274-76, 280-82.

Manson, William. *Jesus the Messiah.* Philadelphia: The Westminster Press, 1946. Pp. 146-54.

IV. The Old Testament conception of the Spirit of God

Anderson, Bernhard W. *Understanding the Old Testament.* Englewood Cliffs, N. J.: Prentice-Hall, Inc., 1957. Pp. 183-88.

Knudson, A. C. *The Religious Teaching of the Old Testament.* New York: The Abingdon Press, 1918. Ch. iv.

V. The Spirit in the New Testament writings

Abrahams, I. *Studies in Pharisaism and the Gospels.* New York: The Macmillan Company, 1917-24. Pp. 47-50.

Richardson, Alan. *An Introduction to the Theology of the New Testament.* New York: Harper & Brothers, 1958. Pp. 103-24.

Scott, C. Anderson. *Christianity According to St. Paul.* New York: The Macmillan Company, 1927. Pp. 141-50.

Scott, E. F. *The New Testament Idea of Revelation.* New York: Charles Scribner's Sons, 1936. Pp. 228-50.

——*Spirit in the New Testament.* New York: Doubleday & Company, 1923. Selected readings.

9

The Temptation

THE REALIZATION WHICH CAME TO JESUS AT HIS BAPTISM—THAT the Kingdom was at hand and that he was the Messiah in the new age—confronted him with the necessity of making some important decisions. What was the character of the Kingdom to be, and how would he fulfill his mission? It was one thing to hear the call; it was another to carry it out. The Father did not do Jesus' thinking for him. He must face the future on his own, seeking the guidance of God and applying vigorous thought to the decisions he must make. This called for meditation and quiet, for prayer and consideration.

When Luke recorded that Jesus "was led by the Spirit for forty days in the wilderness" (4:1-2), and Mark stated that "the Spirit immediately drove him out into the wilderness" (1:12), they were saying that the sojourn in the desert place apart was an outgrowth of the baptism itself. The Spirit which he had received at that time was guiding him.

We refer to this experience in the wilderness as a period of temptation. It was the inevitable result of an actual situation in which a decision concerning the character of the Kingdom and of the messiahship must be made. This decision had to be reached in the face of varying conceptions of the messianic kingdom and of the Messiah, some of which were out of harmony with God's will and character. The temptation was at the point of tension between God's way and other possible and seemingly desirable methods.

I

Messianic ideas had an extended history by this time. For generations deeply religious persons in Israel had looked forward to the coming of God's kingdom and of his chosen representative, the Messiah. An early view was that the Kingdom would be a renewal and glorification of the national life, in which the Messiah would rule. Isaiah (9:7) spoke of a day when

of the increase of his [the Messiah's] government and of peace
there will be no end,

107

upon the throne of David, and over his kingdom,
   to establish it, and to uphold it
with justice and with righteousness
from this time forth and for evermore.

He (11:7, 9) pictured an idyllic society in which peace would
prevail, where

the cow and the bear shall feed;
   their young shall lie down together;
   and the lion shall eat straw like the ox.

.   .   .   .

for the earth shall be full of the knowledge of the Lord
   as the waters cover the sea.

The Messiah would be raised up from the existing order. At one
time Isaiah suggested to King Ahaz that such a one might be an
infant in their midst already (7:13-17). At another time he spoke
of him as a shoot out of the stock of Jesse (11:1).

The experience of captivity in Babylon (586-538 B.C.) resulted
in a new conception of the messianic ideal unlike that of the kingly rule. There emerged from this period of servitude a portrayal
of the Messiah in terms of a servant who would save the people.
This representation appears in several places in the prophecy of
Second Isaiah (42:1-7; 49:1-6; 52:13–53:12; 61:1-3; 62:1, 6-7). He
will announce the salvation of God and become a light to all the
nations, to the Gentiles as well as to the Jews.

In one reference in particular, this messianic figure is represented
as being a suffering servant (Isa. 52:13–53:12). As he attempts to
fulfill his mission he will meet with deep humiliation, but these
very experiences will heal the wounds of the nation. His pain will
be vicarious in that he will suffer in behalf of the iniquities of
others rather than because of his own sins. Without his suffering
the people would not be saved. The actual hardships of Israel
during the exile contributed to this view.

Even though the wording of the servant passages suggests that
the prophet had an individual in mind as the one who saves, the
meaning implies that he was thinking of a group. Sometimes the

servant is the people of Israel as a whole (Isa. 41:8; 43:10; 44:21; 45:4). Again the title refers to the righteous remnant who have remained faithful through the difficult days, and in whom the true Israel is to be found (Isa. 42:1-7; 44:1; 49:1-6, 8-13; 51:1, 7).[1]

There was a later view of the nature of the messianic kingdom and of the Messiah himself which represented another significant change in outlook. Largely because of contact with Persian religious thought following the Exile (538-330 B.C.), and because of the discouragement engendered from being under the heel of a succession of foreign conquerers, the Jews began to think of their destiny in transcendental and apocalyptic terms. At the time when the Book of Daniel in its present form was written, the Syrian overlord Antiochus Epiphanes (175-164 B.C.) was oppressing the nation in an endeavor to Hellenize its culture. Judas Maccabaeus, the son of a Jewish priest, and his brothers opposed this attempt with vigorous military action.[2]

It was a dark hour, so dark that ultimate deliverance by earthly means seemed unlikely. It appeared that only God could save the nation. Therefore, it was concluded that a new Israel, ideal and glorified, would come down from the heavens, This idea was expressed thus (Dan. 7:13):

> I saw in the night visions,
> and behold, with the clouds of heaven
> there came one like a son of man,
> and he came to the Ancient of Days
> and was presented before him.

Some have considered this passage as pointing to an individual. Most scholars today, however, regard the reference as collective in character. As such, it would indicate the saints of God. In writings of this character one does not press for details as to how a renewed and glorified Israel could come down from the heavens. The meaning is clear, however. The initiative in creating this ideal

---

[1] A recommended reading on the servant passages is H. H. Rowley, *The Servant of the Lord and Other Essays*, pp. 3 ff.

[2] Cf. the previous reference to this situation, pp. 32-33.

people lies with God. It was heaven's answer to a situation which seemed by all earthly standards of judgment to be hopeless.

There was yet another conception of a messianic figure and his kingdom which was in the thinking of the nation when Jesus received his call to messiahship. Like the representations in Daniel, this was apocalyptic also. It is found in the parables of Enoch.[3] In this portrayal once again a figure called the Son of man appears. This time, however, the reference is to an individual rather than to the ideal nation. This individual is considered to be a heavenly being, one who is pre-existent and divine. He is the Elect of God, the righteous One, who will raise up the kings and the mighty from their seats. William Manson has pointed out that in Enoch the "concept of the Son of man had thus an inclusiveness, finality, and ultranational range and transcendence belonging to none of the earlier forms of the messianic idea." [4]

This brief review of the development of messianic thought in Israel shows that as the fortunes of the nation rose and fell, the hopes for the coming of the Messiah kept pace with its changing situation. Especially in times of calamity would the dream grow bright. The more spiritual among them saw in the Messiah's coming an expression of the righteousness of Jehovah within history. The less understanding emphasized the nationalistic character of the great event. Their king would reign over all the earth, especially over the enemies under whom they had been subjected politically. These were the hopes of the past.

In Jesus' day the Jews continued to hold to their messianic ideas, although not every group stressed them to the same degree. As we have seen,[5] the Zealots were very eager for the coming of the messianic reign and proposed a program of military action to further that end. The Pharisees maintained likewise an interest in the coming of the chosen One, but they advocated no course of action except the keeping of the Law. The ideal in their hands was religious primarily; however, it did not cease altogether to be political. It was a different story in the case of the Essenes. They thought of these matters solely in mystical terms. The Sadducees,

[3] I Enoch 37-71.
[4] *Op. cit.*, p. 145.
[5] See chap. 2, pp. 37-38.

on the other hand, believed in the Messiah's coming but were careful not to stress any conception which might be regarded by the Romans as politically seditious. This represents briefly the state of thought in Jesus' day concerning the coming of the Messiah. The people followed the Pharisees in their outlook for the most part. There may have been new interest in the apocalyptic portrayals, however, as a result of John the Baptist's preaching. All who were touched by this fiery prophet would be moved to expect transcendent events in the immediate future.

As Jesus faced the coming Kingdom and decided what course he would follow in the role of Messiah, he considered both the traditional hopes of the people and also their current expectations. There was yet another consideration, however, which was more important to him than all the rest, namely, the will of his Father in the present situation. *What kind of Kingdom did God have in mind and what kind of Messiah did God wish him to be?* Every idea out of the past and every conception of the present must be lifted up for his approval or rejection. Temptation lay in the fact that some of the hopes of the people which were appealing because they would be popular were discovered to be out of line with God's character and will. It was not always that they were evil, but often that they were superficial, which made them unworthy.

II

The lower Jordan Valley presents a varied terrain extending sixty-five miles from the Sea of Galilee to the Dead Sea and varying in breadth from three to fourteen miles. Some sections are extremely fertile, while others are weird in shape and desolate in appearance, ridged with clay and gravel. Thorn bushes and broom cover the drier areas, but cane and oleander grow along the streams. Floods are frequent, leaving in their wake swamps and malaria. In those parts where there are plains of sour soil, burnt-out hillsides, and jungle growth, the aspect is stern and forbidding. It is this section of the valley which the New Testament calls wilderness (Mark 1:4, 12), and it was here that Jesus retired into seclusion to consider the course which lay before him. In days past there were wild beasts to plague those who traveled here, lions in particular presenting the greatest difficulty. Besides these there were wolves, leopards, and wild boar.[6] It is understood easily why Mark would note that Jesus was "with the wild beasts" (1:13) during the days of his temptations. The storm within his soul was matched by the rigor of the landscape without and around him.

Both Matthew and Luke record that Jesus fasted during these days. It should not be concluded that he went without food entirely, but rather that he lived on the sparse growth to be found there. Food was secondary; prayer and meditation were primary. It was to be expected that hunger would result from eating such meager fare.

As one reads the records of these days, one should take note that they are presented in a highly symbolical form.[7] Pictorial representation of inner religious experience characterizes the narrative. Outstanding in this regard is the introduction of the devil as a person who spoke to Jesus. It is not to be thought that a camera would have caught the likeness of such a one. The experience was subjective. Evil suggestions were there, to be sure, but they were there as ideas and images, perhaps, within the mind of Jesus. As such they were ever so much more distinct and demanding than if they had been external. Inner voices are more potent always than those which come from without. This is the framework of interpretation within which to approach the gospel account of the temptations.

Not only should we regard the reference to the devil as symbolical in form, but also we should consider the representation of the temptations themselves as pictorial. Turning stones into bread, jumping from the temple, and bowing in worship before the devil (Matt. 4:3-10),[8] all mean more than doing just these things. As a matter of fact, it was not these things which Jesus was asked to

---

[6] See G. A. Smith, op. cit., pp. 467-96, for further information on the Jordan Valley.

[7] Even the "forty days" should be regarded as representative of a time of turmoil and struggle, e.g., the flood-rains in the time of Noah were for a period of forty days and forty nights and the Hebrews wandered forty years in the wilderness.

[8] This is the Matthaean order of the temptations. Luke reverses the order of the second and third. I prefer Matthew's order, because I regard the temptation to bow before the devil as the greatest of the three and, therefore, as the climax of the series.

do. Rather, it was certain courses of action which such things represented that Jesus was tempted to follow. We owe this symbolical presentation of the temptations to Jesus himself. Always the master of simile, metaphor, and parable, Jesus was never more vivid in portraying truth than when he shared with the disciples the account of his temptations. He was alone during these difficult days and only from his own lips could the story have come.

III

The thinking and praying of Jesus in the wilderness of temptation was vigorous and compelling. He was confronted with decisions involving God's intention for the Kingdom and for himself as the Messiah. It was not program building in the sense of making small plans for a temporary movement which concerned him. Instead he was convinced that it was the destiny of the human race that was involved, a destiny in which as Messiah he was to play a major part.

It was at the point where Jesus himself was related to the Kingdom that the temptations first took hold. This was the question: Was the recent conviction which had come to him that he was the Messiah genuine? The tempter suggested that he prove it to be valid, first by turning stones into bread and then by leaping from the temple. "If you are the Son of God," do this, he urged. Like others who have known great religious experiences only to be plagued later as to their validity, Jesus was facing the necessity also of rethinking his experience at the baptism.

Jesus refused steadfastly to apply any miraculous tests to substantiate the reality of God's voice which he had heard in his soul at the Jordan River, announcing to him that he was his Son. He concluded that it was the voice itself which carried within it the accents of genuineness. Turning stones into bread would prove only that he could turn stones into bread. Leaping from the Temple would indicate only that he could leap from the Temple and land safely on the pavement below. Neither would vindicate his conviction that the Father had spoken to him. If Jesus had followed the suggestions of the tempter and had succeeded in doing both feats, he would then have been in the position of trusting the feats rather than the inner voice. This is substituting a material basis for a spiritual one. Jesus refused to do this and established by so doing a principle which he followed throughout his ministry. It was by this same rule that he decided not to provide "signs" as proof that he was the Christ when the Jews asked for them. Jesus regarded the character of spiritual truth itself as the truest indication of its validity. Secondary confirmations were superfluous.

In addition to the temptation to question the conviction which came to him at his baptism that he was the Messiah, Jesus faced several alternatives in the conception of the Kingdom and in the program for carrying out his high commission. There was, as we have seen, an element of appeal in each of them. For instance, the temptation to turn stones into bread carried the suggestion that Jesus seek to interpret the Kingdom in terms of economic reform, and that he attempt to improve the economic status of the nation. This temptation as far as Jesus was concerned did not carry necessarily the idea that a program of excessive prosperity was in order; it was rather that the actual material needs of man should be placed first in the new day. Here was the real basis of appeal to Jesus. Having earned the bread for his own family in Nazareth, he knew the need at this point. The people would have welcomed such release from the burden of worry which they faced daily. They would have responded gladly. Their fathers in Israel of old had lifted high their heads at the thought of a land flowing with milk and honey, and the reign of the messianic king pictured in Isaiah implied prosperity for the nation. Such hopes were alive still. Somewhat later in this century the Apocalypse of Baruch[9] promised that in the new age one vine would have a thousand branches, and every branch would bear a thousand clusters of grapes. Besides this, each cluster would carry a thousand grapes and every grape would produce a core of wine. This is obvious hyperbole, but it expresses the hope that God would send an abundance of material goods. And this same expectation was in the hearts of the people as Jesus wrestled in the wilderness with the decision whether to be or not to be a "bread-giving Messiah."

In facing the suggestion of making economic stability the first

[9] Written in the latter half of the first Christian century for the purpose of encouraging the Jews who had suffered because of the destruction of Jerusalem. See 29:5-8.

consideration in the Kingdom, Jesus reflected on the experience of his nation in the past. Words from Deuteronomy came to his mind, and with these words the situation out of which they grew sprang to life. The author of Deuteronomy was writing of the wilderness days under Moses and reminding the nation that they should remember their dependence upon Jehovah as they were about to come into the inheritance of the land which he was to give them. It was God upon whom they must rely rather than upon material goods. They must come to realize that "man does not live by bread alone, but that man lives by everything that proceeds out of the mouth of the Lord" (Deut. 8:3). Here was the answer. The past had spoken to Jesus with a word that he recognized as coming from God. The Kingdom was not primarily a matter of food and drink. He decided that he would bring the Father to men first of all. If they found him and responded with faith and love, there would be bread enough for all. By this decision Jesus did not turn his back upon the genuine material needs of his generation. He saw deeper than many of his contemporaries. The roots of a sound economy are basically religious, and it was here that Jesus chose to take his stand, knowing that from such a position the needs of the whole man, body and soul, would be met.

IV

As we follow Matthew's sequence, the second temptation was that Jesus should leap from the Temple with the expectation that God would intervene and save him miraculously. This is in the spirit of the apocalyptic tradition of the nation. There is more to this suggestion than is evident at first. It carries with it the idea that as the Messiah, Jesus should inaugurate the Kingdom through spectacular feats that would startle the people into following him. The question was this: Should he undertake an all-out display of miraculous power, and thus introduce and define the character of the Kingdom?

If Jesus had followed the suggestion of the tempter literally, had leaped from one of the parapets of the Temple at the hour of prayer, and had landed unhurt upon the pavement below, what would the consequences have been? Doubtless there would have been much excitement, a great show of interest, and an invitation

to repeat the performance. In time a new routine would have
been needed as the old one became boresome. In the meantime
what of the kingdom of God? Would the message of God's love for
the poor and needy, the sinful and the brokenhearted, have been
heard? Hardly. And what of Jesus' word concerning the character
of God? Would it have been clarified by temple jumping? Not at
all. A temporary following with no understanding of the deep
things of the Kingdom would be all that such actions would
bring. There was no future in this.

Wherein, then, did the appeal lie for Jesus, for unless there was
some element of appeal in it, it was not a temptation? The promise
of the idea lay in the expectation that it would win a following
surely, and Jesus was interested in a following. The people expected mighty deeds when the Kingdom came. Furthermore, the
ninety-first psalm seemed to promise dramatic deliverance for the
followers of Jehovah. It said (11-12):

> For he will give his angels charge of you
>   to guard you in all your ways.
> On their hands they will bear you up,
>   lest you dash your foot against a stone.

Jesus chose not to follow such a course. He recalled that it had
been written, "You shall not put the Lord your God to the test . . ."
(Deut. 6:16). At Massah the people had dictated to God in an
attempt to get him to show his presence among them on their own
terms. Temple jumping was this same kind of dictation. It was
putting God to the test instead of trusting him, and Jesus would
have none of it.

Later Jesus was to understake a healing ministry involving deeds
of unusual character. These were not intended, however, to attract
a following; they were an expression of God's love instead. That
such mighty acts brought great crowds to hear him is a matter
of record. But Jesus was hindered by the numbers which came for
physical help only or were drawn to him largely by curiosity. For
this reason he urged frequently that those who were healed should
keep the fact secret.

V

The third temptation was the greatest of all, both in the sweep of its outreach and the magnitude of its possibilities. It was the "kingdoms of the world and the glory of them" that were offered to Jesus on the condition that he bow down before the evil one. To interpret the Kingdom in worldly terms and to seek to win the world by employing the ways of the world were the issues represented in the tempter's words: "All these I will give you, if you will fall down and worship me" (Matt. 4:9).

The Roman world provided a spectacle such as previous centuries had not known. This was the prize statesmen and generals had lived and died to gain. Its pageantry and power impressed all who had greatness in their souls. The Jews for centuries past had longed for the day when they would be significant politically, and the Zealots in Jesus' time had pledged themselves to overthrow the Empire. Could there be anything unworthy in such a dream?

It was not that the dream of world-submission to God was evil, but rather that the ideal of the Kingdom as an earthly empire and the means of achieving that goal which the tempter was suggesting were unworthy which caused Jesus to reject them. These means involved compromise, killing, misrepresentation, and chicanery. They called for the use of force and military might to compel man's submission. And in this program what would become of the ideals of the kingdom of God? This was the question Jesus had to face. What made it difficult particularly were certain messianic hopes of the past, such expectations as those in First Isaiah where the Messiah was pictured as an earthly ruler (9:6-7; 11:1-10).

Jesus saw that the suggestion was evil, both in its conception of the Kingdom as an earthly empire and in the methods it implied for realizing this end. The program carried at its heart a contradiction which was suicidal. It was, in effect, worshiping Satan rather than God. To worship God meant to follow him and live as he would have men live. It was to be like him in character as far as this was possible humanly. The sixth chapter of Deuteronomy presented Jesus with an insight in this regard where it is insisted that obedience to Jehovah is the only rule for righteous living. Obedience to men and the ways of men where these are contrary to Jehovah's will are sinful. There is no future to it except destruction. In this evil suggestion no possible program for advancing the Kingdom could be found, hence Jesus said: "Begone, Satan! for it is written,

> You shall worship the Lord your God
> and him only shall you serve.
>
> (Deut. 6:13)

VI

The wilderness temptation was ended. Jesus had turned aside from every suggestion which was contrary to the character of the Kingdom as he knew it, and, therefore, to the will of his Father. The revelation of God in the nation's past as he found it in the Scriptures had guided him in his thinking. It is most unlikely that he had any biblical scrolls with him during these days of difficult decision. What he had heard at the synagogue proved to be invaluable, as he remembered it when he needed it most.

Luke concludes his account of the temptation experience by remarking that "when the devil had ended every temptation, he departed from him until an opportune time" (4:13). This is a realistic insight, for Jesus encountered the issues which he considered in prospect during the wilderness days many times throughout his active ministry. Matthew says that after the temptations were ended, "angels came and ministered to him" (4:11). Jesus knew the reinforcement of spirit that comes to those who are loyal to the will of God.

QUESTIONS FOR DISCUSSION

1. The messianic expectations of the Jews in Jesus' day made it necessary for him as the Messiah to face certain alternatives in program. Why were not the answers to this problem available immediately to Jesus, apart from the necessity of spending many days and nights in mental and spiritual struggle? Does the genuineness of Jesus' personal life suggest the answer to this question?

2. Would the wilderness experience of Jesus have been necessary had not the baptism brought to him a tremendous realization of mission? Explain.

3. What modern political and social movements resemble the alternatives

in program which Jesus faced: i.e. making economics central, emphasizing the miraculous, and stressing the virtues of extreme nationalism?

4. During these days of temptation Jesus turned to the Scriptures for guidance. In using them, he entered understandingly into the earlier biblical situation in order to find a principle which would apply to the decision he must make. Is this in line with biblical literalism or with the historical approach to the Bible?

5. To what extent do you think Jesus depended actually upon the Scriptures for illumination?

6. If you assume that Jesus related the experience in the wilderness to his disciples, is it likely that he did it in pictorial and symbolic language? Does his practice of speaking in parables suggest an answer?

7. It has been suggested that Jesus shared this experience with the disciples at a time when they needed to understand his program. How would doing this have quelled their ambition to rule in earthly splendor along with him whom they regarded as the Messiah?

SUGGESTIONS FOR READING

I. The historicity of the temptations

Bundy, Walter. *The Religion of Jesus.* Indianapolis: The Bobbs-Merrill Company, 1928. Pp. 19-24.

Goodspeed, E. J. *Life of Jesus.* New York: Harper & Brothers, 1950. Pp. 43-44.

Lowrie, Walter. *The Short Story of Jesus.* New York: Charles Scribner's Sons, 1943. Pp. 18 ff.

Taylor, Vincent. *The Life and Ministry of Jesus.* Nashville: Abingdon Press, 1955. Pp. 61-63.

II. The symbolical character of the narrative

Barton, G. A. *Jesus of Nazareth.* New York: The Macmillan Company, 1931. Pp. 117-25.

Bosworth, E. I. *The Life and Teachings of Jesus.* New York: The Macmillan Company, 1939. Pp. 71 ff.

Rollins, W. E. and M. B. *Jesus and His Ministry.* Greenwich, Conn.: The Seabury Press, 1954. Pp. 44-60.

III. Interpretations of the temptation to turn stones into bread

The Interpreter's Bible. Nashville: Abingdon Press. VII, 269-71; VIII, 83-85.

Luce, H. K. *St. Luke,* "Cambridge Bible Series." New York: The Macmillan Company, 1936. Commentary 4:1-4.

Robinson, T. H. *The Gospel of Matthew,* "The Moffatt New Testa-

ment Commentary." London: Hodder & Stoughton, Ltd., 1947.
Commentary 4:1-4.

IV. Interpretations of the temptation to leap from the temple

   The Interpreter's Bible. Nashville: Abingdon Press. VII, 271-72; VIII,
   87-88.

   Luce, H. K. *St. Luke*, "Cambridge Bible Series." New York: The
   Macmillan Company, 1936. Commentary 4:9-12.

   Robinson, T. H. *The Gospel of Matthew*, "The Moffatt New Testament Commentary." London: Hodder & Stoughton, Ltd., 1947.
   Commentary 4:5-7.

V. Interpretations of the temptation to bow down and worship Satan

   The Interpreter's Bible. Nashville: Abingdon Press. VII, 272-73, VIII,
   85-86.

   Luce, H. K. *St. Luke*, "Cambridge Bible Series." New York: The
   Macmillan Company, 1936. Commentary 4:5-8.

   Robinson, T. H. *The Gospel of Matthew*, "The Moffatt New Testament Commentary." London: Hodder & Stoughton, Ltd., 1947.
   Commentary 4:8-10.

10

The Ministry of
Teaching and Preaching

J ESUS BEGAN HIS PUBLIC MINISTRY SOON AFTER THE ARREST OF
John the Baptist. The clang of the metal grating over the cell
where his friend was imprisoned sounded in his ears a clarion call
to action. This tragic event brought home to his mind and heart
the realization that this was the time to begin.

The Gospels refer to Jesus both as a teacher (Mark 5:35; Matt.
12:38; Luke 18:18) and as a preacher (Mark 1:14, 38, 39; Matt.
4:17, 23; 9:35; 11:1; Luke 4:44; 8:1) during his ministry. Mark
introduces his career with the words, "Jesus came into Galilee,
preaching the gospel of God" (1:14), while the Fourth Gospel
represents Martha as telling her sister Mary, "The *Teacher* is here
and is calling for you" (11:28).[1] This same writing suggests that
Jesus was called "rabbi" (which means teacher) by two inquiring
followers of John the Baptist (1:38), and was addressed as "rab-
boni" (which means teacher) by the weeping Mary at the tomb
(20:16).

In reporting the ministry of Jesus, the gospel writers did not
distinguish sharply between the functions of teaching and preaching. They are combined frequently to refer to the same general
activity (Matt. 9:35; 11:1). John the Baptist, like Jesus, was represented as doing both teaching (Luke 3:12) and preaching (Mark
1:4, 7). The words must then be taken quite generally as referring
to the oral ministry of Jesus.[2] Behind their use lies the teaching
function of the synagogue where both instruction and exhortation
were combined in the same public service.

In the Greco-Roman world a premium was placed upon oratory.
Civic functions were celebrated by laudatory addresses. Men were

---

[1] Italics mine.

[2] A distinction has been drawn by C. H. Dodd, *The Apostolic Preaching and
Its Development,* between the teaching (didache) and preaching (kerygma) of
the early church. The former refers to the ethical instruction of the church, and
the latter signifies the message. For Paul the gospel and the teaching based upon
it were different. It was the former which saved men. It is not clear as to
whether this distinction should be applied to the ministry of Jesus. His teaching
and preaching in relation to the Kingdom were concerned, it would seem, with
one and the same truth.

swayed by the utterances of politicians and generals alike. Traveling philosophers went from city to city teaching aloud at the corners of the streets. All of this opened wide the way for the Christian preachers and made the outdoor teaching and preaching of Jesus a normal procedure.

I

That Jesus was a forceful speaker is clear from the large following which he drew. They wondered at the words of wisdom which he spoke, and called it a teaching of authority. By its directness and forthrightness it made its appeal for decision. In one of his characteristic summaries Luke says that "he taught in their synagogues, *being glorified by all*" (4:15),[3] indicating that his speaking was well received. It was customary for the Jewish teachers to cite authorities for their statements, pointing either to the accepted Scriptures or to quotations from learned rabbis—much as we employ footnotes in writing. Jesus did not do this except on rare occasions. Instead he spoke on the basis of the authority of the truth itself. It was enough for him to be convinced, and out of this conviction he urged the people to enter the kingdom of God.

One is left to speculation alone when it comes to the character of his voice and expression while teaching or preaching. And yet we are not entirely without some indications in these matters. Jesus was an outdoor speaker primarily, although he did speak frequently in the synagogues. As an outdoor preacher, he spoke under varying conditions. On the hillside (Matt. 5:1; 24:3), standing in a boat pushed out from the shore (Mark 4:1), along the highway (Mark 10:17), inside a home (Luke 5:19)—all these provided the settings for his oral ministry. Such situations as these suggest required a voice that could be heard—strong, full, and resonant. There were no microphones into which one might speak, and no sound systems to amplify the vocal tones. One needed to be deep-chested and vigorous to command attention out in the open, and this Jesus was and did. He could much more easily interpret the meaning of many of his utterances if we could know the exact intonation of his voice when he spoke them. To one with

[3] Italics mine.

his versatile mind the nuances of vocalization would have been appealing especially.

Besides the voice there are the expressions of the face, the gesture of the arms, and the movements of the body to consider in appraising a public speaker. One cannot imagine Jesus speaking with a frigid countenance. He possessed eyes which reflected the measured depth of his soul. They were capable of expressing forgiving love with great tenderness one moment and severe judgment the next. Children were moved to draw near by their kindness, and the sinful were made to feel their guilt by their piercing indictment. All of this added power to his teaching and preaching by giving it a magnestism which held a single person in its grasp or moved great numbers with its drawing power.

The hands of Jesus received special mention throughout the gospel record likewise. He placed them upon the bodies of the sick and raised them in benediction as he blessed the people. To one thus accustomed to use his hands, public speaking offered additional opportunities for gesture. Some of the staccato sentences lend themselves readily to accompanying physical movements, while the frequent use of the imperative mood calls further for such expressions.

The Gospels make it clear that Jesus' teaching and preaching ministry was extensive. Even though the performance of deeds of healing were frequent, this oral expression was more predominant in his approach to the people. He was endowed with a prophetic message to announce—the presence and advent of the kingdom of God—and as the prophets before him, he spoke to his nation. Had we only the Gospel of Mark we might conclude that it was deeds which dominated the picture. Matthew and Luke tell a different story in this regard. Due to their inclusion of large amounts of material from Q as well as special tradition of their own which we designate as M and L, we know that it was the teaching and preaching which held first place. During the wilderness days Jesus had settled this issue. Temple jumping and turning stones into bread as symbols of astounding feats were rejected. Jesus felt himself anointed to preach good tidings instead.

II

The teaching and preaching of Jesus was informal. It showed none of the planned character of an oration or a modern sermon. This does not mean that systematic thinking did not precede it or that it was carelessly put together. One might say that it should be characterized by the words "ordered spontaneity." The only utterance of Jesus which could be called a sermon is what we refer to as the Sermon on the Mount as found in Matthew (5–7). Here we may discover a theme which runs throughout the discourse— the superiority of the new gospel to the tradition of the Jews. Illustration follows illustration, and the sermon closes with a solemn warning to those who hear but refuse to act. We do not have in this instance a sermon, however, in which all the materials are to be found in their original setting. Some of them appear in various other contexts elsewhere in the gospel record.[4] We owe the present arrangement of them to the author of the Gospel in all probability.

The spontaneity of Jesus' utterances is due in part to the fact that they were called forth from his mind and soul by situations mostly not of his own making. Rarely, if ever, did he announce a service for which he had prepared a sermon. Chance meetings along the way (Mark 10:17), unexpected remarks by a passer-by (Matt. 19:3), sudden questions from the disciples (Luke 11:1) — these are typical of the occasions which prompted Jesus' teaching and preaching. There may have been times when he knew he was to attend the synagogue and expected to be called upon to comment upon the lesson. If such were the case, he may have prepared his messages in advance. By and large, however, Jesus depended upon the developments of the day at hand to determine what he would say.

It was possible for Jesus to draw upon the inspiration of the moment without becoming shoddy in his expression or hazy in his ideas because of the intense intellectual life which he lived continually. He interpreted what he witnessed on every hand, finding in it the ever-present activity of the heavenly Father. The people who saw but did not *see*, as well as those who heard but did not

[4] Cf. Matt. 5:15-16 and Luke 11:33; Matt. 5:25-26 and Luke 12:57-59; Matt. 6:9-13 and Luke 11:2-4; Matt. 7:22-23 and Luke 13:26-27.

hear, concerned him. God was at work in their very presence; the Kingdom was at hand actually, but they were blind to it. Good weather prophets some of them might be, but they were poor interpreters of the "signs" in their own generation. "Hypocrites" was what Jesus called such as these (Luke 12:54-56). They posed as intelligent and alert guides and misled others to accept them in that light, but they were walking in darkness instead.

The Gospels represent Jesus' utterances as brief in character. He who said that when talking with God we are not heard for our many words, was not inclined to be wordy himself when he spoke to others. In part this brevity may be due to the fragmentary character of the tradition which came down to us. More likely, however, it is because of the epigrammatical nature of his statements and the directness of his thought.

Reference has been made to Jesus' preaching in the synagogues. This provided an unusual opportunity which his followers also used later in their missionary activities, especially the apostle Paul. The practice of giving visiting teachers a chance to speak upon the lesson for the day made this possible. Open debate followed sometimes and the people gave an eager hearing to what was said. It was an educational procedure which was not to be overlooked. The fact that groups of people met here expecting to be taught meant that their attitude was favorable for learning. They were people with the proper background for understanding what Jesus said likewise. As Jews they had been reared in the sacred traditions of their nation, even as Jesus himself had been, and thus were in a position to understand his message.

It is a matter of conjecture as to how long the synagogues remained open to Jesus. As antagonisms developed, it is reasonable to suppose that he was not welcome always. The account of his preaching in the synagogue at Nazareth makes it clear that uprisings against him occurred as he spoke out frankly concerning the attitude of the leaders among the people (Luke 4:16-30). It is suggested here that mob action followed the meeting and threatened his life. Reports of this outburst were certain to spread, making it difficult to find a speaking opportunity at the synagogues

in some places.[5] His healings on the Sabbath in the synagogues
would tend to make him unwelcome (Mark 3:1-6). As long as
they were open to his presence, however, he attended regularly as
had been his custom from his boyhood days in Nazareth.

III

We have been considering the teaching and preaching ministry
of Jesus from the standpoint of its background, delivery, and
general character. Attention must be given also to its unique form.
He did not speak in the legalistic phrases of the Jewish teachers
at the synagogue. There was nothing formal or academic about his
statements. The language was bright with metaphors and similes,
giving to conventional themes an originality that they did not possess on the lips of others. References to nature, home life, the
market place, and the open road abound. He did not use the
vocabulary of a religious functionary, and there was no suggestion
of the professional priest in his phraseology.

Jesus knew how to express himself so that he could command
the attention of his hearers and be assured that they would not
forget what he said. He used *figurative language* which lent itself
to short pithy sayings. "Beware of the leaven of the Pharisees"
(Mark 8:15), he said when referring to hypocrisy. "Enter by the
narrow gate; for the gate is wide and the way is easy, that leads
to destruction" (Matt. 7:13), he advised when speaking of the
need to discipline one's life. "Beware of false prophets, who come
to you in sheep's clothing but inwardly are ravenous wolves"
(Matt. 7:15), he warned as he counseled his followers. "Do not give
dogs what is holy; and do not throw your pearls before swine, lest
they trample them underfoot and turn to attack you" (Matt. 7:6),
he urged as he counseled them not to waste their attention on
closed and prejudiced minds. Such words as these, spoken as Jesus
would speak them, were moving and effective.

In addition to figurative language, Jesus used *dramatic statements* to convey his teachings to the people. At times they were
so extreme in form that they would stab his hearers into attention.

---

[5] Later the apostle Paul was to be driven out of synagogue after synagogue by
jealous and outraged Jews.

There can be no doubt that he did not intend them to be taken literally, for to do so would be a denial of the intention of the statements themselves. "Give to every one who begs from you; and of him who takes away your goods, do not ask them again" (Luke 6:30) is an illustration of this kind of saying. The teaching "To him who strikes you on the cheek, offer the other also; and from him who takes away your cloak do not withhold your coat as well" (Luke 6:29) is another such statement. An oustanding example of these particular forms is, "If your right eye causes you to sin, pluck it out. . . . If your right hand causes you to sin, cut it off" (Matt. 5:29-30). To comply literally with this injunction would be to deny the good sense of Jesus himself. And yet the effectiveness of this warning against compromise and complacency is as evident to us who read it now as it was to those who heard it from his lips.

In the literary tradition of the Hebrew people the *proverb* had found an important place. Many of them were attributed to Solomon because of his reputation for wisdom. Jesus found this form of expression congenial also.[6] Some of his teachings which were of this character include the following: "Render to Caesar the things that are Caesar's, and to God the things that are God's" (Mark 12:17). "The sabbath was made for man, not man for the sabbath" (Mark 2:27). "Judge not, that you be not judged. For with the judgment you pronounce you will be judged, and the measure you give will be the measure you get" (Matt. 7:1-2). "For every one who exalts himself will be humbled, and he who humbles himself will be exalted" (Luke 14:11). Statements such as these were likely to be repeated over and over again by the followers of Jesus, for their form was conducive to both memorization and repetition.

When we consider the teaching and preaching of Jesus, we discover that the *parable* was the most significant form which he employed. While we cannot say that Jesus invented the parable, his singular use of it makes him its chief exponent. So extensive was his employment of this form of teaching that special mention was made of the fact (Matt. 13:34-35). When asked why he spoke in parables, he replied that is was because of the blindness of the

---

[6] The scribes in the time of Jesus made use of proverbs, cf. the Pirke Aboth in the Mishnah.

people who saw but did not see and heard but did not hear. A story with a meaning which they themselves must deduce as they heard it and caught its teaching, might win an entree into their minds.[7]

A parable is a story, the truth or lesson of which is to be transferred to another area of experience. This application to life may be drawn either by comparison or contrast. The situation in the story is either like a corresponding situation in life or unlike it. To illustrate, the parable of the lost son (Luke 15:11-32) suggests that God is like the father who runs to meet the returning youth, eager to forgive him and to restore him to the family circle. On the other hand, the parable of the unjust judge (Luke 18:1-8) is intended to show that God is unlike the judge who gives in to the widow who pesters him, lest she wear him out with her pleas. Contrast rather than comparison is what Jesus intended here.

In interpreting the parables, it should be remembered that it is the meaning of the story as a whole which is central rather than the details in the narrative. To find a significance in each detail is to allegorize overmuch the parable. An allegory is like a parable in that it applies to an area of experience beyond itself. It differs from a parable, since it is a representation in which every detail should be applied to life.[8] The Fourth Gospel contains two outstanding allegories, that of the good shepherd (John 10:1-18) and that of the vine and the branches (John 15:1-11). It is common practice to allegorize a parable, largely because the distinction between a parable and an allegory is not realized. Even in the New Testament, the parable of the sower is treated as an allegory in the explanation of it which is given (Luke 8:11-15).[9] Such interpretation may sometimes introduce ideas foreign to the intention of the teller of the parable.

Jesus' parables are colorful and dramatic even though they are

[7] See Matt. 13:14-15. Matthew's reference to the fulfillment of prophecy in the use of parables is beside the point. It is not moral to speak in order to blind men to the truth.

[8] "In a well-constructed allegory each detail of the story has its counterpart in the meaning; whereas, in a parable, story and meaning meet, not at every point, but at one central vantage ground of abiding truth." George A. Buttrick, *The Parables of Jesus*, p. xvii.

[9] I regard this allegorical explanation as due to the author rather than to Jesus himself.

brief. The situations which they present are lifelike, such as one might meet any day in first-century Palestine. A man robbed on the highway (Luke 10:29-37), an urgent request for needed bread due to a visit by an unexpected guest (Luke 11:5-8), a farmer enlarging his granary to accommodate his increased crop (Luke 12:16-21), a sheep that wanders from the flock so that the shepherd must go in search of it (Luke 15:4-7), a marriage feast to which an invited guest comes improperly dressed (Matt. 22:1-14)—these and many other occasions provide material for the parables of Jesus. It is assumed frequently that the parables, while true to life and in this respect different from fables, are nevertheless fictional in character. According to this view, they are stories which Jesus composed rather than events which occurred actually. This may be true, although there is no situation in any one of them which might not have taken place. This accounts for their realism as well as for their suggestiveness. They are true to experience.

The parables of Jesus cover a wide range of subjects representing the many facets which make up the Kingdom. Prayer (Luke 11:5-13), money (Luke 16:1-9), the growth of the Kingdom (Matt. 13:31-33), preparedness (Matt. 25:1-13), forgiveness (Luke 15:8-10), the use of one's talents (Luke 19:11-27), reception of the truth of the Kingdom (Matt. 13:1-9), the necessity for putting belief into action (Matt. 7:24-27), and the character of neighborliness (Luke 10:30-37) are all among the themes treated in the parables. In the light of the fact that Jesus put none of his teachings into writing but counted on the impression they made upon the minds of those who heard them, his selection of the parable form was a fortunate one. The people would not forget easily these fascinating stories. They could readily be repeated at family gatherings or while walking along the dusty road engaging a friend or chance acquaintance in conversation.

IV

Jesus made much use of the Old Testament scriptures in his teaching and preaching. Only the Law and the Prophets had been accepted as canonical writings at that time, but the others were being read also. In all probability he did not own a single scroll, so that his knowledge of it came from hearing it read in the synagogues. As a boy he had memorized portions of it by rote, sitting cross-legged before his teacher. This memory work stood him in good stead.

The attitude of Jesus toward the Scriptures was evident in what he said about them. He regarded them as basic: "It is easier for heaven and earth to pass away, than for one dot of the law to become void" (Luke 16:17). He warned also that "whoever then relaxes one of the least of these commandments and teaches men so, shall be called least in the kingdom of heaven" (Matt. 5:19), and said that he had not come to abolish the law and the prophets but to fulfill them.

Jesus was not a literalist as he read his Bible. He preferred the prophetic emphasis upon ethical righteousness to the legalism of the Pharisees in their interpretation of the Scriptures. It was their manifest intention that concerned him rather than their literal statement. Jesus did not hesitate to put one scripture passage above another in preferment. When asked concerning divorce, he inquired what Moses said. The Pharisees quoted Deut. 24:1-4. But Jesus favored the word in Gen. 1:27 and 2:24 (Mark 10:2-9). On occasion he placed his own convictions above the statements of scripture. Quoting the Law regarding killing, adultery, divorce, taking an oath, retaliation, and hatred of enemies, he supplanted what it said with his own injunction, opening his reply with the words "But I say to you . . ." (Matt. 5:21-48). Bornkamm concludes that Jesus in such instances exercises a freedom in interpreting the Law that neither rabbi nor prophets could follow. His "I say unto you" he asserts "cannot have its equivalent in the literature of the rabbis." [10]

Jesus accepted the view of his day regarding biblical authorship. Moses had written the Law, and David had composed the Psalms. Some of the books of the Bible which he used most are our favorites also: Isaiah, Deuteronomy, Psalms, Leviticus, Hosea, Zechariah, Genesis, Exodus, Daniel, First Samuel, Numbers, Nehemiah, and Jeremiah are quoted, or alluded to in his teaching.[11] The biblical personalities which attracted him most are the ones which appeal today: Abel, Abraham, Isaac, Jacob, Moses, Noah, Jonah, Lot and

[10] Cf. Bornkamm, *Jesus of Nazareth,* p. 99.
[11] These are listed according to the frequency of the references to them.

his wife, David, Solomon, the queen of Sheba, Elijah, Elisha, the widow of Zarephath, and Naaman come in for special mention.

In general we can say that Jesus used his Bible in answering questions put to him, replying to enemies, illustrating the character of the Kingdom, warning men of the Judgment, making personal decisions, and interpreting his messianic mission. He applied the spirit of the passages quoted, or situations mentioned, to the problems at hand, always taking into account the context. In this way situations in the past yielded words of wisdom to his own time.

The Scriptures were the thought-world within which Jesus lived. He moved back and forth within the history they related and the ideals and truths they proclaimed. They were not so much a series of writings to him as an area of living, an atmosphere within which he thought, felt, purposed, and acted.

QUESTIONS FOR DISCUSSION

1. Read the Sermon on the Mount (Matt. 5–7). Characterize the form of Jesus' preaching on the basis of this material according to the following: philosphical, theological, didactic, practical, hortatory, educational.

2. How would you evaluate this sermon according to the following: interest appeal, literary style, vocabulary usage, convincing quality, and clarity of thought?

3. Which of the particular literary usages of Jesus do you regard as most effective, the parable, figurative speech, the proverb, or dramatic statement? Explain.

4. Since he did not record them in writing, how do you account for the fact that so many of Jesus' words were remembered? Was it because of the trained memories in that day or because of the pictorial character of Jesus' speech?

5. Read the parable of the good Samaritan (Luke 10:29-37). Paraphrase it in modern speech. Compose a parable based on current life which has the same teaching.

6. Turn to the account of the temptation of Jesus (Matt. 4:1-11) and note his use of scripture as found in the quotations from the Old Testament. Check the biblical sources from which these scriptural references came to determine in what way they applied to Jesus' situation:

a) Matt. 4:4—Deut. 8:3.

b) Matt. 4:7—Deut. 6:16.

c) Matt. 4:10—Deut. 6:13.

7. Use the *Abingdon Bible Commentary* for the interpretations of the Old Testament situations from which these quoted verses came.

SUGGESTIONS FOR READING

I. The parables of Jesus

Barnett, A. E. *Understanding the Parables of Our Lord.* New York and Nashville: Abingdon-Cokesbury Press, 1940. Selected readings.

Beck, Dwight M. *Through the Gospels to Jesus.* New York: Harper & Brothers, 1954. Pp. 185-93.

Buttrick, G. A. *The Parables of Jesus.* New Hampshire: R. R. Smith, 1928. Selected readings.

Oesterley, W. O. E. *The Gospel Parables in the Light of Their Jewish Background.* New York: The Macmillan Company, 1936. selected readings.

Smith, B. T. D. *The Parables of the Synoptic Gospels.* New York: The Macmillan Company, 1937. Selected readings.

II. Jesus' use of Scripture

Gilbert, George Holley. *Jesus and His Bible.* New York: The Macmillan Company, 1926. Selected readings.

Goguel, Maurice. *The Life of Jesus.* New York: The Macmillan Company, 1944. Pp. 553 ff.

Laymon, Charles M. *Luke's Portrait of Christ.* Nashville: Abingdon Press, 1959. Ch. IV.

III. Jesus as a teacher

Branscomb, Harvie. *The Teachings of Jesus.* New York: The Abingdon Press, 1931. Pp. 89-111.

Burney, C. F. *The Poetry of Our Lord.* New York: Oxford University Press, 1925. Ch. i-iii.

IV. The Sermon on the Mount

Beck, Dwight M. *Through the Gospels to Jesus.* New York: Harper & Brothers, 1954. Pp. 164-84.

Bornkamm, Günther. *Jesus of Nazareth.* Translated by Irene and Fraser McLuskey and James M. Robinson. 3rd ed. Harper & Brothers, 1960. Pp. 106-7, 221-24.

Dibelius, Martin. "The Sermon on the Mount and Christ's Mission," *Contemporary Thinking About Jesus,* ed. Thomas S. Kepler. Nashville: Abingdon Press, 1944. Pp. 267 ff.

The Interpreter's Bible. Nashville: Abingdon Press. VII, pp. 279-336.

Windisch, Hans. *The Meaning of the Sermon on the Mount.* Translated by S. MacLean Gilmour. Philadelphia: The Westminster Press, 1951. Selected readings.

11

The Ministry of Service

JESUS WAS NOT A RELIGIOUS PROFESSIONAL AS WAS TRUE TOO often of some of the priests in his day. Instead, he mingled with the people as they walked along the dusty roads, visited with them as they mended their nets beside the sea, talked to them at the doorsteps of their homes, and prayed with them in the synagogue service itself. Great crowds gathered to hear him from time to time. On other occasions he held conversation with individuals. He chose to spend his days with the people, and in this free and happy association his messianic mission was finding expression.

The time came when Jesus felt it best to select a few persons who would be nearer to him than the rest. This was not a matter of favoritism but a question of more effective service instead. From the larger group who followed him he chose twelve men to compose an inner circle of learners. It was customary for teachers in that day to be surrounded by carefully selected pupils wherever they went. When people came to know who these persons were, they would seek them out for instruction if the teacher was occupied. Why the number selected was twelve rather than another figure is a matter of conjecture. To the Hebrews numbers had an esoteric significance which we do not give to them. The number "twelve" was a symbol of completeness. Traditionally there had been the twelve tribes, and now Jesus was choosing twelve disciples. After he left them, as well as during his ministry, these could give a *complete witness* to his teachings. This may have been the significance of the figure.

A deeper motive for choosing the disciples was Jesus' longing for the companionship in service which they would make possible. It was important to him to share the inspirations which came day by day, especially with those who would more nearly understand than the multitudes. The life he lived had an element of loneliness in it. All who see and feel beyond their fellows know what this is. The highest peak of any mountain range which towers above the rest must remain in solitary elevation. It is the same with great persons, and it was true of Jesus. There was a further need for companionship which became acute increasingly as his ministry developed. It grew out of the enmity which the religious leaders exhibited toward him. As we shall see, later disagreement with him on their part led to antagonism and outright persecution. Jesus did not accept this unfeelingly. It hurt him to be rejected by the leaders of the religion which had nurtured him and which he felt he had come to fulfill. Fellowship with the twelve under these circumstances was meaningful.

At what point in his ministry did Jesus select the disciples? Matthew regards it as coming before the break with the Pharisees (Matt. 10:1-4). Jesus saw the people as sheep having no shepherd, and these men were to be their leaders. Mark and Luke relate the call to the rupture between Jesus and the Pharisees (Mark 3:13-19; Luke 6:12-16). Their thought was that Jesus was establishing in the choosing of the Twelve the nucleus of a new order of religious service to replace the old which had rejected him. In any case, each of the Synoptic writers see in this act a reason that is related to his developing ministry.

It was not easy to make the selection. For some months these men, along with many others, had been following Jesus. Some of them he had met, for the first time presumably, where John was baptizing (John 1:35-51); others had left their nets by the Sea of Galilee to accompany him (Mark 1:16-20). One of them had come from the tax collectors' seat (Mark 2:13-14). Jesus had had ample opportunity to observe them, and his judgment of a man's potentialities was marked. Even so, Luke tells us that he spent the entire night in prayer before making his choice (6:12). We can but speculate on the considerations that guided Jesus in the final selection. Here, as always, the Father's will as it was shown him would be determinative finally. Did Jesus attempt to balance the group by seeing to it that the interests of the men were varied? As it turned out, there was considerable variety in their temperaments. Were there some whom he would have liked to include, but whom he knew were not yet ready? Later, in the case of the three would-be disciples this was the situation (Luke 9:57-62), even as it was also with the rich young ruler who could not bring himself to leave his wealth (Mark 10:17-22). We can be sure that Jesus' nightlong vigil in prayer sharpened his judgment and illumined his mind as he chose the disciples. It made a difference in the final selection.

The lists of names of the Twelve vary in the gospel records.[1] Attempts have been made to account for these differences. Bartholomew is identified usually as referring to Nathanael (John 1:45-51) since the Synoptic Gospels never mention the latter, while John's Gospel does not speak of the former. The other disciples named in John are all found in the Synoptics except Nathanael. Matthew and Mark give the name Thaddaeus. Luke does not include this disciple. He does, however, mention Judas, the son of James. He might possibly be the same Thaddaeus which Matthew and Mark know. John's Gospel records also the name of a disciple called "Judas, not Iscariot," who could be Judas, son of James. These differences are interesting since they reflect variations in the tradition which circulated among the churches.

I

After some time in training, Jesus decided to send forth his disciples on an evangelistic tour. (Mark 6:7-13; Matt. 10; Luke 9:1-6.) He felt that they would not only open the way in communities which he would later visit, but also could extend the work more rapidly. The experiences which had come to those who responded to his message might be known by others who would receive the preaching of his disciples. Great enthusiasm on the part of Jesus marked this undertaking. The Father was honoring manifestly the ministry of the Messiah. The kingdom of God was at hand. Let it come! Let it grow!

Two by two, Jesus sent them out. Where one might grow discouraged, the other could encourage. Their separate personalities would supplement each other besides increasing their appeal to the populace. It would be interesting to know how they were paired. Whom did he select to accompany the impulsive Simon? Was it John the mystic or Levi the businessman? He gave them an agenda to follow as far as indicating the type of work they should do. It was not unlike what he had been doing. Luke indicates that they were to preach the kingdom of God and to heal the sick. Matthew is more specific. He informs us that Jesus said: "Preach as you go, saying, 'The kingdom of heaven is at hand.' Heal the sick, raise

[1] Cf. Mark 3:16-19; Matt. 10:2-4; Luke 6:14-16.

the dead, cleanse lepers, cast out demons" (Matt. 10:7-8). Here
was the program of the hour. It was a kingdom-of-God program,
and the tour was a kingdom-of-God undertaking.

All three Gospels agree that the provisions to be taken on the
journey were limited deliberately by Jesus. They were not to be
weighted down with baggage. Bread, wallet, money, and extra
clothing were prohibited. It was not that Jesus favored a lack of
preparedness or that he was announcing conditions for all future
workers. Instead, in this particular situation he wanted to create
in his disciples the feeling of dependence upon God which this
requirement would necessitate. It was good also that the people to
whom they were going should share in the work by caring for the
physical needs of the workers. Deissmann has suggested that the
wallets they were not allowed to carry were begging bowls such as
the many beggars used throughout Palestine. His followers were
not to be classed with this group of mendicants.

Among the instructions Jesus gave them was the injunction not
to move from house to house in the same community. This would
have insulted those in whose house they had last stayed, for it
would have suggested that their hospitality had run out. If they
remained in the same home, the community would associate the
new work with that home; and a permanent headquarters would
be established. They were not, however, to force themselves upon
others. If a home would not receive them when they had blessed
it after the fashion of the Jews, they were to depart immediately,
but not until they had warned the occupants of the opportunity they
were missing. In the case of an entire village which was unfriendly,
Jesus told them to shake the dust off their feet as they departed,
not as a gesture of indignation and resentment, but as a sign that
they were missing a great opportunity.

When the disciples returned from their tour, they were very enthusiastic, reporting that the demons were subject to Jesus' name.[2]
The message had been accompanied by works of healing and expressions of power. Their joy was matched by outspoken delight on
the part of Jesus. In their absence he had been praying for them

[2] This incident is based upon the story of the sending out of the seventy on a
similar undertaking which I regard as another version of the mission of the
Twelve. Luke (10:1-20) alone records it, his source being Q. Matthew (10) com-
bines the accounts of Mark and Q into a single presentation.

and received a vision of their success and of the spead of the work throughout the earth so that evil itself would be overthrown. "I saw Satan fall like lightning from heaven," he told them. In similar figurative language he announced that their victory would be complete; serpents and scorpions would be powerless to afflict them. This was Jesus' way of expressing his supreme confidence in the coming of the kingdom of God.

Jesus' enthusiasm knew no bounds at this season. On every hand there were indications that the seed sown would bear a tremendous harvest. The prospect was nothing short of ultimate victory for the cause; today, tomorrow, and the day after that would witness the realization of his expectations. At last the common people of the nation were being approached in terms that they could understand. Those whom he had characterized as "sheep without a shepherd" were having their high hour of opportunity and were responding. This led Jesus to lift his voice in an exalted prayer. "I thank thee, Father, Lord of heaven and earth, that thou hast hidden these things from the wise and understanding and revealed them to babes; yea, Father, for such was thy gracious will," he prayed. (Luke 10:21.) It was a moment of profound worship for Jesus. Its spontaneous character is the measure of its depth.

He turned to his disciples and told them that the experiences which they were having, the new life which they were seeing wherever people responded to the preaching of the Kingdom, was that which prophets and kings in distant days had longed to see and hear, but had not done so. The deepest religious currents of the nation's past were flowing in the direction of such a flood tide as they were witnessing. It was the great hour of all history, and they were a part of it.

II

The greatness of this hour in history expressed itself in many ways through Jesus' ministry of service. Deeper than the healing of men's bodies and minds was the experience of forgiveness which came to many. Usually sinners are not attracted to idealists such as Jesus. In his case, however, they were moved to seek him out. It was not that he condoned evil in the lives of men or that he was trying to be popular by closing his eyes to it. The very opposite was

true. His denunciations of evil were scathing, and his analysis of
its roots in man's selfishness, revealing. Yet sinners came to him and
felt at home in his presence at the same time that they were acutely
conscious of their sin. What is the explanation of this paradox? It
lies in the fact that at the same moment his judgment moved out to
condemn sin, the love of God which he offered went forth to forgive.

Early in his ministry the Synoptics record the healing of the
paralytic (Mark 2:3-12; Matt. 9:2-8; Luke 5:18-26). This man had
been brought to Jesus by four of his friends who removed sections
from the roof and lowered him into the room.[3] The crowds at
the door made regular entrance impossible. Access to the roof was
had by going up the outside staircase. This man had come for
healing, but curiously enough, Jesus said to him at the outset,
"My son, your sins are forgiven."

The Jews believed that misfortune, sickness, and sin went together. The Talmud states that no man gets up from his sick couch
until he has first been forgiven.[4] Jesus did not accept this interpretation as applicable *always*. An illustration of his attitude at
this point is to be found in his account of the falling tower. He
made it clear that sin was not the reason that the tower of Siloam
fell upon those whom it killed, yet added that unless his hearers
repented they would perish likewise (Luke 13:4-5). In the case of
the paralytic, however, Jesus announced the man's forgiveness before healing him. He may have sought to focus attention on a need
deeper than physical well-being.

The Pharisees regarded Jesus' words concerning forgiveness as
blasphemy. Only God could forgive, they said. Jesus' reply was that
it was no more difficult to forgive than to heal and commanded
the man to take up his couch and go home. This he did to the
amazement of the crowd. There is a difference of opinion among
scholars as to whether Jesus was himself forgiving the man or
whether he was announcing in a priestly way the fact that God had
forgiven him. The accounts in the Gospels seem to say that Jesus
himself forgave the man. This emphasis may be due to the theology
of the church at a later period when Jesus had come to be thought

---

[3] It was a clay roof probably. The Romans employed tile more than the
Palestinians.
[4] Ned. 41a.

of as God in the flesh. Again, it may be that as the Messiah, Jesus felt that the power to forgive was inherently his. This act then would be an expression of the messianic kingdom, no less.

In any case, that sinners sought him out and in his presence experienced forgiveness is clear. On one occasion a woman braved the scorn of the Pharisees and entered the room where Jesus was dining with one of them (Luke 7:36-50). Since the house was directly on the street, access was easy. She had been drawn to Jesus by his preaching, no doubt; and a longing for the new life of the Kingdom had filled her heart. With her tears she washed his feet and dried them with her hair. Jesus was moved deeply by her expression of love and interpreted it as gratitude for the forgiveness she had received. Turning to Simon the Pharisee, he said that "her sins, which are many, are forgiven, for she loved much." Simon, on the other hand, had not shown Jesus even the customary courtesy of providing for the washing of his feet. His lack of such an expression of love had indicated little gratitude on his part.[5] Evidently he had not been forgiven.

On another day the Jews brought a sinful woman into Jesus' presence and asked him to sentence her.[6] They wanted him to pass judgment upon her sin. A marked contrast in attitude between Jesus and the Jews is found here. They were interested in using her as a test case to trap Jesus, for if he had said stone her, he would have been guilty of breaking Roman law; and if he had said release her, they would have charged him with disregarding the commandments of Moses. Considering their religious profession, their unconcern for the personality of the woman, was more sinful than the woman's misdeed. At Jesus' words, "Let him who is without sin among you be the first to throw a stone at her," they went away so that he was left alone with the woman. With extreme tenderness he said, "Woman, where are they? Has no one condemned you?" She

[5] This story may be regarded as another version of the account which Mark (14:3-9) and Matt. (26:6-13) give of the anointing of Jesus' head by a woman in the home of Simon the Leper at Bethany. Again, it shows marked similarity to the story of the anointing of Jesus' feet by Mary, also at Bethany, and found in John (12:1-8). It is difficult to say which is the original story, and the relationship between them is intriguing. Consult the commentaries for suggested solutions.

[6] This story is printed as a footnote to John 8.

replied, "No one, Lord," whereupon Jesus added, "Neither do I condemn you; go, and do not sin again."

This story illustrates Jesus' attitude toward sin and sinners. He did not minimize sin; instead he gave newness of life to the sinner. In his presence they experienced a change. Forgiveness was not a doctrine he taught so much as it was an experience he brought. The sinful woman received it.[7]

III

Outstanding among the expressions of the Kingdom which accompanied Jesus' ministry of service was the recognition of outcasts and foreigners. People of that day were classified by the Jews according to whether they were ceremonially clean or unclean. This was a question of Jewish law and ritual. If one were a Gentile, he was unclean; or if he were a Jew who had circulated among Gentiles, he was in need of ceremonial cleansing. Handling of the dead or eating forbidden foods made one unclean also.[8] This was not a matter of morals; not sin, but of ceremonial evil. Such associations were regarded as affecting one's standing before God.

These views made the Jews snobbish and unfeeling in their attitude toward other races. People were valued not according to their worth as persons but according to their ceremonial status. Such classifications honeycombed life with artificiality. Jesus, with his direct approach to all people because he regarded them as children of the heavenly Father, found this false system of differentiation or caste distasteful exceedingly. It was sinful and unrelated to the real value of persons.

On one occasion when he was dining at the home of a Pharisee, he did not wash himself ceremonially before eating (Luke 11:37-41).[9] It may be that he expected the omission to be noticed and counted on this to provide an opportunity for making his remarks. What he said, in effect, was that by stressing such external matters,

[7] Clearly this story is out of place in its location in the Fourth Gospel. Some ancient manuscripts omit it altogether. Others place it at the end of this Gospel. It has been found also after Luke 21:38. The style of the narrative indicates a closer relation with the Synoptics than with John.

[8] Cf. Acts 10:9-16.

[9] Mark 7:2 indicates that it was some of his disciples who had not washed rather than Jesus.

the Pharisees were missing the point completely. It was *within* the heart that evil desires were born: "Now you Pharisees cleanse the outside of the cup and of the dish, but inside you are full of extortion and wickedness. . . . Give for alms those things which are within; and behold, everything is clean for you." Race, nationality, ceremony, and outward contacts do not determine inherent worth. It is what a person is within his life that counts.

Acting upon this conviction, Jesus disregarded the rules which restricted human associations. For this reason "the Pharisees and the scribes murmured, saying, 'This man receives sinners and eats with them'" (Luke 15:2). When he called Levi to leave his tax office, the new follower gave a feast to celebrate, inviting many of his friends. Among them were tax collectors and others whom the Jews regarded as unclean.

Jesus was the guest of honor. The Pharisees complained and inquired of him: "Why do you eat and drink with tax collectors and sinners?" His reply was that the well had no need of a physician, only the sick (Luke 5:27-32). Wherever he was needed he would go; human need rather than ceremonial standing determined his fellowship with others.

All Gentiles were considered outcasts. They were non-Jews. The enmity of the Jews toward the Romans was especially acute because they were their political overlords. Resentment of this fact provided an additional reason for antipathy toward them. They were not only Gentiles; they were *Roman* Gentiles as well. Samaritans were in a peculiar position likewise. As a people of mixed blood, they were outside the accepted circle.[10] On the other hand, they shared a religious background with the Jews, since they too claimed the Old Testament forefathers for themselves. The Samaritan woman prided herself that it was Jacob's well to which she had come to draw water (John 4:12). She held the view of her countrymen, however, that Mount Gerizim was more sacred than Jerusalem (John 4:20).[11]

[10] The Samaritans were descended from the Hebrews who were left behind when most of the nation was carried as slaves to Assyria. They had intermarried considerably with Gentiles who had moved into Canaan following the captivity.

[11] A temple on Mount Gerizim was destroyed by Hyrcanus in 129 B.C.

The attitude of his fellow countrymen toward non-Jews did not deter Jesus in his service to them. He complimented the Roman centurion whose servant he healed by saying that in all Israel he had not found such great faith (Luke 7:1-10). He cast the demon out of the daughter of the Syrophoenician woman (Mark 7:24-30), and made a Samaritan the hero of the parable in which priests and Levites were insensible to a wounded man's need, while a good Samaritan showed mercy unto him (Luke 10:29-37).

The issue was not race or nationality but human values where Jesus was concerned. Any other basis of recognition was superficial. How could one discriminate where all were the children of the same heavenly Father? This was the question which Jesus asked himself and which he answered in loving service toward all. He was proud of his Jewish heritage, but he was more proud of the universal brotherhood of all men.

QUESTIONS FOR DISCUSSION

1. What would you judge were the responsibilities of a disciple? Was he an onlooker, companion, fellowworker, healer, teacher, preacher? Cf. Mark 6:7-13; Matt. 10; Luke 10:1-20.

2. What considerations would you think went into Jesus' selection of the disciples: aptitude, willingness, family conditions, religious background, teachableness, education?

3. Do you think that the disciples remained with Jesus constantly, or was there a going and a coming from time to time as the ministry and its needs developed?

4. If Jesus were choosing such a company today, would he select twelve or more than twelve? Less than twelve? Explain.

5. What is your thought regarding the practice of Francis of Assisi, who took Jesus' instructions to the disciples as they conducted their preaching tour literally, as a rule for himself and his followers in their ministry? Are there any religious orders today which follow this practice?

6. What does Jesus' enthusiasm over the success of the preaching ministry of the disciples indicate regarding his attitudes? Were they formal or deeply personal?

7. On the basis of the incidents cited in the chapter, summarize Jesus' teaching on sin.

8. Why did sinners feel at home in the presence of Jesus? Was it because he was easy on them, or was it that they felt he was interested deeply

in their welfare in a personal rather than a professional sense?

9. Considering Jesus' attitude toward ceremonial uncleanness, what do you think his feeling would be toward ceremonialism in the church today? Would you regard an extreme formalism in worship and a major stress upon regulations concerning religious practice which exists sometimes among us, as finding favor with Jesus?

10. What parallels do you find in the social attitudes of the Jews in Jesus' day and our own today? Does Jesus' approach apply in the modern world?

SUGGESTIONS FOR READING

I. The practices of traveling teachers and philosophers in the Greco-Roman World

Derwacter, F. M. *Preparing the Way for Paul.* New York: The Macmillan Company, 1930. Selected readings.

Dill, Samuel. *Roman Society from Nero to Marcus Aurelius.* New York: The Macmillan Company, 1905. Pp. 334-83.

McCasland, S. Vernon. *The Religion of the Bible.* New York: Thomas Y. Crowell, Company, 1960. Pp. 215-22.

II. The food laws among the Jews

Asher, Joseph Mayor. "Food and Health Laws," *Encyclopedia Americana.* New York: Americana Corporation. XVI, 120 ff.

The Jewish Encyclopedia. New York and London: Funk & Wagnalls Company, 1902. IV, 596 ff.

III. Ceremonial uncleanness

Asher, Joseph Mayor. "Food and Health Laws," *Encyclopedia Americana.* New York: Americana Corporation. XVI, 123 ff.

The Jewish Encyclopedia. New York and London: Funk & Wagnalls Company, 1902. I, 68 ff.

IV. The background of the Samaritans

Textual material: II Kings 17:24-41; Ezra 4. Cf. *Abingdon Bible Commentary.* Nashville: Abingdon Press, 1929.

Anderson, Bernhard W. *Understanding The Old Testament.* Englewood Cliffs, N. J.; Prentice-Hall, 1957. Pp. 440 ff.

Bright, John. *A History of Israel.* Philadelphia: The Westminster Press, 1959. Pp. 393 ff.

Johnson, Sherman E. *Jesus in His Homeland.* New York: Charles Scribner's Sons, 1957. Pp. 82-87.

Mould, E. W. K. *Essentials of Bible History.* New York: The Ronald Press, 1951. Ch. xix (especially pp. 352, 365-66).

12

The Ministry of Healing

JESUS' ANNOUNCEMENT THAT THE KINGDOM OF GOD WAS AT HAND was more than a proclamation in words, for it was accompanied by dramatic expressions in deeds. As he faced those who were discouraged, burdened with a sense of sin, or bound by sickness and suffering, there welled up within him the desire and disposition to cheer, forgive, and heal. Wherever he went, events of such marked character occurred that great crowds gathered about him and much popular interest developed in his ministry. At his command evil spirits came out of those who were demon possessed so that people said, "With authority he commands even the unclean spirits, and they obey him" (Mark 1:27). Mark tells us of one evening in particular when, at sundown,[1] "they brought to him all who were sick or possessed with demons. And the whole city was gathered together about the door. And he healed many who were sick with various diseases, and cast out many demons; and he would not permit the demons to speak, because they knew him" (1:32-34).

This popular following, based upon his deeds of healing, presented Jesus with a serious problem. He was troubled by the prospect of this kind of activity overshadowing his message. Early in the morning, following the healings at Capernaum, he sought the solitude of a lonely place where he might pray to the Father concerning this issue (Mark 1:35-39). When the disciples found him, he had concluded that he must move on to other communities rather than to remain there and continue the healing. This was not a decision to forego such deeds of mercy, but a safeguard against making them the primary emphasis of his ministry.

I

Healers and healing stories abounded in the first century. In this sense the healing work of Jesus was not *in itself* a novelty. Among the Greeks, Romans, and Jews, it was expected that miraculous wonders would occur, from time to time, as the gods came to the

---

[1] The people waited until the Sabbath had ended before carrying their sick to Jesus, so that they would not break the Jewish law which forbade them to bear burdens on the holy day.

assistance of human beings in need. Some writers have concluded that the miracle stories of our Gospels owe their form, if not their substance, to the Jewish and Greco-Roman miracle narratives.[2]

Most of these healing stories were magical in character. For instance, at the festival of the Lupercalia, two priests arrayed in strips of goatskin ran around the base of the Palatine and struck with thongs the women who were standing in their path. These had placed themselves there in expectation of this happening to them as a charm against barrenness. This feast was on February 15.

Josephus the historian was familiar with incantations which were supposed to have been handed down from Solomon and to be effective for casting out demons.[3] He tells how a certain Eleazar had healed one of demoniacal possession by placing to his nostrils a ring that held a root, "of one of those mentioned by Solomon." This was done in the presence of Vespasian. Another story is told of two rabbis who went to Rome to intercede on behalf of their people. On shipboard they met a demon who joined company with them even to the great city itself. Once there, the demon took possession of Caesar's daughter, whereupon one of the rabbis exorcised it by calling, "Ben Temalion (the demon's name), come out!" Gratified and feeling in their debt, Caesar granted the request of the rabbis, and their mission was successful.

The Jews regarded many forms of sickness as due to demoniacal agencies—leprosy, rabies, asthma, croup, heart disease, and madness.[4] In cases where the demon had "possessed" the person actually, exorcism was practiced as a means of expelling it. Once, when accused of casting out demons by the power of Beelzebul, the prince of demons, Jesus replied by inquiring, "And if I cast out demons by Beelzebul, *by whom do your sons cast them out?*" (Matt. 12:27.)[5] This recognizes clearly the fact that the Jewish priests practiced healing in their ministrations.

Magical formulas were used frequently in the curing of disease. Sometimes these were written out on a small piece of parchment

[2] Cf. Dibelius, *From Tradition to Gospel,* tr. B. Lee Woolf, 1934, pp. 70 ff. Also R. Bultmann, *op. cit.,* pp. 36 ff.

[3] Josephus *Antiquities* VIII. 2. 5.

[4] Cf. Talmudic tractates Horayoth 10a; Yoma 77b, 83b; Gittin 67b; Bekhoroth 44b; Taanith 20b; for references to these diseases and their relation to special demons.

[5] Italics mine.

and attached to one's person, or they may have been spoken orally. For instance, someone with bloody flux would drink wine in which Persian onions, anise or saffron had been boiled, at the same time repeating over and over the formula, "Be cured of thy flux!" The treatment for daytime blindness was to take the spleens of seven calves and put them in a basin used by a surgeon for bleeding. Then a person outside the room would request food from the blind man, who would reply, "How can I open the door? Come in and eat." Upon entering the room, he breaks the basin lest the blindness come upon himself, and the healing is supposed to occur. These remedies were not regarded as medicinal. They partook of magic and depended upon unseen powers to make them effective. And on these superstitious bases healing claims were made.

We can see, therefore, that healing deeds were customary with religious functionaries. Jesus would have been out of line clearly, if his religious teaching had not had its healing accompaniments. This was not the reason Jesus undertook his healing ministry, but from the standpoint of the populace he was expected to be a healer. The wonder is not that we have tales of healing associated with Jesus, but that they are relatively so few in number. The Gospels are an example of considerable restraint in this regard.

II

Why did Jesus include healing as a part of his mission as Messiah? The reason remains his own except as he gives us intimations in a word here and there. A firm background existed for this kind of activity in the Old Testament, which Jesus knew with marked intimacy. For instance, a healing is there recorded in the case of Elisha who healed Naaman, the Syrian captain, of leprosy by instructing him to bathe in the Jordan River seven times (II Kings 5). Then there is the account of the special healing of King Hezekiah who prayed for restored health and whose answered prayer was announced by Isaiah the prophet—a cake of figs was laid on the boil (II Kings 20:1-7). Both the raising of the widow's son by Elijah (I Kings 17:17-24) and the resuscitation of the Shunamite's boy by Elisha (II Kings 4:18-37) are recorded in the Scriptures likewise. These stories provided a background for Jesus' healing ministry as a kind of precedent for such activity.

More to the point, however, were the prophetic statements concerning the day of the Lord, or the new age, at which time marvelous acts of God were expected to occur. Passages such as these (Isa. 29:18; 35:6) would not only lead the people into an attitude of mind and spirit where healings would take place, but would inspire Jesus also to consider such work:

> In that day the deaf shall hear
>   the words of a book,
> and out of their gloom and darkness
>   the eyes of the blind shall see.
>
> .   .   .   .
>
> Then shall the lame man leap like a hart,
>   and the tongue of the dumb sing for joy.
> For waters shall break forth in the wilderness,
>   and streams in the desert.

From the words of Jesus it is clear that he regarded his healing activity as a part of the good news of the kingdom of God. In the controversy already referred to,[6] when Jesus was accused of casting out demons through the power of Beelzebul, he concluded the interview by saying, "But if it is by the Spirit of God [7] that I cast out demons, then the kingdom of God has come upon you" (Matt. 12:28). Clearly Jesus regarded healing not as something added to his message in order to attract the people but as an important part of the good news itself which, as the Messiah, he had come to bring. In the wilderness days he had rejected temple jumping as a too spectacular method of winning a following, but healing, as he understood and practiced it, was something different. God was interested in physical well-being, and sickness with its attending suffering was a form of imprisonment. The impulse to heal was one with the desire to make real in the lives of the people the love of his heavenly Father.

We see this again in connection with the account of Jesus' visit to his home community at Nazareth. Luke (4:18-19) adds to the statements of Matthew and Mark, in reporting this occasion, the notation that Jesus read from the book of Isaiah (61:1-2) the following words:

---

[6] Cf. p. 145.

[7] The Lukan version reads "finger of God" (11:20).

The Spirit of the Lord is upon me,
because he has anointed me to preach good news to the poor.
He has sent me to proclaim release to the captives
and recovering of sight to the blind,
to set at liberty those who are oppressed,
to proclaim the acceptable year of the Lord.

After reading this passage Jesus commented that it was being fulfilled in their presence, clearly a reference to his own work among
them (Luke 4:21).[8]

And yet another indication that Jesus regarded healing as a part
of his vocation is found in words spoken by him to disciples of
John the Baptist who came to inquire if he were the one "who is
to come." "Go and tell John what you have seen and heard: the
blind receive their sight, the lame walk, lepers are cleansed, and
the deaf hear, the dead are raised up, the poor have good news
preached to them." (Luke 7:22).[9] It is possible to interpret these
words of Jesus symbolically. The same is true of the words read
at the time of the Nazareth visit just considered. In view of the
strong tradition regarding Jesus' healing activity, however, a complete symbolization of them would be forced historical interpretation.

There is one further indication that Jesus regarded his healing
ministry as an expression of his mission as Messiah. It is found in
the instruction which he gave to his disciples when he dispatched
them on an evangelistic undertaking. Mark tells us that Jesus
sent them forth and gave them authority over the unclean spirits
(6:7). Luke states, in addition, that this was the power to cure
diseases (9:1). Matthew has the further word that they were to heal
all manner of sickness (10:1). Not only did Jesus consider his healing work as an expression of the Kingdom, but he felt also that
his disciples should undertake it as they went abroad to spread
the word.

In considering the purpose of Jesus' ministry of healing, it should

[8] This verse has been questioned by some scholars since Matthew and Mark
do not carry it. It is not out of line with Jesus' total view regarding his mission.
In any event this is the impression Jesus' ministry made upon the church.

[9] Matthew records these words likewise. Their source is to be found probably
in Q.

be understood finally that he did not heal in order to *prove* that he was the Messiah. He did this work *as* the Messiah, but not to convince men that he was the Messiah. On one occasion, when the Jews asked him for a "sign from heaven," he refused to provide it, saying, "No sign shall be given to this generation" (Mark 8:12).[10] What the Jews had in mind was the performing of a wondrous deed which would back up his claims and vindicate his message. Just as in the wilderness, when Jesus would not turn stones into bread to prove the reality of his experience of call to messiahship, so here likewise, he would not restort to external manifestations to validate his position.

III

What type of healing did Jesus undertake? Outstanding were the numerous cases involving demon possession. There was Mary Magdalene "from whom seven demons had gone out" (Luke 8:2). The probabilities are that she had been quite insane rather than very wicked as she is represented to have been in tradition. Then, there was the daughter of the Syrophoenician woman whose mother exhibited marked faith as a Gentile and would not be sidetracked from her request for healing (Mark 7:24-30). In the synagogue, at the outset of his ministry, Jesus cast out a demon from a man whose outcries were loud and persistent. The result of this act upon the people was one of astonishment: "What is this? A new teaching! With authority he commands even the unclean spirits, and they obey him" (Mark 1:24-27).

Exceedingly dramatic was the casting out of the spirits from the Gerasene demoniac (Mark 5:1-20). The man had changed his name to Legion because he was convinced that there were many demons indwelling him. The conversation between the demons and Jesus, in which they implored him to send them into the swine, was quite in line with the thinking of the first century concerning the nature and disposition of demons. They preferred to live in a creature rather than to wander in the wastelands. It is interesting to note

[10] Matthew and Luke add "except the sign of Jonah." Luke suggests the prophetic idea that the sign of Jonah was a voice, calling men to God (11:30), while Matthew (12:40) regards the sign as the deliverance of Jonah from the whale.

that in many of the cases where exorcism of demons was involved, the sick persons struggled, going into extreme muscular contortions for a short time, and then sank to the ground, exhausted or in a kind of faint (Mark 1:26; 9:26). This was a reflection of the belief of the person that a struggle was going on inside of him as the demon was resisting eviction.[11]

When we inquire as to whether Jesus believed in the existence of demons, we receive different answers to our question. Some hold that he shared with others of his day this outlook. Others insist that he did not believe in them, but found it necessary to accommodate himself to the ideas of the time in order to heal those who *thought* they were plagued or possessed by them. From a reading of the Gospels, however, it appears that Jesus was a true son of his own segment of history, as far as belief in the reality of demons was concerned, and that he accepted their existence.

Jesus' healing activity was not limited to the exorcising of demons. The list of cures involves a variety of conditions. There was the woman who was stooped and could not stand upright (Luke 13:11-17), the epileptic boy (Mark 9:14-29), the single leper (Mark 1:40-45) and the ten who were cleansed at the same time (Luke 17:11-19), the paralytic who was let down through the roof (Mark 2:3-12), and the impotent man at the pool (John 5:1-18). Several cases of the curing of blindness are included. Bartimaeus, the blind beggar (Mark 10:46-52), the blind man at Bethsaida whose healing was gradual (Mark 8:22-26), the two who followed after crying, "Have mercy on us, Son of David" (Matt. 9:27-31), and the man born blind (John 9) are among these. It is recorded also that Jesus healed a man with a withered hand (Mark 3:1-5), a man with dropsy (Luke 14:1-6), Simon's mother-in-law, who had a fever (Mark 1:29-31), a man who was deaf and dumb (Mark 7:31-37), a woman with a flow of blood (Mark 5:25-34), and that he restored the ear of the high priest's servant which had been cut off in the garden (Luke 22:50-51). Besides these, there are three accounts of Jesus' raising persons from the dead: Jairus' daughter (Mark 5:21-24, 35-43), the widow of Nain's son (Luke 7:11-17), and Lazarus (John 11). We can see from these instances

---

[11] Such a struggle with its outcries might account for a stampeding of the pigs, causing them to rush down the bank, in the instance of the Gerasene demoniac.

that the cases cover a varied field: curvature of the spine, epilepsy, leprosy, paralysis, blindness, deaf and dumbness, atrophy, dropsy, fever, flux, a severed bodily part, and death.

IV

In describing these acts of healing, the gospel writers give some indications of the procedure Jesus followed. It varied from case to case, although there was a recognizable pattern in certain types of conditions. In the casting out of demons Jesus employed usually the command (Mark 1:25). He literally ordered the illness to depart. Sometimes Jesus employed physical agents. He touched the eyes of the blind (Mark 8:23-25), placed his fingers in the ears of the deaf and upon the tongue of the dumb (Mark 7:33), and laid his hand upon the leper (Mark 1:40-45). The mixing of clay with spittle was used in the healing of the man born blind (John 9:6).

On the other hand, frequently some act was required of the sick person, and the healing occurred in the process of performing the act. The ten lepers were told to show themselves to the priests (Luke 17:14), the paralytic was asked to pick up his pallet (Mark 2:11), and the blind man was instructed to wash in the pool of Siloam (John 9:7).

A study of the procedures which Jesus followed in his healing ministry suggests that the curative power was not in the method itself. Instead, it was in the attitude which the infirm took toward Jesus. The word which describes his attitude best is *faith*. One can see this is the case of the woman who touched Jesus' garment and was healed. On the surface this appears to be a cure by magic. Closer examination of the record, however, will show that it was faith in Jesus, who wore the garment, rather than the garment itself which brought healing. This is implied in the statement of Mark that Jesus perceived that power had gone from him, and, also, in the words Jesus spoke to her, "Daughter, your faith has made you well; go in peace, and be healed of your disease" (Mark 5:34).

The two blind men who followed Jesus, crying aloud, "Have mercy on us, Son of David," were asked by Jesus, "Do you believe that I am able to do this?" They said to him, "Yes, Lord." Then he touched their eyes, saying, "According to your faith be it done to you." And their eyes were opened (Matt. 9:27-31). In this case Jesus' question to the blind men would seem to be a deliberate attempt to awaken healing faith in them.

The place of faith in healing is shown elsewhere in the story of the epileptic boy, who was brought to Jesus by his distraught father. The disciples had attempted to help and had failed. When the father appealed to Jesus saying, "If you can do anything, have pity on us," Jesus turned to him and said, "If you can! All things are possible to him who believes." Immediately the father cried out and said, "I believe; help my unbelief!" Then Jesus healed the boy (Mark 9:14-27).

There is a further aspect to the place of faith in the ministry of healing which the story of the epileptic boy reveals. This is the fact that the one who would heal, the *healer*, is to possess faith, quite as much as the person who is healed. When the disciples asked Jesus privately why it was that they had been unable to heal the boy, Jesus said to them, "Because of your little faith. For truly, I say to you, if you have faith as a grain of mustard seed, you will say to this mountain, 'Move hence to yonder place,' and it will move; and nothing will be impossible to you" (Matt. 17:20-21).

The Gospels are explicit in indicating that the faith-attitude, which made healing possible, was centered in Jesus. That is, it was awakened in the sick, either by the presence of Jesus, or by the impression he made upon them, through the witnessing of others. The New Testament church illustrates the latter, in its healing activities, by its reference to the name of Jesus.[12] For instance, Peter said to the lame man at the gate of the temple, "In the name of Jesus Christ of Nazareth, walk" (Acts 3:6). Jesus was a factor in this healing.

It was stated at the outset that Jesus undertook his mission as the Messiah by announcing the near advent of the Kingdom. As the healing ministry developed, he regarded it as an expression of the presence of that Kingdom in their midst. It was not that it had come fully, but that where these things occurred, it was present actually.

[12] Cf. Matt. 7:22. The reference here to casting out demons *in the name of Jesus* is a reflection of the practice followed in the New Testament church.

V

The healing ministry of Jesus, considered in this chapter, was a *first-century phenomenon,* and the gospel accounts describing it were written by *first-century writers.* This means that the world view of the first century permeates the records.

The basic assumptions of that day concerning nature differed from ours. These should be called pre-scientific. Modern conceptions of natural law and of an established order in the universe did not exist. All causality was regarded as free, direct, and immediate.

This world view placed a high value upon miracles. Rather than presenting a problem in interpretation, they were welcomed as evidence of the presence of God. Religious functionaries were expected to perform signs and wonders. These provided heartening examples of divine power, and indicated God's victory over evil, demoniacal agencies, which were believed to have control over the lives of men. From this standpoint miracles *had* to occur if a religion were to attract a following.

The healing ministry of Jesus must be approached with this background in mind. As we have seen, the Gospels present a considerable number of instances of healing. Some of them had to do with the physical needs of persons, and others were concerned with mental sickness. In the former group were such conditions as leprosy, lameness, blindness, deafness, and death. In the latter were the many cases of demon possession.

There is a possibility that the reports of some of the healings, in the form in which we have them, have been heightened and enlarged.[13] There is the further probability that, since the explanations given the cures are first century in character, we would interpret the same events somewhat differently today with our particular scientific, psychological, and philosophical outlook.

It is not possible always to probe behind any specific healing, as reported, to the original event. Here lies the problem of modern attempts to "naturalize" the miracles. We are learning much today,

[13] It has been said that some of the stories of wonder deeds in the Gospels had their origin in certain sayings of Jesus. A suggested example is the account of Jesus' turning water into wine in John's Gospel (2:1-11). The saying from which the story is thought to have developed is, "No one puts new wine into old wineskins" (Luke 5:37).

however, concerning the interaction of mind and body. Psycho-
therapy and psychosomatics are helpful at the point of speculation
concerning the *how* of many of Jesus' healings. This is true particularly in relation to the casting out of evil spirits or demons.[14]
The emphasis of Jesus upon faith as a condition of healing is suggestive in making this approach to a study of these cases. Healings
which seem to be predominately physical, however, do not yield
as readily to modern analysis.

It should not be assumed in the attempts to understand some of
Jesus' healing deeds that a psychological explanation discounts or
discredits the fact of the healing. Psychology is a description of the
process. It does not deal with ultimate causes, nor is it the sole
basis of final evaluation.

Contemporary interpreters of the healing deeds of Jesus have
drawn usually one or more of the following conclusions. Not all
of them are mutually exclusive. They may (1) rule out the healings as unhistorical, (2) regard them as stories which developed
from certain sayings of Jesus, (3) take them to be supernatural pres-
entations of natural occurrences, (4) accept them as literal fact,
or (5) reserve final judgment concerning them in the expectation
of further knowledge.

In this chapter we have been considering the healing deeds of
Jesus and the problems they present to the modern mind. Similar
issues are raised by the other miracles of Jesus, those that are
related to materials directly, rather than to matter through personality. These include such events as the feeding of the five
thousand (Mark 6:32-44; Matt. 14:13-21; Luke 9:10-17; John 6:
1-13), and the stilling of the waves of the sea (Mark 4:35-41; Matt.
8:23-27; Luke 8:22-25). For the most part the same considerations
that were indicated in relation to the healing deeds apply here
also. The one main difference is that the personality element of
the individual healed is missing. In its place is the material reality.
With the approach of modern physics to matter in terms of energy,
and the evident ability of mind to use energy for its purposes, it
is suggestive to consider the possibility that the mind of Jesus was

---

[14] Cf. the suggestive and helpful study of demon possession and exorcism in
early Christianity, in the light of modern views of mental illness, found in S.
Vernon McCasland, *By the Finger of God.*

capable of control here, as in the personal realm. In any case the emphasis should be placed upon the *message* of the gospel story rather than upon the procedure or fact of the event itself as described.

Whatever decision is reached concerning the miracles in the Gospels, they remain a tribute to the greatness of Jesus. The impact of his life upon his own generation was such that these accounts were written and believed to be true. It was to be expected that one with his qualities of mind and spirit should perform mighty deeds.

QUESTIONS FOR DISCUSSION

1. Since the healing ministry of Jesus was recorded by persons living in the first century, would you agree that a knowledge of the outlook of that day in regard to sickness and disease is necessary if we are to interpret the healings adequately? Explain.

2. Do you think that a modern medical scientist would have diagnosed some of the pathological conditions Jesus met in the same terms as are to be found in the Gospels? If you answer in the negative, does it imply that the people were not healed actually?

3. What evidence do you find in the book of Acts that the early church continued to regard healing as a part of its service? Cf. Acts 3:1-10; 5:12-16.

4. Might we not consider the healing ministry of the church today through its hospitals a continuation of Jesus' program, or does the use of modern medicine change the picture?

5. Need the approach to healing through modern medical science which the church has fostered be any less spiritual than Jesus' methods?

6. What is meant by the statement that Jesus' healing work was moral in character rather than magical (the mechanical working of a formula)? Did it exist for its own sake, in order to astound the people and secure a following, or was it a part of a larger message of the good news of God's love and care for suffering men?

7. How does our present knowledge concerning the interaction of mind and body help us in our approach to an understanding of these matters?

8. Are we in a position today to "explain" scientifically the healing work of Jesus? If your answer is affirmative, does this subtract from its significance? If your answer is negative, does this add to its value?

9. What does a study of modern faith-healing movements such as are

found in Christian Science, the practices at Lourdes, and in the several Holiness groups contribute to our understanding of Jesus ministry of healing?

SUGGESTIONS FOR READING

I. The miracle story as found in the Gospels

Dibelius, Martin. *From Tradition to Gospel.* New York: Charles Scribner's Sons, 1935. Ch. iii.

Richardson, Alan. *The Miracle-Stories of the Gospels.* New York: Harper & Brothers, 1942. Chs. ii, iii, vi, vii.

II. The treatment of disease and sickness in the first century

Edersheim, Alfred. *The Life and Times of Jesus the Messiah.* New York: Longmans, Green & Company. II, 770-76.

Hyde, W. W. *Paganism to Christianity in the Roman Empire.* Philadelphia: University of Pennsylvania Press, 1946. Pp. 15 ff.

Schuerer, E. *The History of the Jewish People in the Time of Jesus Christ.* 5 vols. Selected readings.

III. The healing ministry of Jesus

Beck, Dwight M. *Through the Gospels to Jesus.* New York: Harper & Brothers, 1954. Pp. 208-17.

Bethune-Baker, J. F. "Early Traditions About Jesus," *The Rise of the Christian Church.* Part III, I, 133-54.

Box, H. Stanley. *Miracles and Critics.* New York: Morehouse-Gorham, 1935. Selected readings.

Kee, Howard C. and Young, Franklin W. *Understanding the New Testament.* Englewood Cliffs, N. J.: Prentice-Hall, Inc., 1957. Pp. 98-103.

McCasland, S. V. *By the Finger of God.* New York: The Macmillan Company, 1951. Selected readings.

Taylor, Vincent. *The Life and Ministry of Jesus.* Nashville: Abingdon Press, 1955. Pp. 106-10.

IV. Healing miracles in the New Testament church

Cairns, D. S. *The Faith That Rebels.* New York: Harper & Brothers, 1929. Ch. i-iii.

Craig, C. T. *The Beginning of Christianity.* Nashville: Abingdon Press, 1943. Selected readings.

Streeter, B. H. *The Primitive Church.* New York: The Macmillan Company, 1929. Selected readings.

13

God the
Universal Father

IN CONSIDERING THE TEACHINGS OF JESUS, UNDER SELECTED CAPTIONS, one might gain the impression that he was a theologian with a carefully developed theological and ethical system. This would not be exactly true. Although his teachings can be systematized according to subjects, Jesus himself did not arrange them in this manner. It is unlikely, also, that they came to him as ideas in a formally developing pattern of thought.

Jesus' teachings were the outgrowth of his living. At a particular moment in history he lived a particular kind of life, meeting the situations which faced him with vigor and imagination. He was intensely religious and the quest of his spirit was to learn the will of God. Out of this search came knowledge of a very special kind. It was intuitive, in the sense that all revelations of truth to sincere seekers are "given" to them; it was moral, in that his mind was dedicated to God, and the purpose of his thinking was completely unselfish.

Jesus discovered that God was loving, as he himself went out to love those whom he met, although some were unattractive and insincere. He learned that God answered prayer, because his own prayers were answered. He was sure that the kingdom of God was at hand; he was living in it already. And he was certain that the pure in heart could see God, for in his own sincerity he had experienced the celestial vision.

In all of this Jesus was an intellectual, but not in the sense of being an abstract thinker. Ideas for him were related always to persons. He was not concerned with concepts in a system of thought, but rather with the pattern of God's purpose in history and in the day which was at hand. To this interest he brought intense concentration, and the insights which resulted became the foundation of his teachings.

I

Jesus' teachings concerning God must be considered in the light of the Old Testament, for their roots reach deep into the past history of the Jews. Behind them lie the aspirations and discoveries of many generations. This religious tradition which Jesus inherited made a direct contribution to his own thinking. He cannot be understood apart from it, and neither can the significance of the movement he originated be determined, except in its light. He did not accept all that the elders of his nation had believed in the past, but whether he adopted their tenets or rejected them, the traditions of Israel furnished the anvil upon which he fashioned his own teachings.

The Old Testament proclaimed and did not question the existence of God. On every hand it was assumed that he was a reality and that he could be known. He was regarded as a personality whose character was distinctly his own. The name "Yahweh" distinguished him from all other gods.[1] This belief in his personal existence showed itself in anthropomorphic representations, where he was pictured as having almost human associations with men (Gen. 3:8; 11:5).

God was thought, also, to have a purposeful relation to historical events. He gave the Covenant and the Law to the nation, and by his hand the Jews had been delivered from bondage in Egypt. The Philistines and Syrians, likewise, had been led by him out of Caphtor and Kir (Amos 9:7); and Assyria, too, had been used as a rod with which to forward his purpose among the nations (Isa. 10:5; 14:24-27). The existence of God was clearly evident in the activity of God.

Outstanding in the Jewish conception of God was his creatorship. He had brought forth the universe through his creative word (Gen. 1:1–2:4; Pss. 148:5; 33:9). The psalmist sang that the glory of God was declared by the heavens, and that his handiwork was made evident in the firmament (Ps. 19:1). The moon and stars he had established (Ps. 8:3), and the foundations of the earth he had laid, likewise (Ps. 104:2, 5), The writings of Deutero-Isaiah are particularly eloquent in their stress upon the creatorship of God. Here (Isa. 40:12) he is spoken of as the one:

Who has measured the waters in the hollow of his hand
   and marked off the heavens with a span,
enclosed the dust of the earth in a measure
   and weighed the mountains in scales
and the hills in a balance.

[1] Cf. Exod. 3:15.

Since Jehovah was the creator of the universe, it was believed that he was present in his creation and aware of what was happening. In its fullest expression this teaching was late in developing. Such writings as Ps. 139 present it movingly:

> Even before a word is on my tongue,
>   lo, O Lord, thou knowest it altogether.
>
> .   .   .   .
>
> Whither shall I go from thy Spirit?
>   Or whither shall I flee from thy presencce?
>
> .   .   .   .
>
> If I take the wings of the morning
>   and dwell in the uttermost parts of the sea,
> even there thy hand shall lead me,
>   and thy right hand shall hold me.

The creatorship, omniscience, and omnipresence of God, in the thinking of the Jews, were one with his power or omnipotence. This power was not hypothetical since on every hand there was evidence of its existence. For this reason the prophet of the exile called upon his people to be observant (Isa. 40:28):

> Have you not known? Have you not heard?
> The Lord is the everlasting God,
>   the Creator of the ends of the earth.
> He does not faint or grow weary,
>   his understanding is unsearchable.

Even in a distant land, God's power was evident.

Of great significance also was God's moral character. He was both holy and loving. This was a distinctive feature in the religious tradition which Jesus inherited. The holiness of God made him unapproachable. To look upon him was to die (Exod. 33:20; Judg. 13: 22). His righteousness set him apart from other gods and from humanity as well. Something was needed to bridge this gap, at least to enable man to stand in his presence. In meeting this need the Jews stressed the keeping of the Law, and ceremonial rites by which one could be purified.[2] The prophetic spirits among them, however,

[2] These emphases changed from time to time and from writer to writer.

placed greater emphasis upon the *attitude* of the worshiper. To the
question (Ps. 24:3) :

> Who shall ascend the hill of the Lord?
> And who shall stand in his holy place?

one psalmist replied (24:4) :

> He who has clean hands and a pure heart,
> who does not lift up his soul to what is false,
> and does not swear deceitfully.

In a similar vein the prophet Isaiah called upon the people of his
day to stress the inner life of the mind and spirit as they sought
union with the holy God. He reacted against the ceremonialism by
which some attempted to purify the soul, and represented God as
saying that he hated their new moons and appointed feasts, and
wanted to have nothing more to do with the multitude of their
sacrifices (Isa. 1:13-15). Amos (5:21) heard God say:

> I hate, I despise your feasts,
> and I take no delight in your solemn assemblies.

While Hosea (6:6) announced on his behalf:

> For I desire steadfast love and not sacrifice,
> the knowledge of God, rather than burnt offerings.

During the days of Jesus' ministry, however, these words of the
prophets seem to have been forgotten, for the religious leaders
among the Pharisees and Sadducees were energetic in their stress
upon both the Law and the ceremonies at the Temple.

In the thinking of the Jews, God was not only holy; he was loving
as well. This love was described both as the love of a father for his
children (Ps. 103:13), and as the love of a husband for his wife
(Hosea 1-3). Although earlier it was thought to be showered upon
the chosen people alone, it was regarded later as embracing the entire human race. The experience of the Jews in finding the love of
God in a foreign land, while captives in Babylon, did much to en-

large their conception of his care for all men everywhere. In that
distant place a prophet heard God say (Isa. 45:22-23) :

> Turn to me and be saved,
>   all the ends of the earth!
>   For I am God, and there is no other.
>
> .   .   .   .   .   .
>
> To me every knee shall bow,
>   and every tongue shall swear.

This enlarged view of the love of God did not gather the majority
of the leaders to its support, however, following the exile. And in
Jesus' day a narrow nationalism prevailed, which regarded foreigners
as outcasts and beyond the pale.

II

Jesus took the best that was in the religious tradition which he
inherited and incorporated it into his daily living. In every instance,
however, the ideals of the past were accepted for the present only
because his own experience confirmed them. He was not interested
in orthodoxy for the sake of conformity to tradition. On the other
hand, he was not adverse to enriching his own ministry and message
through the spiritual discoveries of others. It has been said that every
statement of Jesus can be paralleled in the Old Testament or in the
writings of Judaism contemporary to his day. This claim could be
substantiated quite likely. To do so, however, would not detract from
the uniqueness and originality of Jesus. These lie in his own experience of these truths. The imprint of his personality is upon
them.

Jesus' chosen name for God was Father. As a boy of twelve, he
remarked that his parents should not have wondered that he was in
his Father's house (Luke 2:49). He taught his followers to pray
"Our Father" (Matt. 6:9). When he referred to the coming of the
Son of man, he said that he would come in the glory of the Father
(Luke 9:26). And in a moment of exalted joy upon the return of the
seventy from their successful evangelical mission, Jesus prayed, "I
thank thee, Father, Lord of heaven and earth" (Luke 10:21).[3]

[3] Cf. also John 17, where in prayer Jesus is represented as addressing God as
"Father," "Holy Father," and "O righteous Father."

Finally, at the end of his life he prayed, "Father, into thy hands . . ."
(Luke 23:46).

The word "Father" was an expression of God's character. He
held a fatherly relation to all men and forgave his children when
they looked to him in repentance. This is the meaning of the parable
of the prodigal son (Luke 15:11-32). The lad returned from the life
of a wastrel, and his father received him with open arms, forgiving
him for the wrong he had done. A ring was placed upon his finger,
restoring him to his place in the family, and a great feast was prepared to signalize the joy and happiness of the parent at the return
of his son. This is the truly great picture of God.

Jesus taught that the heavenly Father loved his children and
showed a personal concern for their minutest interests. He said
figuratively, "Why, even the hairs of your head are all numbered"
(Luke 12:7), and told them that every sparrow's fall was marked by
God—sparrows which could be purchased for as little as five for two
pennies—and he counseled, "Fear not; you are of more value than
many sparrows." How inexpressibly real! It is as Bornkamm says,
"The nearness of God is the secret of Jesus' language about God as
Father." [4]

This love of God for his children is extended to all, even to those
who do not recognize it. "He makes his sun rise on the evil and on
the good, and sends rain on the just and on the unjust." (Matt.
5:45.) The same generous attitude is illustrated in Jesus' parable
of the laborers in the vineyard (Matt. 20:1-16). Those who had
begun their work after the first laborers had gone into the vineyard were paid the same wages at the end of the day which the
others received. When those who had labored all day in the scorch-
ing heat objected, the householder inquired, "Do you begrudge my
generosity?" God is a generous householder also.

Jesus was convinced that the heavenly Father, who was motivated
always by love, looked to his children for love in return. Therefore,
in *the great commandment* he said, "You shall love the Lord your
God with all your heart, and with all your soul, and with all your
mind" (Matt. 22:37). These words were taken from Deut. 6:4-5 and
represent a unique quotation from the Scriptures in support of a

[4] Günther Bornkamm, *Jesus of Nazareth,* p. 128.

position Jesus held. To this quotation he added another, this time from Leviticus: "You shall love your neighbor as yourself" (Matt. 22:39; Lev. 19:18). By selecting freely two separate passages from the tradition of the nation, and relating them to each other, Jesus was expressing the spirit of liberal Judaism in his own day.[5]

III

The fact that God loved his children did not mean, however, that his good will was to be taken lightly. Jesus taught that God was to be reverenced and his authority respected at all times. Great love could not be sinned against without serious consequences. In a moving passage he pictured a man on his way to the judgment seat, where he had not the slightest chance of being exonerated, because he was guilty. In this situation he was told to make it up with his accuser out of court, "lest he drag you to the judge, and the judge hand you over to the officer, and the officer put you in prison." To such a person Jesus said, "I tell you, you will never get out till you have paid the very last copper" (Luke 12:58-59). The judge was none other than God himself, the same loving Father whom Jesus had presented to men. To hold men responsible for doing what was right was an act of love. God's love and his demand for righteousness were not contradictory. He who loves and he who judges are the same person.

The loving God was a working God, also, as Jesus knew him. In a Johannine story which has many synoptic characteristics, Jesus healed a lame man at the pool. It was a Sabbath healing and led to a controversy with the Jews. In defending his act, when it was challenged, Jesus said, "My Father is working still, and I am working" (5:17). We have here the picture of a God who is at work constantly in his world. By this statement Jesus was saying that even as his Father was working, he was working also.

It is the working God who sustains the world. The earth is his footstool, even as heaven is his throne (Matt. 5:34-35). He feeds the birds, causes the sun to shine and the rain to fall, clothes the grass of the field, and garbs the lilies with loveliness and beauty (Matt. 6:25-33). It is because God is at work in his world that the many

---

[5] Cf. C. G. Montefiore, *The Synoptic Gospels*, I, 286-88.

parables of Jesus have their point. The growing mustard seed (Matt.
13:21-32), the varied crops of the sower (Matt. 13:1-9), and the
weeds which clutter the ground (Matt. 13:24-30) are each the result
of God's activity in the realm of nature.

God is at work also in the affairs of men, expressing his divine will
within history. This results in the kingdom of God, concerning
which Jesus taught his disciples to pray (Matt. 6:10):

> Thy kingdom come,
> Thy will be done,
>   On earth as it is in heaven.

Whatever the petition for the coming of the Kingdom means in detail—to which consideration we shall turn in the next chapter—in
the broadest terms, it refers to the will and purpose of God, realized
as fully and completely on earth as it is in heaven.

Because there is a will of God for men to follow, Jesus urged that
it was wise to do so with complete dedication. Both Matthew's (5–7)
and Luke's (6:17-49) versions of the Sermon on the Mount close
with a parable, sometimes called the parable of the two foundations.
Here is presented a contrast between the man who hears and does
the will of God, and the man who hears and fails to act. The one
builds his house on the rock, while the other erects his dwelling upon
the sand. Then comes the storm! In language of sharp realism
Jesus pictured the testing hour: "And the rain fell, and the floods
came, and the winds blew and beat upon that house" (Matt. 7:25).
The house built on the rock foundation held firm, but the other,
constructed on the sand, shifted and fell. The meaning of the
parable is clear; hearing and doing of the will of God determines
destiny.

IV

In Jesus' teaching concerning heavenly beings, there is an interesting departure from certain Old Testament writings and from the
Judaism of his day. It is found in the noticeable brevity of his reference to angels. Following their enslavement in Babylon, the Jewish
conception of God became increasingly transcendental. A God who
was "high and lifted up" needed intermediaries if he were to keep

in touch with his created world. These were to be found in the angels who were regarded as the "messengers," "ministers," and "watchers" of God, and who did his bidding.

The Jews had been influenced in their belief in angels by their contact with Persian religion. Sometimes these heavenly beings were said to mediate the word of God to the prophets (Ezek. 40:3; 43:6; Zech. 1:1; Dan. 4:13, 23). Again, they were represented as exercising the divine wrath upon evildoers (Gen. 19:13; II Kings 19:35). At other times they were pictured as administering God's providential care to his own (Ps. 91:11-16).

Of the thousands of angels who are mentioned in apocalyptic writings (Rev. 5:11), only the names of a few are given. These include Gabriel (Dan. 8:16), Michael (Dan. 10:13, 21), Raphael,[6] and Uriel.[7] In time certain classifications into specific groupings developed, leading to the conception of a hierarchy, with angels of greater and lesser rank included. Although there was much splendor and pageantry in this outlook, it was confusing to the humble worshiper, who knew not where to turn in the midst of these myriads of heavenly beings.

Jesus' teachings did not omit completely the mention of angels. He referred to the coming of the Son of man "in the glory of his Father with the holy angels" (Mark 8:38), and during the dark hours in Gethsemane he asked, "Do you think that I cannot appeal to my Father, and he will at once send me more than twelve legions of angels" (Matt. 26:53)? The explanation of the parable of the weeds in the field suggested that the reapers at the final harvest (judgment) would be angels (Matt. 13:39, 41), while the repentance of one sinner was said by Jesus to cause rejoicing before the angels of God (Luke 15:10). These references to angelic beings are not prominent, however, in the teachings of Jesus. They are a part of the traditional background of first-century thought.

The reason for the small place given to angels in the teachings of Jesus is that he thought of God as being very closely related to his world. The activities which the Old Testament ascribed to the sphere of angels, Jesus pictured God as accomplishing directly through personal action. There was no need to introduce inter-

---

[6] Tob. 12:15.
[7] En. 9:1.

mediary agents. Another reason for this limited reference to angels
may have been the fact that they do not seem to have played a significant part in Jesus' personal religious experience. His own sense
of God was immediate, not mediated through heavenly beings.

QUESTIONS FOR DISCUSSION

1. To what extent was Jesus' teaching concerning God dependent upon
Old Testament thought? To what extent was it independent of the Jewish
Scriptures? Does your study of Jesus' use of Scripture help to answer
this question?

2. Had Jesus been reared in a different religious tradition than that
which he met in the Nazareth synagogue, would it have made a difference
in his teaching concerning God? Was he independent completely of the
environment in which he lived?

3. Compare Jesus' conception of God with that of the Old Testament
in regard to the following:

    a) The creation of the world

    b) His character as Father

    c) The love of God

    d) The power of God

    e) The nearness of God

    f) God's relation to history

    g) The forgiveness of sins

    h) The proper form of worship

4. What are the implications of Jesus' teaching concerning God for the
modern day as it relates to:

    a) Standards of ethical conduct

    b) Minority groups, and all others who are considered as outsiders

    c) Strong nationalisms throughout the world

    d) Life-work considered as a profession or a vocation

    e) Respect or disrespect for authority

    f) The goal of society

5. Be prepared to discuss this statement: "Everything in religion grows
out of the character of the God who is worshiped." Would Jesus subscribe
to this idea?

SUGGESTIONS FOR READING

I. The Old Testament thought of God

    His love:

    Richardson, Alan. *An Introduction to the Theology of the New Tes-*

tament, New York: Harper & Brothers, 1958. Pp. 268 ff.

His holiness and righteousness:

Leslie, Elmer. *Old Testament Religion.* New York: The Abingdon
Press, 1936. 188 ff., 170-73, 233-35.

His power:

Knudson, A. C. *The Religious Teaching of the Old Testament.* New
York: The Abingdon Press, 1918. Pp. 115 ff.

His relation to history:

Williams, Walter G. *The Prophets—Pioneers to Christianity.* Nashville: Abingdon Press, 1956. Selected readings.

His creatorship:

Anderson, Bernhard W. *Understanding the Old Testament.* Englewood Cliffs, N. J.: Prentice Hall, Inc., 1957. Pp. 407-11.

His universality:

Oesterley, William, and Robinson, T. H. *Hebrew Religion.* New York:
The Macmillan Company, 1930. Pp. 129 ff.

II. The Hebrew belief concerning angels and spiritual beings

Knudson, A. C. *The Religious Teaching of the Old Testament.* New
York: The Abingdon Press, 1918. Pp. 192 ff.

III. Jesus' teaching concerning God

Bornkamm, Günther. *Jesus of Nazareth.* Translated by Irene and
Fraser McLuskey and James M. Robinson. 3rd ed. New York:
Harper & Brothers, 1960. Pp. 96-143.

Branscomb, Harvie. *The Teachings of Jesus.* New York: The Abingdon Press, 1931. Ch. x.

Manson, T. W. *The Teaching of Jesus.* London: Cambridge University Press, 1935. Chs. iv-viii.

IV. The New Testament view of the love of God

Moffatt, James, *Love in the New Testament.* New York: Harper &
Brothers, 1930. Pp. 83 ff. Also selected readings.

Nygren, Anders T. S. *Agape and Eros.* Translated by A. G. Hebert.
New York: The Macmillan Company, 1932. Selected readings.

14

Preaching the Kingdom of God

JESUS' TEACHING CONCERNING THE KINGDOM WAS AN OUTGROWTH of his conception of God. The character of the Father, as he knew him in his own religious experience, determined for him the character of the Kingdom. To the extent that this experience was traditional, his conception of the Kingdom was traditional; but to the extent that Jesus' experience of God was unique, his thought of the Kingdom was original. The character of God, the religious experience of Jesus, and the nature of the Kingdom belong together in the teachings of Jesus.

Jesus began his public ministry with this announcement: "The time is fulfilled, and the kingdom of God is at hand; repent, and believe in the gospel" (Mark 1:15). From that day until the end of his life, he proclaimed the Kingdom by parable, precept, and deed. In Matthew's Gospel the title "kingdom of heaven" is used rather than the customary "kingdom of God," as in Mark and Luke. Only rarely does Matthew give the usual form (19:24; 21:31, 43). He prefers the other because it is more Hebraic in character and is in line with the Jewish reticence to pronounce the name of God.

References to the Kingdom did not come to those who heard them as something new. It has been noted already that for centuries past the Jews had been anticipating the coming of God's reign. As the state of their nation rose and fell, hopes for a new day or new age for Israel were expressed openly. National independence, economic abundance, peace, judgment for the enemies of the nation as well as for evil persons within the nation, and the reign of the Messiah characterized usually the popular ideal of the Kingdom.

Prior to the ministry of Jesus, there had been several major variations in this outlook, particularly in regard to the nature of the Messiah.[1] At times he was thought of as a reigning monarch, ideal in character and sweeping in power (Isa. 9:6-7; 11:1-10). On yet other occasions it was believed that the spiritual core of the nation, referred to as the servant, would fulfill the messianic function, the nation

---

[1] Cf. the fuller analyses of these conceptions presented previously, pp. 107-11.

purified through suffering and bearing the burdens of the sinful
(Isa. 52:13–53:12) .[2] Still later, the Messiah was conceived in terms of
the apocalyptic Son of man, coming down out of heaven and saving
the nation (Dan. 7:13-14) . This was not an individual person, but a
symbolic figure of the messianic reign of the saints of Israel. In First
Enoch, the Messiah was considered to be an actual heavenly being.[3]

From this brief survey it can be seen that the people who heard
Jesus announce the coming of the Kingdom were familiar generally
with this hope. They read into his words the faith of their fathers
and the thoughts of the times. His own particular conception of the
Kingdom, they were to learn as his ministry continued. Some of
them were to be impressed deeply, while others were to be disap-
pointed in the interpretation of the Kingdom he would present.

I

Jesus regarded the Kingdom as the supreme value of life, and the
search for it as one's major endeavor. He said, "Seek first his kingdom and his righteousness, and all these things [objects of earthly
concern] shall be yours as well." (Matt. 6:33.) As the highest value
of life, the Kingdom is worth all things else that men had held
heretofore to be valuable. To enter it and possess its riches, one
should be willing to follow the example of the pearl merchant in
Jesus' parable, "who, on finding one pearl of great value, went and
sold all that he had and bought it" (Matt. 13:45-46) . Or again, one
should be as alert to the treasures of the Kingdom as another man
whom Jesus represented as finding a treasure hidden in a field while
plowing. It had been put there for safekeeping, no doubt, and then
forgotten. When this astute man found the treasure, he covered
it up quickly and sold all that he had in order to buy that field
(Matt. 13:44). Both of these possessions represented material
wealth, yet the men sacrificed everything to secure them. How much
more should men pursue the Kingdom to possess it at any cost!

The kingdom of God was the reign of God on earth, as Jesus saw
it. He accepted the traditional hopes of his people that one day God
would set up his rule in a new age. Of particular significance in this
connection was Jesus' conviction that the Kingdom was immediately

[2] Cf. Isa. 42:1-7; 49:1-6; 61:1-3, for other servant passages.
[3] I En. 46:3-4; 48:3; 62:5, 14.

at hand. What had been an anticipation was to be a fact. To announce this was to proclaim the "good news." As a divine order
which men might enter, the Kingdom was open to all who would
respond to Jesus' call to repent and believe the gospel. Those who
lived within the new society would exhibit the characteristics of the
Kingdom in their lives.

In the prayer which is known as the *Lord's Prayer,* Jesus taught his
followers to pray (Matt. 6:10) :

> Thy kingdom come,
> Thy will be done,
>   On earth as it is in heaven.

This petition suggests that in the Kingdom God's will is done in
every personal relationship between man and man, as well as between
man and his heavenly Father. One discovers here an important principle for interpreting Jesus' conception of the Kingdom.

What is this will of God which expresses itself in personal relationships as the kingdom of God? To answer this question fully would
call for a review of Jesus' teachings on every point, such as his words
concerning earthly possessions, race, outcasts, discipleship, forgiveness, love, religious ceremonialism, and true worship. It would take
one to the Gospels and to the Sermon on the Mount in particular for
definition and illustration (Matt. 5–7). Viewed in this light, the
Kingdom in the teaching of Jesus is an ethical, or more strictly, a
religious society. As distinguished from the widely accepted traditional Jewish conception, it is nonpolitical in character. In the certain destruction of evil and the enthronement of good which the
coming of the Kingdom would bring, the victory will be ethical and
religious rather than political and military.

II

It has been indicated that in the tradition of Israel there were
several different answers to the question as to how the Kingdom
would come, answers which varied from time to time in the face of
changing circumstances. What were Jesus' convictions in this regard? [4] There is considerable difference of opinion among the scholars in this field as to what Jesus believed concerning the "how" of

---

[4] Cf. the discussion in chap. 9.

the coming of the Kingdom, although their conclusions are based upon the same gospel tradition. One reason for this grows out of the fact that there are several paradoxes at the heart of Jesus' teaching in this regard. Stated briefly, the paradoxes are these: Jesus taught that the kingdom of God was both God's and ours, both present and future, both an achievement and a gift, both in the heart and in society, and both gradual and sudden in its coming. Interpreters tend sometimes to focus on one or the other side of these paradoxes, to the exclusion of the remaining one.

Two views in particular of Jesus' teaching concerning the mode or manner of the coming of the Kingdom have emerged in the works of biblical scholars. There are variations in the presentation, but the several conclusions mostly accept or lean toward the apocalyptic interpretation on the one hand, or the nonapocalyptic, which may be called the social-evolutionary interpretation, on the other. Reference has been made already to the development of apocalyptic thinking in Israel, especially during the intertestamental period.[5] Psychologically, this view grows out of a deep-seated pessimism concerning the possibilities of bettering conditions on earth according to the usual human methods. Instead, the apocalyptists believe that God will intervene in the ordinary routine of living, overthrow the existing society through supernatural agents, judge evil men and nations, and then set up a new order of life that will be ideal and beneficent. These programs are described in some detail in words of highly dramatic character and imagery of striking form.[6]

This kind of thinking was in vogue at the very time Jesus was engaged in preaching, and some of the teaching which is attributed to him is in both the form and idea of apocalyptic expression. In particular we have the threefold apocalyptic tradition which contains a discourse concerning the end of the age (Matt. 24; Mark 13; Luke 21:5-36).[7] Here we find a picture of famine, earthquake, wars,

---

[5] Cf. pp. 32-33.

[6] Read Zech. 6; Joel 2; Rev. 19:11-21, for examples of apocalyptic phrasing and imagery.

[7] These words, in their present form, have been attributed by some to the Christian church rather than to Jesus. They suggest an adaptation, possibly, of a Jewish apocalypse to Christian usage, in which genuine words of Jesus may be found, although it would be difficult to isolate them from the whole. Cf. Branscomb, *The Gospel of Mark*, pp. 231 ff.

tribulations, cosmic upheavals, and the coming of the Son of man on the clouds of heaven with power and great glory.

Besides this discourse, certain of the parables of Jesus suggest an apocalyptic procedure. The explanation of the parable of the weeds of the field represents the angels as reapers at the close of the age: "The Son of man will send his angels, and they will gather out of his kingdom all causes of sin and all evildoers, and throw them into the furnace of fire; there men will weep and gnash their teeth" (Matt. 13:36-43).[8] Another of the kingdom parables which is apocalyptic is that of the dragnet, in which a net was thrown into the sea to gather fish of every kind. These, in turn, were sorted according to quality. The parable closes with the words, "So it will be at the close of the age. The angels will come out and separate the evil from the righteous, and throw them into the furnace of fire; there men will weep and gnash their teeth" (Matt. 13:47-50).

In the light of tradition such as this, and the widespread apocalyptic outlook of the day in which Jesus lived, it might be concluded that Jesus was an apocalyptist in his thought of the Kingdom. This was the conclusion reached by Johannes Weiss in *Jesus' Preaching of the Kingdom of God,* and by Albert Schweitzer in his *Quest of the Historical Jesus.* Others have held and now hold this view likewise.[9] When one inquires as to the ethical teachings of Jesus found in the Sermon on the Mount which do not appear to be apocalyptic in character, interpreters of this school suggest usually that these should be regarded as *interim ethics,* which were to be in force during the interim between the preaching of Jesus and the end of the age, at which time the Kingdom would come apocalyptically.

III

There are considerations, however, which have led others to conclude that Jesus was not a thoroughgoing apocalyptist. The passages cited above may be emphasized to the neglect of other aspects of his teaching which are not apocalyptic necessarily, and which do not themselves suggest that they are pertinent only during an interim period before the apocalyptic end of the age. The Beatitudes, in

---

[8] Jesus did not explain his parables usually, and this explanation may have originated in the Christian church rather than with him.

[9] Cf. M. S. Enslin, *The Prophet from Nazareth.*

which Jesus pronounced a blessing upon the spiritually wistful, the mourners, the meek, the persecuted, and the pure in heart would seem to apply to all men at all times and under all conditions (Matt. 5:1-12; Luke 6:20-26). Jesus' teaching concerning prayer, faith, and love are timeless and universal likewise, and do not call for an apocalyptic framework to make them valid.

A further consideration which may be urged against the idea that Jesus was a thoroughgoing apocalyptist is his decision in the wilderness of temptation not to leap from the Temple. This was a symbolic suggestion that he introduced the Kingdom through miracles and other spectacular methods (Matt. 4:5-7; Luke 4:9-12). There is a strong affinity between the methodology of temple jumping and the psychology of an apocalyptist. In refusing to leap from the Temple, Jesus revealed a psychology that was non-apocalyptic.

In addition to this, it may be pointed out that some of Jesus' statements concerning the Kingdom do not suggest apocalyptic procedures. The parable of the leaven, in which the coming of the Kingdom is compared with the rising of the yeast-impregnated dough, implies a process of growth and development (Luke 13:20-21).[10] The dough in the passage does not rise suddenly by an act of divine intervention. Similar teaching is to be found in the parable of the seed which grows of itself: "First the blade, then the ear, then the full grain in the ear." Here again we find the idea of development rather than that of the sudden destruction of the present age and the establishment of a new one from above (Mark 4:26-29).[11]

Of all the arguments which may be presented to support the conclusion that Jesus was not a thoroughgoing apocalyptist, the strongest, perhaps, is his teaching that the Kingdom in a real sense was present already, *although in its totality it was yet to be realized.* When he was challenged by the Pharisees concerning the source of

---

[10] Bornkamm regards this as a "contrast parable" in which the emphasis should be placed upon the fact that such a small thing contains such great possibilities. He rules out natural development as a modern and unbiblical idea: "The end comes from the beginning, the fruit from the seed, the harvest from the sowing, the whole leavened loaf from the leaven." *Jesus of Nazareth,* p. 72.

[11] The parable does suggest a harvest when the grain is ripe, but this need not mean necessarily that the Kingdom is to come apocalyptically. The idea that at the end of history there will be a final judgment (eschatology) does not carry inevitably the teaching that the Kingdom comes *only* through divine intervention. See M. Goguel, *op. cit.,* pp. 569 ff. for a further treatment of the distinction between apocalyptic and eschatology.

his power to cast out demons, he replied, "If it is by the Spirit of God that I cast out demons, then the kingdom of God has come upon you" (Matt. 12:28). The Kingdom was present actually in the things that were happening wherever Jesus went. And following the visit of emissaries from John the Baptist who were told to report to the imprisoned prophet what had been taking place, Jesus exclaimed exultantly: "From the days of John the Baptist until now the kingdom of heaven has suffered violence, and men of violence take it by force" (Matt. 11:12). Men were laying hold of the Kingdom actually during the period of his ministry.

As the Messiah, Jesus was convinced that his healing, teaching, and preaching were resulting in changes in the lives of persons which represented the presence of the Kingdom, no less. He warned against looking for dramatic portents of its coming and urged that when men announced, "Lo, here it is!" or "There!" they should not be followed, for he said, "The kingdom of God is not coming with signs to be observed . . . for behold, the kingdom of God is in the midst of you" (Luke 17:20-21).[12] These words were spoken in reply to the Pharisees who asked him when the kingdom of God was coming. Coming?—it was there if one had eyes to see it!

In considering the idea that Jesus believed the kingdom of God to be partially present in their midst, the suggestion of Charles H. Dodd should be noted. He holds that Jesus regarded the Kingdom as having been realized already. Salvation and judgment were a present reality, and the apocalyptic expression of this fact would occur immediately in world judgment and renewal. Dodd states in his volume *The Parables of the Kingdom:*

It appears that while Jesus employed the traditional symbolism of apocalypse to indicate the "other-worldly" or absolute character of the kingdom of God, he used parables to enforce and illustrate the idea that the kingdom of God had come upon men there and then . . . This world has become the scene of a divine drama, in which the eternal issues are laid bare. It is the hour of decision. It is realized eschatology.[13]

This suggestion that the Kingdom had been realized already would

[12] An alternate reading is "within you." This places the Kingdom within the human personality.
[13] P. 197.

seem to be extreme.[14] The Gospels indicate that it was present here and there as Jesus ministered, and as men responded to him, but in its fullness it was not yet realized. The parables of the Kingdom contain truths for the future quite as much as for the present. In the preaching of Jesus there was a constant expectation of better things to come. Evil had not yet been routed and God was not enthroned finally in the lives of all men. But a beginning had been made actually! [15] This was the exultant fact and it promised a glorious future. On the last night of his earthly life, Jesus turned to his disciples in the Upper Room and said to them: "I tell you that from now on I shall not drink of the fruit of the vine until the kingdom of God comes" (Luke 22:18). He had just passed the cup of the Lord's Supper and was promising them that once more he would drink of it in the Kingdom. They were about to kill the King, but the Kingdom would come! Clearly this looks to the future when in its fullness the Kingdom would be realized. In the New Testament this expectation is not for the *distant* future. As F. C. Grant has reminded us, "Prophecy always foreshortens the future." [16]

IV

Returning to the original question, how did Jesus expect the Kingdom to come. There is reason to believe that Jesus thought and spoke sometimes of the advent of the Kingdom in apocalyptic terms. On the other hand, indications may be found in the Gospels also that Jesus was not a thoroughgoing apocalyptist, that he regarded the Kingdom as actually, though partially, present, and that growth and development had a place in its full realization. How may these differences be resolved?

A reasonable conclusion would be that, while Jesus was not a thoroughgoing apocalyptist, he did turn to the idea and language of apocalyticism on occasion, especially in the crisis hours of his ministry.[17] His faith in the advent of the Kingdom flamed into bril-

[14] Cf. F. C. Grant, *The Gospel of the Kingdom*, pp. 145 ff.

[15] Bornkamm stresses Jesus' emphasis upon the present as God's present and as the hour of salvation. Because of this the future of God is also salvation, as well as judgment. *Jesus of Nazareth*, p. 93.

[16] *The Earliest Gospel*, p. 11.

[17] Note that the setting for the threefold apocalyptic tradition in the Gospels is during the tense hours of the final week in Jerusalem.

liance at such times, and the apocalyptic assurance and terminology came quite naturally to his lips.

Jesus does not seem to have been concerned with an apocalyptic blueprint of the future in these moments, but was filled with a tremendous conviction that the future was of God's making *finally*.[18] When it became evident that the religious leaders of his nation would turn a deaf ear to the gospel and would reject the Messiah himself, there seemed to be no future except as God would provide it. Under the pressure of this realization Jesus found in the apocalyptic expectation and phraseology of his people an assurance that victory was certain, in spite of rejection by his nation. This, it may be concluded, is the significance of the apocalyptic element in his teaching.

The faith of Jesus in the coming of the Kingdom has been the inspiration of the church through the centuries, as it has directed its efforts toward the making of a better world. During periods favorable to growth her attempts to create a new society through worship, preaching, and Christian social action have been continuous. On the other hand, when great crises have bowed men low and deprived them of the opportunities to change conditions through consecrated human endeavor, the church has turned sometimes to the outlook of apocalyptic thinking, and reasserted her faith that God would act, where men could not. At such times it has urged its members to wait upon God, in the certain confidence that he would overthrow evil and bring in a new day.

In each of these expressions of faith—faith expressed through active Christian service and faith expressed through expectant and humble waiting upon God to act—there is a precedent, both in the religious experience and in the teachings of Jesus. His paradoxes of the Kingdom in this regard have persisted in the life of the church until the present hour.

QUESTIONS FOR DISCUSSION

1. In what sense may it be said that the kingdom of God is a reflection of the character of God? If he were vindictive, would the character of the Kingdom be different than if he were loving?

[18] He disclaimed any knowledge for the coming of the end of the age. Matt. 24:36.

2. Did the fact that there was a background of belief in the coming of the messianic kingdom among the Jews hinder or help Jesus in his ministry as the Messiah and in his preaching of the Kingdom? Is it easier to change man's thinking in some regards or to begin afresh?

3. If we define the Kingdom as an order of life in which the will of God is expressed perfectly in the relations between men and men, and between men and God, what changes would the Kingdom make in modern society:

a) In our attitudes toward race, minority groups, and virulent nationalisms?

b) In family life?

c) In the church?

d) In economics?

e) In international relations?

4. Which is more deadly, the cutting of the nerve of human endeavor which results if we assume that God alone sends down the Kingdom from above (the essential idea of apocalypticism), or the disillusionment which sets in when we realize our human weakness as we attempt to bring the Kingdom to pass by our own efforts?

5. How does Jesus' view concerning the coming of the Kingdom avoid one or both of the impasses represented in the previous question?

6. What encouragements are to be found in Jesus' teaching concerning the coming of the Kingdom for all those in our day who are interested in a more Christian society?

7. Be prepared to argue the case for and against the view that Jesus was a thoroughgoing apocalyptist in his teaching concerning the Kingdom.

SUGGESTIONS FOR READING

I. The Old Testament teaching concerning the Kingdom

Bright, John. *The Kingdom of God.* Nashville: Abingdon Press, 1953. Selected readings. Pp. 17-186.

Knudson, A. C. *The Religious Teaching of the Old Testament.* New York: The Abingdon Press, 1918. Pp. 351-81.

Oesterley and Robinson. *Hebrew Religion.* New York: The Macmillan Company, 1930. Pp. 342-57.

II. The Kingdom found in Jewish apocalyptic writings

Box, George H. "The Historical and Religious Backgrounds of the Early Christian Movement," *The Abingdon Bible Commentary.* Nashville: Abingdon Press, 1929. Pp. 843-47.

Bright, John. *The Kingdom of God.* Nashville: Abingdon Press, 1953. Pp. 156-86.

Charles, R. H. *The Apocrypha and Pseudepigrapha of the Old Testa-*

ment. London: Oxford University Press, 1913. Selected readings.

Rowley, H. H. *The Relevance of Apocalyptic.* London: Lutterworth Press, 1944. Selected readings.

Simkhovitch, V. G. *Toward the Understanding of Jesus.* New York: The Macmillan Company, 1947. Selected readings.

III. Jesus' conception of the Kingdom

Bornkamm, Günther. *Jesus of Nazareth.* Translated by Irene and Fraser McLuskey and James M. Robinson. 3rd ed. New York: Harper & Brothers, 1960. Pp. 64-95.

Branscomb, Harvie. *The Teachings of Jesus.* New York: The Abingdon Press, 1931. Ch. ix.

Bright, John. *The Kingdom of God.* Nashville: Abingdon Press, 1953. Pp. 187-214.

Bultmann, R. "The Kingdom of God," *Contemporary Thinking About Jesus,* ed. Thomas Kepler. Nashville: Abingdon Press, 1943. Pp. 301-7.

Knox, John. *The Ethic of Jesus in the Teaching of the Church.* Nashville: Abingdon Press, 1961. Selected readings.

Manson, T. W. *The Teachings of Jesus.* London: Cambridge University Press, 1935. Chs. v-viii.

Schweitzer, Albert. *Quest of the Historical Jesus.* New York: The Macmillan Company, 1948. Selected readings.

Taylor, Vincent. *The Life and Ministry of Jesus.* Nashville: Abingdon Press, 1955. Pp. 72-83.

Warschauer, J. *The Historical Life of Christ.* New York: The Macmillan Company, 1926. Pp. 77-90.

Wilder, A. N. *Eschatology and Ethics in the Teaching of Jesus.* New York: Harper & Brothers, 1939. Selected readings.

IV. The Kingdom in the New Testament

Barth, Markus. *The Broken Wall.* Philadelphia: Judson Press, 1959. Selected readings. Based upon a study of Ephesians.

Bright, John. *The Kingdom of God.* Nashville: Abingdon Press, 1953. Pp. 215-74.

Filson, Floyd V. *Jesus Christ the Risen Lord.* Nashville: Abingdon Press, 1956. Pp. 42 ff., 93 ff.

Laymon, Charles M. *Christ in the New Testament.* Nashville: Abingdon Press, 1958. Pp. 28 ff.

Richardson, Alan. *An Introduction to the Theology of the New Testament.* New York: Harper & Brothers, 1958. Pp. 84-102.

15

The Place
of Earthly Goods

JESUS HAD MORE TO SAY CONCERNING EARTHLY GOODS THAN ABOUT many other subjects. Both in direct reference and by implication, he dealt with this theme frequently. The economic life of the day provided the background for his teaching in this regard.[1]

As a preacher of the Kingdom, Jesus was not an economic theorist. He was not concerned with changing the structure of society through espousing a revolutionary system of economics. This is one of the reasons that economists through the centuries have been unable to refer to Jesus as a proponent of their favorite systems. His chief concern in this area was for the people who lived under economic tensions. It was what poverty and riches did to persons that interested him most. His emphasis here was the same as that which he made in regard to the religious system of his day. The liberation of personality from the enslavement of all external institutions was his constant crusade, and economics provided one area where such liberation was needed. The issue was religious primarily when reduced to these terms.

I

Jesus recognized the legitimate place of material goods in the lives of persons. He told men not to worry about food and clothes for the heavenly Father knew that they needed them (Matt. 6:25-34). If men would seek the Kingdom first of all, he said, these other material necessities would be theirs as well. The truth of this teaching has been illustrated in the numerous situations where religious concern has enriched personality, and personality in turn has increased the capacity to earn, thus adding to material wealth. Jesus urged men to employ their abilities wisely and encouraged those who had invested their talents.[2] Such endeavors lead to an accruing of earthly goods. This religious obligation to industry and application on the

[1] Cf. the previous treatment of this subject, pp. 23-26.
[2] Cf. the parable of the pounds (Luke 19:11-27) and the parable of the talents (Matt. 25:14-30).

part of the individual has been one of the taproots of capitalism.

The fact that Jesus was not an ascetic, and that he did not join the ranks of the Essenes, is a further indication that he recognized the legitimate place of possessions. He did not take the vows of poverty and thus turn deliberately from economic pursuits. When he said that the Son of man had no place to lay his head (Luke 9:58), he was not arguing against the ownership of property; rather he was stating the practical fact that in order to preach the gospel of the Kingdom he had become an itinerant with no permanent address. His advice to the disciples, likewise, as he sent them on an evangelistic tour, telling them to take with them neither "staff, nor bag, nor bread, nor money" (Luke 9:3), was not intended to forbid ownership of these possessions on the part of his followers as a whole. It was special counsel on a particular occasion for the purpose of helping the disciples to realize their dependence upon the providence of God and upon the generosity of those with whom they were to stay. The mendicant orders of the church were in error when they regarded these words as a command of Jesus which he intended his followers throughout the years to observe literally. There was no asceticism here.

It will be remembered that Jesus decided against becoming an economic liberator as he made his plans for proclaiming the Kingdom. He said that man shall not live by bread alone (Matt. 4:4). These words could be taken as an indication that Jesus was an ascetic, that he regarded material goods as evil. Such an interpretation, however, would be erroneous. What he said was that bread *alone* did not constitute the full resources for living. He did not rule out bread altogether. And later when he gave his disciples a model prayer, he placed a petition for daily bread at the heart of it.

II

The teachings of Jesus include many references to the poor. In a special sense the kingdom of God was for them. When the disciples from John the Baptist came to him and inquired whether or not he were the Messiah, he sent them back with instructions that they tell what they had seen—how the blind had received their sight, the lame had been made to walk, lepers had been cleansed, and the deaf had been cured. Then he added to this list of deeds the statement that the poor had heard the preaching of the "good news" (Luke 7:18-23). This was quite as important as the more showy expressions of the Kingdom.

The poor (οἱ πτωχοί) in the nation were those whose economic status was low; they were the humble and the needy in spirit as well. Lack of wealth had made them dependent upon God, and this dependency had developed in them a capacity for trust. There was a similar group in the Old Testament (Pss. 72:2, 4; 37:11; Isa. 66:2). Unlike the rich, who had assimilated foreign influences during the exile in Babylon and had become independent, the poor turned to God and clung more tenaciously to the traditions of the nation.

The Beatitudes make it clear that Jesus rejoiced that the Kingdom carried a blessing for the humble poor. This is the meaning of the familiar beatitude: "Blessed are the poor in spirit, for theirs is the kingdom of heaven" (Matt. 5:3). Their spiritual longing would be satisfied in the new day. Luke presents this beatitude in a somewhat different form: "Blessed are *you poor*, for yours is the kingdom of God" (Luke 6:20).[3] It is suggested sometimes that Luke had a bias against the rich, and that he embraced a strain of Ebionitic asceticism which regarded poverty itself as a virtue.[4] Another possibility is that Luke shared Jesus' conviction that God's poor, who cried unto him day and night in their humility and need, would find the longings of their hearts fulfilled in the Kingdom. It is clear that Jesus did not regard poverty as an ascetic virtue. He was concerned with what it did to personality. On every hand this was to be seen. While in the lives of some it made for beauty of character, in the case of others it led to dwarfed mentality and immoral acts. The poor were in danger of losing their souls quite as much as the rich. Preoccupation with money because they were desperately in need of it, and bitter resentments toward those who had plenty, were as cancerous for them as greed was for the wealthy.

The Gospel of John reports an incident which is used sometimes

---

[3] Italics mine. This was followed by a "woe" directed against the rich (6:24).

[4] The Ebionites were a Jewish-Christian sect which became extinct about the fourth century. Ebionism took several different forms and on the whole represented a mutilated Christianity. Cf. *Encyclopedia of Religion and Ethics*, ed. James Hastings, V, 139-45, for a treatment of these groups.

to suggest that Jesus approved of the existence of a particular class in society to be known as "the poor" (John 12:1-8). At a dinner in the home of Lazarus, Mary anointed Jesus' feet with precious ointment. When Judas objected, saying that it could have been sold and the money given to the poor, Jesus replied: "The poor you always have with you." These words have been taken to suggest that Jesus regarded poverty as justified. The remaining part of his statement, however, discounts this interpretation of the text. It reads, *"but you do not always have me."* [5] Jesus was to leave them soon, and Mary's act of love would inspire the villagers at Bethany far more than the distribution of the bread which the money from the ointment would have provided. Whereas the bread would have relieved the pangs of hunger temporarily, the example of Mary, under these particular circumstances, would move many to live sacrificially in the days ahead.

Jesus appreciated the humble faith of the poor and rejoiced that the Kingdom would be a blessing to them. He did not approve of poverty itself, either on the grounds of an ascetic bias against earthly goods, or because he regarded the poor as constituting a special social class instituted of God.

III

Jesus' concern for the poor was matched by his understanding of the problem which confronted the rich. His attitude toward them was not one of resentment; rather it was a realization of the temptations which the possession of money brought, and a desire to be helpful. He did not show the antagonism toward the wealthy which the "have-nots" exhibit sometimes. He was free of covetousness at this point, even though his personal financial resources were limited.

Basic in Jesus' teaching concerning earthly goods was his conviction that wealth made it difficult for one to enter the Kingdom. His most frequently quoted statement in this regard is: "It is easier for a camel to go through the eye of a needle than for a rich man to enter the kingdom of God" (Mark 10:25). This is hyperbole rather than a literal statement of fact. What Jesus is saying here is that it is difficult in the extreme for a rich man to find the new life

[5] Italics mine.

in the Kingdom. His disciples, upon hearing these words, inquired as to whether anyone could be saved actually. Jesus replied that all things were possible with God. There is a touch of humor in the statement concerning the needle's eye. The picture of a camel with its droll expression examining the eye of a needle to determine his chances for entering is most suggestive.

The situation in which the rich man finds his wealth a hindrance to entering the Kingdom, however, is not humorous, and Jesus' teachings provide vivid illustration of this fact. The parable of the rich man and Lazarus is one such teaching (Luke 16:19-31). Here we find a rich man "who feasted sumptuously every day." Surrounded by wealth on every hand, he became so encased in the trappings of riches that he was separated from his fellow men who needed him. This meant, also, that he was deprived of the good things that others could contribute to his life. For instance, there was Lazarus the beggar who lay at his gate, full of sores and plagued by scavenger dogs. The rich man had no interest in Lazarus, but God did, and when the beggar died he went to heaven where he was an honored guest, seated next to Abraham. If Father Abraham found delight in the company of Lazarus, the rich man might have enjoyed him likewise, but his money interfered. The parable closes with an ominous note. When the rich man died he went to Hades, where he was separated still from Lazarus, and what was far worse, from God as well. Between them was a great chasm fixed. The chasm which the rich man had allowed his wealth to create on earth was carried over into heaven, only this time he was on the wrong side of it.[6]

IV

In the Lazarus parable riches came between man and man. Jesus taught that they may come between man and God also. The parable of the rich fool illustrates this (Luke 12:13-21). Here we find a man who prospered so greatly that he had to tear down the old barns and build larger ones in order to accommodate his crops. This would seem to have been a perfectly respectable procedure. It may be assumed, also, that the methods by which the man's wealth was gained were thoroughly legitimate. And yet all was not well in the

[6] The parable is not concerned with a geography of heaven. It has to do with personal relationships as they are affected by money.

situation for the man came to trust his wealth rather than God where his future was concerned. He said: "I will say to my soul, Soul, you have ample goods laid up for many years; take your ease, eat, drink, be merry." Instead of finding his security in God, he found it in his goods. To him God said, "Fool! This night your soul is required of you; and the things you have prepared, whose will they be? So is he who lays up treasure for himself, and is not rich toward God." His goods had taken the place of God, and he lost in the end.

The Sermon on the Mount contains a teaching which is a kind of footnote to the parable of the rich fool. It states: "Do not lay up for yourselves treasures on earth, where moth and rust consume and where thieves break in and steal, but lay up for yourselves treasures in heaven, where neither moth nor rust consumes and where thieves do not break in and steal. For *where your treasure is, there will your heart be also.*" (Matt. 6:19-21.) [7] These words do not suggest that earthly goods are evil in themselves. It is only when they become the chief treasure and, as such, the basis of one's security, that they are unworthy. Being temporal and transient in character, they will not sustain the soul which is eternal. Only God can do this.

In addition to believing that earthly goods, when allowed to dominate life, would disrupt man's relationships with his fellow men on the one hand and with God on the other, Jesus held that an inordinate concern for money would interfere in one's response to the call to discipleship. This was the problem of the rich young ruler (Luke 18:18-25). Here was a youth who had all of the qualifications. He had been trained in the Jewish law from childhood. His abilities had been proved for he had achieved a sound financial status. The fact that he had come running to Jesus marked him as an enthusiastic person (Mark 10:17). In addition to this, it is stated expressly that Jesus looked upon him in love (Mark 10:21). He was an ideal candidate for service—but he refused Jesus' invitation to discipleship and turned away sorrowful.

The reason for the young man's refusal to follow Jesus was that he had been asked to sell all of his possessions and give the returns to the poor. The demand was a large one, especially for a person whose pride lay in his wealth. As he saw it, it meant a surrender of

[7] Italics mine.

position and power, and this the young ruler was not willing to do. Riches were keeping him away from *riches!* His love of wealth was costing him the Kingdom. The interesting thing about this situation is that probably the youth might have retained his money and followed Jesus at the same time, had he been willing to lose it for the Kingdom. This is illustrated in the case of Zacchaeus the publican who was a wealthy man also. He offered enthusiastically to share his wealth with the poor and with those whom he had cheated, and Jesus accepted him without making the demand that he give it all away (Luke 19:1-10). The difference between the rich young ruler and Zacchaeus was that the former had identified himself with his money and would not break the connection, while the latter was willing to identify himself first with the Kingdom. The call of discipleship was a call for all of self. This was what Jesus meant when he said: "You cannot serve God and mammon" (Matt. 6:24).

The rich young ruler was not the only person whose attitude toward wealth was responsible for his not becoming a disciple of Jesus. There was another youth, a would-be disciple, who turned away, also, when he learned the conditions of life which discipleship in that day demanded. This man had come to Jesus and had offered to become his follower. When Jesus looked at him, he saw that he had been accustomed to the life which luxury affords. Such living habits as those of an itinerant preacher would be difficult in the extreme for such a person, and so he said to him: "Foxes have holes, and birds of the air have nests; but the Son of man has nowhere to lay his head" (Luke 9:58). There is no record of the man's acceptance of Jesus' challenge, and this silence of the Gospels concerning him has been taken to mean that he turned away. For this reason he is listed as a would-be disciple. Wealth and a love for the kind of security which wealth provides kept him from responding to the call to discipleship.

V

Jesus' final word concerning earthly goods was a positive one. That wealth provided a constant temptation to the poor and rich alike was evident, and that it kept some from discipleship could not be denied. It was equally true, however, that in the hands of those whose first loyalty had been given to God, money provided an opportunity for the extension of the Kingdom. Jesus' parable of the unrighteous steward illustrates this pre-eminently (Luke 16:1-9). It tells of a man whose dishonesty was equaled by his foresight. Knowing that he was to be relieved of his position, he tampered with the book of accounts to the benefit of those who were indebted to his employer. By doing this he won their favor, so that when he lost his job, he could turn to them for sustenance. Clearly he was a rascal, and yet he won the commendation of his master.

In telling this story Jesus was placing a premium upon foresight and intelligence, but not upon dishonesty. The steward had to pay for his crime, undoubtedly, but he had shown himself to be a person of imagination and prudence. Both of these attributes of character Jesus wished to see in the lives of his followers. It grieved him to realize that too often good people were dull people; that, as he put it, "the sons of this world are wiser in their own generation than the sons of light." And in this connection, Jesus commanded his followers to apply intelligence and foresight to their use of money and earthly goods. What he said was: "And I tell you, make friends for yourselves by means of unrighteous mammon . . ." (Luke 16:9).

In urging thus an intelligent use of money, Jesus was not suggesting that the bribe was effective as a means of making friendships. Rather he was asserting that money, if properly handled, could be used to produce Kingdom values. In the children's story of King Midas and the golden touch, we are told of a king who had the power to convert all that he touched into gold, including persons themselves. What Jesus is saying in this teaching concerning earthly goods is that one should turn gold into persons rather than persons into gold. We might call this the golden touch in reverse.

The values of the kingdom of God are personal values. They include joy, peace, love, hope, faith, and similar attributes of the human spirit. Money when properly spent can result in an enlargement of personality so that these qualities of character will be enhanced. Education, decent housing, adequate health service, effective missionary enterprises, and helpful facilities for worship call for capital. These cannot be had without economic support, and yet they are required for the fuller life. Money in the hands of one whose motives are those of Jesus and whose standards are Christian, provides an opportunity for realizing kingdom values on earth.

QUESTIONS FOR DISCUSSION

1. Jesus did not teach a particular system of economics. Are there any systems today which lend themselves more definitely to his teaching concerning earthly goods than others? What of the following: capitalism? socialism? co-operatives? fascism? communism?

2. Would the approach to money which Jesus makes accentuate or diminish one's capacity to earn? Explain.

3. Was Jesus' preoccupation with the poor prompted by a concern for religious or economic values?

4. In the parables of the rich man and Lazarus (Luke 16:19-31) and the rich fool (Luke 12:13-21), is anything stated as to the way in which their money had been earned? What is it that made them good examples of a misuse of money?

5. What was it that was particularly tragic about the rich young ruler's refusal to obey Jesus' command? Was it because the poor were deprived of the use of his money, or because he was deprived of knowing the true riches of the Kingdom which sharing would have brought him?

6. How may the prudence which Jesus enjoined in the parable of the unrighteous steward be applied to other aspects of the Kingdom besides the proper use of money?

7. Be prepared to name several persons whose use of wealth in the modern world exemplifies Jesus' teachings regarding it.

8. The chapter has emphasized Jesus' teaching concerning earthly goods as it relates to the poor and the rich. Does it apply with equal pointedness to the middle-class wage earner today?

9. In a discussion between capital and labor, which side do you think Jesus would support? Explain.

10. To what extent do you regard the practice of economic sharing in the early church (Acts 4:32-37) as a reflection of Jesus' teaching concerning early goods?

SUGGESTIONS FOR READING

I. Economic life in the Greco-Roman world and in Palestine during the first century A.D.

Case, Shirley Jackson. *The Social Triumph of the Ancient Church.* New York: Harper & Brothers, 1933. Ch. i.

Grant, F. C. *The Economic Background of the Gospels.* London: Oxford University Press, 1926. Pp. 54 ff.

Klausner, Joseph. *Jesus of Nazareth.* New York: The Macmillan Company, 1929. Pp. 174-92.

II. Asceticism as a religious practice

General:

Drake, Durant. *Problems of Conduct.* Boston: Houghton Mifflin Company, 1916. Pp. 125 ff.

Encyclopedia Americana. New York: Americana Corporation. II, 378 ff.

Hocking, W. E. *Types of Philosophy.* New York: Charles Scribner's Sons, 1929. Pp. 458 ff.

Jewish:

Foakes-Jackson, F. J. *The Biblical History of the Hebrews to the Christian Era.* New York: Harper & Brothers, 1921. Pp. 396 ff.

Mould, E. W. K. *Essentials of Bible History.* New York: The Ronald Press, 1951. P. 482.

III. Jesus' teaching concerning earthly goods

Bosworth, E. I. *The Life and Teaching of Jesus.* New York: The Macmillan Company, 1939. Pp. 160-62, 180-83, 282-85.

Branscomb, Harvie. *The Teachings of Jesus.* New York: The Abingdon Press, 1931. Ch. xiv.

Cadoux, C. J. *The Early Church and the World.* New York: Charles Scribner's Sons, 1925. Pp. 61 ff.

Grant, F. C. "The Teachings of Jesus and First Century Jewish Ethics," *The Study of the Bible Today and Tomorrow,* ed. Harold R. Willoughby. Chicago: University of Chicago Press, 1947.

Scott, E. F. *The Ethical Teaching of Jesus.* New York: The Macmillan Company, 1924. Ch. xiii.

Wendt, H. H. *The Teachings of Jesus.* New York: Charles Scribner's Sons, 1892. II, 58 ff.

IV. The social gospel of the early church as it relates to possessions and wealth

Bartlet, V. "The Christian and Early Christian Idea of Property," *Property, Its Duties and Rights.* 2nd ed. New York: The Macmillan Company, 1922.

Cone, O. *Rich and Poor in the New Testament.* Pp. 118-58.

Howlett, Duncan. *The Essenes and Christianity.* New York: Harper & Brothers, 1957. Selected readings.

Knox, John. *The Early Church and the Coming Great Church.* Nashville: Abingdon Press, 1955. Ch. II.

Scott, E. F. *The Nature of the Early Church.* New York: Charles Scribner's Sons, 1942. Ch. viii.

Troeltsch, E. *The Social Teaching of the Christian Churches.* New York: The Macmillan Company, 1949. Pp. 113 ff.

16

Teaching Men to Pray

THE GOSPELS PICTURE JESUS AS A MAN OF PRAYER. IN ADULT LIFE
he continued the praying which had characterized his childhood and youth. Luke in particular regarded the prayer experiences of Jesus as a matter of special concern. He made frequent
note of the fact that Jesus prayed at moments of great decision.
In reporting the same event Mark and Matthew may not indicate
that Jesus was praying at the time, while Luke mentions it specifically.[1] On the other hand, Mark and Matthew record some
prayer retreats not found in Luke (Mark 1:35-38; 6:46; Matt. 14:
23).[2]

The occasions when Jesus prayed were those of great decision
for the most part. He turned to prayer at the baptism (Luke 3:
21-22), following the first day's ministry at Capernaum (Mark
1:35-38), after healing the leper (Luke 5:12-16), before selecting
his disciples (Luke 6:12-16), after feeding the five thousand (Mark
6:45-46), at Caesarea Philippi when Peter confessed him to be
the Christ (Luke 9:18-22), at the Transfiguration when he prayed
concerning his coming death (Luke 9:28-29), on the occasion of
the giving of the Lord's Prayer (Luke 11:1-4), in Gethsemane
(Mark 14: 32-42), and from the cross (Mark 15:34). Most of these
prayer experiences have been, or will be, considered in connection
with the life of Jesus, and need not be discussed at length in this
chapter. It should be noted, however, that these represent the hours
of significant choice for Jesus, when the currents of his life were
moving swiftly, and the direction of the future was being determined. At such times Jesus prayed because he needed to pray
actually. This was genuine praying such as sincere suppliants had
known before, and his followers have practiced since.

The results of prayer at these times of decision in the life of
Jesus were marked. A hightening of vision and a renewal of poise
came to him because he prayed. There was strength for living in
communion with his heavenly Father. Refreshment from fatigue

[1] Cf. Mark 1:9-11; Matt. 3:13-17; Luke 3:21-22.
[2] Indications of Jesus' praying which are peculiar to Luke are found in 3:21;
5:16; 6:12; 9:18, 28-29; 11:1.

and encouragement to persist in his difficult mission as the Messiah, resulted likewise. The impression which his prayer life made upon the church is reflected in a passage from the book of Hebrews, which was written toward the close of the first century to strengthen the Christians who were facing the prospect of serious persecution.[3] The unknown author of this writing states, "In the days of his flesh, Jesus offered up prayers and supplications, with loud cries and tears, to him who was able to save him from death, and he was heard for his godly fear. Although he was a Son, he learned obedience through what he suffered" (Heb. 5:7-8). The writer of these words concluded that prayer had a large place in the religious experience of Jesus.

I

In addition to the frequent prayer retreats of Jesus, the Gospels have preserved some of the prayers themselves which came from his lips. One interesting characteristic of these prayers is their brevity. On occasion they consisted of but a single sentence. The Lord's Prayer is the longest of them, and it would not be regarded as a lengthy prayer under most circumstances.[4] The reason for the brief character of the reported prayers of Jesus is that he was in such spiritual union with God that many words were superfluous. He was not concerned to change the mind of God and, therefore, long persuasive arguments were unnecessary.

The prayers of Jesus which the Gospels record were of different types. There was his *prayer of thanksgiving* upon the return of the seventy volunteer workers who had been engaged in evangelistic activities (Luke 10:21-22). Two of them in particular were *prayers of intercession* in which he prayed for Peter that he might not lose his faith following the denial, and for those who were crucifying him that they might be forgiven since they did not realize the full extent of the sin they were committing (Luke 22:31; 23:34). Again, there was a *prayer of inquiry* out of the depths of despair, as from

[3] *Ca.* A.D. 90 when the persecutions of the Roman Emperor Domitian were about to begin.

[4] The high-priestly prayer of Jesus in John 17 is lengthier than the others, but its present form owes much to the author of the Gospel, although a genuine tradition may lie behind it.

the cross he turned toward the Father and asked, "Why? Why?" (Mark 15:34; Matt. 27:46). On one occasion Jesus offered a *prayer of petition* when the prospect of the cross threatened to crush him, and he asked to be delivered from the necessity of drinking the cup (Mark 14:36). And finally, there was a *prayer of committal* as Jesus was dying (Luke 23:46). With this prayer he gave himself into the keeping of God. It is evident that there is much variety in these prayers, touching personal experience in many different situations.

II

Jesus' praying was spontaneous and extempore rather than studied and stilted. Although he recognized probably the regular hours of prayer at the Temple when in Jerusalem,[5] just as he attended the synagogue service customarily, his approach to prayer was in no sense formal. The nearest he came to suggesting liturgical prayer was in the Lord's Prayer itself. While praying in a certain place, his disciples were greatly impressed with what it was meaning to Jesus, so much so that they asked him to teach them to pray (Luke 11:1). The Lord's Prayer was the result. Even here, however, this prayer was not intended to be ritualistic. More specifically, we might say that Jesus was providing an approach to praying on this occasion, by suggesting certain appropriate themes for prayer.

In a very real sense the Lord's Prayer may be said to represent a significant statement of the religion of Jesus. As one author has said, "It sprang from the very depths of his religious experience. It is the richest single word of his that has come down to us. No other one passage gives us so much of Jesus himself. Into no utterance did Jesus pour more of his life, thought, feeling and faith." [6] Within the framework provided by the petitions of this prayer, every teaching of Jesus can be placed. In fact, unless one does interpret its separate statements in the light of the totality of Jesus' teachings, their full meaning will be obscured. Just as the prayer interprets his life, so his life and teachings add new dimensions to the prayer.[7]

---

[5] Note how the disciples of Jesus continued to observe the prayer hours at the Temple. Acts 3:1.

[6] Walter E. Bundy, *Our Recovery of Jesus*, p. 310.

[7] Cf. E. F. Scott, *The Lord's Prayer*, p. 53.

The Lord's Prayer might well be called a perfect prayer. It begins as all prayers should, with a mighty sense of the greatness of God:

"Our Father who art in heaven."

God is exalted above the earth, yet not removed from it. He is Father of all, and men are to pray for their brothers' needs, as well as their own.

"Hallowed be thy name."

Not only is God great above all others; he is also holy and righteous, and his children should revere his name, not in words alone but also in attitude and deed.

"Thy kingdom come."

Life and history are not without purpose. God's Kingdom is in the making here on earth, a great and glorious society, a brotherhood of good will.

"Thy will be done

On earth as it is in heaven."

The kingdom of God will be a perfect expression of the perfect will of God in every human relationship.

"Give us this day our daily bread."

Material needs in the Kingdom are not beneath God's concern. Bread, books, hospitals, clothing, proper housing—all these, and more besides, are required if men are to fulfill their destiny.

"And forgive us our debts,

As we also have forgiven our debtors."

Man is more than a body; he is also a living soul. His nature is moral and spiritual basically; therefore, he needs forgiveness and must himself be forgiving. Only thus can he have fellowship with a righteous God and also with his erring brother.

"And lead us not into temptation,

But deliver us from evil."

The possibilities of evil are on every hand. Man's weakness and lack of foresight may find him unprepared to meet a sudden turn of events that tempt his soul. He needs God's help at this point.[8]

The phrase "For thine is the kingdom and the power and the glory forever" is found sometimes in manuscripts, some of them ancient. It was added probably to provide a liturgical ending and is in full accord with the spirit and meaning of the prayer.[9]

[8] The above interpretation of the several petitions of the Lord's Prayer was taken from my book *Great Prayers of the Bible*, pp. 85-86, published by the Women's Division of Christian Service, The Methodist Church.

[9] Notice should be taken of the difference in the form of the prayer as found in Luke 11:2-4 and Matt. 6:9-13.

III

In Jesus' teaching concerning prayer, incentives for praying are to be found in the nature of God. The life of prayer is a response to his character. It is to be expected that children should turn toward a loving heavenly Father. Accordingly, one does not need to introduce involved arguments in order to establish the validity of prayer. Most of them are beside the point compared with the central truth that prayer is the natural language of personal relationship between a father and his children.

Jesus seemed to be concerned when his hearers did not understand these things readily; they were self-evident to him. He inquired of them (Matt. 7:9-11):

> Or what man of you, if his son asks him for a loaf, will give him a stone? Or if he asks for a fish, will give him a serpent? If you then, who are evil, know how to give good gifts to your children, how much more will your Father who is in heaven give good things to those who ask him?

Surely God will be as loving and responsive as sincere earthly fathers with all their shortcomings! This logic is based on the fact of the revelation of God in human behavior.

Not only does God's love for his children move them to pray; his intimate knowledge of them, likewise, is an incentive to prayer. He who numbers the hairs of their heads (Luke 12:7) is informed and interested in the specific needs of men. Jesus assured them that it was unnecessary to "heap up empty phrases" in praying as the Gentiles did and said, "Your Father knows what you need before you ask him" (Matt. 6:7-8). The realization of this fact would make for confidence as they turned to prayer. God's close knowledge of his children had been a favorite theme of the psalmists of Israel. One of them had said to God (Ps. 139:2-3):

> Thou discernest my thoughts from afar
>
> . . . .
>
> and art acquainted with all my ways.

Jesus believed this earnestly.

Jesus' confidence in the efficacy of prayer was based upon God's power, as well as upon his fatherly love and minute knowledge. Unless God had power to act, by which he could implement his good will, prayer might be an aesthetic expression, but it could hardly become a vigorous force. On one occasion Jesus stated his supreme faith in the power of God, as he replied to an inquiry concerning the salvation of the selfish rich by saying, "With men this is impossible, but with God all things are possible" (Matt. 19:26). It is within this framework of complete confidence in God's power that Jesus' prayer in the Garden of Gethsemane should be understood. As he prayed to be delivered from death, he prefaced his petition with the words, "My Father, if it be possible . . ." (Matt. 26:39). This was not a questioning of the power of God, but a conditioning of the request by relating it to the will of God.

This same prayer closed with the words: "Nevertheless, not as I will, but as thou wilt." It was Jesus' basic assumption, underlying all of his teaching concerning prayer, that in every situation God knows what is best, and therefore men do not pray to change his mind but to discover his will. This kind of praying is possible only when there is supreme confidence in God's love, knowledge, and power. Jesus had this confidence in his heavenly Father pre-eminently.

It was because of convictions such as these that Jesus invited men to pray and assured them of results. He said, "Ask, and it will be given you; seek and you will find; knock, and it will be opened to you. For every one who asks receives, and he who seeks finds, and to him who knocks it will be opened." (Matt. 7:7-8.) This is an invitation to pray within the context of Jesus' total teaching regarding God and the Kingdom. It is not a call to a type of prayer that is sub-Christian in character, one that is based on ideas and ideals that are out of line with the spirit of Jesus. Rather, it is a summons to pray as Jesus himself prayed. Only then will the petitioner receive, the seeker find, and the suppliant at the door discover that it opens.

IV

Jesus taught that man has a contribution to make to the prayer experience, as well as God. His attitudes in prayer make a significant difference. If he is arrogant and self-centered, like the Pharisee in the parable of the Pharisee and the publican, thanking God that he is holy and not like the despised publican, his prayer will be ineffectual. The situation will be exactly as Luke said it was when he indicated that the man "stood and prayed thus *with himself*" (Luke 18:9-14). On the other hand, if he is humble like the publican who beat his breast in sincere repentance and trusted himself to the loving mercy of God, he will go "down to his house justified."

This humility in prayer will show itself in other respects. Lengthy prayers which make a pious display are ruled out. Men are not heard for their "many words," Jesus said (Matt. 6:7). Such oratory in prayer is not only distracting, but altogether unnecessary in order to gain God's attention. Besides this, it leads sometimes to pride and vanity in religion. For this reason, Jesus spoke of going into one's room and shutting the door, in order to pray to the Father who is in secret (Matt. 6:6). This is much to be preferred to standing on the street corner where all men might stare at a flourishing display of words. It would not be justifiable to deduce from this statement of Jesus that he disapproved of all public prayer and looked with favor upon private devotion only.[10] Instead, he was concerned with the temptation to become an exhibitionist in public prayer, a temptation to which he saw men succumbing in his own day. He was not arguing against this expression of prayer as such.

Humility in prayer is urged, likewise, in another of Jesus' admonitions. He was thinking of a man who takes his gift to the altar. This in itself was a prayer act. While praying at the altar, he remembers that there is one who holds something against him—rightly or wrongly Jesus did not say, although the presumption would seem to be that the prayer is at fault. To such a person Jesus said, "Leave your gift there before the altar and go; first be reconciled to your brother, and then come and offer your gift" (Matt. 5:23-24). Prayer for Jesus was not a devotional expression only; it was a moral act as well. Being at odds with others, when one is to blame, blocks the prayer channel and hinders effective praying. Only a humble confession of one's sin to those whom one has sinned against will open the channel again.

A further teaching of Jesus concerning man's responsibility in prayer has to do with persistency. In two parables of dramatic in-

---

[10] This conclusion has been drawn sometimes. Cf. W. E. Bundy, *The Religion of Jesus*, p. 187.

tensity he stressed the need for holding fast to the petition one was offering, in season and out of season. The parable of the friend at midnight tells of a man who gets up grudgingly in the middle of the night to give bread to a neighbor who kept knocking on the door, lest everyone in the house, including the children and the animals, be awakened (Luke 11:5-8). The parable of the unjust judge depicts a woman who plagues a judge constantly, urging him to decide her case in which she had been wronged (Luke 18:1-8). Finally, he listened to her persistent pleas lest she wear him out by her continual coming. In both of these parables the request was granted in order to get rid of the suppliant. Jesus was not teaching that God is like these two, who responded because they did not wish to be bothered. The parables make their point *by contrast* rather than by comparison, as far as the giver is concerned. Their meaning is this: If unexemplary persons, such as the awakened man and the unjust judge, will honor the persistent appeals of those whom they do not love, in order not to be further troubled, how much more will a loving God respond to the requests of his children, who lift persistently their petitions into his presence.

The purpose of persistency in this kind of praying is not to wheedle and whine until God changes his mind or becomes convinced that he should give in to one's prayer request. Rather, the holding fast to one's petition is to the end that one might realize more deeply the nature of his own prayer. During the waiting period he may become sufficiently mature to appreciate the response. Ready answers to thoughtless praying do not make for character that is Christian.

In addition to humility and persistency in prayer, Jesus taught that men should pray with expectant faith. On one occasion he said to his disciples, "I tell you, whatever you ask in prayer, believe that you receive it, and you will" (Mark 11:24). These words do not mean that any reckless request will be granted just because men believe that it will. This is not prayer as Jesus taught it; neither is it prayer as he himself prayed. What Jesus promised was that no petition would go unheeded, and that every prayer had an answer— God's answer. And because it was God's answer it would be the best of all possible answers. To believe this is to have faith where praying is concerned.

Another of the reported sayings of Jesus concerning prayer is found in the Fourth Gospel, as a part of the upper room teaching on the night before he was crucified. Jesus was thinking of the future and regarding it in the most optimistic terms. He told them that they would do greater works than he had done, and promised that if they prayed in his name their prayer would be answered: "Whatever you ask in my name, I will do it, that the Father may be glorified in the Son; if you ask anything in my name, I will do it" (John 14:13-14). It is assumed sometimes that Jesus was suggesting that the addition of the phrase "in Jesus' name" to a prayer was a guarantee that the prayer would be answered, in the very terms in which it had been offered. Such an interpretation is magical and is out of line with Jesus' total teaching. To pray in Jesus' name meant to pray with his spirit, attitude, and outlook, to pray as he himself prayed, no less. We have here an illustration of the need for a principle of interpretation as one attempts to discover the meaning of isolated statements of Jesus. Each single utterance must be interpreted in the light of his total teaching and of his own personal practice. This provides a valuable corrective against a misreading of the gospel tradition at any one point.

QUESTIONS FOR DISCUSSION

1. In what way is the genuineness of Jesus' personal life illustrated by his practice of prayer? Was his praying intended to enrich his own life, primarily, or was it to provide an example for others mainly?

2. What do you think Jesus would say to the person who holds that prayer is a subjective experience only, in which one rearranges his own ideas so that a better integration of personality results?

3. In praying for others Jesus practiced intercessory prayer. As an expression of his loving concern for them, this was a genuinely religious act. If one had inquired of Jesus how this kind of prayer "worked," what reply do you think he would have given?

4. On the basis of the Lord's Prayer construct a creed which might express the religion of Jesus. In what sense does one's own praying represent truly one's personal creed?

5. Prepare a list of what seem to you to be unworthy practices of prayer today, evaluated in the light of Jesus' teaching about prayer.

6. Which elements in Jesus' teaching in regard to prayer do you consider to be basic? Give your reason for the choice made.

7. Be prepared to present the values of both sides of the question in the following: public vs. private prayer, extempore vs. liturgical prayer, brief vs. lengthy prayer.

8. Do you think Jesus' teachings concerning prayer would have been any different had he lived in the twentieth century, with its particular philosophical, psychological and scientific outlook? Explain.

SUGGESTIONS FOR READING

I. The psychology of prayer

Hickman, Frank S. *Introduction to the Psychology of Religion.* New York: The Abingdon Press, 1931. Ch. xii.

Johnson, Paul E. *Psychology of Religion.* Nashville: Abingdon Press, 1945. Ch. v.

Stolz, Karl R. *The Psychology of Religious Living.* New York: The Abingdon Press, 1937. Ch. xvi.

II. The philosophy of prayer

Buttrick, George A. *Prayer.* Nashville: Abingdon Press, 1942. Selected readings.

Heiler, Friedrich. *Prayer.* Translated by Samuel McComb and J. E. Park. London: Oxford University Press, 1937. Selected readings.

Hocking, William E. *The Meaning of God in Human Experience.* New Haven, Conn.: Yale University Press, 1912. Selected readings.

III. The Lord's Prayer

Manson, T. W. *The Teaching of Jesus.* New York: The Macmillan Company, 1932. Pp. 113 ff.

Rollins, W. E. and M. B. *Jesus and His Ministry.* Greenwich, Conn.: The Seabury Press, 1954. Pp. 98-101.

Scott, E. F. *The Lord's Prayer.* New York: Charles Scribner's Sons, 1951. Selected readings.

IV. Jesus' teaching concerning prayer

Bornkamm, Günther. *Jesus of Nazareth.* 3rd ed. Translated by Irene and Fraser McLuskey, and James M. Robinson. New York: Harper & Brothers, 1960. Pp. 133 ff.

Branscomb, Harvie. *The Teachings of Jesus.* New York: The Abingdon Press, 1931. Ch. xvii.

V. Jesus' practice of prayer

Beck, Dwight M. *Through the Gospels to Jesus.* New York: Harper & Brothers, 1954. Pp. 147-48, 205-7, 308-9, 431-34.

Bundy, Walter E. *Our Recovery of Jesus,* Indianapolis: The Bobbs Merrill Company, 1929. Ch. VI.

17

Practicing the Law of Love

IF ONE WERE ASKED TO SELECT THE PREDOMINANT THEME IN THE teachings of Jesus, it would be his emphasis upon love. Whatever the subject—the character of God, the nature of the Kingdom, the significance of prayer, or the importance of forgiveness—he made love central. This fact in particular accounts for the unity which characterizes his teaching. Love gave meaning to all that he taught, and provided the focal point about which it moved.

There was ample precedent for Jesus' stress upon love. The Old Testament, along with its emphasis upon justice and righteousness, contained major strains of teaching concerning love. It does not treat this subject in the abstract; always it is considered in connection with the action of God in history or with the associations of man with man. Hosea regarded God's deliverance of the Hebrews from Egypt as an expression of love. He represents him as saying (11:1):

> When Israel was a child, I loved him,
>   and out of Egypt I called my son.

Isaiah pictured God's relation to the nation as that of a beloved vineyard owner who carefully prepared the hill and planted the choicest vines. He hewed out a wine press to receive the wine and erected a tower where the watchman could guard the vineyard. All was done with the tenderest care; it was an act of love. When the work was completed, he said (5:4):

> What more was there to do for my vineyard,
>   that I have not done in it?

Love had built its lavish best.

The Old Testament taught, also, that man was to be loving in his association with others, even as God was loving in his relation to the nation. In an early legal code known as the Book of the Covenant (Exod. 21-23), it was stated expressly that if one found his enemy's ass going astray, he should return it to his enemy (Exod. 23:4). Strangers, likewise, when passing through the country were to be treated kindly. "You know the heart of a stranger, for you were strangers in the land of Egypt" (Exod. 23:9). It was taught also among the Hebrews that they were not to gather the grain too closely. Some should be left for the poor and the needy to glean (Lev. 19:9). A further word advises a loving treatment of neighbors: "You shall not take vengeance or bear any grudge against the sons of your own people, but you shall love your neighbor as yourself" (Lev. 19:18).

The books of Ruth and Jonah in particular recommended an attitude of love toward other races. They were written at a time of extreme nationalism when the Jews were being urged to separate themselves from all who were not of their own people. Ruth was presented as the beautiful heroine of the story which bears her name, even though she was a non-Jew. As a Moabitess, she was loved of Boaz, a man who was an outstanding symbol of Jewish integrity. And in the Jonah story the Ninevites who lived in the capital city of a heathen nation were singled out for praise. They repented more wholeheartedly at the preaching of Jonah than the Jews had done under the ministry of their own prophets. These non-Jews proved to be examples of faith to the Jews themselves. Jesus made reference to their ready repentance, and said that the men of Nineveh would condemn the Jews of his own generation in the hour of judgment, because they repented at the preaching of Jonah, while his contemporaries would not listen to him (Luke 11:32). The point in both of these accounts is that non-Jews such as Ruth and the Ninevites were worthy objects of Jewish love.

I

The teaching of Jesus concerning love is vivid and direct, indicating clearly that it grew out of his own experience. From childhood through youth and into maturity, he had known an intimate fellowship with the heavenly Father, and love was the life of this fellowship. At the baptism God had addressed him as the beloved Son (Luke 3:22). There was more than a messianic title in these words. They were intimate and personal. Love was expressed here in great measure and love was returned in kind.

Jesus not only lived in the strength of this love, but he passed it on, likewise, to others. It was the motivation which moved him to make the cause of every needy man his own concern. He saw them as "sheep without a shepherd" and spent his energies in their behalf. Sinners, outcasts, the sorrowful, the lonely, and the burdened sick found ready asylum in his love. To them he was support and hope. His love sent them forth as new persons. It enabled them to take up life again when they had been ready to lay it down.

Because Jesus lived the life of love so fully, he was able to teach the way of love with great effectiveness. He was the illustration of that teaching. First in importance with his insistence that men should be aggressive in their love for God. The Great Commandment counseled them to love God with every faculty of their being— heart, soul, strength, and mind (Luke 10:27; Matt. 22:37, Mark 12:30). He was the supreme object of devotion for personal life; all other loyalties and affections were secondary. This teaching was given in response to the question of a sincere scribe who was pleased with the reply he received. Jesus, in turn, said of his inquirer that he was not far from the kingdom of God. In quoting the Shema Jesus was revealing himself to be a true Jew. Montefiore, a Jewish scholar, has commented upon this fact significantly. He said, "This paragraph shows us Jesus as the true successor of Amos and Isaiah; he speaks as they would have spoken. Like the good Jew he is, he at once quotes the Shema as the first and highest commandment. The love of the One God is the supreme ordinance." [1]

Jesus moved beyond the important Jewish commandment however, by adding to it a word from Leviticus (Lev. 19:18). This second injunction followed directly upon the first, almost in the same breath. It was, "You shall love your neighbor as yourself." These two statements belong together. Love toward God and love toward man are part and parcel of a single love, provided the first becomes the motive for the second, and the second becomes an occasion for realizing the first.[2]

Matthew reports that Jesus added a further word at this time, by way of commenting upon the significance of the Great Command-

[1] C. G. Montefiore, *The Synoptic Gospels*, I, 287.

[2] Bornkamm insists, however, that these are two different kinds of love. "Whoever considers both commandments in this sense to be identical knows nothing of God's sovereign rights, and will very soon make God into a mere term and cipher, which one will soon manage to do without." *Jesus of Nazareth*, p. 110.

ment. He said, "On these two commandments [love to God and neighbor] depend all the law and the prophets." (Matt. 22:40.) The fruits of love in human personality were the goal of God's historical revelation to the nation. The implications of this teaching for the religious system of Jesus' day were staggering, if not altogether fatal. Individual teachers among the Jews might have given assent, as the scribe to whom Jesus spoke seemed to have done, but the system could not.

II

In the Great Commandment the word used for love is ἀγάπη. It does not suggest sentimental affection. Rather, it is akin to what we mean by invincible good will. The word carries the idea of value, esteem, and generous concern. As such it implies a response of the entire personality. Such good will underlies many of Jesus' statements concerning man's obligation in human relations. The Golden Rule is based upon it: "So whatever you wish that men would do to you, do so to them; for this is the law and the prophets" (Matt. 7:12). Love given and love received is the picture here. This teaching is found, likewise, in Jesus' word concerning the Roman soldier who commanded a civilian to carry his "duffle bag." He had a legal right to force him to pack it for one mile. Jesus urged, however, that out of good will, the civilian should volunteer to bear it an additional mile (Matt. 5:41). In doing this, from the motive of love, the bearer would lose his resentment toward the soldier, and the soldier would become more humane in his attitude toward the person carrying his pack. In such a relationship there would be no place for a master-slave psychology.

The love which Jesus advocated in one's association with his fellows is the basic principle of his teaching concerning man's obligation to those in need. On the night of the Last Supper he told them that they were to be the servants among men, in the sense that their leadership was to be expressed through service. "I am among you as one who serves," he said (Luke 22:27). This service, based upon love, was exemplified by the Samaritan in the well-known parable of the man who had been beaten and robbed (Luke 10:29-37). Organized religion in the persons of the priest and Levite had passed him by, but the Samaritan had interrupted his journey and cared for the needs of the unfortunate traveler. He had proved himself to be a neighborly person to his neighbor, the man half-dead by the side of the road. It is suggestive that in this parable Jesus selects a non-Jew for the hero. The contrast between the love shown by a heathen and the lack of love shown by the Jewish religious officials is impressive. There is subtle sarcasm, born of sorrow, in the comparison.

The loving concern which Jesus urged his followers to show toward the neglected and unfortunate may be seen, also, in his advice concerning whom to invite to a festive dinner. He said, "When you give a feast, invite the poor, the maimed, the lame, the blind, and you will be blessed, because they cannot repay you. You will be repaid at the resurrection of the just" (Luke 14:13-14). To make a law out of this injunction and invite only the unfortunate would be to sabotage the situation it was intended to create. Jesus was condemning social cliques which excluded the persons particularly in need of normal fellowship. If only the tragic sufferers came to a feast, the absence of the unafflicted would make their affliction all the more noticeable. It would not be a loving gesture. But to welcome all manner of men would make for hearty and happy human relations.

Another of Jesus' teachings which is misunderstood frequently, because it is interpreted apart from the obligations of love, is his injunction, "Give to every one who begs from you; and of him who takes away your goods, do not ask them again" (Luke 6:30). Matthew reports the saying somewhat differently: "Give to him who begs from you, and do not refuse him who would borrow from you" (5:42). The intention of both statements is similar. Jesus is urging his followers to do the loving thing in meeting human need. To give indiscriminately whatever one was asked to give, however, might not be a loving thing to do, and to lend under certain circumstances might not prove to be helpful. On the other hand to be niggardly and calculating in responding to requests for aid is not loving or generous; it is not the attitude of invincible good will which Jesus taught. Each situation must be assessed thoughtfully.

The importance of love as it moves out in a bold and adventurous attempt to meet human need is illustrated effectively in the parable of the last judgment (Matt. 25:31-46). This parable has a surprise ending. Those who were invited to inherit the Kingdom expressed amazement at being chosen. The reason given for their selection was that in feeding the hungry, satisfying the thirsty, welcoming the lonely, clothing the naked, visiting the sick, and calling upon those in prison, they had been serving the King. The King said to them, "Truly, I say to you, as you did it to one of the least of these my brethren, you did it to me." Their destiny depended upon the love they had shown toward suffering men, love that had expressed itself in practical ways. The others, presumably quite orthodox in belief but less loving in service, were deprived of their inheritance.

III

Men have not found it difficult overmuch to love those who love them. Jesus recognized this by pointing out that sinners, tax collectors, and Gentiles returned regularly love for love (Luke 6:32-34; Matt. 5:46-47).[3] On the other hand, it has been easy always to hate those who are one's enemies, those who are harming one deliberately. Men enjoy the rough justice of the *lex talionis* found in the Jewish Law, and calling for an eye for an eye and a tooth for a tooth (Exod. 21:24).[4] On the plane of uncritical egoistic impulse, returning evil for evil comes naturally. This is the reason that Jesus urged his followers to embody a higher righteousness in their personal relations, calling upon them to go further than others (Matt. 5:20).

Included in this higher righteousness was the command to turn the other cheek and to love one's enemies (Matt. 5:39, 44). No other word of Jesus has been found more difficult to follow than this. It demands so much. Consequently, it has been interpreted on occasion as pure hyperbole, requiring no more than a genial graciousness toward others, as long as they do not irritate one too greatly. Sometimes it has been interpreted on the level of the playground where one boy strikes another, and the latter is expected to invite a second blow on the opposite cheek. Both interpretations are in error. The first does not go far enough, and the second is childish, exhibiting in no sense Christian love.

The aim of Jesus in this teaching concerning love for enemies was

[3] This material came from Q. It is suggestive that where Luke has "sinners," Matthew uses "tax collectors" and "Gentiles."

[4] In Jesus' day, however, it was possible to substitute a fine for actual physical return.

the fullest possible life for both the offended and the offender. Retaliation in kind was finally futile. It might cause the offended to feel that he had justified himself, and restrain the offender from further acts of offense, but it would not change either of them basically. Turning the other cheek, however, would ennoble the life of the injured one and invite a change of heart in the offender.

How does one return good for evil and love one's enemies? Jesus answered this question by referring to God's way of relating himself to his children. He directs the warm sun to shine upon the fields of good and evil men alike, and sends the soft rain to fall upon the thirsty crops of saints and sinners without discrimination (Matt. 5:45). God does not strike back because he has been offended personally. He continues to love in order that he may help men to become their intended best. He stands by in good will looking for an opportunity to serve them.

Love of this kind is not passive and sentimental. It is fiercely alive and aggressive. On occasion it might express itself severely. The character of the universe and the reality of judgment are not relaxed or changed because God is loving. They were the creation of his love from the first. To set love and judgment in opposition to each other is to miss the point entirely. Each becomes an occasion for the expression of the other. Judgment becomes love in action rather than retaliation in anger.

Jesus did not elaborate upon what love toward one's enemies means in the many specific situations which confront men, both in times of war and peace. It is for the individual to decide what invincible good will requires, day by day and event by event. Ready-made answers are not available.

In expressing love toward enemies men are called upon to forgive the offender. It was in response to Peter's question, "Lord, how often shall my brother sin against me, and I forgive him? As many as seven times?" that Jesus said: "I do not say to you seven times, but seventy times seven" (Matt. 18:21-22).[5] Rabbinic teaching held that three times was the correct number for forgiving one's enemy. Rabbi Jose ben Jehuda said, "If a man commits an offense once they for-

---

[5] The Lukan form of the reply is: "If he [your brother] sins against you seven times in the day, and turns to you seven times and says, 'I repent,' you must forgive him." Luke 17:3-4. Cf. Gen. 4:24.

give him, a second time they forgive him, a third time they forgive him, the fourth time they do not forgive him." [6] In placing the number at seventy times seven, Jesus was not indicating a specific figure but was urging an indefinite number of times. As often as one showed a repentant spirit, he should be forgiven. A calculated expression of forgiving love was not sufficient.

Following this teaching concerning forgiveness, Luke presents a tradition indicating that one of the disciples said to Jesus, "Increase our faith" (17:5). Whether these words were spoken on this occasion would be difficult to establish. They do seem to suggest, however, that the disciples thought that this kind of forgiveness made great demands upon their faith. At this point Matthew places the parable of the unforgiving servant (18:23-35). It tells of a servant who had been forgiven generously of a great debt amounting to about ten million dollars. He, in turn, refused to forgive a small debt of twenty dollars which another owed to him and sent the man to prison till he should pay it. When the lord heard of the servant's ungenerous act he said to him, "You wicked servant! I forgave you all that debt because you besought me; and should not you have had mercy on your fellow servant, as I had mercy on you?" This parable teaches that men are required to be as forgiving as God is forgiving, that they are expected to love as the heavenly Father loved.

IV

The teaching of Jesus in regard to love finds another area of application in the question of marriage and divorce. Because of the ease with which a man could divorce his wife in that day, the home was in constant danger of collapse at the whim of the husband. Wives could not divorce their husbands, but the husband could divorce the wife at will. This situation made for instability in personal relations within the home. Its one-sidedness revealed a disrespect for the personality of the wife which, in itself, denied love as Jesus taught it.[7]

---

[6] Cf. the Babylonian Talmud, Yoma, 86b., 87a.

[7] The Law of Hammurabi of the Babylonians, by way of contrast, did provide for the right of a woman to divorce her husband and to marry another.

It is over against such a background as this that Jesus' words concerning marriage and divorce should be interpreted. Mark suggests that the question was raised first by the Pharisees who wished to find something by which to test Jesus. "Is it lawful for a man to divorce his wife?" they inquired. Jesus replied by referring to the law of Moses which permitted it (Deut. 24:1-4), but then went on to say that this permission was a concession to the weakness of the flesh. In the beginning of creation, divorce was not in the plan of God who made his children male and female and intended that they should marry and "become one." Therefore, Jesus said that what "God has joined together, let not man put asunder" (Mark 10:9). This is the ideal. Marriage was to be permanent. As an expression of love it was not to be dissolved.

What then of divorce? This was the question which the disciples asked Jesus later, in the privacy of the house. His reply was this: "Whoever divorces his wife and marries another commits adultery against her; and if she divorces her husband and marries another, she commits adultery." (Mark 10:11-12).[8] On the surface these words seem to forbid divorce under all circumstances. In Matthew, however, Jesus' statement includes one condition under which divorce would be permissible, namely, in the case of unchastity (5:31-32; 19:3-9).[9] Whether the inclusion of this condition came from Jesus himself, or whether it was added by the church when a literal keeping of Jesus' teaching was found to be all but impossible, is an open question.

In Jesus' statement concerning divorce, we do not have legislation as such; instead, we have a strong assertion of an ideal of marriage as a permanent relationship, making easy divorce impossible. This was a correction of the practice which prevailed within Judaism in the first century. That there are marital situations, however, in which a continuance of the relationship is demoralizing, and in which infidelity may not be a contributing cause, is undeniable. The question at issue is what happens to personality in these marriages. Is the situation such that Jesus' ideal of personality has a chance of being realized, both in the case of the married partners and of the children

---

[8] Since women could not secure a divorce, the latter part of the statement must refer to the remarriage of a woman who had been divorced by her husband.

[9] Matthew's version seems to be dependent upon Q rather than upon Mark.

who are members of the family? If not, then divorce could be in
harmony with the spirit of Jesus' teachings.

The person who is interested in divorce should not conclude,
however, that a nonliteralistic interpretation of Jesus' words suggests
that they may be taken lightly. The decision must be made when
face to face with Jesus' teaching that God intended marriage to be
permanent. And only when the situation is viewed in the light of the
responsibilities of love toward every member of the family can a
decision be reached that is worthy of being followed. Unless divorce
is a love act in the best interests of all parties concerned, as Jesus
interpreted love, it is out of line with his teachings.

In these matters of personal relationship Jesus placed the emphasis
not upon legal and external aspects, but upon the motive and intention of the heart. Adultery for him was not limited to the commiting
of the act. Lustful thinking in which the mind dwells deliberately
upon unchaste desires, Jesus regarded as being quite as sinful as the
overt act itself (Matt. 5:27-28). Teaching of this kind was most dis-
turbing to the legalistic-minded Pharisees. There was no way in
which Jewish law could measure and regulate the attitude of the
heart. They had legal grounds for stoning one who was an adulteress
actually (John 8:5),[10] but what could one do when adultery was
interpreted as lustful thinking? Truly they were facing a dilemma
in such teaching as this.

V

It has been noted already that Jesus questioned the Mosaic divorce
law on the ground that marriage was intended to be permanent.
A further consideration may have been that it did not show proper
respect for the personality of the woman involved. This reaction
is characteristic of the emancipation Jesus brought to the women in
his day. They were made to feel that they had a place in the Kingdom movement. Some of them followed him from time to time, contributing to his necessities from their savings (Luke 8:1-3). The
names of Mary Magdalene, Joanna, and Susanna are listed as among
this group. Joanna was the wife of Chuza, Herod's steward, and
may, therefore, have been a person of means. Montefiore suggests

[10] This section is found in the footnotes of the R.S.V.

that Jesus' recognition of woman was not only unusual in a rabbi, but also represented a break with orientalism in this regard.[11]

Many of the stories in the Gospels concern women. Jesus was welcomed in the home of Mary and Martha and shared with them the good news of the Kingdom (Luke 10:38-42). The Syrophoenician woman begged him to cast out a demon from her daughter, and he responded to her call (Mark 7:24-30). He was moved with compassion at the sorrow of the widow of Nain who had lost her only son (Luke 7:11-17). When a woman who was a sinner braved her way into the home of a Pharisee, and bestowed her love upon Jesus by washing his feet with her tears, he accepted the act as an expression of her gratitude because she had been forgiven (Luke 7:36-50). He dealt kindly with the woman who was healed when she touched his garments in the crowd (Luke 8:43-48). And while bearing the burden of the cross, on his way to the hill of crucifixion, he turned to the women who were following tearfully and said: "Daughters of Jerusalem, do not weep for me, but weep for yourselves and for your children" (Luke 23:28). He knew that the years ahead would be difficult for mothers of babes and little ones. In a day when the cause of women had few to represent it, he was considerate of their needs.

Jesus' interest in marriage and the family included a loving concern for children. Mothers sensed this and brought their little ones to him that he might lay his hands upon them and bless them. Such blessings were customary in an oriental society. When the disciples sought to discourage the mothers, Jesus rebuked them and said, "Let the children come to me, and do not hinder them; for to such belongs the kingdom of heaven" (Matt. 19:13-15). In these children Jesus found a living expression of his own faith in the limitless possibilities of life. Their enthusiasm for every new tomorrow was akin to what he felt as he envisaged the coming of the Kingdom. To adults who had forgotten that life held beautiful surprises, that evil could be overcome and sorrow turned into joy as they bore hopelessly their burdens, Jesus counseled: "Truly, I say to you, unless you turn and become like children, you will never enter the kingdom of heaven" (Matt. 18:3). He was not suggesting that they become

---

[11] C. G. Montefiore, *Rabbinic Literature and Gospel Teachings*, p. 217.

childish; rather, he was urging them to be childlike in their confidence that great and good experiences lay ahead.

Family ties were not unimportant to Jesus. It has been suggested already that one of the reasons he may have postponed his ministry until he was nearly thirty years of age was that he was needed in his own home circle to provide for the family. The time came, however, when he must surrender the comforts of home and take up his ministry on behalf of the kingdom of God. He was uncompromising with himself when this hour struck. And he was equally uncompromising with others whom he called to follow him. To the man who wanted to remain at home until his aged father died, Jesus said, "Leave the dead to bury their own dead; but as for you, go and proclaim the kingdom of God" (Luke 9:60). There were others at home who had not heard the call. Let them care for his father.

Jesus spoke another word concerning the necessity of putting the Kingdom first when he said to the multitudes, "If any one comes to me and does not hate his own father and mother and wife and children and brothers and sisters, yes, and even his own life, he cannot be my disciple" (Luke 14:26). On yet another occasion when he was facing the future and envisaging the struggle which his followers would meet, he saw that families would be divided over the issue of the Kingdom, and said, "For I have come to set a man against his father, and daughter against her mother, and a daughter-in-law against her mother-in-law; and a man's foes will be those of his own household." And then he added, "He who loves father or mother more than me is not worthy of me; and he who loves son or daughter more than me is not worthy of me" (Matt. 10:35-37). These are sobering words intended to emphasize the primacy of the Kingdom. There was no thought in Jesus' mind of taking family relationships lightly as he spoke them.[12] Rather he was stressing the absolute character of the call to discipleship. If one loved the Kingdom as intensely as this, his normal love for the family would be increased immeasurably.

---

[12] Jesus criticized the practice of giving money for religious purposes which one's parents needed, and marking it "corban" (given to God). Cf. Mark 7:9-13. For a discussion of this issue cf. C. G. Montefiore, *The Synoptic Gospels*, I, 163 ff.

QUESTIONS FOR DISCUSSION

1. Defend the thesis that Jesus' teaching concerning love had its roots in the best thinking of the Old Testament.

2. Develop the idea that there was an original element in Jesus' teaching concerning love. Did it consist in the breadth of the conception or in the extent of his practice of love?

3. What difference is there, if any, between love defined as affection, and love interpreted as invincible good will?

4. In the Great Commandment (Mark 12:30-31), men are told to love God with all their heart, soul, mind, and strength. What does love mean in relation to these various faculties? Give illustrations of love expressed in these ways.

5. Jesus' combining of love for neighbor with love for God was an original exposition of the law. Is there a basic relationship between these two loves? Does love for man lead to a deeper love for God, or does love for God increase one's capacity to love man?

6. To what extent does Jesus' own practice of love illustrate the Great Commandment? The answer to this question should be specific, one in which illustrations from his ministry are cited.

7. How does the life of Jesus provide a commentary on his teachings to love one's enemies?

8. What truth is there in the claim that loving one's enemy and turning the other cheek is a counsel of weakness? Can it be made to be a counsel of strength?

9. How would one apply the teaching to love one's enemies in the case of modern wars, especially since one rarely comes into personal contact with them?

10. Summarize Jesus' teaching concerning divorce. Does it make the securing of a divorce easy or difficult?

11. To what extent may we say that the position of women in the modern world is the result of a new attitude toward them in the teaching and practice of Jesus? Be specific in the answer.

SUGGESTIONS FOR READING

I. The teachings of the Old Testament concerning love

Anderson, Bernhard W. *Understanding The Old Testament*. Englewood Cliffs, N. J.: Prentice-Hall Inc., 1957. Pp. 245 ff, 314 ff.

Knudson, A. C. *The Religious Teaching of the Old Testament*. New York: The Abingdon Press, 1918. Pp. 173-91.

II. The Hebrew family

Abrahams, I. *Studies in Pharisaism and the Gospels*. New York: The
Macmillan Company, 1917-24. Ch. ix.

Cole, William Graham. *Sex and Love in the Bible*. New York: Association Press, 1959. Selected readings.

The Jewish Encyclopedia. New York and London: Funk & Wagnalls
Company, 1902. V, 336 ff.

Moore, George F. *Judaism in the First Three Centuries of the
Christian Era*. Cambridge: Harvard University Press, 1927. II, 119 ff.

Patai, Raphael. *Sex and Family in the Bible in the Middle East*. New
York: Doubleday & Company, 1959. Selected readings.

III. The family in Greco-Roman society

Friedländer, Ludwig. *Roman Life and Manners Under the Early
Empire*. 4 vols. New York: E. P. Dutton & Company, 1908-13.
Selected readings.

Goodsell, Willystine. *A History of the Family as a Social and Educational Institution*. Selected readings.

Moore, George F. *History of Religions*. New York: Charles Scribner's
Sons, 1913-19. I, 517. (Cf. God's) Pp. 423, 543.

IV. Jesus' teaching concerning the family

Branscomb, Harvie. *The Teachings of Jesus*. New York: The Abingdon Press, 1931. Ch. xv.

Cadoux, C. J. *The Early Church and the World*. New York: Charles
Scribner's Sons, 1925. Pp. 58 ff.

Scott, E. F. *The Ethical Teaching of Jesus*. New York: The Macmillan
Company, 1925. Ch. xiv.

Walker, Rollin H. *Jesus and Our Pressing Problems*. New York:
The Abingdon Press, 1930. Pp. 113-134.

V. Love and war

Lee, Umphrey. *The Historic Church and Modern Pacifism*. New York
and Nashville: Abingdon-Cokesbury Press, 1943. Selected readings.

Macgregor, G. H. C. *The New Testament Basis of Pacifism*. New
York: Fellowship of Reconciliation, 1937. Selected readings.

Moffatt, James. *Love in the New Testament*. New York: Harper &
Brothers, 1930. Selected readings.

18

Immortal Life

T HE TRUE CHARACTER OF A TEACHING IS FOUND IN ITS IMPLICATIONS regarding ultimate issues. In this regard eschatology is an important subject.[1] This is true particularly where man is concerned. What is to be the end or goal of his existence as a person? Is death the last word concerning him, or is there life fulfillment beyond the grave to which he may look forward? If extinction of personality is the answer to this question, we have one kind of universe; if immortality is the answer, we have another.

The future life is not one subject merely among many, not a postscript to be added to religion or philosophy. It is constitutionally a part of religion and philosophy. What one teaches concerning death determines the character of what one teaches concerning life. For instance, the question as to whether the values we experience in this world are temporary and transient, or whether they are timeless and eternal, is answered by what happens to personality at death, for personality is the seat of all values.

It is doubtful whether Jesus was concerned with a philosophical rationale of death and immortality. His approach to these questions was not metaphysical; rather it was religious and intuitional. A loving God who held a deep concern for his children would regard death seriously. He would not turn a deaf ear to the crying of the bereaved, nor would he allow his own to pass away as the light of a candle that is snuffed out by a wind in the night. Jesus was sure of this, so sure that he did not argue the case for immortality, but accepted it as a basic assumption for much that he taught.

I

Jesus inherited from his own people a belief in immortality that had been many centuries in developing. Although the Egyptians, the Persians, and the Greeks had each their own ideas of life after death, the Jews in large measure did not borrow from them but arrived at their conception independently. Persian influence is not completely

[1] Eschatology is the study of last things, involving such subjects as death, judgment, the end of the age, and immortality.

absent, however, from their eschatology.[2] At certain stages in its development, the Jewish doctrine was inferior to that of their neighbors. Only when the teachings of the prophets who stressed the ideal of righteousness had done its work, did Jewish thought on this subject begin to move in the direction of the thinking of Jesus.

Basic in the Old Testament view of the future life was the idea of a place beneath the earth to which the dead went, known as Sheol. Here they lived a kind of indeterminate existence without ethical distinctions which was uninviting decidedly. In describing this life, Job said of it (14:11-12):

> As waters fail from a lake,
>   and a river wastes away and dries up,
> So man lies down and rises not again;
>   till the heavens are no more he will not awake,
>   or be roused out of his sleep.

The psalmist who feared he would die was so disturbed at the thought of Sheol, particularly because he believed his fellowship with God would there be terminated, that he prayed (Ps. 6:4-5):

> Turn, O Lord, save my life;
>   deliver me for the sake of thy steadfast love.
> For in death there is no remembrance of thee;
>   in Sheol who can give thee praise?

A. C. Knudson writes of Sheol saying:

Sheol was a land of forgetfulness (Ps. 88:12). It was called Abaddon, "destruction" (Ps. 88:11; Job 26:6; 28:22). It was synonymous with silence (Ps. 115-17). From it there was no return (Job 7:9; 14:12), and in it there was "no work, nor device, nor knowledge, nor wisdom" (Eccl. 9:10). The dead had no consciousness of themselves and no knowledge of others (Eccl. 9:5 f.). They had no interest in their living descendants and no acquaintance with their affairs (Job 21:21; 14:21). Life to them was a blank nothingness. Everything connected with it had ceased except bare existence.[3]

---

[2] Cf. Oesterley and Robinson, *Hebrew Religion*, pp. 351-52.
[3] A. C. Knudson, *The Religious Teaching of the Old Testament*, p. 391.

There was nothing much to hope for there. Death was a tragedy on this basis.[4]

This view of life after death could not remain permanently satisfying to the Jews. As their thinking developed, it was found to be out of line with their understanding of the character of God and the nature of man. In time, therefore, the traditional view of Sheol was modified. The God of righteousness which the prophets taught could not, it was felt, leave his children to such a fate and be unconcerned for morality in the afterlife. Adam Welch has stated the issue in this way: "Mere existence without spiritual content and without moral issue, could not ultimately fulfill the greatness of a faith which was teaching Israel that its life on earth became full of enduring content as soon as it accepted the standards and served the purposes of Yahweh." [5]

There is one passage in the book of Job which has been taken by some scholars to suggest a higher conception of immortality than that which the traditional Sheol teaching offered. In the midst of an experience of great tribulation, the reason for which he could not understand, Job was given an intuition of profound faith in God, which led him to say (19:25-27) :

> For I know that my Redeemer lives,
>   and at last he will stand upon the earth;
> and after my skin has been thus destroyed,
>   then without my flesh I shall see God,
> whom I shall see on my side,
>   and my eyes shall behold, and not another.

The original Hebrew text of these verses is difficult, and the passage may be translated to read either *"without* my flesh I shall see God" or *"from* my flesh I shall see God." The Revised Standard Version prefers the former reading. Those who find here a developing faith in immortality on moral grounds hold that Job came to the conclusion that he would be vindicated *after death* for the seeming injustice of his great suffering.[6] The total message of the Book of Job,

---

[4] There was an earlier view of Sheol which attributed more life and activity to the dead. Saul was represented as calling Samuel back from the dead through the woman of Endor (I Sam. 28) in order to inquire concerning the future.

[5] Adam C. Welch, "Hebrew and Apocalyptic Conceptions of Immortality," *Immortality,* ed. James Marchant, p. 61.

[6] Cf. Knudson, *op. cit.,* p. 398; and *Ibid,* p. 72.

however, implies that in God's revelation to Job vindication is to be found on earth and not in a future life.

Much of the time prior to the prophet Jeremiah, the Jews regarded the group as the unit with which God was most concerned. The messianic kingdom was considered to be a national entity. Sheol itself was looked upon as a place of graves more truly than as the location of a single grave. The growing sense of individualism which developed, however, restored the individual to his proper place in society, and gave to him a new importance as a person in life after death. Until this occurred, the only way in which an individual thought he could express himself actively after death was through his offspring.[7] Now, there was hope for individual survival.

This belief in individual survival was enlarged later to include the doctrine of bodily resurrection. The persons who died before the coming of the messianic age, particularly the righteous, it was thought, would be resurrected to enjoy the new life (Isa. 26:19). The author of Daniel envisaged this resurrection to include both the good and the evil. He said, "And many of those [the Israelites] who sleep in the dust of the earth shall awake, some to everlasting life, and some to shame and everlasting contempt. (Dan. 12:2).[8] The messianic age which in times past had been considered a substitute almost for personal immortality, now is regarded as the reward of righteousness, both for the living and for the dead who will be restored to the earth at the last day.[9] It was to be bodily resurrection because the Jews found it difficult to think of the soul without a body, just as they conceived of the body always as possessing phychical expressions. Even in Sheol the soul had a body (Isa. 14:9-11).

The Greeks, on the other hand, stressed the spirit rather than the body. During a person's lifetime, this spirit was regarded as living in the body. At the time of death with the decay of the flesh, however, the spirit was free to continue its existence apart from the

---

[7] The levirate law (Deut. 25:5-10) outlining the responsibility of a brother to marry his deceased brother's widow in order to raise up children for the brother deceased was considered important in this connection.

[8] Cf. Ps. 49:14-15. The wicked are to dwell in Sheol, while the righteous shall be taken by God to heaven.

[9] It is not clear as to whether the "many" in the Daniel passage (12:2) includes all those in Israel who have died, or the unusually good and the particularly evil. In either case, they are Israelites and not the heathen.

body.[10] The Platonic school of philosophy held to the doctrine that man was composed of a spirit called "nous," a soul referred to as the "psyche," and a body. The spirit was considered to be divine and eternal, while the soul and body were thought of as mortal and temporary. This belief in an immortal spirit that was noncorporeal was more advanced than that of the Jews, who as we have seen, stressed bodily resurrection. The Greek view of immortality was philosophical, largely, growing out of a particular conception of man, while the Jewish view was religious and based upon a specific idea of the character of God.[11]

During the intertestamental period the belief of the Jews concerning immortality underwent further changes. There was a heightening of the differentiation between the good and the wicked. Even Sheol came to be regarded as a place where these were separated. A new transcendentalism entered the picture also, so that life in the new age became less materialistic. The final resurrection as a supreme demonstration of God's power continued to be anticipated.

First Enoch, in particular, reveals the enlargement of eschatological concepts at this time:

And in those days shall the earth also give back that which hath been
    entrusted to it,
And Sheol shall give back that which it hath received,
And Hell shall give back that which it owes.

For in those days the Elect One shall arise,
And he shall choose the righteous and holy from among them:
For the day hath drawn nigh that they should be saved.

. . . .

And the earth shall rejoice,
And the righteous shall dwell upon it,
And the elect shall walk thereon.[12]

And the Lord of Spirits will abide over them,
And with that Son of Man shall they eat

---

[10] Ps. 73:23-26 approaches the Greek idea. Although the body will decay, fellowship with God will remain.
[11] Cf. Oesterley and Robinson, op. cit., p. 329, for a discussion of this difference.
[12] I En. 51.

And lie down and rise up for ever and ever.

And the righteous and elect shall have risen from the earth,
And ceased to be of downcast countenance.

And they shall have been clothed with garments of glory,
And these shall be the garments of life from the Lord of Spirits;
And your garments shall not grow old,
Nor your glory pass away before the Lord of Spirits.[13]

Passages such as the above were influencing the faith of the pious
in Israel when Jesus taught the gospel of the kingdom of God. Immortality was an openly expressed hope among them, although its
association with extreme apocalypticism in some quarters had made
it an involved theme.

II

In the discussion of the religion of the Jew it was noted that the
Sadducees did not believe in the survival of the soul after death.
Along with their denial of bodily resurrection they rejected also the
teaching of the time regarding angels and spiritual beings. In the
background of this disbelief lay their view of God as one who was
remote from the world, without a real concern for human events and
persons as individuals. The Pharisees, on the other hand, were em-
phatic in their belief in immortality, as well as in their acceptance of
angels and spirits. This was, in part, an outgrowth of their faith in
divine Providence.

Most of the teachings of Jesus concerning life after death are by
implication; they are implied in what he says about other subjects.
For instance, when he speaks concerning the judgment he presup-
poses immortality. He warned men not to fear the one who can kill
only the body but rather to "fear him who can destroy both soul and
body in hell" (Matt. 10:28). It was God who determined eternal
destiny and not the person who deprived one of his physical existence on earth and after that could do no more. There was something beyond death. The reference here to both body and soul suggests that Jesus held to the Jewish belief in bodily existence after
death.

The idea of the judgment which implies immortality appears, also,

[13] I En. 62:14-16.

in Jesus' warning to the Jewish people who would not respond repentantly to his preaching. Even the non-Jews of Assyria repented when Jonah preached in Nineveh, and the queen of the South made a long journey to hear the wisdom of Solomon. They took seriously what these two had to say, even though both Jonah and Solomon were far less significant than Jesus. Therefore, these figures of the past will rise up at the Judgment and condemn the nation for not heeding his message (Matt. 12:41-42). One's response to the gospel must be faced; judgment and the future life are at stake.

Life after death is basic, likewise, in interpreting Jesus' parables of the rich man and Lazarus (Luke 16:19-31), the rich fool (Luke 12:16-21),[14] and the last judgment (Matt. 25:31-46). The first two suggest that one's eternal destiny may be involved in the proper use of money, and the last asserts that it may depend upon the kindness that is shown to others. All three bear telling witness to the fact that Jesus did teach the existence of a future life, and indicate that entering it involves ethics and morality. Eternal life is concerned with character as well as with the continuation of personality.

It should not be assumed that Jesus was attempting to frighten people into goodness with these teachings concerning the Judgment and life after death. He was being realistic rather than making a negative appeal to the emotions. If character counted, and the attitudes one took toward God and other persons made an eternal difference actually, then it was important to say so.

In the Fourth Gospel, Jesus is represented as placing the emphasis upon judgment as a process at work continuously in personality, as men respond to or reject the truth (3:19-21):

And this is the judgment, that the light has come into the world, and men loved darkness rather than light, because their deeds were evil. For every one who does evil hates the light, and does not come to the light, lest his deeds should be exposed. But he who does what is true comes to the light, that it may be clearly seen that his deeds have been wrought in God.

Judgment in this sense takes place at every moment of consciousness.

---

[14] Cf. the parable of the weeds of the field (Matt. 13:36-43), and the parable of the dragnet (Matt. 13:47-50).

In the Synoptic Gospels the stress is upon a judgment at the end of the age. This was true particularly in those parts of Jesus' teaching which are apocalyptic in character. He spoke of the glorious coming of the Son of man surrounded by angels, and of the nations appearing before him to be judged (Matt. 25:31-46).[15] This was to be the final judgment at which time man's eternal destiny would be determined. And this teaching implies immortality as a serious fact in the universe.[16]

III

Jesus' teaching upon life after death is found in several additional situations reported in the Gospels. In the first he was seeking to innoculate the disciples against disillusionment and discouragement as they faced hardships. One way to meet this emergency would be to detach oneself from a love of this world and its treasures. And therefore, Jesus said, "Sell your possessions, and give alms; provide yourselves with purses that do not grow old, with a treasure in the heavens that does not fail, where no thief approaches and no moth destroys. For where your treasure is, there will your heart be also." (Luke 12:33-34.) [17] In this same vein, when the rich young ruler came to Jesus, he was urged to free himself from the hold his riches had gained upon him, to sell his goods and distribute to the poor. Then, Jesus said, he would have "treasure in heaven" (Luke 18:22). There was another world where treasures were to be found, eternal and timeless, beyond the transient earth.

There was yet another occasion, during the final week of his life, when Jesus dealt with the belief in immortality. The Sadducees, who did not accept bodily resurrection, confronted him with an argument by which they sought to discredit both him and his belief in life after death. Quoting the teaching of Moses regarding the duty of a man to marry his deceased brother's widow in order to raise up children for his brother (Deut 25:5-10), they presented a hypothetical case where seven brothers in succession had been married thus to the same woman. Then they inquired: "In the resurrection whose

[15] Cf. the consideration of the Son of man figure, pp. 242-44.

[16] Jesus did not present a detailed sequence of events in connection with the last judgment such as is found in Rev. 20.

[17] Luke 12:33-34. The Matthaean version of this saying is found in the Sermon on the Mount (6:19-21). The original of both versions was most probably Q.

wife will she be?" It was a perplexing question, but Jesus made reply. He indicated that difficulty in understanding this situation lay in the fact that they did not know the Scriptures and were not acquainted with the power of God. Besides this, in heaven they are as the angels, who neither marry nor are given in marriage (Mark 12:24-25) .

It was as the God of the living that Jehovah addressed Moses in the burning bush, saying, "I am the God of your father, the God of Abraham, the God of Isaac, and the God of Jacob" (Exod. 3:6) .[18] He was not a Lord of cemeteries but of living souls. Furthermore, the power of God was sufficient to make provision for any situation, including the one in which a woman had been married to seven brothers. The shortsightedness of the Sadducees lay in their limited view of God. As Jesus knew him, the heavenly Father could take care of his own after death, whatever the case might require. Again, it was Jesus' conception of God that was central in his teachings concerning immortality, even as it was pivotal in his teaching on all subjects.

We are accustomed to think of heaven as the abode which men may enter at the very moment when life on earth ends for them. Jesus' reported word to the dying thief on the cross, "Truly, I say to you, today you will be with me in Paradise," seems to suggest that the righteous dead experienced some kind of beatific living immediately following death, although this may not be their final state (Luke 23:43) .[19] On the whole, however, in the first century entering the eternal home was thought of largely in connection with the coming Day of Judgment. These two ideas are not in opposition to each other necessarily, and were soon to be combined. As Harvie Branscomb has indicated:

Even in Jesus' day these two ways of thinking of God's reward were merging into each other. The basic conception is the same. It is the embodiment by faith of humanity's greatest hope, that of a life that is not bound to decaying flesh, but is as boundless and glorious as is the life of the spirit.[20]

[18] Note that although these worthies had been dead for many decades, Jehovah spoke as though he were their God at that very moment.

[19] The word "Paradise" is Persian in origin. In Xenophon it means a park. As it is used in this statement, it refers probably to Hades. Cf. R. H. Charles, *Eschatology*, pp. 473-74.

[20] Harvie Branscomb, *The Teachings of Jesus*, pp. 256-57.

Jesus' teaching concerning immortality must be considered as a part of his total message. It was not something in addition to the Kingdom as a kind of appendage or afterthought. The God of the Kingdom and the God of the future life were one and the same. This means that the values in the reign of God on earth were identical with those which prevailed in heaven. Had not the petition in the Lord's Prayer called for the realization of the will of God on earth even as it was in heaven? Just as the ideals of the messianic age influenced Jewish thought concerning immortality, the nature of the kingdom of God defined the character of the life-everlasting in the teaching of Jesus.

QUESTIONS FOR DISCUSSION

1. What ideas in the Old Testament concerning immortality do you think contributed most to Jesus' teachings on this subject?

2. In the face of their limited view of life after death, how does one explain the optimism and courage of the Jewish people during many centuries of hardship? Does the character of the God they worshiped suggest an answer?

3. How do you account for the fact that the Jews were late in arriving at a conception of personal immortality that was individual and conscious? Had the prophets come into the picture earlier, would it have made any difference? Why?

4. To what extent do you think that Jesus' view of the Kingdom as nonpolitical and universal in character contributed to his view of life after death? Would the fact that it was essentially a matter of spiritual and personal relations make it a suggestive prototype for the future life in heaven?

5. Explain: "The character of God as Jesus knew him made a belief in personal immortality inevitable."

6. Does the absence of descriptive details in Jesus' teaching concerning life beyond the grave add or detract from its impressiveness? Why?

7. Would ideas concerning immortality in terms of perpetual sleep, influence on earth after death, and absorption into the being of God with the consequent loss of individuality satisfy Jesus? Explain.

8. Does the inclusion of judgment and moral values in Jesus' teaching on immortality add or detract from its worth? Why would not the idea of life beyond death, altogether apart from the question of moral worth, have been sufficient for Jesus?

9. In what sense is Jesus' own life an argument for immortality?

SUGGESTIONS FOR READING

I. The Egyptian view of immortality

Moore, George F. *History of Religions.* New York: Charles Scribner's Sons, 1913-19. I, viii-ix.

Petrie, Flinders. "Egyptian Conceptions of Immortality," *Immortality,* ed. James Marchant. New York: G. P. Putnam's Sons, 1924.

Soper, E. D. *The Religions of Mankind.* New York: The Abingdon Press, 1921. Pp. 91 ff.

II. The Babylonian view of immortality

Moore, George F. *History of Religions.* New York: Charles Scribner's Sons, 1913-19. I, x.

III. The Persian view of immortality

Moore, George F. *History of Religions.* New York: Charles Scribner's Sons' 1913-19. I, xv-xvi.

Soper, E. D. *The Religions of Mankind.* New York: The Abingdon Press, 1921. Pp. 135 ff.

IV. The Greek view of immortality

Cornford, F. M. "Greek Views of Immortality," *Immortality,* ed. James Marchant. New York: G. P. Putnam's Sons, 1924.

Moore, George F. *History of Religions.* New York: Charles Scribner's Sons, 1913-19. I, 406-510, selected readings.

Soper, E. D. *The Religions of Mankind.* New York: The Abingdon Press, 1921. Pp. 114 ff.

V. The teachings of the Old Testament concerning life after death

Anderson, Bernhard W. *Understanding the Old Testament.* Englewood Cliffs, N. J.: Prentice-Hall, 1957. Pp. 482, 495, 519, 529-30.

Oesterley and Robinson. *Hebrew Religion.* New York: The Macmillan Company, 1930. Pp. 317-32.

Welch, Adam. "Hebrew and Apocalyptic Conceptions of Immortality," *Immortality,* ed. James Merchant. New York: G. P. Putnam's Sons, 1924.

VI. The Christian view of immortality

Baillie, John. *And the Life Everlasting.* New York: Charles Scribner's Sons, 1933. Selected readings.

Kee, Howard C. and Young, Franklin W. *Understanding the New Testament.* Englewood Cliffs, N. J.: Prentice Hall, Inc.: 1957. Pp. 181 ff.

Macintyre, R. G. "The Christian Idea of Immortality," *Immortality,* ed. James Marchant. New York: G. P. Putnam's Sons, 1924.

Streeter, B. H., *et al. Immortality.* New York: The Macmillan Company 1917. Selected readings.

19

Jesus and His Critics

IT WAS INEVITABLE THAT, SOONER OR LATER, OPPOSITION TO JESUS would develop. He came into an environment which was weighted down with established religious practices and heavy with fixed interpretations of law and ceremonial observances. Instead of conforming to what he found, he faced the situation with originality and personal conviction, refusing to let others do his thinking for him. In all of this he did not seek deliberately to be irritating. He desired only to be honest with himself and sincerely open in his relations with others.

The situation which developed between Jesus and the religious leaders was an outgrowth in part of the decisions he made during the wilderness days when he faced the question as to what methods he should follow in fulfilling his mission as the Messiah.[1] In turning from an economic program, refusing to stress "signs," and in rejecting the nationalistic conception of the Kingdom, Jesus embarked on an upstream course where the currents were swift and tortuous.

The issue between Jesus and his critics is expressed best in his own words when he said that no one tears a piece from a new garment and puts it upon an old garment (Luke 5:36). When washed, the new and unshrunken patch would pull away leaving a larger hole than before. Jesus pointed out also that no one puts new wine into old wineskins (Luke 5:37). As the fermentation developed the already stretched skins would burst from the pressure of the gasses within. These two parables suggest the reason Jesus could not conform to the religious forms and practices of the scribes and Pharisees. There was too much vitality in the gospel of the Kingdom to be contained in their religion as it was practiced. It would spill over the legalistic refinements of the scribes and outrun the ceremonies of the priests. The new spirit of life in Jesus' religion must create new forms of expression. The traditional ones were inadequate.

It was not to be expected that the Jews could be wooed away easily from their religious practices. Jesus did not anticipate this. He understood the ties that bound them to their past. This is the

[1] Cf. chap. 9.

reason that he said, "And no one after drinking old wine desires new; for he says, 'The old is good' " (Luke 5:39). Such understanding as this gave Jesus an objectivity of outlook that was helpful in evaluating the enmity which developed against him.

To chart the course of the conflict between Jesus and his critics is problematical. The nature of the chronology that we possess does not allow for detailing a step by step accounting. It was not the purpose of the authors of the Gospels to present a progressive telling of these events. If we conclude, therefore, that the enmity between Jesus and his critics developed from an early stage of simple irritation, through successive levels of increasing animosity, to a climax of open opposition, the conclusion must be regarded as one that we have drawn. This does not mean that it is, therefore, necessarily unhistorical. We choose to make this assumption, in any case, because it is logical as one considers the character of the issues between them, as well as their own personal temperaments as these are found in the Gospels.[2]

At first the issue between Jesus and the scribes and Pharisees must have seemed to be a minor one regarding certain regulations and ceremonial practices. As he continued to challenge them, however, it probably became evident increasingly that the differences between them were basic. If the position Jesus took were carried out to its logical conclusions, it would mean the death of their cherished system. This was no storm in a teapot, but a tempest of hurricane possibilities. He must be stopped even if it meant putting him out of the way, they concluded.

I

It is likely that the Jews reached the decision gradually to put Jesus aside. They came to it as a result of a series of open breaks. Mark presents in succession a number of such meetings (2:1–3:6). That these did not occur one after the other is probable. The arrangement is the author's who intended by it to provide some exhibits of the conflict between Jesus and the Jews, in response to questions asked by members of the Christian community. Other similar incidents are scattered through each of the Gospels.

[2] For a view that rules out the idea of development in this regard, based upon his analysis of the Gospels, cf. Bornkamm, *Jesus of Nazareth*, pp. 153 ff.

We have seen already that there were differences between Jesus and the Jews in connection with his attitude toward sinners.[3] They resented his announcement of forgiveness to the paralytic, regarding it as blasphemy (Luke 5:21). Only God could forgive sins. In addition to this they disliked Jesus' free association with outcasts and sinners. Following the call of Levi, Jesus attended a feast given by this new disciple to which some of the tax collector's friends were invited (Luke 5:29-32). They had been his companions in a business which the Jews regarded as unpatriotic and therefore ungodly. They were ceremonially unclean besides. Jesus accepted the invitation unquestioningly, rejoicing in the enthusiasm of his follower. To do so was the loving thing. When the Pharisees objected, Jesus replied: "Those who are well have no need of a physician, but those who are sick; I have not come to call the righteous, but sinners to repentance." There is a subtle sarcasm here. The Pharisees who were "healthy," as they saw it, had no need of Jesus. Why, then, should they object to his association with sick men who did? Should they not have been with the needy ones also?

The occasion for the giving of the parable of the prodigal son is suggestive likewise in this connection (Luke 15:11-32). Luke tells us that Jesus related the story at a time when the Pharisees and scribes murmured because the Teacher was receiving sinners and eating with them. They were objecting especially because he ate with them in complete disregard of the food laws which they insisted upon as necessary. This made Jesus ceremonially unclean himself. The setting provides an enlightening background for interpreting the parable. The lost son in the story suggests the sinners who gathered around Jesus to hear him, while the elder brother, who was respectable and complained at the favors shown the prodigal, was exhibiting the same attitude as the Pharisees who murmured at Jesus' friendliness with sinners.

In this same vein the Pharisees objected to Jesus' allowing the sinful woman from the streets to wash his feet with her tears and wipe them with her hair (Luke 7:36-50). Their logic is evident in the remark of Simon the host that if Jesus were a prophet he would have known what sort of woman it was who was ministering to him.

[3] Cf. pp. 137-40.

Touching sinners or being touched by them made one ceremonially unclean. In taking this attitude toward sinners, the religious leaders were disregarding Jesus' fundamental approach toward persons. They were children of his heavenly Father, and even in their sinning were to be approached in this light. Jesus was not condoning sin in these associations but showing respect for persons who might yet repent and live as the children of God they were made to be.

II

Another point of conflict between Jesus and the Jews concerned fasting (Mark 2:18-22; Matt. 9:14-17; Luke 5:33-39). This was a practice of long standing among the Jews. The Pharisees fasted and the disciples of John the Baptist fasted likewise.[4] This was one of the ceremonies in John's movement which identified him with the old age of the Law rather than with the new day of the gospel. Fasting in its purest expression was associated with humility and repentance. It represented a form of prayer by which the worshiper made himself available to God. As the ceremony itself came to be regarded as the desired goal, however, it lost much of its spiritual value and became a magical act by which to get something from God.

Jesus and his disciples did not fast regularly. It would be incorrect to say that they did not fast at all. During the wilderness days Jesus may have eaten sparingly of the berries and roots which were to be found there, but he did not observe the customary hours for eating. In a very real sense this was fasting although it would not be regarded as such from a strict ceremonial standpoint. In regard to the latter the rules for fasting were as prescribed as were those for ablutions. Neglect here would be very noticeable, and notice the Pharisees did. They came to Jesus and inquired why he did not keep the rules in this matter.[5]

In replying to this question Jesus said, "Can you make wedding guests fast while the bridegroom is with them? The days will come, when the bridegroom is taken away from them, and then they will fast in those days" (Luke 5:34-35). Public opinion would have

---

[4] Fasting was required by the Law only on the Day of Atonement, but the Pharisees urged frequent abstinence on all orthodox Jews, fasting themselves usually on Monday and Thursday.

[5] In Mark it is the people who make inquiry, while in Matthew it is the disciples of John who question Jesus. Luke implies that it was the Pharisees.

agreed with Jesus where an actual wedding was concerned. Nonobservance of the rules was followed under such circumstances. But Jesus acted as though life were a wedding every day in the week. He regarded his ministry and the expression of new life in the Kingdom which attended it as a continual wedding festival, and himself as the bridegroom. This is an unusual note in his thought of himself as the Messiah. The beauty of poetry lies lightly upon it. As the Messiah he brought joy and happiness to men. In his presence conventional fasting was out of order.

In spite of this glad recognition of the fact that his presence was an occasion for rejoicing, Jesus looked beyond to the time when he would be taken from them. There is just a hint of it in his statement that the bridegroom would leave (Luke 5:35). Had Jesus concluded finally that the cross awaited him? Although we cannot be sure just where these words belong in the chronology of Jesus' ministry, it is not likely that the cross had been decided upon definitely at this time. It is enough to say that they suggest that dark shadows lay ahead. The issue between Jesus and the Pharisees was taking shape; its outlines were becoming clear increasingly at each encounter with the opposition.

Jesus' suggestion that there would come dark hours in which fasting would be proper gives the clue to his interpretation of its meaning. As an end in itself, it was impersonal and fruitless. As an expression of the sorrow of the soul, it was eloquent. But even then, one must not appear before others to fast. It was hypocritical to disfigure one's face in order that his fasting be seen of men. Such practices were of concern to God only. Jesus' followers were not to parade their woes before others. Rather let them anoint their heads and wash their faces, let them look their attractive best so that their fasting will not be seen by men. God will see, understand, and make ready answer (Matt. 6:16-18).

III

The Sabbath issue more than any other set the enmity of the Jews against Jesus. Association with sinners and outcasts, and disregard for the rules concerning ceremonial cleansing and fasting were serious enough, but his violation of the Sabbath was considered as flagrant and not to be tolerated. Here the rabbis had given extreme care to defining the rules of conduct in order that the holy day might be a delight truly. They intended to safeguard it from all secular practices so that it would be Jehovah's. Absolute rest was the goal behind the multiple restrictions.

It was not an easy matter to draw up Sabbath regulations. When one sought to decide what constituted rest and what was labor, the definitions became involved in a hopeless refinement of meaning. For instance, it was no sin to carry water which fell from the sky as rain; but if it had flowed down the side of a wall, it must not be borne. Women were not to look into a mirror on the Sabbath lest they be tempted to pull out a gray hair, which would be labor. One rabbi taught that to bathe oneself with hot water should be forbidden. In the process the vapor might spread or the floor thereby be cleaned, and this would be labor likewise. A man could wear a wad of material in his ear but if it fell to the ground he dare not pick it up again. To soak the wad in oil was forbidden expressly, because it might possibly lead to healing which was considered as labor. One could walk on a wooden leg but not on stilts. In great detail the Mishnic tract *Sabbath* defines these regulations together with many others. To keep these in mind was a constant burden and to a sensitive conscience must have been unbearable.

In the case of some of the Sabbath laws the burden was eased by special interpretations. The casuistry involved here was ingenious. Places that were out of bounds for carrying things could be brought within lawful distance by connecting them to the permitted area. If several small houses opened into a common court, it was forbidden to carry articles from one house to another. Food might be placed in the court before the Sabbath began, however, and this would connect the several houses so that they would be regarded as one dwelling. The limit placed upon Sabbath-day travel was two thousand cubits. A two-meal supply of food laid at the travel limit before the holy day, however, would constitute a residence. This permitted one to travel an additional two thousand cubits.

These are just a few of the large number of interpretations and special case legislations by which the simpler Sabbath laws of the Scriptures (Exod. 20:8-11; 31:12-17; Deut. 5:12-15) had been made confusing, and the keeping of them futile. It was impossible *not* to break the laws on these terms. The limitations of human memory alone made keeping them an impossibility. Relaxation, restoration of body and mind, and unhampered worship were out of the question. Between God and his children was a mesh of intricate requirements. On these terms the humble Jew could not know free fellowship with Jehovah on the holy day set aside specifically for that purpose.

This situation was distasteful to Jesus beyond measure. His direct approach to God and men was stifled in such an atmosphere. Likewise his conception of righteousness as rooted in the motives of the heart rather than in external practices was contrary to the contemporary Sabbath system. It was not only irreligious as he knew religion, but inhuman as well. Here was an area where compromise was impossible. The differences were more than surface deep. Open challenge could not be avoided.

There are several illustrations of Jesus' break with the scribes and Pharisees over the Sabbath issue in the Gospels. Some have to do with situations in which Jesus healed on the Sabbath (Mark 1:21-45; 3:1-12, 20-30; Luke 14:1-6; John 5:1-47), and one is concerned with plucking and removing the hull from grain (Mark 2:23-28). Both acts were regarded as labor.

The Sabbath restrictions were not heartless completely in the case of the sick. A sufferer might employ means of healing provided his life was in danger actually. If this were not the case, he was expected to wait until the next day. It was difficult to apply this ruling, however, since in some cases one could not tell what constituted a threat to life. And in the presence of great suffering it was inhuman to delay relief. Jesus' revealing question to the Pharisees who were watching to see if he would break the Sabbath by healing the man with the withered hand has sounded down through the centuries: "Is it lawful on the sabbath to do good or to do harm, to save life or to kill?" (Mark 3:4.) They did not reply but their silence was vocal as it cried aloud their disregard for human need. Mark states that in this case Jesus looked around at them with anger, grieved at the hardness of their hearts. This is a thoughtful comment in its insight concerning the character of Jesus' anger. In a similar situation Jesus confounded the Jews by pointing out that they would lift an ass or an ox out of the pit on the Sabbath but not relieve the sufferer who was standing before them (Luke 14:5).[6]

[6] Some manuscripts read "son" instead of "an ass."

Jesus' encounter with the Pharisees when his disciples plucked grain and hulled it on the Sabbath involved the same issue as the healings. Which was pre-eminent, the Law or genuine human need? It was hunger which led to the disciples' act. It was the Law which pronounced it sinful.[7] Jesus used the customary form of defense by finding a precedent in the Scriptures for the disregard of the Law. Had not David himself allowed his followers to eat the bread of the Presence which only priests were permitted to eat? And did he not do it because of the human need for food? The situations were too similar for comfort as far as the Pharisees were concerned. To this question Jesus added words which served as a principle in interpreting all Sabbath regulations: "The sabbath was made for man, not man for the sabbath; so the Son of man is lord even of the sabbath" (Mark 2:27-28).[8] Any interpretation of the holy day which enslaves the human spirit rather than liberating it is contrary to the intention of God. Contrariwise, it was proper on the Sabbath to do anything which glorified God and ministered to the enrichment of personal life.

IV

The conflict between Jesus and the religious leaders would seem to have flamed into open rebuke as his ministry continued. In a series of statements Jesus pronounced "woes" upon the scribes and Pharisees for their attitude and practice. These are presented as a discourse in Matthew and Luke (Matt. 23:1-36; Luke 11:37-52).[9] It is unlikely that they were spoken on any single occasion; they probably represent instead remarks that were made from time to time in the face of specific situations to which they would apply.

Some of the sins which are included in these denunciations represent abuses in religious practice which the system of the day might encourage. They need not be regarded as characteristic of every Pharisee or scribe. Among them are callousness, pride, hypocrisy,

[7] The Rabbinic statutes would find two sins in this act: plucking the ears which was regarded as reaping, and rubbing them, which was considered to be threshing.

[8] The phrase "Son of man" in this statement refers to man in general. This is not always the case.

[9] It is probable that Q is the source of this material in the main. Matthew's version is considerably longer.

and stupidity, and beneath them all is the stressing of rites and regulations to the neglect of feeling for the inner life of the worshiper himself. The system rather than personality was supreme. For instance, Jesus accused the Pharisees of being overly meticulous in the matter of tithing even at the expense of a consideration of the tither: "You tithe mint and dill and cummin, and have neglected the weightier matters of the law, justice and mercy and faith" (Matt. 23:23). In many respects they were like their ancestors who had killed the prophets. By showing the same attitude toward truth, they were, in a sense, participating all over again in the rejection of God's messengers. The blood, therefore, of all the prophets "shed from the foundation of the world, may be required of this generation," Jesus said (Luke 11:50).

The language used in these denunciations was crisp and colorful. Seldom has it been employed more pungently than here. In staccato phrases it presents its penetrating analysis of the sins of the saints. This was the tragedy of the situation. These were good people who in the name of a good cause were confused and heartless. On occasion these passages are accredited to the early Christian community as an example of anti-Semitism following the crucifixion of Jesus. This may be questioned seriously. In the first place the words are too original to be the invention of a group, and in the second place they are typical of the attitude Jesus took consistently toward the religious system of his day.

Jesus' denunciation of the scribes and Pharisees should not be classed as name calling. He is not using words blindly in a fit of anger. A close study of what he said will show it to be a diagnosis of sin rather than an outcry of prejudice. His words here are as penetrating in their insight into human motivation as they are dramatic in their phrasing. Although there is anger beneath them, it is not personal, either in its source or in its goal.

QUESTIONS FOR DISCUSSION

1. Discuss the question of the inevitability of the conflict between Jesus and the scribes and Pharisees. Was there room for an honest difference of opinion between them?

2. Could the open break between Jesus and the religious leaders have been avoided by an effective compromise? Explain.

3. What motives do you think were most responsible for the critical attitude of the Jewish leaders—pride, jealousy, resentment, insecurity, concern for orthodoxy, concern for position, concern for truth?

4. What must have been the reaction of the people who witnessed these open breaks between Jesus and the Jews? Were they proud of their leaders, impressed by the courage of Jesus, or merely curious?

5. Which group in modern life does Jesus most resemble in these situations, the conservatives, the liberals, the middle-of-the-road persons?

6. Discuss the origin and development of the Sabbath law. Is there any similar controlling law in church life today?

7. What is meant by "legalism" in relation to the interpretation of Jewish legal tradition? Is legalism a dead issue today?

8. Did Jesus exhibit a callous disregard for the law of the Jews? Interpret Matt. 5:17-20 in this connection.

9. What does it mean to fulfill the law? Does it call for a carrying out of each minute detail, or for a realization of the intent of the law through adventurous and dynamic living?

10. Consider Jesus' denunciations of the religious functionaries of his day as found in Matt. 23:1-36 and Luke 11:37-52 as diagnosis rather than name calling. What is the difference?

SUGGESTIONS FOR READING

I. The Law (legalism) in the Old Testament

Anderson, Bernhard W. *Understanding the Old Testament.* Englewood Cliffs, N. J.: Prentice-Hall, Inc., 1957. Pp. 457 ff.

Oesterley and Robinson. *Hebrew Religion.* New York: The Macmillan Company, 1937. Pp. 358-68.

II. The Sabbath institution

Edersheim, Alfred. *The Life and Times of Jesus the Messiah.* New York: Longmans, Green & Company, 1899. II, 51-62, 777-87.

Oesterley and Robinson. *Hebrew Religion.* New York: The Macmillan Company, 1937. Pp. 93-96, 244, 246.

III. Pharisaism

Abrahams, I. *Studies in Pharisaism and the Gospels.* New York: The Macmillan Company, 1919. Selected readings.

Bornkamm, Günther. *Jesus of Nazareth.* Translated by Irene and Fraser McLuskey and James M. Robinson. 3rd ed. New York: Harper & Brothers, 1960. Pp. 39-42, 77.

Herford, R. T. *Judaism in the New Testament Period.* Selected readings.

The Jewish Encyclopedia. New York and London: Funk & Wagnalls
Company, 1902. Selected readings.

Johnson, Sherman E. *Jesus in His Homeland.* New York: Charles
Scribner's Sons, 1957. Pp. 10-16.

Riddle and Hutson. *New Testament Life and Literature.* Chicago:
University of Chicago Press, 1946. Pp. 19-29.

IV. Jesus' relation to the Pharisees

Barton, G. A. *Jesus of Nazareth.* New York: The Macmillan Company, 1931. Pp. 194 ff.

Beck, Dwight M. *Through the Gospels to Jesus.* New York: Harper
& Brothers, 1954. Pp. 152-63.

Bosworth, E. I. *The Life and Teaching of Jesus.* New York: The
Macmillan Company, 1939. Pp. 98-125.

Bowie, Walter Russell. *The Master.* New York: Charles Scribner's
Sons, 1928. Pp. 111-30.

Marlatt, Earl B. "Jesus and the Pharisees," *New Testament Studies,*
ed. Edwin P. Booth. New York: Abingdon Press, 1942.

20

The Great Decision

THE MINISTRY OF JESUS IN GALILEE WAS BOTH VIGOROUS AND
extensive. Ultimately this was responsible for the opposition
which developed against him and for his departure from Galilee into
the north country of the Gentiles. Our records concerning this
northern venture are sketchy and incomplete (Mark 7:24–8:26).
Mention is made of Tyre, Sidon, the region of Decapolis, and Bethsaida as well as of the district of Dalmanutha. Except for Tyre and
Sidon, these communities lie east of the Jordan. The brevity of the
record concerning these travels may imply that the ministry itself
in these parts was inconclusive. The tradition in Mark contains
accounts of the healing of the daughter of the Syrophoenician
woman (7:25-30), the healing of one who was deaf and dumb
(7:32-35), and the restoring of sight to a blind man (8:22-26) as
well as a few brief words concerning signs (8:11-12).

The reconstruction of the situation which follows recognizes
loosely the order of events in Mark as having some chronological
significance despite its theological interests. It is unreasonable to
assume that, broadly considered, the significant events of Jesus'
ministry were preserved in the tradition with complete disregard
for chronology, and with concern only for theology. Even the brief
summary of the kerygma (preaching message) in Acts 10:36-43
implies an interest in procedural activity that preceded and resulted
in the death on the Cross.

All was not going well in Jesus' preaching of the kingdom of God.
Immediately prior to Mark's notation of this departure into the
north country, the evangelist had recorded strong words of Jesus
concerning ceremonial defilement in connection with eating which
would have incited rigorous resentment from the Jews. In the previous chapter we have seen how deep-seated were the differences in
outlook between Jesus and the religious leaders. It had become
evident on both sides that there could be no compromise and no
thoughtful meeting of minds between them. Could it be that the
Messiah would be rejected by the religious leaders of his own people?
It was unthinkable! But it was actually happening.

Another cause of concern for Jesus might be found in the attitude of the people themselves who had made up his enthusiastic following. At the outset they gathered about him in such numbers that the word "multitudes" was used again and again by the gospel writers to describe them. Although they did not grasp the full signficance of what was happening, they came to see and hear, responding with great emotion to what they witnessed. On occasion he found it necessary to withdraw into the country in order to find sufficient solitude for prayer and meditation (Mark 1:45). Popularity with the crowd was stimulating to Jesus, for all its uncertainty. What if the entire nation would believe and accept the gospel? What if? What if?

The response of the crowd reached its peak at the time of the feeding of the five thousand (Mark 6:32-44; Matt. 14:13-21; Luke 9:11-17; John 6:1-15). With the great Feast of the Passover at hand, the roadways were lined with pilgrims on their way to the beloved festival. These, along with others in the community, stopped to hear Jesus teach and were so impressed that they remained all day with him near the sea. At the close of the day they ate together a meal which was more than a simple evening repast. We might conclude that it was an experience of fellowship in the kingdom of God in which Jesus showed himself to be a new Moses. Like the ancient leader who had fed the people with the manna in the wilderness (Exod. 16), Jesus made possible a common meal in which the needs of all were met in abundance. In my judgment, here was a symbolic meal in anticipation of the Lord's Supper.[1]

Whether these ideas took definite shape in the minds of the multitudes at this time, it would be difficult to say. It is my opinion that they become a part later of the thinking of the early church. It is clear, however, that the people were so impressed with the meal that they were ready to announce their allegiance to Jesus as the Messiah.[2] His popularity with them was at its peak. But he would not allow himself to be pushed into a public proclamation. There

[1] Cf. B. Harvie Branscomb, *The Gospel of Mark*, pp. 115-16; Dwight M. Beck, *Through the Gospels to Jesus*, pp. 214-15.

[2] John 6:15: "Perceiving then that they were about to come and take him by force to make him king, Jesus withdrew again to the hills by himself." Although the Synoptic Gospels do not record this reaction of the populace, it need not be regarded, therefore, as being unhistorical. At this and other points, particularly in regard to the final days in Jerusalem, the Fourth Gospel is especially illuminating.

was too great a likelihood of misunderstanding. He did not regard himself as an earthly king, which was what the populace had in mind. To give assent to their wishes would be to accede to the old temptation of bowing down before Satan. Firmly he turned from the crowd and went into the hills "by himself to pray" (Matt. 14:23). It was a staggering hour in which Jesus' soul was shaken to its depths. He was so near—and yet seemingly so far from his goal, tragically far.

The old adage concerning the enmity of "love spurned" might apply to the feelings of the people when Jesus refused to be pressed into service as their king. They began to lose interest, to resent this one who had awakened their supreme allegiance, only to spurn, as they saw it, their offer of fealty. As they slipped away one by one, Jesus was faced with deep questionings, even as he had been when the religious leaders rejected him.[3] First the scribes and Pharisees, and now the people themselves—could it be that the nation would not accept his messiahship in the only way he could offer himself?

There was yet another cause for concern in the mind of Jesus as he moved out of Galilee and passed over into the territory ruled by Philip. Herod Antipas had begun to take notice of him, and it was not a hopeful sign. This is the ruler who had beheaded John the Baptist (Mark 6:14-29). In the activities of Jesus which had been reported to him, Herod recognized certain characteristics of the prophet he had killed. So much was this the case, that he concluded that Jesus was John come back to life from the grave. Luke tells us that because of this, Herod wished to see Jesus (9:9). The threat of the ruler's interest complicated further the questionings in Jesus' mind at this juncture in his ministry. It was best to remove himself from Herod's jurisdiction, he concluded, in order that he might think through without interruption the issue of his mission, a mission as the Messiah which had become confused because of his rejection by the religious leaders and his loss of favor with the people themselves.[4]

[3] The Gospel of John has captured the psychology of this situation pre-eminently. Cf. John 6:25-71. Note especially vss. 60 and 66.

[4] It has been suggested also that this northern retreat was for the purpose of training the Twelve for the days ahead.

I

Toward the close of this period in the north country, Jesus moved into the region round about Caesarea Philippi. This distinguished city had been rebuilt by the Tetrarch Philip in honor of Augustus and should not be confused with the Judean Caesarea which Herod had constructed. Jesus' mind was occupied still with the outcome of his mission as the Messiah. Since leaving Herod's domain, he had had considerable time for thinking, and an answer to his questioning had begun to take shape. It was a daring answer, one that he may not have countenanced earlier in his ministry. Luke makes it clear that Jesus had been praying at this time. The issue which confronted him was the greatest which he had yet faced, and prayer alone would bring poise and perspective into this tense hour.

As a final move in making his decision regarding the future, Jesus turned to the disciples and asked them a question which indicates clearly the line of thought which was absorbing his attention: "Who do men say that I am?" It was an open attempt to secure information. Jesus wanted and needed to know. In his own presence the populace was not always expressive. The disciples had ample opportunity, on the other hand, as they mixed, unrecognized, with the crowds to hear what was being said in the market place and along the highways. What had the people been saying? Jesus trusted the basic religious intuitions of the people. Their judgment at this time was important to him.

The answer to Jesus' question was reassuring. The people had classified him with the truly great in the life of the nation. Some had thought him to be John the Baptist; others, Elijah; and still others, one of the prophets. This was distinguished company with which to be grouped. The people had felt that there was something unusual about Jesus. He had come from God in a special sense, even as Elijah and John. It was a reassuring fact that he had been regarded thus, reassuring at a time when his mission was failing seemingly—either failing or about to take a new turn!

A second question followed hard upon the answer to the first. Turning to the Twelve he asked, "But who do you say that I am?" It was important to know what the people had been thinking; it was even more significant to learn what the disciples had concluded. They had been with him in close proximity during the days of popu-

larity. They had heard him preach and teach, witnessed his healing
of the infirm, and stood by as he met the opposition among the
religious leaders. More than this, they had known the intimacy of
fellowship with him in devotion and prayer. Surely their judgment
concerning himself would have more than passing significance.

It was Peter who replied. Impulsive and outspoken, he became
the self-appointed representative of the Twelve: "You are the
Christ," he cried.[5] By these words he was declaring his conviction
that Jesus was the Messiah.[6] Turning to Peter and moved with great
emotion, Jesus said: "Blessed are you, Simon Bar-Jona! For flesh and
blood has not revealed this to you, but my Father who is in heaven"
(Matt. 16:17). It was a heaven-sent inspiration, this insight of Peter.
Jesus heard in these words the voice of the Father who had been
speaking within his own soul. It was as though the Father himself
was addressing him through Peter. He had not been in error when
he read the meaning of the voice at his baptism. The strange turn of
circumstances in the rejection of the religious leaders and the loss of
following by the populace did not mean that he had been mistaken.
The answer to this dilemma lay elsewhere; it was not an indication
that he was incorrect in his conviction that he was the Messiah.[7]

We have suggested already that a daring answer to the problem
Jesus was facing had been forming in his mind during the northern
pilgrimage, an answer that hinged upon whether or not he were the
Messiah in the face of the developments which occurred. Now that
he was in full assurance of his mission as Messiah, what was the
answer? It was a simple one, yet costly. Ostensibly his mission would
fail, in that he would not only be rejected by his own but actually be

[5] Matthew represents Peter as saying, "You are the Christ, the Son of the
living God" (16:16), and Luke has a different reading: "The Christ of God"
(9:20). The Fourth Gospel contains a word which may refer to the same event.
Here Peter says in reply to Jesus' question as to whether the disciples would
leave him: "Lord, to whom shall we go? You have the words of eternal life;
and we have believed, and have come to know, that you are the Holy One of
God" (6:68-69).

[6] The word "Christ" (χριστός) is the Greek word for "Messiah."

[7] Matthew records other words at this point concerning Jesus' reply to Peter:
"And I tell you, you are Peter, and on this rock I will build my church, and the
powers of death shall not prevail against it" (16:18). Clearly the reference here
is to Peter's confession rather than to Peter as a person. Although this apostle
held an honored position in the early church, his word and authority were in
no sense regarded as final by Paul and others. In apostolic times Jesus as the
Christ was central, not Peter or any other person.

put to death by them. This death, however, would turn out not to be defeat but victory. By it he would win the world ultimately. The answer was as daring as it was drastic.

It is my judgment that Jesus was inspired to find this answer not only through his quest in prayer but also by his contemplation of a passage from one of the great prophets of the past.[8] The Prophet of the Exile had discovered during his days of servitude in Babylon that there was power to redeem through suffering love, which met the worst that could be meted out with good will and faith. He had seen it happen in that foreign land far from Jerusalem, and it led him to conceive of the Hebrew nation, or at least the spiritual core of it, as fulfilling its destiny not by becoming a glorified, earthly, political power, but by being a fellowship of sufferers. He put into writing this tremendous conviction, and Jesus found his words in the scroll of Isaiah (53:3-5) :

> He was despised and rejected by men;
> a man of sorrow, and acquainted with grief;
> and as one from whom men hide their faces
> he was despised, and we esteemed him not.

> Surely he has borne our griefs
> and carried our sorrows;
> yet we esteemed him stricken,
> smitten by God, and afflicted.
> But he was wounded for our transgressions,
> he was bruised for our iniquities;
> upon him was the chastisement that made us whole,
> and with his stripes we are healed.[9]

Just as the Scriptures had proved helpful to Jesus in the wilderness of temptation by making clear God's will for his life, they were once more shedding their light upon his path. Here was a true interpretation of his own experience, a light in the darkness. Although this prophecy was not popular in Jesus' day as a messianic

[8] The fact that the early church used Isa. 53 (cf. Acts 8:32-33) to interpret the death of Jesus suggests that he may have referred to this passage himself in his talks with the Twelve during the last days, as he sought to strengthen them for what was coming.

[9] These words are taken from a section of Isaiah dated usually ca. 586-538 B.C., i.e. during the time of the Exile. Other messianic passages in Isa. e.g. 7:14-16, 9:1-7, 11:1-9, 32:1-8, 33:17, involve different dates and authorship.

expression, he took it to his heart. The nation had missed it, but he would bring it to life in his own personal experience of suffering and death. It was his Father's will.

But how could Jesus make this clear to Peter and the rest? When they had expressed their faith in him as the Messiah, they had quite a different future in mind. They envisaged his ruling upon the throne of David, no less. The Messiah as a suffering servant would not only be distasteful to them but also disillusioning in the extreme. It would be difficult but, nevertheless, Jesus knew that the disciples would have to understand the plan of God for lifting the world through the mission of the suffering Messiah, just as surely as he himself would have to embrace it. And so Mark notes that "he began to teach them that the Son of man must suffer many things, and be rejected by the elders and the chief priests and the scribes, and be killed, and after three days rise again" (8:31).[10]

It was as he had anticipated; Peter protested immediately, saying, "God forbid, Lord! This shall never happen to you" (Matt. 16:22). Just as quickly as Jesus had commended Peter for his insight concerning his messiahship, he now upbraided him for his outspoken brashiness. "You are speaking like Satan when you talk this way," in effect he told him. "That is exactly what he is saying to me now; I recognize the voice of the Tempter in your words. They are a hindrance to me, for they are not the words of God but of men." [11] Peter was wrong this time. He was not only incorrect concerning Jesus' future but uninformed in regard to his own as well. This too Jesus must make clear. His followers needed to be willing to follow all the way. There was no escaping this necessity: "If any man would come after me, let him deny himself and take up his cross and follow me. For whoever would save his life will lose it, and whoever loses his life for my sake will find it" (Matt. 16:24-25).[12] Hard words

[10] The details here must surely have been read back into the record following the events of the Crucifixion and Resurrection. But that Jesus by faith foresaw suffering and ultimate victory in the future at this time seems assured.

[11] This represents a paraphrasing of Matt. 16:23. The preservation of this tradition concerning Peter is unusual, considering his prominence in the church, and argues strongly for its authenticity.

[12] It has been suggested that the reference to the cross in these words is evidence of the fact that they did not come from Jesus, since crucifixion was the Roman and not the Jewish method of capital punishment. Such a conclusion is beside the point, since it fails to recognize that the Jews were subject to the Romans and very familiar with crucifixion.

were these, but the times were hard also. Could Jesus convince his disciples of the rightness of the course God wanted him and them to take? Only the future would tell.

II

All three of the Synoptic Gospels make it clear that on this occasion Jesus commanded his disciples to tell no man that he was the Messiah. He knew that the people would find it impossible to accept the announcement on his terms. Instead, in their misunderstanding they might well be encouraged to instigate a messianic movement which could have nothing but tragic consequences. Opportunities for future teaching would be engulfed in such a development, and bitter disillusionment would follow his refusal to become a political figure among his countrymen. It was best to say nothing at all, for the time being, attempting rather by teaching, service, and death to redefine the messianic ideal as the Father had revealed it to him.[13]

In speaking at this time of the suffering and death which lay before him, Jesus used the title "Son of man" with reference to himself (Mark 8:31; Luke 9:22). This was a term with a history behind it. It is to be found many times in the writings of Ezekiel as a designation of the prophet (2:1 et al.). Later it appears in Daniel where it probably refers to the messianic reign of Israel rather than to an individual Messiah (7:13-14). We find the term again in the parables of Enoch where it is personalized and applies to a heavenly being who takes his place in the presence of God, "the Lord of Spirits":

This is the Son of Man who hath righteousness,
With whom dwelleth righteousness,
And who revealeth all the treasures of that which is hidden,
Because the Lord of Spirits hath chosen him,

[13] A different interpretation of the messianic secret is found in Wrede, *Messianic Secret in the Gospels* (1901), where it is attributed to the disciples rather than to Jesus. Wrede concludes that, in his ministry, Jesus did not call himself the Messiah. When the disciples realized that he was, because of the resurrection experiences, they were perplexed at Jesus' silence on this point during his lifetime. Hence the idea of a messianic secret developed to explain this silence. It is suggested also that this idea was pointed up by stressing the fact that only the demons in the demon-possessed perceived Jesus' secret, and that the hearts of unbelievers were hardened so that they would not understand the parables.

And whose lot hath the pre-eminence before the Lord of Spirits in
uprightness for ever.
And this Son of Man whom thou hast seen
Shall raise up the kings and the mighty from their seats.[14]

The Son of man in Enoch fulfills the function of a judge who will
pass upon men and nations at the Judgment. His office bears directly
upon the destiny of mankind. The figure is that of a dramatic and
ecstatic individual, yet one whose person is vague and mysterious.

When Jesus spoke of the Son of man with reference to himself,
what meaning was he putting into the words.[15] Was he thinking
of Ezekiel, Daniel, or Enoch? On occasion he used the title simply
as a synonym for the pronoun "I" (Matt. 8:20; Luke 9:58; Matt.
11:19; Luke 7:34; Matt. 12:32; Luke 12:10). At other times it was
employed as he envisioned *a glorious return* with the clouds of
heaven (Mark 14:62).[16] Again, it is found on his lips as he contemplated his own suffering, death, and final exaltation (Mark 8:31,
9:31, 10:33-34, 10:45, 14:21). This was the intent when the term
appeared following the announcement of messiahship to the Twelve
at Caesarea Philippi.

These uses of the title, especially the latter two, would seem to suggest that Jesus was thinking of it as applying to his own mission, a
mission that was taking him to an untimely death. This need not
mean that he identified himself wholeheartedly and completely with
the heavenly man of Enoch,[17] or with the representations in Ezekiel
and Daniel.[18] Here was a title that suggested a special function in
connection with God's ordering of the destiny of men and nations,
whether as prophet, a messianic nation, or as a heavenly being. Jesus
was a prophet, but he was more than a prophet. He was identified

[14] I En. 46:3-4.
[15] Bornkamm, *Jesus of Nazareth*, p. 231, suggests that it was the "prophets"
in the early church who were responsible for the formation of the words concerning the Son of man, and that it is probable that Jesus himself did not use
the term.
[16] In Aramaic the term means simply "man" in general (barnasha).
[17] It might even be questioned whether or not Jesus had actually read the
Enoch passage. The "idea" was a part of the environment in which he lived.
[18] Schweitzer in his *Quest of the Historical Jesus* finds in Jesus' use of the title
"Son of man" an identification of himself with an apocalyptic figure which calls
for a specific program that he must carry out. To fulfill prophecy, he takes the
last messianic woes upon himself and goes to Jerusalem deliberately in order
to die so that he might return in glory.

closely with his nation and their messianic mission, but this did not describe fully his significance. He was truly the Messiah who would suffer and die for the people, only to rise again, exalted even as the heavenly man of Enoch. The very elasticity of the term "Son of man" made it highly adaptable to his purpose. *To limit his use of it solely to any one of its historical meanings in a technical sense, however, would be to do violence to the originality of Jesus.* It seems to me that he employed the title in order to express the unique character of himself and his mission. His use of it was suggestive rather than official.

III

It was characteristic of the greatness of Jesus that he found significance in the inspired ideas of the past as he sought to discover the full meaning of his messiahship in the present. Only one of bold imagination would have combined the humiliation of the suffering servant in Isaiah with the exalted splendor of the Son of man in Enoch. And yet he was more, far more, than a carbon-copy combination of these two representations. The uniqueness of his personal experience of God, the vitality of the Kingdom which under his ministry was beginning already to manifest itself, and the manner in which he met the particular challenge of the historical situation which confronted him—all these gave to Jesus a grandeur of being beyond those who had preceded him, as well as those who would follow.

A few days after the Caesarea Philippi pronouncement,[19] Jesus took with him Peter, James, and John, and climbed one of the lesser summits of Mount Hermon.[20] As he had done many times before, he once again was leaving the cities, seeking solitude where he might turn to the heavenly Father in prayer. Although the direction of the roadway into the future was clear, it took strength to walk that road. Fortitude and courage were needed. And so Jesus went to the familiar source, to his Father.

This prayer experience on the top of the mountain was one of mystical union with God. Matthew and Mark have presented it from the standpoint of the disciples who were, in a sense, looking on rather

[19] Mark (9:2) and Matthew (17:1) state that it was six days later; Luke (9:28) records the figure as eight.
[20] Mount Tabor has been suggested also as the site of this prayer retreat, but Mount Hermon is nearer to Caesarea Philippi and therefore was more accessible.

than participating (Matt. 17:1-13; Mark 9:2-13). Luke approaches
the event as it occurred within the soul of Jesus (9:28-36). It is
Luke who mentions the fact that in this high hour Jesus was concerned with his coming death. All three suggest that as Jesus stood
before them (Luke adds, "praying") his entire being was illumined
and that his garments became white.[21] All three relate, likewise, that
Moses and Elijah talked with Jesus as he prayed. Because of the
great impression which this experience made upon them, the disciples asked Jesus if they might not erect "booths" for Moses, Elijah,
and himself, and remain on the top of the mountain. Before they
descended from its summit, the voice of the heavenly Father was
heard, speaking from out of a cloud which enveloped them and
saying, "This is my Son, my Chosen; listen to him!" (9:35).

In understanding this great event in the life of Jesus it is necessary
to realize that the record of the event was phrased by the early
church, which may have objectified inner religious experiences in
the telling of them. A spiritual voice could be described easily as an
external voice coming from a cloud, while a light shining within the
countenance and reflecting the glory of the soul may be interpreted
concretely as dazzling garments, white as light. Because of this, we
must look beneath the "form" of the account and find the inner
spiritual reality which lies at the heart of the transfiguration of Jesus.

As he prayed concerning the future, Jesus was united with his
heavenly Father in spiritual union so that the presence of God
filled his entire being. The prospect of the cross had been difficult to
face. Rejection and apparent defeat were hard to bear. In this prayer
hour Jesus came to realize, however, that both Moses and Elijah had
to meet similar humiliation and suffering. Each had walked the
lonely road of heartache and seeming failure, *yet they were never
more fully God's true servants than in their darkest hours when they
held firm to their purpose.* It would be the same with him. This is
the meaning of the reference to the presence of Moses and Elijah on
the Mount of Transfiguration. It was their experience that God was
using to strengthen Jesus for his "departure which he was to ac-

[21] Luke states that they were "dazzling"; Mark suggests that they were "glisten-
ing," and Matthew indicates that they were "as light." There is a possibility
that the post-resurrection glory of Jesus provided the language that described
these high moments on the mount. It has even been suggested that this is a
post-resurrection experience that has been read back into the ministry of Jesus.

complish at Jerusalem" (Luke 9:31). And when he gave willing assent, confirming a decision made already at Caesarea Philippi, God's voice of praise was heard within his soul.

What did these hours on the mountain mean to the disciples? Although the Transfiguration was Jesus' experience primarily, they were privileged to witness the impressiveness of his person in this high hour.[22] They may well have heard him call out the names of Moses and Elijah as he prayed. It is not impossible, also, that they may have had a vision in which they saw them talking with Jesus. With thoughts of the Messiah in their minds, this would not be improbable since these two persons were expected to appear on earth again at the advent of the Messiah. Furthermore, they felt the presence of God with an acute perception as he was opening their eyes to the glory of Jesus.

The disciples would not forget soon this experience. It would be eclipsed by the sorrow of the days ahead, but the ecstasy of the resurrection would revive it in their memories. One thing further, however, must be said concerning the significance of the Transfiguration for the three disciples. Although they saw here the glory of Jesus, they did not realize that he was accepting the cross on these lofty heights of Mount Hermon.[23] If they had, they would not have revealed the lack of understanding during the following weeks which they showed at each mention of the coming crisis.

IV

The assumption behind the interpretation in this chapter of Jesus' experience at Caesarea Philippi and on the Mount of Transfiguration is that he regarded himself as the Messiah. The baptism and temptations in the wilderness have been presented in these terms also. All four of the Gospels proceed upon this same assumption as they tell their story. The early church as reflected in the New Testa-

[22] There is an interesting treatment in Berguer, *Some Aspects of the Life of Jesus*, pp. 230-31.

[23] Some scholars (Schweitzer, *op. cit.*, pp. 380 ff.; Lowrie, *St. Mark*, pp. 306-10; Warschauer, *The Historical Life of Christ*, pp. 200 ff.) reverse the order of the Caesarea Philippi pronouncement and the Transfiguration, because they are convinced that the disciples first needed the vision of Jesus at the Transfiguration to realize that he was the Messiah. It was because Peter had seen Jesus transfigured, they hold, that he could say, "You are the Christ."

ment epistles held firmly, likewise, to this conviction concerning Jesus.

Some writers have concluded that Jesus did not take this view regarding himself.[24] It is suggested that the church decided that Jesus was the Messiah following the resurrection experiences and set forth the story of his ministry in those terms.[25] Attempts are made to separate the material in the Gospels into earlier and later strands by way of showing that the earlier strands indicate a non-messianic point of view on Jesus' part. In demonstrations of this kind the process of getting behind Q and Mark (the major earliest written sources) is too subjective frequently to commend itself widely.

It must be recognized that it is difficult exceedingly to get beyond the faith of the first Christians in the question as to whether or not Jesus regarded himself as the Messiah. Among their number were those who had been intimate companions of Jesus. The tradition as it took form was subject to constant check by them. Whether they exercised this opportunity or not is a matter of conjecture. Since they believed that their personal destinies were involved in their allegiance to Jesus, it may be assumed that they would have been concerned to avoid any serious difference between the faith they held and the facts as they knew them concerning his views. And the question as to whether or not Jesus regarded himself as the Messiah was not a minor one, since it was basic to the faith they both cherished and proclaimed.

In reporting individual stories and sayings, the church may have fallen heir to the weakness of subjective interpretation here and there, but in regard to a major idea such as this it would not have been easy to do so. There were too many people alive who had heard Jesus and had known him intimately for the church to have been in error consistently concerning what Jesus thought of himself. It is my conclusion that the gospel writers recorded the tradition that Jesus believed himself to be the Messiah because he had taken this view himself, and the church was aware of this fact, having con-

[24] Cf. Guignebert, op. cit., p. 295. Goguel, op. cit., 577-78, suggests that at the baptism Jesus received a prophetic sense of mission which later developed into a messianic consciousness.

[25] Cf. Bornkamm, op. cit. p. 174, "the tradition understood and transmitted Jesus' words not only as words spoken in the past, but as the words of the risen and present Lord."

firmed it by the reports of those who walked with him in the days
of his flesh.[26]

QUESTIONS FOR DISCUSSION

1. Does the fact that there were crisis hours in the religious experience
of Jesus contribute to or detract from his greatness? Explain.

2. It was stated in the chapter that Jesus' retreat into the north country
was for the purpose of thinking his way through the impasse which had
developed in his career as Messiah. Can this view be harmonized with the
idea that Jesus knew from the very first, even as far back as his visit to
the Temple at the age of twelve, the fate which awaited him at Jerusalem?

3. When Jesus asked the disciples whom the people thought him to be,
was his inquiry based on a desire to know, or was the question for the
sake of leading the disciples into a declaration of his messiahship?

4. Since he had announced to the disciples at Caesarea Philippi that he
was to suffer and die, why was it necessary for him to pray to his Father
about this prospect on the brow of Mount Hermon several days later?
Does this reveal a vacillating person, or was the issue of such significance
that to face it again and again was necessary?

5. Within the chapter, note was taken of the fact that Schweitzer and
others reverse the order of the Transfiguration and Caesarea Philippi
incidents in order to give Peter a reason to have discovered Jesus to be
the Messiah. Did Peter need the experience on the mountain in order to
realize this fact? What experiences had he known already with Jesus
that might have led him to conclude this, apart from the Transfiguration?

6. Would an attempt to interpret *psychologically* the transfiguration
experience of Jesus and the disciples discredit the *ideas* which lay at the
heart of it?

7. What is meant by the statement that the transfiguration of Jesus
was intended primarily for Jesus himself? At this time who needed most
the strength which came from it, Jesus or the disciples?

SUGGESTIONS FOR READING

I. The purpose of Jesus' journey into the north country
    Bosworth, E. I. *The Life and Teachings of Jesus.* New York: The
    Macmillan Company, 1939. Pp. 209 ff.

[26] Exceedingly suggestive discussions of this question are to be found in a
chapter by Clarence Tucker Craig, "The Problem of the Messiahship of Jesus,"
New Testament Studies, ed. Edwin Prince Booth, pp. 95-114; and also in B.
Harvie Branscomb's commentary, *The Gospel of Mark,* pp. 149-52.

Taylor, Vincent. *The Life and Ministry of Jesus.* Nashville: Abingdon Press, 1955. Pp. 140-44.

Warschauer, J. *The Historical Life of Jesus.* New York: The Macmillan Company, 1926. Ch. xii.

II. The meaning of Peter's announcement that Jesus was the Christ

Bosworth, E. I. *The Life and Teachings of Jesus.* New York: The Macmillan Company, 1939. Pp. 222 ff.

Goguel, Maurice. *The Life of Jesus.* New York: The Macmillan Company, 1944. Pp. 378 ff.

Goodspeed, E. J. *Life of Jesus.* New York: Harper & Brothers, 1950. Pp. 123 ff.

Manson, William. *The Gospel of Luke.* New York: Harper & Brothers, 1930. Pp. 107-11.

III. Jesus as the Son of man

Blair, Edward P. *Jesus in the Gospel of Matthew.* Nashville: Abingdon Press, 1960. Pp. 68-84.

Cadoux, C. J. *The Historic Mission of Jesus.* New York: Harper & Brothers, 1943. Part I, viii.

Enslin, M. S. *The Prophet from Nazareth.* New York: McGraw-Hill Book Company, Inc., 1961. Pp. 137-48.

Foakes-Jackson and Lake. *Beginnings of Christianity.* New York: The Macmillan Company, 1920. I, 374 ff.

Manson, William. *Jesus the Messiah.* Philadelphia: The Westminster Press, 1946. Pp. 158 ff.

Taylor, Vincent. *The Names of Jesus.* London: St. Martin's Press, 1953. Selected readings.

Warschauer, J. *The Historical Life of Christ.* New York: The Macmillan Company, 1926. Pp. 91-104.

IV. The character of the transfiguration experience of Jesus

Berguer, G. *Some Aspects of the Life of Jesus.* New York: Harcourt, Brace & Company, 1923. Pp. 228 ff.

Bosworth, E. I. *The Life and Teachings of Jesus.* New York: The Macmillan Company, 1939. Pp. 256 ff.

Bowie, Walter Russell. *The Master.* New York: Charles Scribner's Sons, 1928. Pp. 206 ff.

Rollins, W. E. and M. B. *Jesus and His Ministry.* Greenwich, Conn.: The Seabury Press, 1954. Pp. 184-203.

V. The messianic consciousness of Jesus

Bornkamm, Günther. *Jesus of Nazareth.* Translated by Irene and Fraser McLuskey and James M. Robinson. 3rd ed. New York: Harper & Brothers, 1960. Pp. 169-78.

Branscomb, B. Harvie. *The Gospel of Mark.* New York: Harper & Brothers, 1937. Pp. 149-52.

Craig, C. T. "The Problem of the Messiahship of Jesus," *New Testament Studies,* ed. Edwin P. Booth. New York and Nashville: Abingdon-Cokesbury Press, 1942. Pp. 95 ff.

————"The Teachings of Jesus," *The Interpreter's Bible.* Nashville: Abingdon Press, 1951. VII, 149-50.

Duncan, G. S. *Jesus, Son of Man.* New York: The Macmillan Company, 1949. Selected readings.

Goguel, Maurice. *The Life of Jesus.* New York: The Macmillan Company, 1944. Pp. 385-92.

Guignebert, C. A. *Jesus.* New York: Alfred A. Knopf, Inc., 1935. Pp. 295-96.

Laymon, Charles M. *Christ in the New Testament.* Nashville: Abingdon Press, 1958. Pp. 146-50.

21

The Journey to Jerusalem

FOLLOWING THE EXPERIENCE OF HIS TRANSFIGURATION, JESUS directed both his steps and his heart toward Jerusalem. The decision had been made and he must carry it out to the very end. There would be occasions when it must be faced again as the time of his death drew near, especially during the final period in Jerusalem and on the eve of the last day, but the turning of the road had been accomplished.

Mark makes it clear that the journey from the north country through Galilee was made under a cloak of secrecy: "They went on from there and passed through Galilee. And he would not have any one know it" (9:30). Jesus did not wish to be arrested by Herod and thus be interrupted in his purpose. Nothing must be allowed to interfere with the will of his Father as his ministry was moving toward its fulfillment.

He tried again during these days to make the future plain to his disciples, and predicted once more his passion (Mark 9:31). It was important that they should know what lay ahead. As the Messiah, he was counting on these men to carry through—through the tensions of tragedy and beyond into victory. But they did not understand as he told them of the end and were afraid to ask him what he meant. An explanation might confirm the fears which were beginning to confuse their minds—fears too undefined to be vocal, yet too menacing to be faced.

En route through Galilee Jesus visited the town of Capernaum for the last time. This had been the headquarters for his ministry. Here were some of his first successes and to this community he had returned from visits to the villages round about. Presumably Peter's home was here (Luke 4:38), and James and John may have lived here also, since they were fishing partners of Peter (Luke 5:10). A return to Capernaum would give these men an opportunity to see their families before they made the dangerous journey to Jerusalem. It was quite like Jesus to be concerned with the families of his disciples.

Within the privacy of the house (Peter's?) Jesus asked the disciples what they had been discussing along the way. He had noticed that they were engaged in heated conversation. In fact, some of their words may have been audible and Jesus knew that they had been concerned with the question as to which of them was the greatest. This was an outgrowth of the messianic hopes which the recent experiences at Caesarea Philippi had awakened in them. Since these men were thinking of the messianic kingdom in earthly and political terms, it was natural that they should begin to eye the places of honor in the new order. Jesus' question caught them offguard. They were too embarrassed to reply and a telling silence followed Jesus' inquiry. Then it was that he said to them: "If any one would be first, he must be last of all and servant of all" (Mark 9:35). There was a little one standing close to Jesus in the room. He took the child in his arms and said to them: "Whoever receives one such child in my name receives me; and whoever receives me, receives not me but him who sent me" (Mark 9:37). These must have been frustrating words to the disciples at a time when their ambition was keyed to high pitch. Becoming servants and receiving children seemed far removed from political rule. But this was just the point. Jesus was redefining the Kingdom for these men who were misunderstanding, and during the days ahead he would continue to do so again and again.

Before leaving Capernaum, Jesus uttered some of the most serious words which are to be found in the Gospels. Storms lay ahead for himself and for the disciples also. Strong winds call for strong measures. Therefore, he said to his men (Mark 9:43-47):

If your hand causes you to sin, cut it off; it is better for you to enter life maimed than with two hands to go to hell, to the unquenchable fire, And if your foot causes you to sin, cut it off; it is better for you to enter life lame than with two feet to be thrown into hell. And if your eye causes you to sin, pluck it out; it is better for you to enter the kingdom of God with one eye than with two eyes to be thrown into hell.

Scarcely can one imagine more forceful words than these under the circumstances. But there were more to come when Jesus added the statement concerning salt. He said: "Every one will be salted with fire. Salt is good; but if the salt has lost its saltness, how will you

season it?" (Mark 9:49-50.) [1] Yes, in the immediate future, the
disciples must endure the discipline of suffering and hardship and
they must hold fast, lest they lose the very qualities in their lives that
made them significant. When this happens, it is all but impossible to
restore such a one to his original verve. Like salt without flavor
there is little that they can accomplish.

I

The exact itinerary of Jesus and his disciples as they made their
way toward Jerusalem is difficult to determine. Mark and Matthew
suggest that they moved over into Perea, "beyond the Jordan,"
recrossing the river again over the Roman bridge near the city of
Jericho. Luke implies that Jesus traveled through Samaria, or attempted to do so. He tells how one Samaritan village refused to
give them lodging when they perceived that they were Jewish
pilgrims on their way to the Feast at Jerusalem (Luke 9:51-55).[2]

Considerably later in his narrative Luke places Jesus "between
Samaria and Galilee" (17:11) [3] and relates how ten lepers were
healed, only one of whom turned back to express his gratitude, this
one being a Samaritan. Later, Luke presents the visit to Jericho even
as Mark and Matthew, and this suggests the trans-Jordan route.
One reason for this confusion is that Luke contains at this point a
lengthy section of material organized around the idea of a last journey to Jerusalem (9:51–18:14). The arrangement is literary and edi-
torial predominantly. Some of the material included is found in an
entirely different context in the other Gospels, and parts of it are
reminiscent of the Sermon on the Mount. This is a further illustration of the difficulty one faces in attempting to deduce a close
chronology from the gospel records.

One day as they journeyed along the road in Perea, Jesus was walking ahead of them. There was something about his bearing, the measured and determined character of his stride and the lift of his head

---

[1] In Matthew these words are found in the Sermon on the Mount (5:13).
Mark's setting for them is situationally ideal.

[2] Because of this refusal, Klausner suggests that Jesus crossed over beyond
the Jordan (cf. Mark 10:1).

[3] The phrase means probably "along the border of Samaria and Galilee" (cf.
H. K. Luce, op. cit., p. 178), i.e. traveling eastward.

as his visage pointed toward the future, that amazed the disciples. Mark tells us that they were afraid. It was a fear born of uncertainty and dread of the unknown. They had traveled the roadways of Palestine for many months with Jesus as part of a very close fellowship in which they came to know his every mood. But since the recent days in the north, a change had come over their leader. Never had he seemed more masterful; never were they more sure that they were correct in their estimate of him. And yet—he had begun to talk of death and suffering, of plucking out eyes and of saltless salt. They were accustomed to his speaking in parables. This, however, was something different, and they were afraid. Abruptly Jesus stopped in the way, turned to them directly, and again told them of what awaited him at Jerusalem (Mark 10:32-34). Clearly this was what had been absorbing his thought as he preceded them on the road.

When they spoke up and asked for a favor, it would seem almost that James and John were seeking to divert Jesus' attention from such dark thoughts with a realistic facing of the traditional kingdom. "Grant us to sit, one at your right hand and one at your left, in your glory," they asked. (Mark 10:37.) [4] This petition would confront Jesus with the necessity to express himself concretely, *and on their terms*. But he was not to be diverted from his absorption with the cross. "You do not know what you are asking. Are you able to drink the cup that I drink, or to be baptized with the baptism with which I am baptized?" he inquired. Later in this same journey Jesus cried out: "I came to cast fire upon the earth; and would that it were already kindled! I have a baptism to be baptized with; and how I am constrained until it is accomplished!" (Luke 12:49-50) [5] The cross! It was always the cross these days.

When James and John replied that they were able to drink the cup and to accept his baptism, Jesus did not argue the case with them. They did not know fully what they were agreeing to bear. Perhaps they could face such suffering. Who could say? This much was certain; they would have to do it surely. But the granting of the

[4] Matthew (20:20-21) represents the mother of James and John as making the request. This suggests that the women who followed Jesus from time to time were with him during the Perean journey.

[5] This may be Luke's version of the Markan reply to James and John. (Cf. Mark 10:38-40.)

petition to give seats of honor to these two in the messianic kingdom was not Jesus' to grant. Only the Father could do this. When the other disciples became aware of the priority James and John were seeking, they resented it. Their own ambitions flared high; each wanted precedence over the other. And again Jesus was called upon to check their grasping spirit, and at the same time to modify their views of the nature of the Kingdom. He told them that among the Gentiles, the rulers expressed their authority by lording over their subjects. It was not to be so among his followers, for they were to show their true position by humbly serving their own: "Whoever would be first among you must be slave of all" (Mark 10:44).[6] It was a sober hour at an unknown location on the other side of the Jordan. Jesus may have been thinking of Herod Antipas for he was still in his territory when he compared his kingship to that of a traditional overlord. This could not be the way for himself or his followers; the transfiguration experience had settled this issue once and for all.

II

In the account which Luke gives of the journey to Jerusalem the impression is made that again the people followed Jesus in great numbers. He speaks of the crowds increasing (11:29), of many thousands gathering together so that they "trod upon one another" (12:1), and of multitudes accompanying him (14:25). Since Luke used this mission to Jerusalem as a focal point about which to organize many sayings and stories of Jesus, apart from a consideration of their original context, it is difficult to evaluate the character or extent of Jesus' popular following in Perea. On the other hand, Mark states also in his introductory statement concerning this journey that beyond the Jordan crowds came together unto him again (10:1).[7] All things considered, it would seem that there was a renewal of popular interest in Jesus, not as great as in the busy days in Galilee but considerable even so.

Jesus' work among the people during this last-journey ministry

[6] These words do not appear in Luke in this context but are found on the lips of Jesus at the Last Supper, where a similar (or the same?) controversy develops (22:24-27). Cf. Luke 9:46-48.
[7] Cf. Matt. 19:2.

does not seem to be different from his earlier endeavors. He continued to heal and to teach as he had done before, with the teaching activity in the foreground. The note of intensity which is found in Jesus' words to his disciples at this time appears in his public utterances likewise. He said that it was an evil generation that insisted upon signs and failed to read *the sign* of his presence and preaching in their midst (Luke 11:29).[8] He urged them to be prepared for the coming of the Son of man with their loin girded and their lamps burning (Luke 12:35-40). He warned them not to take their goodness for granted in the reference to the falling tower of Siloam, and urged them not to procrastinate in repentance in the parable of the fig tree which was cut down finally because it bore no fruit (Luke 13:1-9). Again, he encouraged them to "strive" to enter by the narrow door for many would seek to enter and would not be able (Luke 13:24-30).[9] In addition to these admonitions Jesus insisted that the people count the cost of discipleship before undertaking it, lest they fail to follow all the way because they were not prepared for what it required. To illustrate this point, he referred to the builder who was ashamed because he could not complete the tower he had begun since he had not figured fully as to its cost, and to the king who suffered defeat at the hands of an enemy because he had not estimated the fighting force necessary for victory before the battle was undertaken (Luke 14:28-33). And finally, Luke tells us Jesus counseled men to keep praying and not to faint, in the parable of the unjust judge (18:1-8). These are sobering teachings for a sober time and reflect the resolute purpose of Jesus during these days.

The journey to Jerusalem was marked also by frequent contact with the Pharisees in the account which Luke gives, and Mark confirms this partially by including in the Perean ministry the test question which this religious group asked Jesus concerning divorce (10:2-12). On two occasions Jesus was invited to dine in the home of a Pharisee. One of these was the time when he did not indulge in the ceremonial washings and spoke out concerning the need to cleanse

---

[8] Matthew (12:39) gives this teaching an earlier setting.
[9] Matthew (7:13) has a parallel to these verses in the Sermon on the Mount.

the heart from which evil sprang (Luke 11:37-41).[10] Then followed the "woes" against the Pharisees in an analysis of the weaknesses of their system and practice, as well as Jesus' words to the people condemning the hypocrisy of these religious functionaries. Later, the Pharisees warned Jesus that Herod was seeking to kill him, but he was not concerned with this word. The end was near in any case and soon he would be finishing his course (Luke 13:31-32). The telling of the parables of the lost sheep, the lost coin, and the prodigal son belongs to this period in Jesus' ministry also, according to Luke, who says that they were called forth by the murmuring of the Pharisees because Jesus ate with sinners (Luke 15).[11] And lastly, the Pharisees asked Jesus when the Kingdom was to come, a question which led him to say that it was in their midst, or within them (Luke 17:20-21).[12] The earlier break with the Pharisees is confirmed by these later contacts en route to the Holy City. In fact, there is revealed in these meetings an intensifying of the tension between them along the way.

III

At the heart of Luke's account of the journey to Jerusalem is a section of the teachings of Jesus which fitted significantly the need of the hour for preparation to meet the difficult days ahead (Luke 12). Many of these words are recorded by Matthew within a variety of settings (16:6, 10:26-33, 12:31-32, 10:19-20, 6:25-33, 6:19-21, 24:43-44, 24:45-51, 10:34-36, 16:2-3, 5:25-26), and some of them are to be found in the Gospel of Mark in a different context also (8:15, 8:38, 3:28-29, 13:11, 10:38). With an unusual sense of drama Luke made them a part of the Perean ministry. He seems to regard these words as an attempt of Jesus to inoculate his followers against discouragement when the testing hour at Jerusalem arrived. Then they would not fall away through disillusionment. Being forewarned they would find themselves forearmed.

[10] Matthew (23:25-26) includes this teaching in the account of the last week in Jerusalem. Cf. also Luke 14:1 ff.

[11] Matthew (18:12-14) places the giving of the parable of the lost sheep in Galilee just prior to the trip to Jerusalem and following Caesarea Philippi.

[12] Matthew (24:23, 26-27) and Mark (13:21) locate this teaching during the final week in Jerusalem.

What are some of these teachings by which Jesus hoped to fortify his followers for the future? At the outset he warned them against hypocrisy, since there would be a temptation to keep their allegiance to him a secret when the enmity of the nation's leaders was heaped upon him. It would be little use to dissemble, however, for "nothing is covered up that will not be revealed, or hidden that will not be known" (Luke 12:2). Even those secrets which are whispered behind locked doors shall be broadcast from the housetops.

Another temptation in their tomorrows would be to hold back because of fear, especially a fear of death. In a most tender way Jesus spoke to them of God's minute concern for their welfare. If he cares for the sparrows which fall—and he does—he will surely stand by his own children in their need. God's love for them was based on his detailed knowledge of their situation, knowledge as specific as though he had numbered the hairs of their heads. In any case they should not fear those who can harm their bodies only, but who have no control beyond that over their eternal destiny. They should fear God instead, fear in the sense of profound respect and trust. The antidote for an unhealthy fear of man was a healthy fear of God (Luke 12:4-7).

There was yet a more threatening temptation than any previously mentioned which would plague soon the followers of Jesus. They would be tempted to turn a deaf ear to the Spirit of God speaking in their hearts. To deny the truth deliberately would be an easy way to escape the necessity of facing up to its painful consequences, come what may. But if one did this insincere thing again and again and again with persistent and dogged refusal to admit what he knew to be true, he would lose the capacity to recognize the truth. There was no surer way to destroy the moral nerve than this. It was certain to be sucidal. Jesus called it the sin against the Holy Spirit and said that it would not be forgiven (Luke 12:8-10). This was not because God would cease ever to be loving, but because the sinner would lose the power to see his sin and therefore could not repent. Forgiveness for Jesus was not a canceling of the evil record which God would or would not effect, as he chose. Rather, forgiveness was a restored personal relationship between God and his child, in which both must participate.

At this time, also, Jesus foresaw the probability that his followers would be arrested and brought before judges because of their loyalty to him (Luke 12:11) .[13] They should not become distraught, he told them; it would be given them what to say in such a crisis. The Holy Spirit would be their teacher and, therefore, their replies would come from God. These words of Jesus were a great comfort to the church during the days of persecution. It was a promise that they would not be alone in the time of trial.

Another important thing to remember in the future, Jesus said, was that worry was fatal. The birds, the lilies, and the fragrant grass of the field received trustfully what God gave them day by day. This the disciples must learn to do also. Anxiety was not foresight; rather it was futility. No one has ever added to the span of his life through trustless fear. God knew already what they needed, Jesus told them, and he was prepared to give them the Kingdom and all else besides, if they would but seek it (Luke 12:22-34).

These words of promise concerning God's providential care must not be taken, however, to imply that living was to be without its difficulties. Jesus, therefore, turned back again to a prognosis of the future. He pictured broken homes and severed personal relationships as men and women took sides in the issue of the Kingdom. "Do you think that I have come to give peace on earth?" he asked. "No, I tell you, but rather division." (Luke 12:51.) [14] Here was a choice which all must make and which could not be sidestepped. Yes, they must and they would make a stand, and a costly stand it would be.

An important element in the background of these serious teachings of Jesus during the southward journey to Jerusalem was his conviction that in the events which were transpiring, as well as in others which were to come, judgment was taking place. Men were on their way to face the judge at that very moment, he believed. In no uncertain terms he counseled them to make peace while there was yet time, saying (Luke 12:58-59):

As you go with your accuser before the magistrate, make an effort to settle with him on the way, lest he drag you to the judge, and the judge

---

[13] "Before the synagogues and the rulers and the authorities" the *wording* of this passage may reflect later developments.

[14] Matthew (10:34) has this in a more pictorial form: "I have not come to bring peace, but a sword."

hand you over to the officer, and the officer put you in prison. I tell you, you will never get out till you have paid the very last copper.[15]

The settlement Jesus had in mind was not a compromise, but rather a full dedication to the Kingdom as an expression of God's will on earth even as it was in heaven.

IV

When Jesus and his company recrossed the Jordan River near Jericho, they were in the territory of Judea. This meant that they were not far from Jerusalem, and Jerusalem represented the suffering and death which he anticipated. There was a finality in this fact which Mark as an author does not miss in the account he presents. As the party was leaving Jericho, Jesus was recognized dramatically as the Messiah by a poor blind beggar named Bartimaeus, whom he healed (10:46-52).[16] "Jesus, Son of David," he called him. Although the rulers of the nation were soon to deny Jesus the right to this title, Bartimaeus did not hesitate to use it.

At this point in the narrative Luke places the conversion of Zacchaeus, a chief publican, who was much hated by the people. The very qualities which had made him efficient in his business were in evidence as he climbed a tree to see Jesus. Even though he was short of stature, he would not be denied a look at this man who had gained already a reputation for fairness in his dealings with tax collectors. Jesus responded enthusiastically to Zacchaeus' interest and invited himself to dine with the outcast. He cared little that there would be self-righteous men in the crowd who would murmur that he had become a guest of a sinner (Luke 19:1-10).[17] Before the interview had ended, Zacchaeus looked into the face of Jesus with wholehearted sincerity and offered to restore fourfold from his great wealth all that he had secured dishonestly. He volunteered, in addition, to give half of his goods to the poor. Because of this change of attitude Jesus called him a true son of Abraham. The salvation of the Messiah had come to his house.

[15] Matthew (5:25-26) places these words in the Sermon on the Mount.
[16] Matthew (20:29-34) suggests that *two* blind beggars were healed as Jesus left Jericho. Both called Jesus the Son of David. Luke (18:35-43) holds that the healing occurred as Jesus was *entering* Jericho. He too includes the messianic title.
[17] The healing of Bartimaeus would account for the crowd.

QUESTIONS FOR DISCUSSION

1. Luke has a dramatic conception of the last-journey ministry of Jesus as he makes his way to Jerusalem. Review this account (9:51–18:14) noting the literary impressiveness of the narrative.

2. Prepare an imaginative narrative of Jesus' last visit to Capernaum using situations and ideas which you regard as having historical probability, even though they are not found in our records.

3. Describe the mood or temper of Jesus during the southward journey, illustrating your points with reference to the gospel narrative.

4. What would you say to the person who held that Jesus was somewhat morbid in his preoccupation with death at this time?

5. The prophets experienced what has been referred to as the "dark night of the soul." Compare Elijah's experience (I Kings 19:1-18) and also Jeremiah's (Jer. 20) with Jesus' facing of the dark future. What basic differences among them do you note? Which one of them seems most to have found a significant meaning in his experience?

6. What impression do you think Jesus' last-journey teachings made upon the disciples, the people, and the Pharisees? Which of these three groups was in a position to understand him best? Why?

7. How does Jesus show a moving combination of tenderness and severity during this journey? Do you find a conflict here in his point of view.

8. In what way do the variations among the Matthaean, Markan, and Lukan accounts of this journey, as noted in the footnotes, illustrate the difficulties one faces in constructing a closely-knit chronology of the life and ministry of Jesus?

SUGGESTIONS FOR READING

I. The Lukan idea of a last-journey ministry for Jesus

Crownfield, Frederic R. *A Historical Approach to the New Testament.* New York: Harper & Brothers, 1960. Pp. 147 ff.

Manson, T. W. "The Sayings of Jesus," *The Mission and Message of Jesus,* Major, Manson, and Wright, New York: E. P. Dutton & Company, 1938. Pp. 276 ff.

Manson, William. *The Gospel of Luke.* New York: Harper & Brothers, 1930. Pp. 119 ff.

Taylor, Vincent. *The Life and Ministry of Jesus.* Nashville: Abingdon Press, 1955. Pp. 156-65.

II. The Lukan idea of a last-journey ministry for Paul

Foakes-Jackson, F. J. *The Acts of the Apostles.* New York: Harper & Brothers, 1931. Pp. 183-84.

Rackham, R. B. *The Acts of the Apostles.* Boston: Gorham Press, 1912. Pp. 373-74.

III. The Perean ministry of Jesus

Beck, Dwight M. *Through the Gospels to Jesus.* New York: Harper & Brothers, 1954. Pp. 242-57.

Goguel, Maurice. *The Life of Jesus.* New York: The Macmillan Company, 1944. Pp. 392-99.

Stauffer, Ethelbert. *Jesus and His Story.* Translated by Richard and Clara Winston. New York: Alfred A. Knopf, Inc., 1960. Pp. 105-8.

Warchauer, Joseph, *The Historical Life of Christ.* New York: The Macmillan Company, 1926. Pp. 221-40.

22

Last Days in the Holy City

FROM JERICHO TO JERUSALEM IS NOT A FAR JOURNEY IN TERMS OF miles. The thoughts which filled Jesus' mind, however, as he and the company which followed him walked along the road, were extended thoughts. It was one thing to set one's face in the direction of Jerusalem; it was quite another thing to decide upon a course of action which one would follow upon arrival. And it was this latter decision which concerned Jesus as he journeyed in the way. A likely reconstruction of our Lord's decision and how it was carried out based upon the record, the issue, and the historical situation is in order.

It was festival time and the eve of the Passover was close at hand. As was usual at this season of the year, pilgrims from far and wide took to the open roads en route to the Holy City. The sight of these faithful in Israel with their faces aglow in expectation of the great feast was an inspiration to Jesus. It was as their Messiah that he was making this eventful journey, and he must tell them his secret, tell them in such a way that they would not be misled. It was too much to expect that they would understand fully, and yet, he must give them something which they would remember in the days ahead. They must be told.

A plan took shape with the passing of the miles. It was a daring one because it was subject to great misunderstanding by both the Romans and the Jews. He would ride into the city as the king of the nation, not as a traditional ruler, to be sure, but nevertheless, as the one in whom the deepest longings of the past were to be realized. The Romans might regard it as treason and the Jews could conclude easily that he would rule as King David had done. He would be Jesus-Caesar in their thinking. Both judgments would be erroneous but both were likely to result.

As was the case frequently with Jesus, the Old Testament spoke to him in living terms at this significant hour of decision. One of the less prominent portrayals of the Messiah was to be found in the writings of Zechariah. He was seen there as a humble king, one whose interests lay in justice and salvation. Peace rather than war was to concern him primarily (9:9-10):

Rejoice greatly, O daughter of Zion!
  Shout aloud, O daughter of Jerusalem!
Lo, your king comes to you;
  triumphant and victorious is he,
humble and riding on an ass,
  on a colt the foal of an ass.
I will cut off the chariot from Ephraim
  and the war horse from Jerusalem;
and the battle bow shall be cut off,
  and he shall command peace to the nations;
his dominion shall be from sea to sea,
  and from the River to the ends of the earth.

This was the answer—a king who rides in humble grandeur rather than in lordly splendor. To enter Jerusalem upon a beast of burden would be a far cry from the triumphal return of a victorious ruler from the field of battle. And yet to ride thus into the sacred city could be a public announcement of his messiahship. At least *he* would know what it meant, and later they would recall the occasion, understand its meaning, and find strength in it for living in the Kingdom.[1]

It was with a definite purpose in mind, therefore, that Jesus made plans with a friend in a village near Jerusalem to borrow an ass upon which to ride into the city. Just who this person was and how the agreement was reached, we are not told in the Gospels. This much only is said: "And when they drew near to Jerusalem, to Bethphage and Bethany, at the Mount of Olives, he sent two of his disciples, and said to them, 'Go into the village opposite you, and immediately as you enter it you will find a colt tied, on which no one has ever sat; untie it and bring it.' If any one says to you, 'Why are you doing this?' say, 'The Lord has need of it and will send it back here im-

---

[1] It is said sometimes that the Christian Church discovered the Zechariah prophecy and applied it to Jesus, by way of interpreting the ride into Jerusalem, or that the prophecy itself suggested the account of the ride, which may not even have occurred. The tradition of the Triumphal Entry is firmly established, however, in all four Gospels, and Jesus' practice of turning to the Scriptures for guidance and inspiration is discernible on other occasions besides this one. Much depends upon one's total view of Jesus and upon one's particular theory of gospel origins when it comes to his judgment in such matters as this.

mediately'" (Mark 11:1-3).[2] When the two disciples did as they
were instructed to do, all turned out according to the arrangements.

I

It is the planned character of the entry which suggests that it was
messianic particularly in the mind of Jesus. There was intention and
purpose behind it. The demonstration which met him as he neared
Jerusalem was spontaneous and unorganized, but the ride itself was
the result of decision. Just what reception Jesus contemplated his
act would inspire is uncertain. Did he foresee the possibilities of a
public outburst or did he think only of what he knew he must do?
Because of the unpredictability of the popular reaction, it is not
likely that Jesus counted upon a specific response from the people;
rather, he was following the will of the Father to the very end, and
that will, as he saw it, called for an announcement to Jerusalem that
her Messiah was visiting her.

When the two who had been sent into the village brought the ass
to Jesus, his followers placed their garments over its back to provide
a saddle. Then Jesus mounted the small animal and the humble procession began to move. The disciples followed, at first with bated
breath and uncertain emotion. Could this be that for which they had
been waiting? Had it happened at long last? Step by step their enthusiasm increased as they whispered excitedly to one another. They
were afraid to be too outspoken lest they be chided once more by
Jesus and compelled to restrain themselves. And yet it seemed to be
taking place before their very eyes. Jesus was riding as Jehovah's
King. It was impossible for them to hold back their joy which
showed itself on their faces and was reflected in their excited movements.

The people along the road noticed soon the stirrings in the group
surrounding Jesus. Excitement attracts a crowd invariably, and by
this time the disciples were openly enthusiastic. It did not take much
time to draw together a large number of people from the pilgrim

[2] The village of Bethany is familiar, but the site of Bethphage is uncertain,
known only from statements in the Talmud as located on the edge of the city.
Matthew (21:1) names only Bethphage. The order of mention in Mark is
irregular, since Jesus would have reached Bethany first as he approached
Jerusalem.

throng, people whose hearts were stirred already by the prospect of entering Jerusalem for the celebration of the Passover feast. For many days and nights these loyal Jews had contemplated this moment. Around the evening fires and in small groups during the daytime they had joined in singing the Songs of Ascents (Pss. 120–134). Such words as these had been inspiring them to rejoice in the goodness of Jehovah and to contemplate deliverance from their enemies:

> I lift up my eyes to the hills.
>   From whence does my help come?
> My help comes from the Lord,
>   who made heaven and earth.
>   (Ps. 121:1-2)

> I was glad when they said to me,
>   "Let us go to the house of the Lord!"
> Our feet have been standing
>   within your gates, O Jerusalem!
>   (Ps. 122:1-2)

> Pray for the peace of Jerusalem!
>   "May they prosper who love you!
> Peace be within your walls,
>   and security within your towers!"
>   (Ps. 122:6-7)

> As the mountains are round about Jerusalem,
>   so the Lord is round about his people,
>   from this time forth and for evermore.
>   (Ps. 125:2)

The expectant attitude which these songs had awakened in the Passover pilgrims found a moving stimulus in the figure of Jesus as he rode in humble dignity along the way. Many who looked upon him that day had seen his deeds of mercy and healing in Galilee during the early ministry there. They remembered and rejoiced. Spontaneously they burst forth in shouts of praise, placing their clothes on the road in front of him, according to the custom when royalty passed, and waving branches before him which they had broken from the bushes beside the way, this latter act also being customary in the presence of rulers and nobility.

It was not by act alone that they honored Jesus on that eventful day of his life. They found fitting words to express what they felt concerning him, likewise, and cried out: "Hosanna! Blessed be he who comes in the name of the Lord! Blessed be the kingdom of our father David that is coming! Hosanna in the highest!" (Mark 11:9-10) .[3] Luke and Matthew are more explicit than Mark in reporting that the pilgrims ascribed messianic prerogatives to Jesus in their praise (Luke 19:38; Matt. 21:9) . In Luke the words of the multitude were: "Blessed be the King who comes in the name of the Lord!" and in Matthew they cried: "Hosanna to the Son of David!"

As Jesus heard the words of the multitudes and saw their moving expressions of adoration and praise, his spirits were lifted. He knew that they did not understand fully what all of this meant to him, but they were paying tribute to his ministry and thus glorifying the heavenly Father. In their voices he heard the Jewish nation pay him honor and in their plaudits he was convinced that God was recognizing him as the Messiah. Lifting himself to the full dignity of his person, Jesus rode toward the gates of Jerusalem. His eyes were gazing toward the Father because his thoughts were there also. The Messiah was coming to his own city.

Luke (19:39) tells us of an attempt at this time by the Pharisees to induce Jesus to discourage this public display of loyalty. There was danger in such an exhibition. "Teacher, rebuke your disciples," they said. These leaders faced the possibility that the Romans might regard this outburst as treasonable and curb their privileges, even to the point of denying them the right to control their own practice of religion, including the celebration of the feasts. For this reason Jesus was urged to quell the demonstration. But he would not do it! The heavenly Father and all the cosmic forces of the universe were behind it. "If these [the people] were silent, the very stones would cry out."

II

Upon entering Jerusalem, Jesus went directly to the Temple. The Messiah must go to the House of Jehovah first of all because the

---

[3] Cf. Ps. 118:26.

Temple was historically *the* place of prayer for the nation. As a boy of twelve, Jesus was stirred deeply upon his first visit to this sanctuary. The enthusiasm of youth was his even yet as he looked about its sacred precincts. The house of his Father was home to him. It was the end of the day and he could not remain long. He would return tomorrow when the activities were in full swing, heightened by the coming of the faithful who were crowding into Jerusalem from the surrounding Mediterranean world for the Passover.

Jesus spent the night in Bethany, a village only a short distance from Jerusalem (Mark 11:11).[4] He was a guest probably in the home of Mary and Martha.[5] It was difficult to secure lodging in the city and to visit his friends was a helpful experience indeed. The loneliness of the great was bearing down upon him. There was strength in friendship such as could be found in Bethany.

Early the following morning Jesus and his disciples started toward Jerusalem again. They passed a fig tree by the side of the road and stopped to pick some figs. Finding none upon the tree, the Gospels state, Jesus cursed the tree, saying, "May no one ever eat fruit from you again" (Mark 11:14). The next day the disciples discovered that the tree had wilted and, remembering Jesus' cursing of it, they were impressed greatly. When they called Jesus' attention to its condition, he urged them to have faith in God, speaking at length concerning the power of positive trust and counseling them to pray expectantly (Mark 11:20-25). The incident raises some questions for the thoughtful reader. It seems unlike Jesus to curse an impersonal entity, and it was not the season for figs. Attempts have been made to explain the situation by noting that figs on a tree left over from the former year would ripen as the new leaves came out in the spring, and, therefore, some fruit might have been expected. While this takes care of the botanical aspects of the story, it does not answer the question as to why Jesus would curse a tree.[6]

When Jesus arrived at Jerusalem he went to the Temple at once,

---

[4] Luke (21:37) notes that Jesus spent his nights on the Mount of Olives rather than in Bethany.

[5] It has been held by some, however, that Jesus stayed in the home of Simon the leper in Bethany.

[6] It is possible to regard the entire incident as a parable on the moral obligation to bear fruit. Jesus' mind was much engrossed at this time with the prospect of the issue of his own sacrifice at Jerusalem.

anticipating an uplifting fellowship in worship with his disciples and
the visiting pilgrims. But what he found moved him more to protest
than to pray. The environment resembled that of a market place, no
less, where the noise of the animals being sold for sacrifice drowned
out the chanting of the priests, and the odor of the refuse turned the
fragrance of incense into a stench. Added to this was the clatter at the
tables of the money-changers where the worshipers exchanged their
various coins for temple tokens (Tyrian money of silver), as they
prepared to make their payments into the ecclesiastical treasury.
They were not permitted to contribute the assorted and variable
coinage from abroad.[7]

As Jesus watched these procedures in the temple area a deep
indignation rose within him, such indignation as belongs to the
"terrible meek." This was not the first time that he had witnessed
them but, somehow, he saw them in a new light. As one who was
about to give his life for the people, this business in worship seemed
callous exceedingly. Always the prophet at heart, he found here the
same crass materialism which Amos and Isaiah had cried out against
so eloquently in words that were, even yet, sounding down through
the years (Amos 5:21-24; Isa. 1:10-17). This particular sin of his
nation's leaders was of concern to Jesus as a Jew; it was important
especially to him, also, because as the Messiah he felt a responsibility
to those who wished to worship at the Temple, desiring thereby to
draw into closer union with the heavenly Father. Nothing could be
allowed to come between the humble worshiper and the God he was
seeking, not even the temple procedures themselves.

With determined movements Jesus overturned the tables of the
money-changers and released the sacrificial animals and doves. Dramatically, John's Gospel says that he made a whipcord and drove
those who were responsible outside the Temple. This was not
primarily an act of physical violence; rather it was the power of
moral indignation that emptied the sacred place of the traffickers.

---

[7] Klausner, op. cit., p. 314, calls attention to the fact that the Talmud states
that booths for the sale of pigeons and doves were not in the Temple but in
"the hill of anointing," i.e. the Mount of Olives, but adds: "In Jesus' time the
Sadducee-Boethuseans controlled the temple, and they may not have treated the
outer court as too holy to permit the sale of doves and pigeons or of money-
changing for the purchase of seals for the various temple offerings; and such
may have been allowed in the Herodian basilica to the south of the outer court,
the site of the present Mosque el-Aska."

The raised arm was more than a material weapon of attack. Had it been this only, there were many who would have turned upon Jesus. They might have attempted to resist his physical strength, but they were unable to face his anger of soul, an anger that was devastating because it was utterly selfless. Those who were using the Temple as a short-cut to places beyond were stopped, also by Jesus: "And he would not allow any one to carry anything through the temple" (Mark 11:16) .[8]

The Temple was built for worship. This is what Jesus meant when he said on this occasion: "Is it not written, 'My house shall be called a house of prayer for all the nation'? But you have made it a den of robbers" (Mark 11:17). These quoted words are found in Isaiah, where they are a part of a prophecy holding out hope to the eunuchs and proselytes under the coming rule in Jerusalem following the return from exile (Isa. 56:7). Both were members of neglected groups and both were fearful of their situation in the new day. The prophet assured them that Jehovah cared and that they would have their rightful status. The Temple was intended as a place of prayer for all. In the context within which Jesus used these words from Isaiah, they are most appropriate. It was the common people who were suffering from the temple system. Even as the Sabbath had come to be an end in itself at the hands of the Pharisees, just so, the Sadducees had caused the Temple and its procedures to become the master and not the servant of men. This constituted out and out robbery. Worship and prayer apart from the machinations of the temple leaders—this was the issue when Jesus cleansed the Temple.

III

The entry of Jesus into Jerusalem brings us face to face with the problems of chronology. This is his first and last visit to the Holy City, according to the Synoptic Gospels. It should be inquired, however, whether one as greatly interested in the traditions of his nation as Jesus would not be likely to have sought out the seat of those traditions long before the very close of his ministry.[9]

---

[8] The Mishnah forbids this also. Berakoth 9. 8.

[9] Goguel suggests that Jesus entered Jerusalem not a few days before his final Passover, but in September or October at the Feast of Tabernacles, and remained there until December at the time of the Feast of Dedication. After this he

Actually the Synoptic Gospels themselves contain statements of Jesus which infer that he did visit Jerusalem on more than one occasion. Matthew gives us a saying in which Jesus cries out with great emotion: "O Jerusalem, Jerusalem, killing the prophets and stoning those who are sent to you! *How often* would I have gathered your children together as a hen gathers her brood under her wings, and you would not!" (Matt. 23:37). This suggests more than one visit to the city. Luke has preserved another word of Jesus which implies more than one, likewise. He notes that when he approached Jerusalem at the end, he wept over it, saying, "Would that even today you knew the things that make for peace! But now they are hid from your eyes" (Luke 19:42). If this were Jesus' only ministry to the city during his entire public service, such tears would have been premature. It would appear, then, that the Synoptic record of one visit only to Jerusalem is incomplete. There were others, possibly, which these writings do not give us.

The Gospel of John, on the other hand, mentions several visits to the Holy City. Jesus attended the Passover (2:13), at the beginning of his ministry, at which time he cleansed the Temple.[10] The next Passover found him in Galilee (6:4) where he remained, choosing not to make the journey. When the Feast of Tabernacles arrives, however, he visited Jerusalem again (7:14), and was still there at the Feast of Dedication (10:22). A final trip to Jerusalem was made for the next Passover (11:55). There he met his death at the hands of the Jews. The chronology in John, therefore, involves three Passover feasts, only two of which Jesus attended, and one Feast of Tabernacles and one of Dedication, for which Jesus went to Jerusalem.

To determine the length of Jesus' ministry on the basis of this data is difficult. The Synoptic Gospels do not give us the complete record, as we have seen; and if we follow their lead, we may conclude that the period of his teaching and preaching covered a time span of

---

retired to Perea and did not return to Jerusalem until several days before the end. The Fourth Gospel plays a large part in Goguel's chronological reckoning.

[10] The Synoptic Gospels place the cleansing of the Temple at the close of Jesus' ministry. This position is preferable to that found in the Gospel of John. It is more logical to assume that this would come at the close of Jesus' ministry as a culmination of his prophetic challenge rather than at the outset. Cf. G. H. C. Macgregor, *The Gospel of John*, "Moffatt Commentary Series," p. 64.

about a year. The Gospel of John, on the other hand, is more interested in drama than in strict chronology. The great feasts it mentions are introduced to provide the background for Jesus' major
teachings, without too much concern for an outline of events. If,
however, we take them and the notations regarding Jesus' attendance
as factual, we may estimate that his ministry lasted somewhat over
two years. Traditionally a three-year ministry has been suggested,
due largely to the mention of the three Passover feasts in the Gospel
of John.

The order of events during Jesus' final week in Jerusalem, according to Mark, is as follows: Immediately after the Triumphal Entry,
Jesus visited briefly the Temple and returned to Bethany that same
evening (11:11). En route to Jerusalem the next day he noticed a
fig tree without fruit and cursed it (11:12-14). Upon his arrival in
the city he cleansed the Temple, driving out those who bought and
sold within its sacred precincts (11:15-18).[11] That night he left
Jerusalem again, going (presumably) to Bethany (11:19). The day
following on their way to Jerusalem, Jesus and his party passed the
fig tree, and notice was taken of the fact that it had withered (11:20-
25). Once again Jesus went to the Temple, where open argument
with the religious leaders followed (11:-27–12:40). Jesus observed,
also, the sacrificial giving of the widow who placed her mite in the
offering box (12:41-44). He predicted then the destruction of the
Temple (13:1-2). Later, sitting on the Mount of Olives, Jesus spoke
at length concerning the end of the age (13:3-37). At this juncture
Mark says that it was two days before the Passover, and tells of the
anointing of Jesus at Bethany, and of the arrangements Judas made
to betray him (14:1-11). This is followed by the account of the
Last Supper "on the first day of Unleavened Bread, when they sacrificed the passover lamb" (14:12-25). The prayer retreat in Gethsemane, the arrest, the trial, and the Crucifixion are next presented
(14:26–15:47), leading up to the Resurrection (16:1-8).[12]

[11] Because of the fact that the money-changers were scheduled to set up their
tables in the Temple between Adar 25 and Nisan 1, it may be that the Temple
was cleansed from two to three weeks before the Crucifixion rather than on the
traditional date at the beginning of the final week. This would call for an
adjustment in Mark's chronology.

[12] In Matthew the Jerusalem ministry covers two days. Luke does not emphasize the division into days.

QUESTIONS FOR DISCUSSION

1. Where was the triumph in the Triumphal Entry:

   a) In the plaudits of the crowd?

   b) In the joy of the disciples?

   c) In the heart of Jesus as he held steadfastly to his purpose?

2. To what extent was this outcry of praise from the crowd the result of conviction and to what extent was it group suggestion?

3. It has been pointed out by some that the riding of this ass which had not yet been broken called for considerable skill on Jesus' part. Does this fact imply anything in particular concerning Jesus' capabilities?

4. By way of summary, what did this entry into Jerusalem mean to Jesus, to the disciples, to the crowd, to the religious leaders among the Jews?

5. If Jesus had at no time proclaimed himself to be the Messiah publicly, what would have been the results in the church which announced that he was? Would the church's claim have been discredited, or was its conviction that Jesus was the Messiah so deep-seated that whether or not he had announced that he was would have made little difference?

6. The section at the close of the chapter is concerned with chronology. It indicates the difficulties of the historian in arriving at an accurate order of events for the ministry of Jesus due to the fragmentary character of the Gospels. Because of this fact does it follow that the portrait of Jesus as presented in the tradition is unhistorical essentially? To what extent does accurate personality portrayal depend upon precise chronology?

7. Would the cleansing of the Temple have been more characteristic of the personality of Jesus had it come at the beginning rather than at the close of his ministry? Explain fully. Do you regard this as a type of action which one would undertake twice?

8. What practices, if any, in the life of the church today correspond with the Sadduceean trafficking in the Temple?

SUGGESTIONS FOR READING

I. The Songs of Ascents which the Jerusalem pilgrims were accustomed to sing

   Abingdon Bible Commentary. Nashville: Abingdon Press, 1929. Pp. 586-93.

   Leslie, Elmer. *The Psalms.* Nashville: Abingdon Press, 1949. Selected readings.

II. The messianic character of the Triumphal Entry

   Goodspeed, E. J. *Life of Jesus.* New York: Harper & Brothers, 1950. Pp. 163-65.

Klausner, Joseph. *Jesus of Nazareth*. New York: the Macmillan Company, 1929. Pp. 308-9.

Taylor, Vincent. *The Life and Ministry of Jesus*. Nashville: Abingdon Press, 1955. Pp. 187-89.

III. The nonmessianic character of the Triumphal Entry

Craig, Clarence T. "The Problem of the Messiahship of Jesus," *New Testament Studies*, ed. E. P. Booth. New York and Nashville: Abingdon-Cokesbury Press, 1942. P. 103.

Lowrie, Walter. *The Short Story of Jesus*. New York: Charles Scribner's Sons, 1943. Pp. 157-60.

IV. The character of the trafficking in or near the Temple

Branscomb, B. Harvie. *The Gospel of Mark*. New York: Harper & Brothers, 1937. Pp. 202-6.

Manson, William. *The Gospel of Luke*. New York: Harper & Brothers, 1930. Pp. 218-19.

Rollins, W. E. and M. B. *Jesus and His Ministry*. Greenwich, Conn.: The Seabury Press, 1954. Pp. 213-17.

V. The chronology of the ministry of Jesus

Goguel, Maurice. *The Life of Jesus*. New York: The Macmillan Company, 1944. Pp. 233-52.

Macgregor, G. H. C. *The Gospel of John*. New York: Harper & Brothers, 1929. P. xii.

Stauffer, Ethelbert. *Jesus and His Story*. Translated by Richard and Clara Winston. New York: Alfred A. Knopf, 1960. Pp. 6-8.

23

The Final Conflict

THE LAST WEEK IN JERUSALEM BROUGHT THE ENMITY OF THE religious leaders toward Jesus to its climax. In the cleansing of the Temple he had confronted them in their own domain, not in the privacy of seclusion but publicly before the many hundreds of pilgrims who had come to Jerusalem for the feast. Self-appointed prophets dared not oppose the religious hierarchy and expect to escape rigorous censure. Jesus was to be no exception to this rule.

It was a direct question which the chief priests and the scribes and the elders put to him: "By what authority are you doing these things, or who gave you this authority to do them?" (Mark 11:28). The form in which they phrased their question indicates the authoritarian character of the religion they represented. It was the authority of office and position which counted most with them. Although it was as the Messiah that Jesus had opposed the temple system, his reason for doing so was prophetic. It was not their right to officiate which was in question, but rather their immorality as they changed worship into a matter of buying and selling, justified by pedantic, legalistic requirements. In this they were no longer priests but thieves, depriving the people of an experience of free worship and prayer.

In replying to their question Jesus used the method of counter-questioning. He interrogated them in return, thus placing the responsibility for sincerity upon them. He said: "I will ask you a question; answer me, and I will tell you by what authority I do these things. Was the baptism of John from heaven or from men? Answer me." (Mark 11:29-30.) They were in a quandary. If they replied that John's baptism was from heaven and vindicated in this fashion John's position as a prophet, Jesus would answer, "Why do you not follow me, then, since John pointed me out as the Messiah?" On the other hand, if they disowned John, they would draw the ire of the crowd upon themselves because the common people regarded John as a prophet. Caught thus between the horns of a dilemma, they claimed not to know the answer to Jesus' question. Their insincerity was evident in this obvious evasion and Jesus refused to say more.

I

The Pharisees and some of the Herodians put another question to Jesus during these last days in Jerusalem. The previous attempt of the Jews to lead Jesus into a statement by which they could accuse him had failed. This one might succeed, they hoped. It was presented with clever accents of praise for Jesus' fearlessness: "Teacher," they said, "we know that you are true, and care for no man; for you do not regard the position of men, but truly teach the word of God" (Mark 12:14). These were praiseworthy sentiments if they were sincere. A person of less insight might have shown considerable susceptibility to this flattery and have given the desired reply to the question which followed: "Is it lawful to pay taxes to Caesar or not?" Not so with Jesus. He recognized the trap, for trap it was. If he had said "no" to their question, they would have had him arrested for political treason. On the other hand an affirmative reply would have sent them to the people with words of ridicule against Jesus. "He sets himself up as your leader yet he advocates subservience to an idolatrous government," would have been the charge. Either answer would have placed Jesus in a difficult situation. What could he say?

Turning to the group, Jesus asked for a coin on whose surface the image of Caesar had been imprinted. Then he inquired whose visage it was. When told that it was Caesar's, he said, "Render to Caesar the things that are Caesar's, and to God the things that are God's" (Mark 12:17). Mark records that they were amazed at him. Not only was his answer above reproach politically, as far as Rome was concerned; but it was sound religiously also. There was an area in which Caesar had a right to make claim to loyalty even as there was one in which God could with justice expect obedience. Caesar had given the Jews good roads, courts of justice, police protection, and considerable freedom. To govern in this way was costly, and a tax was justified as a means of securing revenue with which to defray the expenses of government. On the other hand, God had bestowed upon his children the gift of life itself and had, in addition, surrounded them with love and constant care. They were in his debt beyond their ability to pay. To him they should give their allegiance and deepest affection.

This is one of the few remarks of Jesus concerning political matters. He seems to have avoided deliberately all questions dealing with a philosophy of government. One reason may have been that he did not wish to give occasion for misunderstanding in an area where his messiahship might be interpreted largely in political terms. Another possibility was that for him the kingdom of God was a universal corporate life above any and all political lines. Governments were not unimportant but they were not as significant as the Kingdom. History has vindicated Jesus' decision in this regard. Great states have risen and fallen through the centuries, but the reign of God remains.

A third question was asked Jesus by the Sadducees during these days. It concerned the case of the woman who had married seven brothers in succession. "In the resurrection whose wife will she be?" they inquired. They thought that here was a situation so ridiculous as to discredit belief in the resurrection of the dead. Jesus replied very simply that God's power was equal to this seemingly impossible state of affairs, a fact which the Sadducees had not faced. Their basic view of God was too limited. Besides this, their understanding of Scripture was at fault. As far back as Moses and the burning bush, Jehovah had revealed himself as a God of the living and not of the dead when he called himself the God of Abraham, Isaac, and Jacob, even though these worthies had died many years before. (Mark 12:18-27.)

In the midst of all this questioning Jesus turned to the leaders of his nation with a question of his own (Mark 12:35-37) .[1] They were standing in the Temple where he had been teaching. Referring to a psalm in which the author (assumed to be David) had called the coming Messiah his Lord (Ps. 110:1), Jesus asked how could the Messiah then be regarded as David's son, implying that Lordship was superior to Davidic sonship. The question together with the quotation resembles the rabbinical type of argumentation and is unlike Jesus' usual method of speaking. It may well be a tradition that represents what the Christian church was saying in the fifties rather than what Jesus said in A.D. 30. On the other hand, Jesus may have been turning from his usual type of utterance to the characteristic Jewish form of argumentation in order to meet them on their own

---

[1] The passage does not name actually those to whom the question was put, but the character of the interrogation is such that it suggests persons in authority.

ground. The point of Jesus' question would seem to be that he wished to turn them from traditional thinking regarding himself. The title "David's son" suggested a type of Messiah that Jesus had abrogated. It was too political in character and implied an earthly rule and kingdom rather than the nonpolitical kingdom of God.

II

At this juncture in the record of these events, Matthew presents Jesus' denunciation of the scribes and Pharisees in a somewhat lengthy series of utterances (Matt. 23:1-36). That all of these words were spoken during the last week in Jerusalem is improbable. Luke places many of them earlier in Jesus' ministry (Luke 11:46; 11:52; 11:39-42, 44, 47-51). Matthew's practice of grouping the sayings of Jesus at intervals in his gospel may account for their appearance in this manner at this time. It is not unlikely, however, that an open break such as these denunciations represent took place during these days in Jesus' ministry. Tensions were great and the issue between Jesus and the religious leaders was sharply drawn. Under these circumstances an open clash was inevitable. As was suggested in an earlier chapter these statements of Jesus directed against the scribes, Pharisees, and lawyers must not be regarded as angry name calling but as prophetic diagnosis of the sins of the saints.[2]

The final conflict in Jerusalem called forth from Jesus several significant teachings. Among them was the parable of the vineyard (Mark 12:1-12). In one sense this is a religious epitome of history which recalls God's futile attempts to win his people to himself throughout the centuries by sending prophets and teachers to arouse them from their indifference. Almost in desperation he decides to send his son, saying, "They will respect my son." But in this he was mistaken for they killed the son even as they had maltreated those who had preceded him in this ministry of reconciliation. The final act of disloyalty, God could not disregard. The Kingdom would be taken away from the Jews and given to others, presumably the Gentiles. In some respects this statement is more of an allegory than a parable for each of the several figures in it—the vineyard owner, the husbandmen, the servants, the son, and the "others"—represents a particular person or group of persons. In any case the meaning

[2] See p. 232.

and application is clear. Jesus is warning his own generation of the dire results that will befall them if they turn from him as the Son whom the Father sent finally to win them, after a succession of other attempts had failed.[3]

A second parable of Jesus which is found within the setting of these last days is that of the ten maidens, five of whom were wise and five of whom were foolish (Matt. 25:1-13). Matthew alone reports this parable. Its place during the period of final conflict is logical, for it was intended to alert the faithful to the necessity of preparedness for the hour of revelation when Jesus would return from heaven. Proceeding on the principle that to be forewarned is to be forearmed, Jesus suggested that his own should not lose their enthusiasm during the days ahead for they could not be certain as to what hour he would appear. In referring to his return at the very time of his death, Jesus was giving a supreme expression of his faith that the Father would vindicate the Messiah. The early church which held to Jesus' literal second coming found in this parable encouragement to persevere during days of disillusionment and suffering. It could not forget the sorrow of the five maidens who missed the wedding procession because they had allowed the oil in their lamps to run out. Among the Jews weddings were regarded as sacred especially, even to the point of relaxing certain religious obligations to allow one to attend.[4] This parable is of interest to us apart from its main teaching because once again Jesus is represented as a bridegroom.[5]

The parable of the talents represents yet another teaching which both Matthew and Luke locate toward the close of Jesus' ministry (Matt. 25:14-30; Luke 19:11-27).[6] Here the responsibility for investing one's abilities in the service of the Kingdom is illustrated graphically. And along with this Matthew includes the parable of the last

[3] There is a strong likelihood that the present "form" of this parable owes much to the Christian community who put it to apologetic use, but this does not mean that Jesus did not view his place in history much as the parable suggests, and that he made this clear during these final days at Jerusalem.

[4] Cf. Berakoth 2. 10

[5] Cf. Mark 2:18-22.

[6] We are considering the parable of the talents (Matthew) and the parable of the pounds (Luke) as essentially the same. Luke locates it just prior to the final entry into Jerusalem, while Matthew places it within the last week. A talent was worth about a thousand dollars, while a pound would be valued around twenty dollars.

judgment (Matt. 25:31-46), which teaches clearly that there will be a final reckoning at which time one's service to the Messiah, either directly or through kindness to his brethren, will determine his ultimate and eternal destiny. In all of this Jesus is sharpening the issue at the very time that the outcome of his own ministry as Messiah is reaching a razor-edge denouement.

III

The experience of facing the cross was a challenge to the faith of Jesus. On the slopes of Mount Hermon he had met the inevitability of death as the Father's will, and when he accepted this way, his countenance was illumined with the brightness of heaven. Before him lay the journey to Jerusalem and the days of teaching and preaching which remained. Now however, the final hour was at hand. What had been a matter of prospect was an immediate fact.

Under circumstances such as these faith may falter and expire. On the other hand, it may flare up as a flame and burn more furiously than before. And this is what happened in the soul of Jesus. He looked at the Temple as it stood in its beauty and grandeur. The disciples had commented upon its great stones. Here was a structure which appeared able to outlast time itself. But it would not! Jesus saw clearly that it was doomed to fall. A new order and a new day were at hand. The Messiah's kingdom would supplant the outworn system of the past. He would raise up a new temple of the spirit. He turned to his disciples and announced: "Do you see these great buildings? There will not be left here one stone upon another, that will not be thrown down" (Mark 13:2).[7] Faith was expressing iself, a triumphant faith in the future. God would act!

Jesus then proceeded to extend his faith beyond the destruction of the Temple and out to the ultimate victory of the Kingdom. Before the end, he told them, there would be disturbances in nature, and a persecution of his followers, who would be brought into the presence of governors and kings for judgment. In all of this, however, they would not be alone; the Holy Spirit would counsel them. And finally

[7] John's Gospel has preserved an interesting reflection of this saying. Jesus is represented as saying, "Destroy this temple, and in three days I will raise it up" (2:19). John adds that Jesus spoke of the temple of his body. The new worship would not center in a building but in a Person.

the Son of man would come with great power and glory. The exact hour of this consummation was unknown even to himself. Only the heavenly Father knew. Mankind's responsibility was to be ready, to watch lest the coming find men sleeping.[8]

In forecasting the coming of the Son of man whom he identified with himself, Jesus was asserting his faith in the final advent of the Kingdom. Just as in his ministry the Kingdom was related to his person, so at the end of the age he would make it finally real with his presence. Jesus, it would seem, believed that the kingdom of God and himself were linked together inseparably. He would die shortly at Jerusalem, but this would not be the end of his ministry. Instead, it would be the enlargement of his service.

IV

As the last week in Jerusalem drew to a close, Judas Iscariot, one of the Twelve, made arrangements to deliver Jesus into the hands of the Jewish religious leaders.[9] Betrayal is an evil act always, for it means the denial of love and a breach of personal confidence. This is true especially when the love is such love as Jesus held for his own, and the confidence such confidence as existed between Jesus and the Twelve. Men have speculated from the very first concerning the betrayal act of Judas. Very early in the church it was regarded as having been foretold in scripture.[10] A leading motive behind this conception may have been to save the sovereignty of God. It *seemed* that Judas' act had thwarted the ministry of God's anointed, and thus God himself had been outdone. His power had been challenged and his love obstructed. Hence the insistence of the church in that early day that the betrayal of Jesus by Judas did not take God by surprise, but was rather a part of a foreordained drama of redemp-

[8] This analysis of Jesus' message is based largely on the Markan account of the threefold apocalyptic tradition (Mark 13, Luke 21, Matt. 24). Matthew in particular gives a heightened apocalyptic touch to this material. It is held usually that in the text itself the words of Jesus are mingled with a Jewish apocalypse belonging to sometime before the destruction of Jerusalem.

[9] Why this was necessary is not clear. Jesus was a well-known public figure. It may have been that Jesus' private place of prayer in the Garden of Gethsemane was unfamiliar to the rulers at the Temple.

[10] See Peter's sermon at Pentecost: "Brethren, the scripture had to be fulfilled, which the Holy Spirit spoke beforehand by the mouth of David, concerning Judas who was guide to those who arrested Jesus . . ." (Acts 1:16-20). Cf. Mark 14:21; Luke 22:22.

tion—this explanation sought to give meaning to a situation that was tragic in its impression, even as it was tragic in fact.

Along with this interpretation of the betrayal of Judas, somewhat contradictorily, the New Testament holds Judas responsible personally for his dark deed.[11] If it were a part of God's plan that one named Judas Iscariot would betray the Messiah, then Judas, it would appear, could not have helped himself. It would have been mechanically foreordained, and his act would have contributed actually to the salvation of the world. Under these circumstances it is difficult to see the justice in insisting upon the guilt of Judas. A more considerate interpretation suggests that God was not taken by surprise when evil in the human heart made a stand against love. It was the nature of an evil personal will to do this, and whether it were evil in the will of Judas or in the soul of somebody else, the inevitability of the dark outcome was the same. In this sense one might say that betrayal was foreordained truly.

When it comes to Judas, however, the reason for *his* betrayal of Jesus must be sought in his own personal situation. And we are left here with practically no data for reconstructing the case. Some have claimed that he was a thoroughly evil person, but it is unthinkable that Jesus would have called him into his inner circle or that he would have responded had this been true. Others have suggested that Judas did not intend actually to betray Jesus, that he was impatient with his Master's slowness in announcing himself and sought only to place him in a position where he would be forced to do so, or else to face defeat. This is a plausible suggestion. A further idea on the part of some is that Judas began as an idealistic and enthusiastic disciple, one of the very best, but that he could not keep heart in the face of the tragic turn of circumstances. As Jesus met rejection, Judas became a prey to evil men. Such experiences are not unusual. Yet another theory is that Judas sold out when he discovered that Jesus was not going to be the traditional earthly ruler. At least he would get some return out of the misadventure. This too is a possibility.

In the betrayal of Judas we are face to face with the breakdown

---

[11] Mark 14:21: "For the Son of man goes as it is written of him, but woe to that man by whom the Son of man is betrayed! It would have been better for that man if he had not been born."

of a personal life, one that was basically fine and sensitive. The sui-
cide which followed his realization of what he had done marks him
as a person who cared. He could no longer live with himself because
he had betrayed his friend.[12] Whether it was weakness, ambition,
emotional sickness, frustration, or any other of the many states of
the human soul, the result was the same. It ill befits one to stand
smugly in the presence of Judas with an accusing finger. It remains
for men to be deeply thoughtful and exceedingly humble as they
consider his act. To the very end, Jesus was loving in his attempt to
hold on to Judas. He gave him the sop at the Last Supper, a custom
reserved for the honored guest, in order to assure Judas of his concern for him.

V

It was under the cover of secrecy that Jesus made preparations for
a final fellowship meal with his disciples before he was separated
from them.[13] The time that was left had all but run out and a few
last words with his close companions were needed. Jesus knew that
Judas had made contact with his enemies. They would be closing in
upon him at any time, and he did not wish to be interrupted until
these hours with his own were ended. Arrangements had been made
quietly to secure a room for the meal and the two disciples who
were dispatched to Jerusalem were told that they were to follow one
bearing a pitcher of water. He would lead them to the place of meeting where they were to make ready for the evening fellowship.
(Mark 14:13-16.)

As they gathered about the table the occasion outwardly was not
unlike many others when they had eaten with Jesus. The element of
secrecy may have added a tenseness to this particular situation, and

[12] There are two distinctly different traditions concerning the death of Judas
in the New Testament. One has it that he hanged himself (Matt. 27:3-5), and
the other suggests that he fell headlong and was disemboweled (Acts 1:18).

[13] Notice should be taken of the difference between the date of the Last Supper
in the Synoptic Gospels and in the Gospel of John. In the latter the meal occurs
as a memorial fellowship on the evening before the Passover supper, the evening
of Thursday, Nisan 13 (which is the beginning of Nisan 14). Jesus was crucified
the day following at the time when the Jews were killing their paschal lamb. In
the Synoptic Gospels, however, the Last Supper is regarded as the Passover meal
itself, eaten on the evening of Thursday, Nisan 14 (which is the beginning of
Nisan 15).

the seriousness of Jesus may have been more marked than at other times, but otherwise the fact that they were eating together was not unusual. Although the Synoptic Gospels identify the meal with the Passover feast, many of the elements which went with such an occasion are not mentioned in the description of the supper. A brief review of the procedures followed at the Passover meal will show that it was decidedly ritualistic, calling for certain foods which are not indicated as being present on the table when Jesus ate with his disciples for the last time before his death

A cup of red wine, mixed with water, was poured for each guest. . . . and over it a blessing was spoken. . . . The Paschal table, with its appropriate viands, was then placed in position. These comprise the lamb, the bitter herbs. . . . and the *harōseth,* a paste of dates, raisins, etc., with vinegar, which was held to represent the mortar of Egypt, and salt water. The president of the company took some of the bitter herbs, dipped them in salt water, ate a portion the size of an olive, and gave a similar portion to his companions. A second cup of wine was now poured out. . . . After this the president explained the significance of the feast. . . . The first part of the Hallel (Pss. cxiii, cxiv) was sung, and the second cup of wine drunk. . . . One of the two unleavened cakes was broken, and pieces containing between them bitter herbs were, after dipping in the *harōseth,* handed to each one. . . . After this the Paschal lamb was eaten, a third cup of wine filled, a blessing said and the cup drunk. . . . There remained another cup to be drunk . . . the second part of the Hallel (Pss. cxv-cxviii) was sung; and the feast ended with a benediction.[14]

All of this appears to be quite elaborate when compared with the account of the Last Supper in the Gospels.[15]

What did Jesus hope to accomplish as he sat about the table with his disciples? There was much confusion still in the thinking of this group. They had not yet grasped the interpretation of the Kingdom

[14] "Passover" in Hastings, *Dictionary of Christ and the Gospels.*

[15] For this and other reasons some scholars prefer to regard the Last Supper as a fellowship meal rather than as the Passover feast. It remains an open question as to whether a number of the activities described would have been permitted by Jewish law on the first day of the feast. These include such matters as the carrying of arms on a feast day, the purchase of spices for embalming the body of Jesus, the trial, and the Crucifixion itself. All things considered, it would seem that the Johannine date is preferable. Cf. G. H. C. Macgregor: *The Gospel of John* "Moffatt Commentary Series," pp. xiii-xiv: "The balance of evidence is strongly in favor of John's date."

which he had given them. Ambition was clouding their vision as they pictured themselves in positions of authority. Luke indicates that a dispute arose among them that very night as to which of them was to be regarded as the greatest. To meet it Jesus said (Luke 22:25-27) :

The kings of the Gentiles exercise lordship over them; and those in authority over them are called benefactors. But not so with you; rather let the greatest among you become as the youngest, and the leader as one who serves. For which is the greater, one who sits at table, or one who serves? Is it not the one who sits at table? But I am among you as one who serves.

The Gospel of John tells of Jesus' washing the feet of the disciples as they sat about the table. This too would correct their pride, especially when he said, "If I then, your Lord and Teacher, have washed your feet, you also ought to wash one another's feet. For I have given you an example, that you also should do as I have done to you" (John 13:14-15). It is possible that in the absence of a servant who would have washed the feet of all as a matter of custom, the disciples were too proud to perform the menial task. Their refusal gave Jesus an opportunity to teach this lesson.

Another need in this last hour was to strengthen certain individuals who were facing terrific temptations. One of these persons was Peter. His confusion during these days was obvious to Jesus. Always a person of sensitive feeling, Peter had not missed the tide of tensions that was enveloping them all. Secretive whisperings in the market place and dark glances in the precincts of the Temple were all too evident to be ignored. Jesus had sensed Peter's desperation, and knowing the man, foresaw the storm that lay before him. He decided to tell him, and did so, that rough days were upon them, that he would be sorely tempted to disclaim any connection with the band of disciples and—this is the unthinkable part of it—that he would deny any knowledge of Jesus himself. At the same time Jesus added that he had prayed for Peter and that he was convinced that this disciple would find his soul again, return to his first loyalty and become the mainstay of the others. It was a bold and daring prediction, one that sent Peter to the depths of despair, and yet one that would lift him up in the days ahead.

There was yet another person in this group who stood in greater need of help than Peter. This one was Judas. Already he had made arrangements to betray Jesus by promising to lead the temple soldiers to his secret place of prayer. Even so, Jesus would not give up in his attempt to win Judas. He decided to tell them all as they sat about the table that one of them would betray him. They were shocked, stunned into silence, and then they burst into questions, "Is it I, Lord?" (Matt. 26:22).[16] Jesus hoped that Judas would feel the enormity of his deed as the disciples reacted to his statement, that he would see himself and his act in their true light. Matthew indicates, however, that even Judas joined in the questioning: "Is it I, Master?" he said. He was carrying out his intention with a gesture of innocency. The Gospel of John states, in addition, that Jesus pointed out the betrayer by dipping a morsel of bread into his own cup and handing it to Judas. This was, in reality, an expression of love toward Judas for the giving of the sop was intended customarily for the honored guest. Judas accepted it without a murmur of protest, giving the appearance of good faith. At this point John states with great insight, "Then after the morsel, Satan entered into him." The light of his soul had gone out. He continued in his determination to sin against love. John states further that Judas, after receiving the morsel went out and that "it was night."

VI

The Last Supper is remembered primarily by most Christians not for these experiences we have been considering but, instead, for the sacrament of the Lord's Supper which tradition has associated with this occasion.[17] The earliest descriptive record of this sacrament is found in Paul's first letter to the Corinthians (11:23-26) where the Apostle is attempting to shame the Corinthians for their greed by pointing to the sacrificial and unselfish spirit of Jesus as exemplified

[16] It is significant that they would have questioned their own loyalty in this fashion, indicating a feeling of insecurity in their own minds as to the fate of their undertaking and their own abilities to hold out.

[17] Strictly defined, a sacrament is a ritual in which some kind of efficacy or magical power is thought to be in the elements themselves. The word is often used however, to refer to any act which enriches life because of its particular associations and the depth of its meaning to the participants. For a consideration of the sacraments of the Christian Church see Hugh Thomson Kerr, *The Christian Sacraments,* and G. H. C. Macgregor, *Eucharistic Origins.*

in his death for them. And in doing this, Paul relates how on the night when Jesus was betrayed he "took bread, and when he had given thanks, he broke it, and said, 'This is my body which is for you. Do this in remembrance of me.' In the same way also the cup, after supper, saying, 'This cup is the new covenant in my blood. Do this, as often as you drink it, in remembrance of me.' " It is clear that in this recital Paul is repeating phrases which have achieved already a ritualistic formulation through constant repetition in the church.

The Synoptic Gospels tell of this act, likewise, in connection with their accounts of the Last Supper (Mark 14:22-25; Matt. 26:26-29; Luke 22:14-20). On the other hand, the Gospel of John omits the instituting of the Lord's Supper in connection with the final meal because John has treated it symbolically already in his sermon on Jesus as the bread of life (6:25-65). In the Synoptic accounts there are some differences in detail as well as differences in emphasis. Mark and Matthew, following Paul, stress the new covenant in the shed blood of Jesus, while Luke emphasizes the coming of the Kingdom when once again Jesus shall drink of the cup with his own.[18]

The question which must be answered here is what took place actually around the table on the momentous occasion of Jesus' final meal with his disciples. Did Jesus institute a formal sacrament which became known as the Lord's Supper, or did he perform a simple act of breaking bread and passing a cup, such as he may have done many times before, *only this time did he punctuate the act with words that referred to his death for his own loved ones?* Then did he suggest that every time his followers ate together in the future, breaking the bread and passing the cup, they were to remember him, his death, and his faith in the coming of the Kingdom? It seems to me that Jesus did not establish a *formal* sacrament, ritual and all. Rather he transformed a simple act of eating and drinking into a symbol of his death for them, something they could do everyday in their own homes as they remembered him in the days to come until he returned. If one chooses, one might call it an informal sacrament.

[18] Luke mentions the new covenant (22:20), but the emphasis is upon the future Kingdom. Some manuscripts, however, omit verse 20 altogether. If it is included, we have two cups, one in verse 17 and the other in verse 20.

Later, however, the church came to regard the passing of the cup and the bread as a formal sacrament involving a theology of redemption. By the time Paul wrote First Corinthians this sacramentarian emphasis had progressed considerably. Finally the Lord's Supper was taken out of the home and made a special service in the sanctuary, to be observed in a specific way, using a ritualistic formula, and administered by a duly ordained priesthood or ministry. As the church became sacramentarian, this development was inevitable. It was intended to preserve the meaning of Jesus' death and to make the benefits of his sacrifice available to believers.

Considerable speculation has taken place in regard to a possible relation between the Lord's Supper and the sacred meals of the Dead Sea group. The communal meal of this Essene community had a somewhat sacramental quality as the chosen brethren ate together, partaking of the bread and wine, and enjoying a ritualistic blessing. But the full meaning of the Eucharist in the early church, as Paul understood it, was missing. In the sacred meal described in the "two columns" in the Palestine Museum, probably an early phase of the Qumran Movement, the Messiah of Israel is present, but the priest who blesses the bread is given a higher place.[19] Whatever similarities that exist here are probably due to common backgrounds.

However much we may have come to appreciate the formal sacrament of the Lord's Supper, it is to be hoped that its homely and simple origin will not be forgotten. The Last Supper in the Upper Room with its intimate fellowship between Jesus and the Twelve, with our Lord's attempt to stem the mounting tide of tragedy and to surround his death with a meaning and significance by associating it with the breaking of bread and drinking from the cup—this Last Supper itself is the environment within which the Lord's Supper must be understood finally.

QUESTIONS FOR DISCUSSION

1. Do the questions which Jesus was called upon to answer concerning the source of his authority, the propriety of paying taxes to Caesar, and the nature of marital relations in the next world seem appropriate as a climax to his ministry? What type of mind would regard these questions

[19] Cf. Burrows, *The Dead Sea Scrolls* pp. 237, 332-33; Gaster, "The Dead Sea Scriptures," pp. 19-20.

as central? the legal type? the prophetic type? the practical type?

2. How does one decide what he should do when the demands of Caesar and the claims of God appear to conflict? Can you think of actual situations where this might occur?

3. How can one be a Christian within an unchristian totalitarian state? By coming to regard his principles as relatively binding only? By taking an ideal stand regardless of the consequences?

4. It was suggested that the parable of the vineyard represented an epitome of history, indicating God's attempt to save his world prior to and including the advent of Jesus. Is it possible to enlarge its scope to encompass the centuries since Jesus? How would it be interpreted if you attempted to do this?

5. In the discourse of last things (Mark 13, Matt. 24, Luke 21) separate the material according to the following headings: (1) The fall of Jerusalem; (2) The return of Jesus; (3) The end of the age. Consult the several commentaries for suggestions as to the sources of the material in these chapters.

6. If Jesus expected *literally* to return to the earth shortly after his death, thus vindicating his faith in God and the Kingdom, would you say that he was a discredited prophet since this did not occur? Or does the resurrection and the widespread enthronement of Jesus in the lives of millions of persons throughout the world constitute a greater vindication than a return on the clouds of heaven?

7. What do you think of the point of view of John's Gospel which holds that Jesus returned spiritually to indwell the lives of his followers? Is this a real return or is it begging the question?

8. Prepare a character analysis of either Peter or Judas on the basis of the entire story thus far. Why did Peter return, after denying Jesus, to strength, while Judas took his own life? Was it because Peter's act of denial was impulsive whereas Judas' betrayal was premeditated? Can you think of other reasons for the difference here?

9. How can one keep alive in his thinking the historical situation surrounding the Lord's Supper, when the churchly environment within which we celebrate it today is so different? Can this be done through teaching? preaching? Bible study?

SUGGESTIONS FOR READING

I. The conflict with the religious leaders

Johnson, Sherman E. "Matthew," *The Interpreter's Bible*. Nashville: Abingdon Press. VII, 527-41.

Klausner, Joseph. *Jesus of Nazareth.* New York: The Macmillan Company, 1929. Pp. 317-22.

Rollins, W. E. and M. B. *Jesus and His Ministry.* Greenwich, Conn.: The Seabury Press, 1954. Pp. 218-24.

II. The parable of the vineyard

Grant, F. C. "Mark," *The Interpreter's Bible.* Nashville: Abingdon Press. VII, 836-39.

Montefiore, C. G. *The Synoptic Gospels.* New York: The Macmillan Company, 1927. I, 276-79.

III. The parable of the pounds (talents)

Buttrick, George A. *The Parables of Jesus.* New York: Harper & Brothers, 1931. Pp. 240-50.

Johnson, Sherman E. "Matthew," *The Interpreter's Bible.* Nashville: Abingdon Press. VII, 558-62.

IV. The Son of David passage

Bornkamm, Günther. Translated by Irene and Fraser McLuskey, and James M. Robinson. 3rd ed. New York: Harper & Brothers, 1960. Pp. 227-28.

Bosworth, E. I. *The Life and Teaching of Jesus.* New York: The Macmillan Company, 1924. Pp. 329-31.

Branscomb, B. Harvie. *The Gospel of Mark.* New York: Harper & Brothers 1937. Pp. 222-25.

V. The Lord's Supper

Grant, F. C. *The Passion of the King.* New York: The Macmillan Company, 1955. Pp. 13-20.

Major, H. D. A. "Incidents in the Life of Jesus," *The Mission and Message of Jesus,* Major, Manson, and Wright. New York: E. P. Dutton & Company, 1938. Pp. 169-72.

Manson, William. *The Gospel of Luke.* New York: Harper & Brothers, 1930. Pp. 239-43.

Smart, W. A. *The Spiritual Gospel.* New York and Nashville: Abingdon-Cokesbury Press, 1946. Pp. 55-60.

Taylor, Vincent. *The Life and Ministry of Jesus.* Nashville: Abingdon Press, 1955. Pp. 192-96.

VI. The date of the Last Supper

Beck, Dwight M. *Through the Gospels to Jesus.* New York: Harper and Brothers, 1954. Pp. 300-301.

Macgregor, G. H. C. *The Gospel of John.* New York: Harper & Brothers, 1929. Pp. xiii-xiv.

Montefiore, C. G. *The Synoptic Gospels.* New York: The Macmillan Company, 1927. I, 308 ff.

VII. The threefold apocalyptic tradition

Branscomb, B. Harvie. *The Gospel of Mark.* New York: Harper & Brothers, 1937. Pp. 231-40.

Manson, William. *The Gospel of Luke.* New York: Harper & Brothers, 1930. Pp. 228-36.

24

The Arrest, Trial,
and Crucifixion

THE LAST SUPPER ENDED WITH THE SINGING OF A HYMN (MARK 14:26). It may have been the second part of the Hallel which they sang (Pss. 115-118). Here are moving words for such an hour as this, words with which all were familiar but which took on a special significance at this time:

> O Israel, trust in the Lord!
> He is their help and their shield.
> O house of Aaron, put your trust in the Lord!
> He is their help and their shield.
> You who fear the Lord, trust in the Lord!
> He is their help and their shield.
>
> (Ps. 115:9-11)

> The Lord is God,
> and he has given us light.
> Bind the festal procession with branches,
> up to the horns of the altar!
> Thou art my God, and I will give thanks to thee;
> thou art my God, I will extol thee.
> O give thanks to the Lord, for he is good;
> for his steadfast love endures forever.
>
> (Ps. 118:27-29)

Triumphant faith marks the sentiments of these verses. Their very familiarity brought stability into the confusion of the disciples' minds. In the years gone by they had sung them with mounting confidence. Now they were singing them in the face of uncertainty, and they were impressive in their declared faith in Jehovah. Jesus too would have responded to their reiterations of historic truth. God ruled over nations and the affairs of men. Another verse had stated (Ps. 118:9):

> It is better to take refuge in the Lord
> than to put confidence in princes.

292

He would remember this as he stood before Pilate and the princes of the Temple. Refuge in the Lord God!

From the Upper Room, Jesus and the eleven disciples made their way toward the Mount of Olives, where there was an olive orchard. We know this traditionally as the Garden of Gethsemane. Here was to be found quiet and seclusion, asylum from the clamor of the city, and therefore a place for meditation and prayer. Jesus had come to this retreat before. The olive trees had heard his prayers on more than one occasion, but never such prayers as they were to hear this night. It would be as though a great wind were sighing through their branches.

It was the cup, as he called it, from which Jesus prayed to be delivered. Need he drink it? Was it the Father's will? Could there not be another way? Three times he prayed: "My Father, if it be possible, let this cup pass from me" (Matt. 26:39). Devout men have speculated as to the contents of the cup to which Jesus referred. Some have found in it the sins of the human race. Others have suggested that it contained deep sorrow for the nation, his own nation, that had rejected her Messiah when he came. Still others have stressed the physical pain and suffering which the cross involved as the bitterest dreg in the cup. All this and more besides went into the making of its contents. The historical situation which surrounded him provides our best guidance in interpreting the cup and what it contained. Abstract theologies must be silent in the presence of the reality of what he was facing. Violent death, disappointment, an evil will in his enemies, separation from his friends, the loneliness of the truly great—this is what made the cup so dreadful, and this is why Jesus prayed to be delivered from drinking it.[1]

The entire prayer is not to be found in Jesus' petition for deliverance, however, although this part of it provides the background that gives significance to its final words: "Nevertheless, not as I will, but as thou wilt" (Matt. 26:39). After expressing his own feelings with complete frankness in such intimacy as Jesus always knew when he came before his Father in prayer, he submitted his petition to the wisdom and will of his Father for answer.

---

[1] It is to the credit of the early church that they recorded Jesus' reaction to the cup. They might have been less understanding and regarded his recoil as a sign of weakness. Such honesty contributes to our confidence in their reporting.

Jesus had taken three of his disciples, Peter, James and John, with him as he pressed farther into the garden for prayer. Companionship was comforting and strengthening besides. Having moved apart from them as he communed with his Father, he returned intermittently to speak with them.[2] It was of little use, however, for they had great difficulty in not succumbing to sleep. Grief and confusion over the strange turn of events which had befallen their walk with Jesus had taken its toll in nervous energy, and exhaustion had consumed them. Even Peter, excitable Peter, was too spent for keeping awake so that Jesus said to him: "Simon, are you asleep? Could you not watch one hour? Watch and pray that you may not enter into temptation; the spirit indeed is willing, but the flesh is weak" (Mark 14:37-38). Jesus understood, but this did not mean that his loneliness was abated.

I

The stillness on the Mount of Olives was broken by the sound of muffled voices, punctuated with the noise of clanking armor, as Judas and the temple guards drew near to the place of prayer. The account of what occurred is realistic. Judas approached Jesus and kissed him upon the forehead (Mk. 14:45; Matt. 26:49; in Luke 22:47-48 Jesus restrains Judas). There was nothing unusual in this greeting since it was a customary one between a teacher and his student. What was out of the ordinary about it this time, however, was that Judas was using it as a sign by which to point out Jesus to the soldiers. He was employing the kiss which is the symbol of affection as the seal of betrayal.

All three Gospels record that, at this point, someone drew a sword in an attempt to protect Jesus. It was a brave act against overwhelming odds, but it was a futile one. In his nervousness he missed the head of his opponent and the blow glanced to the side, cutting off his ear instead.[3] The afflicted man was a special bond servant of the high priest and, presumably, had been a leader in the arrest proceed-

---

[2] The gospel writers suggest that this happened at least three times during the vigil.

[3] John's Gospel (18:10) identifies the attacker with Peter. Luke alone states that Jesus restored the ear. It is characteristic of this writer to intensify the narrative at dramatic moments. He alone noted also that Jesus' sweat was like drops of blood (22:43-44).

ings. Matthew makes note of a statement of Jesus at this time which is significant: "Put your sword back into its place; for all who take the sword will perish by the sword" (26:52).

One thing stands out pre-eminently in the account of the arrest of Jesus. It persists also in the story of these dark hours to the very end. Jesus had found an answer through praying in Gethsemane. He was in full possession of his spirit when the soldiers interrupted with military harshness his communion with the heavenly Father. Instead of attempting an escape, he confronted them boldly, speaking courageous words: "Have you come out as against a robber, with swords and clubs to capture me? Day after day I was with you in the temple teaching, and you did not seize me" (Mark 14:48-49). They should have known of what metal he was made. A sneak arrest such as this showed clearly that not only these soldiers but the high priests also who had sent them did not understand Jesus.

The Fourth Gospel, which goes its own way at many points in telling the story of Jesus does not depart far here from the narrative in the Synoptics. It represents Jesus as taking the initiative in these circumstances, even to the point of approaching the soldiers himself and inquiring, "Whom do you seek?" Jesus suggests further that the disciples be given their freedom, since it was himself that they sought rather than the Twelve. And the disciples were not adverse to leaving. Mark says of them: "They all forsook him, and fled." [4]

II

The examination of Jesus before the high priest was tense and confused, according to the Gospels.[5] Caiaphas held the office at this time, having been appointed by the procurator Valerius Gratus.[6] He was the son-in-law of Annas, who had been a high priest also and who was known by the title still (John 18:13). John's Gospel states that Jesus was brought first before Annas. The place of meet-

[4] Mark notes also the predicament of a young man who was friendly to Jesus, and who escaped capture by stepping out of the linen cloth that was wrapped about his body (Mark 14:51-52), as they grabbed for him. He fled clad only in his undergarment. Some have suggested that this youth was John Mark himself, but this ingenious suggestion cannot be substantiated factually.

[5] There is a question as to whether this should be called a trial, since the rules for a formal trial seem not to have been observed fully.

[6] He held office for nearly eighteen years and was deposed finally by Vitellius. This was an unusually extended rule.

ing, while uncertain, may have been in the "bazaars of the sons of Hanan," on the Mount of Olives not far from Gethsemane. This Gospel indicates that Jesus was taken later to the house of Caiaphas. The Synoptic Gospels, however, know only the questioning before Caiaphas.

As witnesses were brought to testify, it was found that there was considerable disagreement among them concerning the evidence. Words that Jesus had spoken relative to the destruction of the Temple were remembered, but there was no unity of report. Throughout the argument he remained silent, so much so, that it became noticeable and the high priest said to him: "Have you no answer to make? What is it that these men testify against you?" But it was of little use. One does not waste words in the presence of minds that are closed by blind prejudice. Finally the high priest asked him outright, "Are you the Christ, the Son of the Blessed?" Here was an opportunity to make a forthright messianic claim, and Jesus took advantage of it, saying, "I am; and you will see the Son of man sitting at the right hand of Power, and coming with the clouds of heaven" (Mark 14:62). The response of the high priest was immediate. Jesus had made a claim which, under the circumstances, appeared to be sacrilegious. He had assumed identity with an office that was reserved for the Chosen One. It was nothing short of the spirit of blasphemy! [7] The chief officer tore his garments, crying, "Why do we still need witnesses?" They found him deserving immediately of death.

Before taking Jesus to the court of Pilate for a civil trial, the temple soldiers, presumably the same ones who had arrested him in the garden, made sport of him. It may be assumed that the high priest and his followers were preparing themselves for the trial which would follow, thus providing an interval during which these indignities took place.[8] They blindfolded Jesus and after striking him asked him to name the one who had struck him. Sarcastically they chided that a true prophet should be able to do this. They spat in his face besides and humiliated him without mercy.

During the arraignment before the Jewish officials, a sad figure of

[7] Jewish scholars assert that to claim to be the Messiah was not to be guilty of blasphemy actually.

[8] It is possible that this sportive action is but another version of that which the Roman soldiers perpetrated later (Mark 15:16-20).

a man moved uncertainly in the courtyard of the high priest's house. It was Peter. Although it had been but a few hours earlier that Jesus had told Peter he would deny him three times before morning, it seemed to be ages ago.[9] So much had happened since then. The final words of Jesus on that occasion were heartbreaking words for Peter. Death, separation, the announcement of a traitor in their midst, and the prophecy of denial had been sufficient almost to unseat his reason. And then there had been the hours in the Garden of Gethsemane, hours of great fatigue and consternation for the disciples, which were ended rudely by a noisy band of soldiers from the temple guard. When one had sought to defend Jesus with his sword, the brave gesture had been rejected with strange words about taking the sword and dying by the sword. The prospect of the Messiah refusing to allow his followers to fight for him was unthinkable. Little wonder that Peter's world had fallen to pieces, and little wonder also that in the chill of the high priest's courtyard he refused to reveal his identity as one of Jesus' disciples when the question was put to him three times, even swearing with an oath that he did not know this man. His final word of denial and the realization that it was morning came at one and the same moment. Luke states that at this very time Jesus, who had returned to the courtyard, looked at Peter and the disciple remembered and went out weeping bitterly.[10]

III

The court of Pilate was a civil court. In its decisions the voice of Rome was heard. Certain judicial rights had been granted by the state to the Jewish courts, but others had been withheld from them as being beyond their domain. Among the latter was the right of capital punishment when it concerned a political felon (John 18: 31).[11] Pilate himself did not have a good reputation. He was re-

[9] The words "before the cock crows" may be taken as a colloquial expression meaning before morning, although Mark concludes that Jesus meant an actual crowing cock (Mark 14:72).

[10] It is significant that the early church preserved a tradition regarding the denial of Jesus by a leader in the movement of such stature as Peter. Evidently the facts were too well known to be ignored, and the restoration of Peter to his honored place in the church too great a witness to the lordship of Jesus to be neglected.

[11] This is a debated question, but it seems unlikely that the Jews would have taken Jesus to Pilate for sentencing, had they had the right to sentence him themselves.

garded as greedy, cruel, and unyielding. Appointed procurator of Judea in A.D. 26 by Tiberius, he was removed from office in A.D. 36 because he had governed badly. His distaste for the Jews can be seen clearly in the New Testament references to the trial. The feeling between them was mutual.

Luke records that Jesus was charged on three counts by the Jews, as they brought him before the Roman court—he perverted the nation, forbade the payment of taxes to Caesar, and claimed himself to be a king (Luke 23:2). Each was a political crime. The latter was the most serious of the three. Pilate therefore asked him outright: "Are you the King of the Jews?" and Jesus replied "You have said so," meaning, "I am" (Mark 15:2).[12] According to the Synoptic Gospels these are the only words spoken by Jesus in the presence of Pilate. The Gospel of John, however, represents Jesus as being more willing to speak on this occasion. He interprets the kingship he has just claimed for himself as being of a spiritual nature. He is a king of truth. (18:33-38.)

From this point on, as the story is told, the issue became one between Pilate and the Jews rather than one between Jesus and the state, Pilate attempting to release Jesus, and the Jews holding fast to their demands for his death. It may be concluded that Pilate was impressed with the nobility of Jesus, that something fine within himself, which he had regarded as dead long since, stirred into life as he stood in the presence of this Galilean. He desired, therefore, to free him if possible. Again, it may be decided that Pilate was being careful lest a judgment against Jesus would lead to an uprising on the part of this teacher's followers. If he could release him, therefore, and pacify the Jews at the same time, he would have kept Roman order and preserved the peace. Still another alternative is that the favorable attitude of the Procurator toward Jesus was written into the record by the evangelists themselves, in order to place the responsibility for the death of Jesus upon the Jews and, at the same time, convince the Greco-Roman world that the Lord of the Christians was not regarded as being anti-Roman. Through the years the first of these alternatives has been the one most widely held. Scholars

[12] For a discussion of the meaning of Jesus' reply here, words that have been interpreted variously, see Harvie Branscomb, *The Gospel of Mark*, pp. 285-88. Branscomb concludes that Jesus was noncommittal.

have not been unmindful, however, of the historical possibilities resident in the remaining two.

One of the gestures by which Pilate sought to be relieved of the necessity for passing judgment upon Jesus was to send him to Herod for sentencing (Luke 23:6-12).[13] Instead of sentencing him however, the ruler tried to induce Jesus to perform a miracle. When Jesus refused, Herod and his soldiers made fun of him, "arraying him in gorgeous apparel" in order to ridicule his supposed claims to kingship. Evidently Herod was not impressed with the danger of Jesus' becoming a revolutionary leader.

The Gospel of John records a second attempt of Pilate to free Jesus. The soldiers scourged him, placed a crown of thorns upon his brow, and draped a purple robe about his shoulders. Then Pilate brought Jesus before the people, hoping that the sight of such humiliation might lessen their desire for his death. (19:1-5.)[14] But such was not the case. When the chief priests and officers saw him they cried out: "Crucify him, crucify him!"

Finally, Pilate gave the Jews the opportunity to choose between Jesus and Barabbas, a murderer and an insurrectionist, as it was the custom at the Passover for the Jews to request the release of a criminal as an act of mercy.[15] He thought that surely they would not select such a one as Barabbas in preference to Jesus. But Pilate was mistaken, tragically mistaken. Blindness prevailed that darkest of days. Barabbas was elected for freedom; Jesus elected to die on the cross.

Even after the Jews chose Barabbas, Pilate hesitated to pass the sentence. Mark says that he asked them again what evil Jesus had done actually. The question made little impression; they would not diminish their demand for Jesus' death. The Gospel of John reports at this point that the Jews told Pilate that if he released Jesus, he was no friend of Caesar (19:12), and Mark says that in order to content the multitude he released unto them Barabbas and delivered

[13] Luke alone reports this story.

[14] The Synoptic Gospels represent this scourging and mocking as occurring *after* Pilate had finally passed the sentence of crucifixion. It was the custom of soldiers to plague condemned criminals before their execution.

[15] It should be said that this action of Pilate was very irregular, and outside the Gospels there is no other evidence that this custom existed among the Jews. This need not, however, mean that it was unhistorical. Pilate may have taken matters into his own hands in order to win the favor of the Jews in this instance.

Jesus to be crucified. It is related also that, after this, he asked for a basin of water that he might wash his hands as a sign that he was innocent of Jesus' blood (Matt. 27:24). And yet it was he who gave the final order to crucify Jesus. Whatever part that Jews played in the events that led to the crucifixion of Jesus, it was a Roman procurator who passed sentence upon him, and Roman soldiers who carried it out.

IV

Before executing the order of death imposed by Pilate's court, the soldiers scourged Jesus and then ridiculed him by doing mock obeisance before him. They had dressed him in purple robes and had prepared a simulated crown out of thorn twigs, which they pressed upon his brow. In a gesture of contempt they placed a reed into his hands as a scepter, later using it to smite him. "Hail, King of the Jews!" they shouted between spitting at him and bowing on their knees before him. This was the customary sadism which the Roman world expended upon the condemned, a burly brutality empty of human feeling. What suffering this meant to Jesus, whose sensitivity was extremely marked, can hardly be imagined.

Such treatment as Jesus received from the soldiers left prisoners frequently in a state of collapse. Besides the physical debilitation in his case, however, there were the other dregs in the cup—deep sorrow and longing for the welfare of his followers. These alone would diminish his strength, but when the violence of the scourging was added, the effect was such weakness that he could not carry the crossbar of his cross to the place of crucifixion. This was the customary procedure. Another man from the crowd of onlookers was forced, therefore, into service, one Simon of Cyrene in North Africa. He was a Jew who had in all probability come to the feast at Jerusalem. It is doubtful whether Simon had seen or heard Jesus before this, but he was never to forget him afterwards. Two of his sons, Alexander and Rufus, are named with such familiarity in Mark that it may be concluded that they were Christians in the church at Rome (15:21). It may be, also, that the details of the passion story came from these two, just as their father who witnessed Jesus' death in person had repeated them again and again. It was a never-to-be-forgotten experience that Friday morning, when Simon had been conscripted into the ugly business of a crucifixion.

Death on a cross was a tortuous experience and unsightly to see. The victim was stripped first of his clothes. When his arms had been extended to their full length, his hands were nailed to the crossbar which was fastened then to the upright already set into the hole in the earth. A peg in the upright fitted into the groin, giving some support to the body which hung from the nails in the hands. Finally the feet were nailed to the upright, and the crucifixion was done. Death came slowly in most cases. It took as long as two or three days on occasion, but usually the time was briefer. Hunger, dehydration, exposure, and the strain of suffering combined to bring the end at last. There was no privacy, no protection from insects, and no relief hour after hour. This was the prospect which lay before Jesus, the Jewish Messiah and preacher of the kingdom of God, when he was crucified between two thieves on a hill north of Jerusalem called "the Skull." [16]

V

The Gospels record seven statements which Jesus made from the cross. As no one of these writings contains all seven, it is impossible to tell in what order they were uttered. Besides this, piety has woven its flowers of prophecy and fulfillment around these words so that one cannot be sure where history begins or ends. All seven of them, however, fit the situation and are characteristic of the attitude and outlook of Jesus. Mark and Matthew tell of his cry of dereliction: "Eloi, Eloi, lama sabach-thani?" meaning, "My God, my God, why hast thou forsaken me?" (Mark 15:34; Matt. 27:46). These are the opening words of the twenty-second psalm where they represent a sob of anguish on the part of one who has borne more suffering than he feels he can stand. As Jesus used these words, however, he was not quoting scripture but was expressing his own sense of desolation in the phrases he had learned as a boy, phrases which helped now to carry his heartache to God. Plagued by passers-by who

[16] The exact location of Golgotha (Aramaic meaning "skull") is unknown and is beyond recovery probably. Wars and excavations have changed the landscape beyond recognition. It is said the hill was called "the Skull" because of its peculiar shape.

wagged their heads and quoted his own words to him concerning the destruction of the Temple; harassed by the chief priests who mocked him saying: "Let the Christ, the King of Israel, come down now from the cross, that we may see and believe"; and railed upon by two thieves crucified on either side of him, Jesus tasted the final despair of life, the despair of those who feel for the moment that God has forgotten them. Yet all the while, above Jesus on the placard placed there by Pilate as naming his crime, were the words "the King of the Jews."

Luke has preserved for us three additional words of Jesus which were spoken from the cross. In the first he prayed for the forgiveness of his persecutors (23:34), and in the second he promised life in Paradise to one of the two thieves who had asked to be remembered when Jesus came in his kingly power (23:43). The ministry of the Messiah was continuing even as he was dying. The third and final word of Jesus from Golgotha, which Luke has given us, is represented as the very last word which he spoke. It is this: "Father, into thy hands I commit my spirit!" (23:46).[17] It was uttered with a loud voice, and the hour was three o'clock in the afternoon (the ninth hour).[18] Darkness had fallen upon the hill since noon, blending well with the heaviness in the hearts of many who looked on, including some women, Mary Magdalene, Mary, the mother of James and of Joses, and Salome. These may have been among the women to whom Jesus had spoken earlier this same day, as he struggled toward the skull hill, urging them not to weep for him but to pray for strength with which to meet the future (Luke 23:27-31).

The Gospel of John contains three words more of Jesus which the author locates in the setting of the cross. In the first Jesus placed his mother into the keeping of one called "the disciple whom he loved" (19:26-27). Some, but not all, regard this person as John, the brother of James. The second word is a cry of the flesh: "I thirst" (19:28). Although this writer does not present the word of dereliction and despair found in Mark and Matthew, he does tell us of Jesus' deep physical need. Because of the fever and intense perspiration which comes with crucifixion, Jesus asked for liquid and they

---

[17] Mark and Matthew each represent Jesus as crying out in a loud voice just before he died, but they do not tell what he said.

[18] Mark represents the Crucifixion as having begun at 9:00 A.M. Darkness fell upon the scene at noon, and death came at 3:00 P.M.

gave him sour wine on a sponge.[19] Previously he had refused to take the usual pain-deadening drink, wine mixed with myrrh, which they offered customarily to those who were being crucified (Mark 15:23). The third additional word which John's Gospel records is represented as Jesus' final one before death. It is a word of triumph: "It is finished" (19:30). And with this he bowed his head and gave up his spirit.

There are other details in the gospel accounts of the death of Jesus, some of which are in the manner of the time, and others which are poetical symbols of the cosmic significance of this day in history. The soldiers whose responsibility it was to nail Jesus to the cross were given, as a part of their pay, Jesus' undergarments for which they cast lots (Mark 15:24).[20] The centurion who was in command that day, however, received more than material remuneration for his services. To him was granted insight to see the greatness of Jesus. Observing his majesty in death, he said, "Truly this man was a son of God!" (Mark 15:39). It is unlikely that this statement was intended to name Jesus as the Messiah, or that it was an attribution of deity in the sense of the Christian creeds which were to come later. Instead, it was a witness probably to this soldier's conviction that Jesus was a divine being who had come to walk among men as the gods of the Romans were said to do on occasion.

Some reported that the curtain of the Temple was rent in two from top to bottom, supernaturally, on that fateful day (Mark 15:38). Others related that a great earthquake shook the earth, laying bare the graves so that the bodies of many saints rose up and moved to and fro (Matt. 27:51-53). Such accounts reveal the experience of the human heart in the presence of a tremendous event.[21]

QUESTIONS FOR DISCUSSION

1. Judging from the actions of the disciples in the Garden of Gethsemane, it would seem that Jesus' words to them in the Upper Room had made little impression. Can you explain this fact? Was it because they

[19] Cf. Psalm 69:21. The similarity here is circumstantial rather than prophetic.
[20] In the Gospel of John (19:24) this is regarded as another instance of fulfilled scripture, although the procedure was a usual one.
[21] Cf. F. C. Grant, *The Earliest Gospel*, pp. 175-87 for a textual study which attempts to get behind the Markan account of the arrest, trial, and Crucifixion of Jesus, in order to find the earliest tradition.

were so set in their own thinking that they did not hear Jesus actually? Were they ignoring an ugly truth by acting as though it were not true? Or were they too nervously exhausted to respond to the dark situation?

2. In praying to be delivered from the cup, was Jesus attempting to change God's mind, or was he making sure that he had read correctly his intuitions that death was inevitable? Is this latter procedure Christian or should one follow his spiritual intuitions blindly?

3. What did Jesus mean when he told the disciples to pray lest they be tempted sorely because the spirit was willing but the flesh was weak? Did he mean that physical fatigue or instinctive drives can affect the self, or that the self can help to control our bodily activities? Might the interaction of mind and body work either to our strength or to our weakness?

4. Why did the temple soldiers arm themselves heavily when they went forth to arrest Jesus? Were they afraid of Jesus or unsure of themselves? Could it be that they feared a rebellion from Jesus' disciples?

5. In the examination and later the trial before the high priest, why was Jesus silent mostly? Was it because he was sure already of the outcome and felt it was useless to speak out, or was it due to the fact that he did not regard the inquiry as a sincere attempt to gain the truth? Or was he seeking to fulfill the scripture which said (Isa. 53:7):

> Like a sheep that before its shearers is dumb,
> so he opened not his mouth.

6. Why did Jesus admit to Pilate that he regarded himself to be a king, knowing that what he was saying had all the earmarks of treason upon it? Was this intended to be a public witness before a Roman magistrate and, as such, important to Jesus officially, or did he hope that Pilate would give serious heed to his utterance?

7. How do you explain Pilate's attempt to free Jesus? Fear? Political expediency? Appreciation for Jesus? Dislike of the Jews?

8. Why was the crowd moved so easily by the religious leaders to call for the crucifixion of Jesus? Fear of their overlords? Mob hypnotism? Dislike of Jesus? Craving for excitement? Were these the same people who welcomed him as the Messiah when he rode into Jerusalem shortly before this?

9. Be prepared to argue the case that the Romans were responsible for the crucifixion of Jesus rather than the Jews. Point out the weakest as well as the strongest link in your own argument.

10. Do the seven last words of Jesus spoken from the cross impress you as pertinent to the situation or do they sound artificial and doctrinaire?

Relate each of them to Jesus' character as seen in the Gospels to determine whether or not they are in harmony with his character.

SUGGESTIONS FOR READING

I. The denial of Peter

Goguel, Maurice. "Did Peter Deny Jesus? A Conjecture," *The Harvard Theological Review*, XXV (1932), 1-27.

Major, H. D. A. *"Incidents in the Life of Jesus,"* The Mission and *Message of Jesus*, Major, Manson, and Wright. New York: E. P. Dutton & Company, 1938. Pp. 181-83.

II. The appearance before the high-priest—examination or trial?

Branscomb, Harvie. *The Gospel of Mark*. New York: Harper & Brothers, 1937. Pp. 277-80.

Goodspeed, E. J. *Life of Jesus*. New York: Harper & Brothers, 1950. Pp. 207-10.

Grant, F. C. "Mark," *The Interpreter's Bible*. Nashville: Abingdon Press, 1951. VII, 887-91.

Taylor, Vincent. *The Life and Ministry of Jesus*. Nashville: Abingdon Press, 1955. Pp. 206-9.

III. The trial before Pilate

Enslin, M. S. *The Prophet from Nazareth*. New York: McGraw-Hill Company, Inc., 1961. Pp. 187-208.

Goguel, Maurice. *The Life of Jesus*. New York: The Macmillan Company, 1944. Pp. 513-26.

Klausner, Joseph. *Jesus of Nazareth*. New York: The Macmillan Company, 1929. Pp. 345-48.

Montefiore, C. G. (ed.) *The Synoptic Gospels*. New York: The Macmillan Company, 1927. I, 360-66.

Rollins, W. E. and M. B. *Jesus and His Ministry*. Greenwich, Conn.: The Seabury Press, 1954. Pp. 244-53.

IV. Crucifixion

Josephus *Antiquities* XIII. 14. 2.

Klausner, Joseph. *Jesus of Nazareth*. New York: The Macmillan Company, 1929. P. 349.

Zeitlin, Solomon. *Who Crucified Jesus?* New York: Harper & Brothers, 1942. Selected readings.

V. The historicity of the seven words from the cross

Gilbert, G. H. *The Students' Life of Jesus*. New York: The Macmillan Company, 1900. Pp. 301-4.

Taylor, Vincent. "The Life and Ministry of Jesus," *The Interpreter's Bible*. Nashville: Abingdon Press, 1951. VII, 143.

25

The Resurrection

JESUS DIED ON THE EVE OF THE SABBATH. IT WAS ALSO THE EVE OF the Passover. Accordingly, the Jews, even those who loved Jesus, were eager to remove his body from the cross before six o'clock the very day of the Crucifixion, so that they could prepare for the Passover meal that evening.

Joseph of Arimathea, who was a counselor of honorable estate and a devout Jew, went to Pilate to secure the right to bury Jesus. He is described in the Gospel of John as a secret devotee who did not follow Jesus openly because of what his fellow countrymen might think. The tragedy of the Crucifixion, however, drove all fear from his mind, and he sought out the very official who had sentenced Jesus to death. Pilate found it difficult to believe that Jesus had died already, and withheld permission until the centurion who had supervised the Crucifixion confirmed the fact. Once this was done, he granted the corpse to Joseph.[1]

After purchasing a large piece of linen with which to incase the body of Jesus for burial, Joseph, assisted by Nicodemus (John 19:39) and others, removed him tenderly from the cross. Within the folds of the linen precious spices and herbs were inserted to embalm the body. The Gospel of John suggests that there were about a hundred pounds of a mixture of myrrh and aloes used. This implies a through embalming. Mark and Luke, however, indicate that it was a hurried burial, and regard the visit of the women to the grave on the first day of the week as for the purpose of completing the preparation of the body for its stay in the tomb.

Jesus was buried without ceremony in a sepulcher located in a garden not far from the hill of crucifixion. It was a new burial place for the family of Joseph, a walk-in tomb, large enough for entry. No one had yet been interred here. Both Luke and John make special mention of this fact, seeing in it an appropriate significance. The contamination of death had not touched it (Luke 23:53; John

---

[1] The Gospel of John relates that previously Pilate had granted the Jews the right to break the legs of the three on the crosses in order to hasten their death. This was done usually with heavy mallets. It seems cruel enough but was regarded as an act of mercy. Jesus was found to be dead already when they came to him.

19:41) .[2] Within were shelves carved out of the rock and upon one of these the body of Jesus was placed lovingly. Before the door a circular stone was rolled into position. This would keep out scavenger animals as well as thieves who made a practice of robbing graves.

As the little company left the burial garden—Joseph, Nicodemus, Mary Magdalene, Mary the mother of Jesus, and a few others perhaps—a numbed exhaustion settled upon them. They had seen it through to the very end. Conspicuous for their absence were the disciples who had fled at the arrest of Jesus.[3] Their prominence in the kingdom-of-God movement which Jesus had inaugurated made it unsafe for them to be seen. But the Romans could excuse these others their grief; and besides, their burying of Jesus relieved the officials of the necessity of performing the task.

At long last quiet covered the garden, and the fragrance of the earth rose with the falling of the evening dew. The clamor of the Crucifixion was ended and the raucous cries of angry and frustrated men were stilled. There was a peace in death after the furor of such a day.

I

The Crucifixion sounded the death knell for the hopes and expectations of the followers of Jesus. All seemed to be over, done with, finished. Not only had the dream of the Kingdom been dashed rudely to earth, but also the presence of their greatest friend had been taken from them. Loneliness and disappointment were added to their fear of further violence from the Romans. As soon as it was safe to travel, the disciples wanted to get as far away from Jerusalem as possible, to return to their homes (mostly in Galilee) where the air was free of this disease of the heart which had settled upon the Holy City even before the Feast of the Passover had begun. In the meantime they would remain in hiding.

[2] On the other hand, it was forbidden to bury in a tomb with one's fathers one who had been executed.

[3] Peter remained nearby until after his denial of Jesus in the courtyard of the high priest. John is thought by some to have been present at the Crucifixion. He may be the person referred to as "the disciple whom Jesus loved" (John 19:26) , but this is a disputed identification.

Then it happened! Some of the women[4] who had gone to the tomb early on the first day of the week to complete the embalming of Jesus' body, found the stone rolled away from the sepulcher, and saw a young man [5] seated within (Mark 16:4-5). He told them that Jesus had risen, that he was no longer in the grave, but had gone before them to Galilee. They were instructed then to inform the disciples and Peter that Jesus would meet his followers there. What did it mean? Jesus, alive? Great fear came upon the women, who fled immediately. (Mark 16:1-8.) [6]

From this point on the account of the resurrection appearances of Jesus as found in the Four Gospels is varied and disconnected. This is what one would expect, considering the nature of the event. An ordered recital of such a tremendous experience, while highly desirable from the historian's viewpoint, is hardly to be anticipated from a psychological position. It was too intense. All of the writers testify to the reality of an experience of the resurrected Jesus, but the location, the details, and the content of the experiences as reported vary.

The earliest written account of the resurrection appearances is found in Paul's first letter to the Corinthians. It appears in what seems to be a creedal statement almost, a formulation of basic beliefs within the church which Paul did not compose but which came to him from a former day (I Cor. 15:3-8):

> For I delivered to you as of first importance what I also received, that Christ died for our sins in accordance with the scriptures, that he was buried, that he was raised on the third day in accordance with the scriptures, and that he appeared to Cephas, then to the twelve. Then he appeared to more than five hundred brethren at one time, most of whom are still alive, though some have fallen asleep. Then he appeared to James, then to all the apostles. Last of all, as to one untimely born, he appeared also to me.

Some of these appearances can be paralleled with those enumerated in the Gospels, but not all. Of special interest in Paul's state-

---

[4] Mary Magdalene, Mary the mother of James, and Salome (Mark 16:1).

[5] In Luke it is two men, and in Matthew it is an angel, who informed the women of the Resurrection.

[6] The remainder of the material in Mark (vss. 9-20) was added later. The older and preferred manuscripts do not have these verses.

ment is the eyewitness atmosphere which pervades the listing. Clearly it was written at a time when many of those who experienced the Resurrection were living still. As such it remains our most significant *written witness* to these experiences. Particularly suggestive also is the fact that Paul names himself as one to whom Jesus appeared. We know something of the character of this experience, for it is described three times in the Acts of the Apostles (9; 22; 26) and referred to elsewhere in Paul's letters (Gal. 1: 15-16). If it can be assumed that Paul's experience of the risen Jesus was similar to that of the others, we have an indication that it was a spiritual and not a material presence which the disciples knew, since Paul's experience would seem to have been spiritual in character.

The Matthaean record of the Resurrection follows the first eight verses of Mark, with some heightening of detail. Then it continues on its own, but continues *in the direction of the original Markan story*. This has suggested to some scholars that the lost ending of Mark is to be found in Matthew.[7] Jesus had told the disciples (Mark 16:1-8) that he would meet them in Galilee, and Matthew's story of these days continues with a Galilean appearance on the mountain. There the risen Lord gave them the commission to evangelize the world. John's Gospel reports a Galilean experience with the risen Jesus also.[8] It is found in chapter twenty-one, a chapter which many scholars regard as an addition to the original form of the Gospel. Here the disciples discovered Jesus on the shore of the Sea of Galilee where they were fishing. As in the beginning he had called some of them from their nets, so now again, it was as they were using their nets that he met them. This chapter tells also of Jesus' reconciliation with Peter, who three times having denied Jesus, now three times affirms his love for him. One cannot help asking whether the tradition behind these Johannine stories might constitute the missing sections of Mark's final chapter. The answer to the question as to whether or not the lost ending of Mark is found in Matthew or John, however, is conjectural.

Luke, in comparison with Matthew and John, knows of no Galilean appearance of Jesus following the Resurrection. He is fa-

---

[7] E. J. Goodspeed, *op. cit.*, pp. 224-25.
[8] John 20, however, presents Judean appearances.

miliar, however, with an account of Jesus' appearance to two followers who journeyed from Jerusalem to the village of Emmaus
(24:13-35). Then he tells of the experience of the disciples who were
visited by the resurrected One as they met together in a Jerusalem
room. And finally, Luke relates that the risen Jesus led them as far
out as Bethany where he was parted from them.[9]

II

As has been said previously, the sketchy and disconnected character
of the gospel accounts of the resurrection of Jesus is not surprising.
It was to be expected that the striking nature of this event would
have been reported variously by persons of different temperaments
and dispositions. And with the passing of time, as men struggled to
find words with which to describe the experience, it is likely that the
narrative tended to take on aspects which it did not possess originally.
This explains some of the confusion within the several stories as
they now stand.

The fact that some of the writers know of appearances of Jesus
only in Judea, while others imply that they were limited to Galilee,
suggests two separate traditions coming from different sections of
Palestine. These reflect the fact that wherever the disciples went,
they found Jesus to be with them. He was known thus in Galilee
and his presence was realized, likewise, in the Jerusalem area. Each
community developed its own tradition accordingly.

Yet another contradiction in the narratives is the fact that the
resurrection experience is represented as being both spiritual and
material in character. Jesus appears and disappears at will, and
enters rooms to which the doors are locked (Luke 24:31, 36). A
material body does not act in this way within our kind of universe.
Such activity implies a spiritual reality.[10] On the other hand, the
risen Jesus is pictured as eating material food and as calling attention
to his flesh and bones (Luke 24:36-43). Basically, there is a marked
difference between these two representations, the one a spiritual

---

[9] In the Acts of the Apostles, Luke represents the resurrected Jesus as charg-
ing the disciples specifically to remain in Jerusalem (1:3-5). Cf. also Luke 24:49.

[10] One might use the words "spiritual body" if one knew exactly what such a
term meant. Paul uses it in I Cor. 15:42-50, where it implies a reality, by way of
contrast, that is the direct opposite of the material body. It was impossible for
the Jew to think of a disembodied spirit; hence there must be a spiritual *body*.

reality and the other, material. A possible explanation of this difference may be that, as time passed, language supplied material representations for what was spiritual originally. The difficulty of
describing a spiritual experience in words would contribute to this
confusion.

The statement that the disciples' experiences of the resurrected
Jesus were spiritual in character does not imply that they were
illusory, imaginary, or unreal. What it means is that they were non-
material. Consciousness, intuition, and thought are of this nature
also, yet they are very real and, subject to critical examination, we
accept them as representing life as it is. The same is true of psychical
experiences in which visions are seen and voices are heard. In the lay
mind these are thought often to be wholly pathological, but to one
acquainted with psychology these may be unusual but legitimate
forms under which the experience of reality comes. Such types of experience need to be subject to the tests of reason, to be sure, but we
should not conclude that all psychical experiences involving visions
and voices are misleading and not to be trusted. They are normal
with certain types of persons and in certain situations.

Did the disciples have an experience of the reality of Jesus as alive
within their consciousness, an intuition of his presence with them?
Or did they experience visions in which they saw him stand before
them and heard him speak? [11] Or was it a spiritual perception of
what we may choose to call a "spiritual body"? Who can say? This
much is certain. They acted in one way *before* the resurrection experience and in another and quite different manner *after* the resurrection experience. Something had happened to them which made
this difference. Frustrated, discouraged disillusioned, fearful and
filled with sorrow on Crucifixion Friday, they became jubilant,
courageous, hopeful, and dynamic on the first day of the week. The
reality of the resurrection experiences in which Jesus was known to
them as alive and possessing the magnetism and power which they
had found in him during the days of his flesh—this reality is the only
adequate explanation of the change.

[11] The question of a group's having the same vision simultaneously, as when
Jesus appeared to the eleven gathered together, presents a problem. Visions are
solitary experiences usually.

III

Among the various aspects of the resurrection stories which call for consideration is the question of the empty tomb. Without exception the gospel narratives report that the grave in which Jesus was buried was empty on that memorable morning when the women came to complete the embalming of his body.[12] And the New Testament does not record that the early Christians frequented the site as a burial shrine, which they might have done had his body been there. An inevitable question follows: What happened to the body of Jesus? Since there is no incontrovertible answer, several suggestions have been made. Joseph Klausner has concluded that Joseph of Arimathea removed secretly the body and buried it in another grave, unknown to the rest. He decided that it was "unfitting that one who had been crucified should remain in his own ancestral tomb." [13]

In Matthew's Gospel it is suggested that the priests circulated the story that the disciples came by night and took Jesus' body away (28:11-15).[14] This idea has been entertained seriously by some in our own day. It is difficult to accept because it imputes deceit to the disciples who, following the Resurrection, became preachers of great spiritual power. How could they have been so effective in their witness as preachers, and later in their testimony as martyrs, had they known they were living a lie? It would be the same with Joseph of Arimathea.

Yet another conjecture to explain the empty tomb is that Jesus did not die really. He merely swooned on the cross.[15] Later, as he lay in the grave and the aroma from the spices which had been inserted in the folds of the burial clothes reached his nostrils, he was revived. After this he left the environs of Jerusalem and went into hiding on the other side of the Jordan River perhaps. The problem in this speculation is the character of Jesus himself. His kind of person

[12] There is no way of telling whether Paul implies or does not imply an empty tomb in I Cor. 15:4. But cf. James Denney, *Jesus and the Gospel*, pp. 112-14.

[13] *Op. cit.*, p. 357.

[14] Could it be that the priests themselves had stolen the body, for fear that the tomb containing it might provide a focal point about which the followers of Jesus could unite? Cf. Walter Lowrie, *The Short Story of Jesus*, p. 220.

[15] Accounts are known of persons in the first century who were removed from a cross and resuscitated.

would not live out his days in hiding. The consciousness of a mission which took him to the cross would have driven him still on the other side of the cross. Back to the people and back to the Temple he most surely would have gone.

It has been suggested further that the women only thought they saw the empty tomb. It was an hallucination brought on by taut nerves and deep grief. In the half light of the morning and with eyes filled with tears, they experienced what they regarded as an unoccupied grave, but actually it was not thus. We are told, furthermore, that the women informed the disciples of their experience and, since these men were supposed to be expecting Jesus to rise again, they had false intimations of his presence. The problem with this view is twofold. First of all, hallucinations are but temporary experiences. In time they are shown to be unreal. In the second place, the accounts do not suggest that the disciples were expecting the Resurrection. It came to them as a surprise. They were stunned and incredulous, even to the point of expressing doubt openly (Luke 24:41). Since this is so, their experience could not have resulted from excited expectations.

What became, then, of the physical body of Jesus? The tomb was reported to be empty, and the body was not present in the resurrection experiences of the disciples, for they seem to have been spiritual experiences. This question remains unanswered.[16] Some may attempt to solve it by suggesting a speedy dematerialization or, again, a kind of evanescence.[17] Such explanations are to be regarded, however, as hypothetical finally. But the reality of the disciples' experience is not hypothetical, and here the case for the historicity of the Resurrection must rest ultimately. Whatever one concludes regarding the tomb, the primary fact is the resurrection experience.

IV

As the Gospels present it, the resurrection experience was not the seeing of a series of apparitions which filled the disciples with

[16] Some explain the empty-tomb stories as a logical deduction from the resurrection experiences of the disciples. The disciples reasoned, they say, that since Jesus was seen by them, the grave must be empty.

[17] Leslie Weatherhead, *His Life and Ours*, pp. 282-86.

wonder. Instead, what they experienced was similar in character to an interview in which Jesus counseled with them. A classic illustration of this is found in Luke's account of the walk to Emmaus (24: 13-35). It tells of an unrecognized figure who joined himself to two travelers. These were grieved at the death of Jesus and in consternation over reports that he was alive. After enlightening them concerning these things, he departed from them. They knew then that it was the Lord who had been with them. In this narrative the literary artist has woven about the traditional story which came to him a garment of verbal beauty and symmetry. The idea which he has preserved in this fashion, however, is not his own creation but belongs instead to the experience of the church. In content it says that the resurrected Jesus interprets the Scriptures for his followers, dispels their gloom and disappjointment over the recent tragic events and lifts their inner life to the level of the "burning heart." Their experience of the presence of the risen Lord renews their faith and joy, and re-establishes their courage.

Another instance of the ministry of the resurrected Jesus is found in Matthew's story of the meeting with the eleven on a mountain in Galilee (28:16-20). At this time Jesus is represented as giving the great commission: "All authority in heaven and on earth has been given to me. Go therefore and make disciples of all nations, baptizing them in the name of the Father, and of the Son and of the Holy Spirit, teaching them to observe all that I have commanded you; and lo, I am with you always, to the close of the age." It appears that the wording here is late, especially the trinitarian formula, and the world-wide evangelistic commission may reflect the missionary movement as it developed under the apostle Paul. Behind these words, however, is a conviction which goes back to the resurrection experience itself, the conviction that the preaching of the Kingdom is to continue and that the followers of Jesus should count upon his presence in their undertakings. Again we can see that there was a positive content to the resurrection experiences of the disciples.

It was these convictions, sometimes referred to as the resurrection faith, that welded the disciples once more into a dynamic union and gave a unique character to the Christian Church. The new fellowship was the old fellowship revived, with the risen Jesus at its center.

QUESTIONS FOR DISCUSSION

1. What was it that caused Joseph of Arimathea to come forward openly and reveal his loyalty to Jesus following the Crucifixion? Was he shamed by the courage of Jesus, outraged at the injustice of the trial, or incensed with the prejudice of the religious leaders?

2. Prepare a statement on the burial customs of the Jews.

3. Compare the accounts of the Resurrection in Mark (16:1-8), Matthew (28:1-20), and Luke (24:1-53).

   a) Which account shows the most literary beauty?

   b) Which account seems to be the most matter of fact?

   c) Which account appears to be most interested in the miraculous?

   d) What differences and inconsistencies do you find among the accounts?

4. Read the account of the Resurrection in the Gospel of John (chapters 20 and 21) and verify the following:

   a) Resurrection appearances in both Judea and Galilee.

   b) Emphasis upon conversation between Jesus and individuals.

   c) Assertions of belief in Jesus.

   d) An emphasis upon details in the narrative.

5. Where is the strongest evidence for the historicity of the Resurrection to be found? in the gospel records? in the origin of the Christian Church? in the fact that the New Testament was written? in the continued faith of Christians through the centuries that Jesus is alive? Explain your answer.

6. Does final belief in the Resurrection depend upon having all of one's questions concerning it answered in full? Is it unscientific to believe unless all of one's questions are answered and all hypotheses verified?

7. Be prepared on the basis of the chapter to state the following theories which attempt to suggest explanations for the empty tomb other than the New Testament representation of it:

   a) The swoon theory.

   b) The theft theory.

   c) The hallucination theory.

What do you regard as the strength and the weakness of these suggestions?

8. Review the words which the resurrected Jesus is represented as speaking to his followers in the gospel stories of his appearances to them. On the basis of these statements what would you say was the content of the resurrection faith in the early church?

SUGGESTIONS FOR READING

I. The lost ending of Mark

Barnett, Albert. *The New Testament: Its Making and Meaning.*

Rev. ed. Nashville: Abingdon Press, 1958. *Ad loc.*

Moffatt, James. *Introduction to the Literature of the New Testament.* New York: Charles Scribner's Sons, 1911. Pp. 238 ff.

Streeter, B. H. *The Four Gospels.* New York: The Macmillan Company 1952, Pp. 335-60.

II. The twenty-first chapter of John

Macgregor, G. H. C. *The Gospel of John.* New York: Harper & Brothers, 1929. Pp. 367-69.

Wright, C. J. "The Revelation of God," *The Mission and Message of Jesus,* Major, Manson, and Wright. New York: The Macmillan Company, 1941. Pp. 944-46.

III. The Synoptic accounts of the Resurrection

Branscomb, B. Harvie: *The Gospel of Mark.* New York: Harper & Brothers, 1937. Pp. 304-14.

Johnson, Sherman E. "Matthew," *The Interpreter's Bible.* Nashville: Abingdon Press, 1951. VII, 615-25.

Luce, H. K. *St. Luke,* "Cambridge Bible Series." New York: The Macmillan Company, Pp. 249-58.

Manson, William. *The Gospel of Luke.* New York: Harper & Brothers, 1930. Pp. 263-70.

IV. The Johannine account of the Resurrection

Dodd, C. H. *The Interpretation of the Fourth Gospel.* London: Cambridge University Press, 1953. Pp. 440-43.

Macgregor, G. H. C. *The Gospel of John.* New York: Harper & Brothers, 1929. Pp. 354-78.

Strachan, R. H. *The Fourth Gospel.* New York: The Macmillan Company, 1952. Pp. 324-40.

V. The place of the Resurrection in the early church

Bornkamm, Günther. *Jesus of Nazareth.* Translated by Irene and Fraser McLuskey, and James M. Robinson. 3rd ed. New York: Harper & Brothers, 1960. Pp. 180-88.

Knox, John. *Christ the Lord.* Chicago and New York: Willett, Clark & Co., 1945. Pp. 59-81.

Laymon, Charles M. *Christ in the New Testament.* Nashville: Abingdon Press, 1958. Pp. 13-17, 27-28.

Scott, E. F. *The Nature of the Early Church.* New York: Charles Scribner's Sons, 1942. Pp. 50-63.

26

Jesus as Lord

IN THE PRECEDING CHAPTERS WE HAVE BEEN CONSIDERING THE LIFE and teachings of the Jesus of history as they have been preserved for us in the Gospels. These records close with accounts of his resurrection. Luke-Acts, however, carries the story into the period of the early Christian fellowship.[1]

Why should the story of Jesus be continued beyond his death and resurrection? The answer to this question is that following the Resurrection, Jesus was regarded as present still within the fellowship of those who believed in him. As John Knox has written, "Jesus was not merely remembered and interpreted in the Primitive Church; he continued to be known there." [2] The fact is that it was because he continued "to be known" that the Christian community came into being in the first place. It existed only incipiently in the group that walked with Jesus during his earthly ministry. Following the Resurrection, however, a fellowship was created which centered in the consciousness of his continuing presence.

In a very real sense the New Testament epistles and the Revelation to John also contain the story of Jesus, even as the Gospels. He is presented in these writings as a living Lord [3] who is spiritually present in the church and who is concerned with the fortune of his followers. There was a contemporary character to this relationship, as the members of the church were conscious of it, that moved beyond what would be usually referred to as due to memory. In the unfolding panorama of the church's growth and development which these writings record, Jesus was a living factor.

I

The followers of Jesus at the first Feast of Pentecost after the Resurrection experienced the coming of the Holy Spirit (Acts 2:4).

[1] The Christian fellowship immediately following the Resurrection is sometimes referred to as the Primitive Church. It is in the first twelve chapters of the Acts section of Luke's material mainly that the account of these days is presented.

[2] *Op. cit.*, p. 59.

[3] The meaning of "Lord" will be considered later in this chapter. Cf. p. 320.

When Peter preached the sermon interpreting this event, he expressed his conviction that Jesus himself had sent the Spirit: "Being therefore exalted at the right hand of God, and having received from the Father the promise of the Holy Spirit, he [Jesus] has poured out this which you see and hear" (Acts 2:33). In this sense what is called Pentecost among Christians was an experience with Jesus. At the conclusion of his sermon Peter stated that God had made Jesus both Lord and Christ, the same Jesus who had been crucified.[4]

The continuing work of Jesus in the early Christian community may be seen, likewise, in the healing of the lame man at the gate of the Temple which was called "Beautiful." When Peter and John saw him there begging, Peter bade him walk *in the name of Jesus* (Acts 3:6). Whereupon the man stood, walked, and entered the Temple with loud expressions of praise. The crowd which gathered was amazed and looked approvingly upon Peter and John. Then it was that Peter assured them that he was not responsible for the healing. Rather, it was "by faith in his [Jesus'] name" that the man walked. As he said, "The faith which is through Jesus has given the man this perfect health in the presence of you all" (Acts 3:16). Again, Jesus is named as responsible for the event.

The first record of martyrdom in Acts tells of the death of Stephen. He was one of seven persons appointed to serve the needy among the Hellenists. As the account continues, however, Stephen became an effective speaker or debater in the synagogues where the Hellenists gathered. The impression he made was so incendiary that finally he was seized and brought before the council where he presented his defense. The result was mob violence in which Stephen was taken out of the city and stoned. In the martyr's experience during these dreadful hours, Jesus played a central part. Acts states it in this fashion: "But he [Stephen], full of the Holy Spirit, gazed into heaven and saw the glory of God, and Jesus standing at the right hand of God" (7:55). In addition, at the moment of death Stephen prayed, "Lord Jesus, receive my spirit," and added in a loud voice, "Lord, do not hold this sin against them" (7:59-60). This prayer for his enemies was not only directed to Jesus as Lord but also reflected

---

[4] Whether these words as we have them be regarded as coming from Peter himself or not, they reflect the convictions of the early church.

Jesus' prayer from the cross for his persecutors.[5] Jesus was acutely real to Stephen in this tragic experience.

II

The religious experience of the apostle Paul should be characterized as a new life "in Christ." This was his favorite phrase in describing it. To explore this aspect of Paul's experience fully would take one deep into the field of Pauline mysticism.[6] In this study, however, it is sufficient to indicate briefly the place Jesus held in the life and ministry of Paul, by way of showing the continuing influence he exerted in the developing Christian community.

The call of Paul into the service of Jesus as Lord was regarded by Luke as being of such great significance that it is related three different times in the Acts of the Apostles (9; 22:3-21; 26:2-18). In each case Paul is represented as being conscious of Jesus as a presence, personally calling him to give up his persecution of the Christians and to become his follower. When Paul wrote to the church in Galatia some years later, he referred to this experience in terms of a revelation of Christ: "But when he who had set me apart before I was born, and had called me through his grace, was pleased to reveal his Son to [7] me, in order that I might preach him to the Gentiles, I did not confer with flesh and blood" (Gal. 1:15-16). In these words Paul makes it clear that his call was a revelation of Jesus to him, and that God was the ultimate source of the revelation.

There are several instances in the course of Paul's missionary journeys that indicate further the place Jesus held in his experience as a Christian. At one point in his second missionary journey, he and his companion attempted to go into Bithynia, but Luke says that "the Spirit of Jesus did not allow them" (Acts 16:7). Here was a consciousness of prohibition which was associated with the will of Jesus. On another occasion when this missionary was fearful of his life because of the opposition at Corinth, Luke records that "the

[5] As a Jewish Christian, Stephen would be a monotheist. His prayer to Jesus could not mean that he regarded him as another God, apart from the heavenly Father. What it does suggest is that in praying thus, Stephen was finding the presence and power of God himself in his fellowship with Jesus the Lord.

[6] Cf. bibliography references at the close of this chapter.

[7] Greek "in."

Lord said to Paul one night in a vision, 'Do not be afraid, but speak and do not be silent; for I am with you, and no man shall attack you to harm you; for I have many people in this city' " (Acts 18:9-10).

In yet another situation Paul was comforted by a word from Jesus as Lord. He was in prison at Jerusalem following his arrest on the false charge of having taken a Gentile into that part of the Temple where they were forbidden to enter. Feelings against him were so marked that his life was in danger. The meeting of the council before which he was examined had disbanded in a riotous clamor. At this point Luke says that "the following night the Lord stood by him and said, 'Take courage, for as you have testified about me at Jerusalem, so you must bear witness also at Rome' " (Acts 23:11). Other Christians besides Paul were having experiences of this same character in the early church, experiences which centered in Jesus as a presence with them.

A most revealing characterization of this new life in Christ is found in Paul's distinctive word to the Galatians. It comes at the close of a section in which he has been presenting his credentials as an apostle of the Lord. "I have been crucified with Christ," he said, and then added, "It is no longer I who live, but Christ who lives in me; and the life I now live in the flesh I live by faith in the Son of God, who loved me and gave himself for me" (2:20). In these words Paul is not looking back in remembrance to the Jesus of history. Instead, he is looking to one who is his contemporary and with whose life he has identified his own; he is looking to Jesus as Lord.

Reference has been made already to the title "Lord" (ὁ κύριος) which was given to Jesus. It appears in that part of Acts which deals with the primitive church (2:36) and is found rather frequently in the Letters of Paul (I Cor. 12:3; 16:22-23; II Cor. 4:5; Rom. 10:12; Phil. 2:9-11).[8] It has been urged that the title may have its origin in the mystery religions where it signified the presiding deity. In this connection some have suggested further that it was first used by Christians in a Christ cult altogether apart from Judaism and the Palestinian community. Bousset regards Syria and Egypt as locales of the phrase.[9] On the other hand, the Septuagint, or Greek version, of

[8] The phrase ὁ κύριος as a title is not found in Mark and is used only rarely in the other Synoptic Gospels.

[9] *Kyrios Christos,* pp. 98-99.

the Old Testament employed it in referring to God, whose own name was too holy to be uttered.[10]

For the purpose of this chapter, a close study of the origins of the title "the Lord" is a secondary consideration. What is significant, however, is the fact that such a title was given to Jesus following the Resurrection, a title that in its origin and context suggested that Jesus was the head of the Christian fellowship. And of even greater significance is the fact that the members of this fellowship gave to him a loyalty and devotion such as they would give to God himself. Jesus as Lord was the central and determining reality in their religious experience.

III

The place of Jesus as Lord in the growing Christian community as it developed in the first century may be seen further in the Epistle to the Hebrews and in the Revelation to John. These writings belong to the period of Domitian's rule toward the close of the century.[11] The first suggests a time of approaching persecution, and the second indicates that it is actually taking place at the time of writing. Both represent a condition in which a steady ballast was needed if the church was to weather the storm.

The Epistle to the Hebrews is quite in line with the Synoptic Gospels in the human apects of its portrait of Jesus. He is pictured here as one who prayed with great emotion (5:7) and who faced the Cross as an adventure of faith and joy (12:2). Like all other children of God, Jesus trusted his heavenly Father (2:13), was patient in tribulation (12:3), and was made perfect through suffering (5:9). At the same time that the author presents these human traits, he finds in Jesus one who is a great high priest, "seated at the right hand of the throne of the Majesty in heaven" (8:1). He is a priest forever who holds his priesthood permanently. As such, he fulfills the function of bringing men to God: "He is able for all time to save those who draw near to God through him, since *he always lives to make intercession for them*" (7:25).[12] As the eternal high priest, Jesus con-

---

[10] The fact that the Aramaic *Maran* ("Our Lord") is used by Paul suggests a Palestinian source for the title. Cf., however, Wilhelm Bousset, *ibid.*, pp. 114 ff.

[11] The date of Domitian's rule is A.D. 81-96.

[12] Italics mine.

tinues the ministry begun on earth and his followers continue likewise to look to him as they draw near to God.

The Revelation to John considers the lordship of Jesus in the highest conceivable terms. He is the King of kings and the Lord of lords (19:16). In a passage of tremendous force the seer-author pictures Jesus, the Lord of lords, as riding a white horse when he moves into the final struggle with the forces of evil, a battle in which he is victorious. In characteristic apocalyptic fashion, he writes (19:11-16):

Then I saw heaven opened, and behold, a white horse! He who sat upon it is called Faithful and True, and in righteousness he judges and makes war. His eyes are like a flame of fire, and on his head are many diadems; and he has a name inscribed which no one knows but himself. He is clad in a robe dipped in blood, and the name by which he is called is The Word of God. And the armies of heaven, arrayed in fine linen, white and pure, followed him on white horses. From his mouth issues a sharp sword with which to smite the nations and he will rule them with a rod of iron; he will tread the wine press of the fury of the wrath of God the Almighty. On his robe and on his thigh he has a name inscribed, King of kings and Lord of lords.[13]

The above representation does not resemble the carpenter-preacher of Galilee, and yet the author regards him as the same person.[14] He is one with the historical Jesus, only now his true place in the unfolding drama of history is being revealed. As such, in this book he is the divine agent of God in the judgment of evil men, nations, and the Antichrist (13:8; 17:14).

The Revelation to John pictures Jesus the Lord also as the object of worship. Both the church on earth and the angelic hosts of heaven praise him. He is worthy of adoration because he was slain and by his blood ransomed men for God, men "from every tribe and tongue and people and nation" (5:9).[15] It is as the slain lamb that the high-

[13] The Revelation to John is an apocalyptic writing. For a description of this outlook the reader may turn to an earlier consideration of this viewpoint. Cf. pp. 32-33.

[14] The author speaks of Jesus as the "Lord" in Rev. 11:8 when referring to his crucifixion.

[15] Cf. the vision of the multitude clothed in white robes who worship (7:9-12).

est exaltation is given to Jesus.[16] A consideration of the atonement as such is not necessary in this connection at this point. It is sufficient to indicate that Jesus was worshiped as an object of faith and devotion, even as God was revered. Beckwith has stated that in the Revelation

worship is offered to him [Jesus] in common with God,—a worship which angelic beings are forbidden to receive; doxologies are raised to him as to God; the throne of God is his throne, the priests of God are his priests; life belongs essentially to him as to God.[17]

The exaltation of the one-time historical Jesus, when he is served and revered as Lord in the writings of the New Testament, did not mean that God's place in the universe had been supplanted. Throughout, Jesus remained the Son. As the Father, God was greater than Jesus (John 14:28). And at the end of the age Jesus was to be subject to God: "When all things are subjected to him, then the Son himself will also be subjected to him who put all things under him, that God may be everything to every one" (I Cor. 15:28).

The New Testament church held both to the subordination of Jesus to God and to the exaltation of Jesus in divine terms, at one and the same time. On the one hand, it continued to identify Jesus the Lord with the historical Jesus. On the other, it elevated him to a position beyond that of a human being. In doing this the church was interpreting the experience of its members with Jesus both before and after his resurrection. The creeds which were to come later took cognizance of this fact in their definitions of the person of Christ and in their delineations of the trinitarian nature of the being of God.

IV

The recognition of Jesus as Lord in the New Testament church continued throughout succeeding centuries. To consider in detail his influence in this regard would require an additional volume and take us too far afield from the purpose of the present study. Some

[16] Cf. I. T. Beckwith, *The Apocalypse of John*, pp. 314-15, for Jesus as the Lamb.
[17] *Ibid.*, p. 313. Cf. Rev. 1:6 3:21; 5:13; 7:10; 20:6; 22:1.

indication of the character of this influence, however, is desirable. On occasion men have turned to Jesus for confirmation of the best that was in their culture. Sometimes they found in him a criticism of their established patterns of living and modified their standards and habits accordingly. Always the result of the impact which he made upon society was the transformation of culture.[18]

The impulse to find in Jesus a confirmation of the noblest elements in any contemporary society has persisted through the centuries. It proceeds from a conviction that there is a basic unity in all that is reasonable and good and, therefore, that Jesus as Lord will support any recognized truth and value. This viewpoint appeals to persons of highly developed cultural sensitivity. Richard Niebuhr has pointed out that men such as John Locke, Leibnitz, Kant, Jefferson, Schleiermacher, Hegel, Emerson, and Ritschl have found this approach congenial.[19] The limitation of this philosophy is that it sometimes leads to an identification of the will of Jesus as Lord with contemporary ideas or mores that are sub-Christian. The Gnostics of the early centuries sought to do this by including Jesus in their philosophical-religious systems. This was regarded by the church as heresy because it resulted in an eclectic creed that compromised the Christian message. The same thing happens in our time when an amalgamation of the Christian faith with other religious systems is attempted.

The church has continued from the first to find in the call of Jesus as Lord an absolute demand for loyalty, whether it was directed to individuals or to social and political institutions. In the forming of the monastic movements, for instance, he was represented as calling those of his followers who had a special vocation to withdraw from family life and the pleasures of the world, and to live according to his law of perfection. Although there were marked differences in the monastic orders, all held the same ideal in this respect. The rule of their order was regarded as Jesus' law for the perfect life which he as Lord expected the members to obey.

Loyalty to Jesus as Lord has led to reform movements in society from time to time. These were frequently undertaken by those who

---

[18] See the definitive study *Christ and Culture* by H. Richard Niebuhr, which has suggested in part the approach in this section.

[19] *Ibid.*, p. 94.

heard a special call to confront an evil order. It was the Jesus on a crucifix who spoke to Francis of Assisi and summoned him to rise and rebuild the chapel which through disinterest had been allowed to fall into ruin. As the conviction that he was called to serve Jesus as Lord mounted in fervor, his vision of the field of service was enlarged to include the entire church, entrenced in its power and wealth. Others such as Bernard of Clairvaux and Dominic in medieval society were moved also by Jesus as Lord to undertake reform. And in the centuries since, men like William Wilberforce, Walter Rauschenbusch, and Washington Gladden have received similar summons and responded with conviction and vigor.

In the area of man's loyalties devotion to the state is prominent, and Christians have sometimes been required to examine this devotion in the light of the loyalty which Jesus as Lord demands of his followers. The centuries have shown the same differences in viewpoint here that are found in the New Testament.[20] On the one hand, an honored church father such as Tertullian wrote, "As those in whom all ardor in the pursuit of honor and glory is dead, we have no pressing inducement to take part in your public meetings; nor is there aught more entirely foreign to us than affairs of state." [21] On the other hand, kings have been regarded as the servants of Jesus, no less, and the doctrine of the divine right of kings has been given serious support by his followers. Out of loyalty to Jesus as they interpreted it, some Christians have refused military service which the state required in a time of national crisis; while others have borne arms in behalf of such a cause because they regarded it as one with his own. Each of these positions, contradictory as it may seem, have been taken by persons who were convinced that they were under orders to Jesus as Lord. The point is that they believed that they were following his will in the course they took.

V

There are great paradoxes in the career and influence of Jesus of Nazareth. He walked the roads of Palestine in flesh such as ours, and

[20] The Revelation to John (13:1-4) regarded the Roman state as an idolatrous servant of Satan, while Paul (Rom. 13:1-7) advocated obedience to the state as an institution ordained by God.

[21] Apology, xxxviii, in the translation of Tertullian's writings in *Ante-Nicene Fathers*.

yet men worship him as divine. He possessed practically nothing while on earth, and yet the material value of the property held by his followers is fabulous. He was crucified as a criminal, yet he is revered as the highest ideal for character.

Jesus died, and yet his own are convinced that he is alive. He was definitely a citizen of the first century, and yet there have been those in every century since who have found in him as Lord the highest authority in their particular generation. He left no formal creedal statement, yet it has been necessary to express the significance of his life, death, and resurrection, as these relate to God and history, through the words of many creeds.

These paradoxes exist because of the kind of person Jesus was, and also because of the character of the religious experiences of his followers. They rest upon the authority of life itself, his life and the lives of those who are committed to him. For nearly two thousand years the account found in these pages has been told and retold. There is every reason that it will continue to be so as long as time shall last.

QUESTIONS FOR DISCUSSION

1. The Resurrection brought to the followers of Jesus the assurance that his personality had persisted beyond the grave. Did it also add new dimensions to their portrait of Jesus? Explain.

2. Why should Peter have regarded the coming of the Spirit at Pentecost as the gift of the crucified and risen Jesus? Cf. Acts 1:6-8; John 16:7-11.

3. Do you see any relation between Jesus' belief in himself as the Messiah and the church's faith in him as Lord? Which conception is greater—Messiah or Lord—or do they mean the same things expressed in different terms? Explain.

4. What convictions concerning Jesus as Lord did the Primitive Church, the apostle Paul, and the authors of Hebrews and the Revelation to John hold in common?

5. How would you define the relationship between the Jesus of history and Jesus as Lord? In what sense are they one and the same person, and in what regard are they different?

6. Explain: Knowledge of the Jesus of history kept the conception of Jesus as Lord from becoming lost in vague generalities.

7. Explain: Knowledge of Jesus as Lord kept the portrait of Jesus of history from remaining only a static memory.

8. Which do you regard as the most fruitful channel through which Jesus as Lord makes his impact upon society: the New Testament? the church? individual religious experience? idealistic social crusades? the fine arts?

9. In what areas of contemporary life is the influence of Jesus as Lord felt most acutely?

10. What does it mean in the twentieth century when a Christian refers to Jesus as Lord?

11. What is the relationship between the experience of Jesus as Lord and the trinitarian conception of God?

SUGGESTIONS FOR READING

I. Concerning the Primitive Church

Craig, Clarence Tucker. *The Beginning of Christianity*. Nashville: Abingdon Press, 1943. Selected readings.

Cullmann, Oscar. *The Early Church*. Philadelphia: The Westminster Press. 1956. Selected readings.

Klausner, Joseph. *From Jesus to Paul*. New York: The Macmillan Company, 1943. Pp. 255-300.

Scott, Ernest F. *The Nature of the Early Church*. New York: Charles Scribner's Sons, 1942. Pp. 1-24.

II. Concerning Pauline mysticism

Schweitzer, Albert. *The Mysticism of Paul the Apostle*. New York: Henry Holt & Co., 1931. Selected readings.

Scott, C. Anderson. *Christianity According to St. Paul*. New York: The Macmillan Company, 1927. Pp. 107-14.

III. Concerning Christ the Lord

Blair, Edward P. *Jesus in the Gospel of Matthew*. Nashville: Abingdon Press. 1960. Selected readings.

Deissmann, Adolf. *The Religion of Jesus and the Faith of Paul*. New York: Harper & Brothers, 1926. Selected readings.

Filson, Floyd V. *One Lord, One Faith*. Philadelphia: The Westminster Press, 1943. Selected readings.

Knox, John. *Christ the Lord*. Chicago and New York: Willett, Clark & Co., 1945. Selected readings.

Wilhelm Bousset. *Kyrios Christos*. Selected readings.

IV. Concerning Christ and culture

Bennett, John C. *Social Salvation, a Religious Approach to the Problems of Social Change*. New York: Charles Scribner's Sons, 1935. Selected readings.

Cailliet, Emile. *The Christian Approach to Culture*. New York: Harper & Brothers, 1953. Selected readings.

Case, Shirley Jackson. *The Social Triumph of the Ancient Church*. New York: Harper & Brothers, 1933. Pp. 97-199.

Hyde, Walter Woodburn. *Paganism to Christianity in the Roman Empire*. Philadelphia: University of Pennsylvania Press, 1946. Pp. 164-225.

McGiffert, A. C. *History of Christian Thought*. New York: Charles Scribner's Sons, 1932. Selected readings.

Maus, Cynthia (comp.). *Christ and the Fine Arts*. New York: Harper & Brothers, 1938. Selected readings.

Niebuhr, H. Richard. *Christ and Culture*. New York: Harper & Brothers, 1951. Pp. 1-44.

Rauschenbusch, Walter. *Christianity and the Social Crisis*. New York: The Macmillan Company, 1920. Selected readings.

V. Concerning the person of Christ

Cullmann, Oscar. *Christology of the New Testament*. Philadelphia: The Westminster Press, 1961. Selected readings.

Horton, Walter. *Our Eternal Contemporary*. New York: Harper & Brothers, 1942. Selected readings.

Laymon, Charles M. *Christ in the New Testament*. Nashville: Abingdon Press, 1958. Selected readings.

Mackintosh, H. R. *The Doctrine of the Person of Jesus Christ*. New York: Charles Scribner's Sons, 1912. Pp. 427 ff.

Smart, W. A. *The Contemporary Christ*. New York and Nashville: Abingdon-Cokesbury Press, 1942. Selected readings.

Index of Scripture

329

Index of Subjects